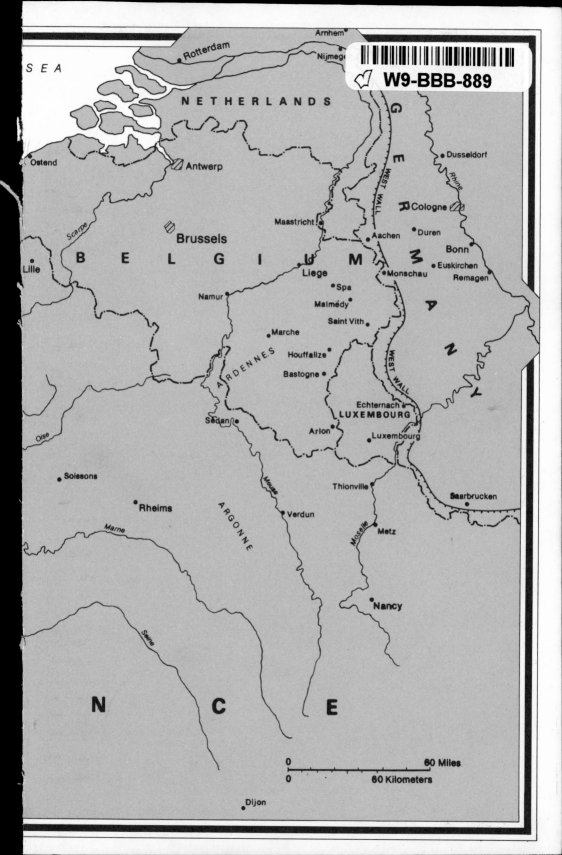

S E A

NETHERLANDS

Rotterdam

Arnhem

Nijmegen

W9-BBB-889

Ostend

Antwerp

Dusseldorf

Rhine

Maastricht

Cologne

Brussels

Aachen

Duren

WEST WALL

BELGIUM

Liege

Monschau

Bonn

Euskirchen

Remagen

Namur

Spa

Malmédy

Saint Vith

Lille

Scarpe

Marche

ARDENNES

Houffalize

Bastogne

GERMANY

WEST WALL

Echternach

LUXEMBOURG

Sedan

Arlon

Luxembourg

Oise

Soissons

Thionville

Saarbrucken

Rheims

ARGONNE

Meuse

Verdun

Moselle

Metz

Marne

Nancy

Seine

F R A N C E

0   60 Miles

0   60 Kilometers

Dijon

THE WAR BETWEEN THE GENERALS

DAVID IRVING

ALLEN LANE

ALLEN LANE
Penguin Books Ltd
536 King's Road
London SW10 0UH

First published in the United States of America by Congdon & Lattes, Inc., 1981
Published simultaneously in Canada by Thomas Nelson & Sons Ltd
Published by Allen Lane 1981

ISBN 0 7139 1344 4

Printed in Great Britain by
Butler & Tanner Ltd, Frome and London
Endpaper map by J. P. Tremblay

Contents

I am tired of dealing with a lot of prima donnas. By God, you tell that bunch that if they can't get together and stop quarreling like children, I will tell the Prime Minister to get someone else to run this damn war.

—GENERAL DWIGHT D. EISENHOWER

The real trouble with the Yanks is that they are completely ignorant as to the rules of the game we are playing with the Germans. You play so much better when you know the rules.

—FIELD MARSHAL SIR BERNARD MONTGOMERY

God, I wish we could forget our egos for a while!

—LIEUTENANT GENERAL EVERETT S. HUGHES

PROLOGUE

Cover Plan

MAY 10, 1945, two days after the surrender of Nazi Germany. Five generals sit around an oaken table in the Frankfurt headquarters of one of the most powerful men in the world, Dwight D. Eisenhower. On his shoulders are the five stars of his rank as General of the Army. The other four generals have sixteen more stars between them—they are the commanders of the four American armies that, in one spectacular year, have penetrated the French coastline at Normandy, have hurled themselves at the Germans at Avranches, have battled forward through rains and mud and snow to the German frontier, have recoiled under Hitler's counterattack, and have finally, just three weeks before, shaken hands with Marshal Georgi Zhukov's troops coming from the ravaged east.

Five generals—Eisenhower, Hodges, Patton, Simpson, Patch. Their faces bear the congratulatory grins of men who have done a job they are proud of. But already there are worries clouding the minds of some. George Patton has relished the war, and he fears the peace that is now to come. He actually dreams of using the surviving German divisions in his army sector for a drive against what he now considers the true

1

enemy—the Soviet Union. He is still furious with Eisenhower for restraining him, and for toadying to his particular bêtes noires, the British. The others in the room, while far more temperate, harbor their own
grudges, disappointments, resentments. Alliance—with the British and
especially the French—has often been an agony. So much misunderstanding, some of it willful; so much outright hatred. So many decisions
that, in the minds of the dissenters, occasioned so many hundreds of
thousands of needless deaths. Indeed, the running contest between the
Allies on the cruelest issue—whose troops should bear the brunt and
thereby perish—has caused deep psychic trauma. These five chiefs and
their close colleagues must live their remaining lives with knowledge
too fierce to forget.

After the meal is cleared away, Eisenhower pulls out a cigarette and
rams it into his wide, expressive mouth. There is something important
he wants to tell these generals—because they have shared his troubles,
with him they have seen opportunities slip through American fingers,
they have witnessed his rages and fury at the behavior of America's
Allies. Yet Eisenhower wants history to remember him for the great
Allied partnership that he has cemented, here on Europe's blood-sod-
den soil. It would be a tragedy, he thinks, if the shameful realities
should leak out. He has pledged himself to prevent it.

White-jacketed flunkies rattle away the last plates and cutlery and
scrape crumbs from the wine-splotched tablecloth. Brandy and li-
queurs, captured from the Wehrmacht's finest stocks, are served. Eisenhower clears his throat. What he is going to say now, he warns the men,
is very confidential. Some of them, he says, may well be called before
a congressional committee. He talks on the urgent need for continued
solidarity, and says, without explanation: "Let's agree on the right form
of organization."

Patton's clear blue eyes are expressionless. He does not speak, but he
has realized suddenly what Eisenhower is saying: he is talking solidarity
for one reason only—the big cover-up is beginning. There is to be no
criticism of the strategic blunders that Eisenhower has unquestionably, in Patton's view, committed during the campaign. There is to be
no searching analysis as to whether these have been Eisenhower's own
fault, or whether too much cooperation with the British was to blame.
Patton is not surprised. He has, he believes, personally suffered, for
three long years, from Eisenhower's craven anglophilia . . . .

Eisenhower had indeed had an almost obsessive desire to be liked and admired by the British. During the Mediterranean campaigns, he had searched the British newspapers in vain for references to his initiative and boldness but had found those words being applied only to generals Alexander and Montgomery; the British begrudged him any recognition except as a manager who had "welded an Allied team." He thought of all the operations he had ordered which had seemed so daring at the time, like the invasions of Salerno and Pantelleria, and he sighed. "It wearies me to be thought of as timid," he wrote on February 7, 1944, "when I've had to do things that were so risky as to be almost crazy." He bit his pencil, wrote, "Oh hum," and laid it aside. And British criticism continued.

Anglo-American tension, to be sure, was not the only variety to fray the sinews of the Grand Alliance. Just before the day of victory in Europe, Eisenhower warned General Charles de Gaulle: "I am deeply concerned . . . that the American public will become aware of what has actually transpired as I know this would awaken a storm of resentment which would be most unfortunate in its results." But it was British hostility that concerned him most.

There had in fact been one Briton who above all others had tried his patience sorely, a fact that Eisenhower strove to disguise. After the end of the war he tried to convince everyone that, in spite of occasional differences of conviction, there existed between Field Marshal Sir Bernard Montgomery and himself only mutual respect and friendly regard. From the official publication *The Papers of Dwight D. Eisenhower* he expunged certain passages highly critical of Montgomery—for example, lines from one letter to General George Marshall criticizing Montgomery's overcautiousness. He wrote to his aide Harry Butcher, ordering him similarly to censor the diaries he had been keeping for Eisenhower.

The suppression became a life's work. Long after D-day, when Montgomery made outspoken remarks on British television about Eisenhower, he refused to make any retort. "British newsmen staying over here were on the phone very quickly to get my reply," he wrote to General Sir Hastings Ismay, "but I gave them nothing but silence." He added, "Actually, I feel sorry for the man. He had it within his grasp to be one of the legendary heroes of his nation; I fear he has hurt himself badly during the past decade." When Eisenhower's own writings were

appearing and were carried in English newspapers, there was another
set-to. Eisenhower himself thought they were lenient to Montgomery,
but the British general erupted when he saw the headline on a *Sunday
Dispatch* article about the Battle of the Bulge: HOW MONTGOMERY
UPSET AMERICANS. Worse was the announcement at the end of the
article: "Next week: British Methods That Always Shocked Me." Stung
to reply, Montgomery wrote: "My dear Ike . . . you can hardly wonder
at my dislike of the whole matter in the headlines such as the enclosed
appearing in London papers. I fear you have lost many friends in
England. Yrs. ever, Monty."

Thus the war between the generals continued long after the guns had
fallen still. In 1965 Eisenhower was shocked to learn that the British
government had invisibly punished some of those who had collaborated
with the Americans. General Sir Frederick Morgan, one of his closest
partners in planning Operation Overlord, was living in poverty, he was
told, without much food or money to buy coal for the fireplace before
which he sat huddled, an exhausted, half-frozen old man. Eisenhower
could not believe the government's lack of charity. "Knowing how
vindictive our own Pentagon can be about its own officers," an aide
remarked to him, "I can imagine that Freddie, who literally sacrificed
himself to be of help to the American side in general and to you in
particular, might be in the very bad books of the War Office. I remember many sneering remarks by top British military brass to the effect
that Freddie had 'deserted to the Americans.' "

And so it went. Despite occasional eruptions of the hot sulfurous lava
of indignation, the crust of secrecy hardened until there was nothing
but rocklike imperviousness to inquiry. Documents, diaries, letters—
almost anything containing wounding allegations—went under the veil.
There were occasional rumors, mumblings, slips, but the myth of Allied
unity persisted. And then the titans died, and their junior colleagues
and heirs were less reticent. The ineluctable deadlines erected by the
Official Secrets Act fell, one after another, and formerly restricted
materials became available to anyone who remembered to look. There
were other impediments, however, not of Eisenhower's creation. The
materials were dispersed through archives of twenty different agencies,
scattered over thousands of miles, and some were penned so execrably
that they were all but unreadable. Once found and analyzed, they
proved not only immensely revealing in themselves, but also full of

clues leading to other papers—memos, informal private memoirs, yellowing scraps squirreled away in drawers and trunks across two continents. Together it all amounted to an astounding contemporary record. Eisenhower's labor of Sisyphus, his benign but futile effort to cheat history, had failed. At last there emerged the untold story of the generals' war.

 CHAPTER ONE

Bedfellows

AT FIRST they were alone—crowding apprehensively into their islands, looking across the twenty-mile-wide Channel to Nazi-occupied Europe, searching the skies for the glint of Luftwaffe bombers, huddling underground as their homes collapsed above them. They had been humiliated, defeated, and driven out at Dunkirk; they had been pushed back across North Africa almost to the gates of Cairo. For more than three years their chances of survival had faded with each passing week.

But the British had returned. And by January of 1944 they were no longer alone. In the east the Red Army had turned on the Wehrmacht and smashed it at Stalingrad. And from the west, from across the Atlantic, there had arrived the legions of fresh-faced young soldiers of Britain's erstwhile colony. The Americans had crowded into Northern Ireland and into England. London was raucous with their presence, athrob with their energy, glad that they had come but eager to see them move on.

Always there was a nervous ambivalence between these two kindred peoples. What was it about the newcomers that antagonized the British

—was it their casualness, their wealth, their way of acting as though they owned the place? What was it about the British that chilled the Americans—was it a residue of eighteenth-century resentment, aggravated by the insecurity of the parvenu? The tension came from too deep in each nation's character and past to be excised. They were Allies in the great forthcoming venture, but perhaps more from necessity than from inclination. Alliance would not be easy.

The American influx, that winter, had become a tidal wave of khaki; each week brought another division of thirteen to fifteen thousand men. London had never seen anything like it. The young Americans, on their part, had never seen anything like London. The buildings were low and gnarled and barnacled with sooty decorations. The policemen wore odd helmets, office workers wore bowlers, and passersby wore blank expressions—no eye contact. What shocked them most, perhaps, these kings of the American road, was to find themselves suddenly impotent in the flow of wrong-way traffic.

The city was also full of women. They poured into London to help staff the wartime bureaucracy, or simply to be near all those men. One American soldier wrote of his surprise to see these cosmopolitan Englishwomen smoking in public, with the cigarettes negligently drooping from their lips and the ash crumbling to the ground as they talked. The Anglo-American mutual attraction, in this respect, was considerable, and from the back streets of Soho to the clubs of Mayfair, nighttime London swung. The mood was almost carefree. It had been two years since the Nazis last bombed the capital.

For weeks now, however, as senior Allied officers continued their planning for the most stupendous military operation of history, the return by force of arms to continental Europe, they had been aware of a darkening threat. High-flying planes had photographed more than a hundred baffling construction sites in northwestern France. Some theorists thought it was all a fantastic hoax—that the Nazis had created a decoy to divert Allied bombing from their cities and factories. Or could Adolf Hitler have a war-winning secret weapon after all? Through agents and captured prisoners came seemingly conflicting rumors about the development of pilotless aircraft and long-range rockets. Obviously the gigantic construction sites were for missiles. Several large supply depots had been identified near these sites, so it was not all just bluff.

Photo analysts could see the truckloads of concrete being poured into the installations, and precise measurements showed them to be aligned on London, on Southampton—even on New York. Some agents whispered that Hitler had developed an atomic bomb.

American army code breakers toiling in Washington intercepted secret German and Japanese messages strongly suggesting that Hitler had something dreadful waiting. From one intercept, in December 1943, they learned that the chief of staff of Field Marshal Gerd von Rundstedt, Hitler's western commander in chief, had gravely confirmed to a Japanese military attaché that there were indeed such weapons. Two weeks later the code breakers intercepted a Berlin circular to German air attachés, reassuring them that the "reprisal installations" had not been damaged by Allied bombing. Official London began to empty, as word of this ugly development was passed among the privileged few.

Even as the nervous exodus began, a general arrived from Washington. His face was the shade of pinkish tan that fair-skinned people take on in the Mediterranean sun. Only forty days had passed since General Dwight D. Eisenhower had learned that he was to command all the Allied forces in the mightiest military operation ever launched.

On the day Eisenhower arrived, there were already some 870,000 Americans in Britain. An American executive of Time, Inc., reported to his publisher, in confidence, "There is not a single square inch of London on which an American is not standing, and add to that the fact that, if he is standing after dark, he is standing unsteadily; I think that there is plenty of trouble brewing." The current gag was that if the helium-filled barrage balloons were ever hauled down, the island would sink under the sheer weight of Americans. They had commandeered whole areas of the capital. The most opulent hotels had become officers' billets, with efficient cafeterias and famous open messes like the Grosvenor House's Willow Run; the Run served fluffy American bread and ice cream too, despite parochial British criticism of the squandering of fuel for refrigeration.

The local gripes were beyond counting. Americans left big tips where British didn't—for barbers, for example—and that rankled. In Mayfair, Oxford accents could be heard sneering about the damned Yanks who had let Britain stand alone until December 1941. There was a popular

notion that Yanks were blowhards, inflated with bluster and brag-
gadocio but capable only of military fiascos like Kasserine. Eisenhower
had devoted two years in the Mediterranean to proving that the British
and Americans could fight as one unit. But the mutual mistrust was
difficult to dispel.

A few days after his arrival in London a bitter letter from an English-
man landed on his desk. "Dear Sir," it read. "While I offer you personally a welcome to England, I do not do so [to you] as C in C of the Allied
Forces because I consider that either General Montgomery or Alexander should have held that position. Remember we have been in this
war for over four years. Our troops have done some very hard fighting,
especially in Africa where we chased Rommel for over a thousand miles
out of Africa. . . ." Eisenhower smiled, and dictated a courteous reply.
In it, he agreed that any one of a number of generals would have been
a better selection than himself. "However," he added, "I hope you will
agree that as long as this duty has been placed upon me by Great Britain
and the United States, I have no recourse except to do my very best to
perform it adequately."

Eisenhower was well aware that the Americans had received from
the British what he called the "priceless gift" of combat experience.
Inarguably, the Americans were profiting, at no price, from lessons that
British veterans had learned and paid for in blood and tears. It was not
just that British scientists had sent some of their most precious inven-
tions to their American colleagues to develop—among them the radar
magnetron, the proximity fuse, and the atomic bomb; now British
combat officers were showing the Americans how to fight in all the
elements.

It seemed like an unbeatable coalition—British brains and experience
harnessed to the immense American industrial and human resources.
But only if this coalition held right through to final victory could
Germany be defeated. History had proved this. John J. Pershing had
stubbornly tried to keep the American high command independent in
World War I, but nobody could deny that it was the appointment of
a supreme Allied commander, Marshal Ferdinand Foch, that made all
the difference in the war's final months. Eisenhower refused to compromise on this principle. He bluntly told one of the most anglophobic U.S.
commanders: "If you or anyone else criticizes the British, by God I will
reduce you to your permanent grade and send you home." Eisenhower

became one of England's truest friends, while never being less of an American for it.

Many saw him, indeed, as the quintessential American. With his open, warm, Great Plains manner, his wide, ready grin, his tangy and colloquial speech, he seemed like a figure out of the Western pulp novels he loved to read. He doted on mush with chicken gravy and on hominy grits. And yet behind all this homeliness there was a subtle, relentless intelligence.

His career had been meteoric. He had graduated from West Point in 1915 and gone on to the Army Staff College at Fort Leavenworth, Kansas. Of this period, classmate William ("Big Bill") Simpson, who would command the Ninth Army under him, recalled, "He was jovial [and] easy to talk to. In a group he stood out because he always had something to say." One of his classmates, General Paul J. Mueller, said, "If you want to know anything about anything in the military or most any other subject and Ike's around, ask him." He worked hard and did well, and when he came out of Leavenworth at the top of his class he was marked for success. Douglas MacArthur took him to the Philippines as his right-hand man. Eisenhower spent nine years with MacArthur, and found that he did not like the general. Later in the war he joked to his staff: "I would not exchange one George Marshall for even fifty MacArthurs." Then he corrected himself and said, "Hell! What am I saying? What would I do with even one MacArthur!"

After Pearl Harbor, General George C. Marshall, the commander of the United States Army, summoned Eisenhower to Washington for a choice assignment. It surprised few people who knew his excellence. Swiftly rising careers—such as that of Pershing, who rocketed from captain to brigadier general almost overnight—usually caused a lot of bellyaching among the older officers. But there was nothing of this about Eisenhower's new appointment. When George Marshall put him in charge of the War Plans Division, there were few people who thought that he was getting an undeserved post. Yet he remained unassuming and, outside the military, unknown. When his photograph appeared in *Life,* the caption identified him as Colonel D. D. Ersenbean.

If fame did not concern him much, reputation did. Above all, he wished it to remain immaculate. He was deeply concerned that his actions should not only be honest, but should be seen by posterity as such. After the invasion, he would be offered a major Hollywood movie about his life; he wrote indignantly to his wife, Mamie: "My own convictions as to the quality of a man that will make money out of a public position of trust are very strong! I couldn't touch it—and would never allow such a thing to occur. We don't need it anyway, it's fun to be poor."

His code of honor was extraordinarily rigorous. Just before the end of the war a U.S. Army trainload of German prisoners of war was being shipped across Germany. Upon its arrival at its destination, the doors were opened and it was found that 130 of the prisoners had been suffocated to death in the jam-packed boxcars through inadequate ventilation. Eisenhower ordered a complete investigation by the Inspector General. Four days later he asked the American legation in Berne, Switzerland, to forward his apology—of all unheard-of things—to the German high command. "If it is found that United States personnel were guilty of negligence," said his message, "appropriate action will be taken with respect to them. The Supreme Commander profoundly regrets this incident and has taken steps to prevent its recurrence."

How differently Winston Churchill would have reacted to the incident! And yet relations between the British Prime Minister and the man he unfailingly addressed as "Ike" were cordial to the point of mutual admiration. They had been so from the moment they met and continued to be until Churchill's death. Eisenhower spoke at Churchill's funeral, extolling Churchill, and he later wrote: "His little foibles were understandable and his virtues were gigantic."

Their first meeting had occurred in 1942, during Churchill's visit to America just a few weeks after Pearl Harbor. President Franklin D. Roosevelt had asked Eisenhower—then only a colonel—to the White House to see the Prime Minister. "Ike came in twice," recalled Churchill. "The first time to introduce the American Eagle (that's the way I always called General Mark Clark) and the second time to introduce [Walter] Bedell Smith, the American Bulldog." Colonel Eisenhower had inspired Winston's puckish imagination.

Years later, each man still lounged pleasurably in the memories of their wartime friendship. There existed between them a mutual confidence and trust; no harsh words were exchanged or even thought. Eisenhower knew of Churchill's essentially aggressive outlook and

counted on it as a factor in strategic calculations. Churchill for his part
was careful to avoid any suggestion of controversy between them. On
the contrary, when Eisenhower arrived in England as the Allies' Supreme Commander, Churchill told him that, if ever Eisenhower had
any dissatisfaction with any British commander, no matter what his
rank or his position, the man would be relieved instantly on his request.
From that moment Eisenhower saw Churchill with new eyes: he meant
business. To the general, the survival of the Anglo-American accord
became a holy mission.

CHAPTER TWO

Uneasy Alliance

To THE British, the notion that they would one day return to the Continent, with their Allies, was self-evident ever since they were ejected from it in 1940. Just three weeks after the Japanese strike at Pearl Harbor, Churchill had hurried over to the United States and had spoken, even then, of the liberation of Europe. At the Casablanca Conference between the British and American leaders in January 1943, the Combined Chiefs of Staff had directed that preparations for an invasion be begun. A joint planning staff was set up in London, known eventually as COSSAC—Chiefs of Staff, Supreme Allied Commander. The commander still had to be designated, but the chief of staff already existed: the British general Sir Frederick Morgan. Morgan began groping through the minefield of Anglo-American relations.

Any invasion plan would have to respect the prima donna qualities of the British and American field commanders who would be fighting this, the fiercest battle on this scale in world history, the first gigantic collision with the massed armies of Nazi Germany. The plan drawn up by Morgan's staff envisaged a landing on the coast of Normandy, in northwestern France, by three divisions—about forty thousand men.

For a time, the community of purpose between London and Washington was complete. The British were militarily powerful and heavily engaged, while the Americans were still weak. But as the balance shifted, major strategic differences emerged. These differences were to affect all that followed. The first arose over the decision, reached at August 1943 in Quebec, that an American should command the invasion operation called Overlord—the United States would eventually be supplying most of the troops. Since Churchill had originally intended that direction of Overlord go to General Sir Alan Brooke, the Chief of the Imperial General Staff, the decision did not cause universal rejoicing in the United Services, the Pall Mall club that was the haunt of Britain's military establishment.

Overlord could succeed only if the cooperation between British, Americans, French, and Canadians was complete and unquestioning. But ever since the Tunisian campaign, when British and American troops began operating in the same narrow theater, rivalries had festered between them. At the ground level, hostility between the GIs and British had run strong. Higher up, British officers were appalled by the differences of style and in particular were baffled by the womanizing of the American commanders. "We did not have the same primeval need to prove our manhood that the Americans did," said one British officer. The Americans mimicked the Britons' accents and squirmed before their effortless ease. The British always seemed to be one up. One colonel, Ben Sawbridge, encapsulated the U.S. Army attitude by remarking shortly before Independence Day, 1943: "We should celebrate July the Fourth as our only defeat of the British. We haven't had much luck since."

In Tunisia that year, the tension had begun to shimmer between the British and American armies as they limbered up for the assault on Sicily. Eisenhower, as theater commander, had tried to cool the passions, but George Patton, commander of the U.S. Seventh Army, had scoffed at his attempts. Over lunch with deputy theater commander Everett S. Hughes, he had described Eisenhower as crazy and "too pro-British in [the] combat zone." "I told Ike," said Patton, "that some day a reporter is going to get home but fast the story of American cooperation to the British tunes." Hughes, too, was powerfully suspicious of the British, noting in his diary that Patton had been restricted to planning, and speculating: "I wonder if [the] British got him out?" Later Patton complained to Hughes about the arrogance of the two top British commanders, Sir Harold Alexander and Sir Bernard Montgomery. "He doesn't like Alex or Monty," observed Hughes. "God, I wish we could forget our egos for a while!" Next day he wrote of Patton: "How he hates the British."

The ensuing campaign in Sicily was a textbook example of how alliances should not operate. The Americans were treated as greenhorns who could not be trusted with a lead role in a campaign. The British laughingly assigned the Seventh Army to guard the rear—as Patton heatedly put it—of Montgomery's Eighth Army as it advanced victoriously around the island. Alexander relieved Clarence R. Huebner of command on the grounds that he was too American for his British staff. The BBC broadcast an infuriating announcement that Patton's Seventh Army was eating grapes and sitting under the pine trees of Sicily. Not much tact was shown on either side, and for a time the Allies were taking more flak from each other than from the Nazis. Halfway through the campaign, after the British suffered a costly reverse, Patton wrote to Hughes a triumphant note: "Our cousins got a bloody nose!"

Patton seemed to regard Montgomery as his real opponent, and not the Nazi commander in Sicily, Hans Hube, the grizzled one-armed veteran of Stalingrad who was directing a brilliant retreat across the island toward Messina. To Montgomery, the GIs officially were "wonderful chaps." But to the Americans, Montgomery was a Gilbert and Sullivan caricature. If it rained, he carried an umbrella onto the battlefield. He was pernickety, methodical, and deadly slow. It did not help that Patton now trounced him in Sicily, scooting around the wrong side of the island and getting into Messina before the British. Montgomery's face was a picture. Patton boasted that according to Eisenhower he had ruined Montgomery's career by getting to Messina first. At any event, from that moment, a bitter feud raged between them.

Into this cockpit of personal ambitions, the Mediterranean, had now sailed the world's great leaders to confer on the momentous issues thrown up by the approach of the invasion year. Roosevelt and Churchill had hopes of resolving their own differences before meeting Stalin. The British now held the weakest hand: their manpower resources were stretched to the limit; by January 1944 the United States would have eleven million people in uniform and more were coming under arms every day, compared with Britain's four and a half million. "We will soon have as many men in England for Overlord," Roosevelt commented to General Marshall at one shipboard meeting, "as the total British forces now in that place." Marshall corrected him—the United States already had more troops there than the British. And Air Force General H. H. "Hap" Arnold chimed in: "By January 1, 1944, we will have over twelve thousand operational planes while the British will only have about eight thousand."

So Churchill would have to accept whatever terms were dictated to him by Roosevelt and Stalin. He and his staff could put up a fight, however. They sailed from Plymouth in a battle cruiser on November 14, 1943, determined to get Overlord postponed in order to permit what they considered more promising operations in the Mediterranean in the interval. Things had changed since the Quebec Conference, they would argue: Italy had been defeated, and the Soviet armies had made enormous gains. By realigning their strategy, the Allies could inflict cheap victories on the Germans; these victories would make Overlord a pushover. The British were bitter at the American "drag" on British strategy in the Mediterranean, which, they felt, had seriously affected Allied successes and the conduct of the war.

As their two warships neared the Mediterranean rendezvous, the British and American staffs had consulted on how to outsmart each other. At Malta, the British chiefs discussed the agenda with Churchill. It was obvious to his top soldier, General Sir Alan Brooke, that real trouble was brewing. Churchill was lying in an enormous bed, the color of a pink wax cherub; he had been stricken with a cold, and he was grouchy and suspicious. He rehearsed to his chiefs the tirade which he proposed to deliver to the evil Americans on their duplicity and on the recent British losses in the Aegean Sea. He just could not reconcile himself to allowing them any say in strategic affairs on his side of the Atlantic. Brooke winced when Churchill told him that he intended to say: "If you won't play with us in the Mediterranean, then we won't play with you in the English Channel!" Brooke predicted that the Americans would then threaten to direct their main effort to the Pacific. Churchill pouted. "Then I shall say, 'You are welcome to do so if you wish.'" Churchill was aiming to cut off his nose to spite his face, as Brooke noted with horror in his diary. Such tactics were unlikely to pay.

Almost simultaneously with the British, the American leadership had sailed by battleship from Plymouth Roads, near Washington. Their aims were diametrically opposed to Churchill's. They wanted Overlord to go ahead, as agreed, on or about May 1. They had not the slightest intention of becoming bogged down in Italy or the Balkans, let alone the Dodecanese or Turkey, merely to satisfy an imperial whim of the British, as they saw it. Roosevelt was counting on Stalin's help in thwarting Churchill's ambitions. Roosevelt intended to offer himself to Stalin as an "honest broker" between East and West.

And the Russians? What unfathomable motives inspired them as Premier Josef Stalin, with his two top advisors on military affairs and diplomacy, flew toward the meeting place at Teheran a few days later? Stalin, it turned out, came only to inquire affably, to smile benignly, to exact promises, and to return to Moscow, having revealed nothing of his own plans or intentions. Brooke would admit after Teheran that Stalin had a military brain of the very highest caliber. "Never once," wrote Brooke, "in any of his statements, did he make any strategic error, nor did he ever fail to appreciate all the implications of a situation with a quick and unerring eye." He outshone Roosevelt and Churchill in this respect. Hitler once said of Stalin, full of admiration: "That man thinks in terms of centuries." That was the danger for the British.

For six days as the battleship *Iowa* had ploughed eastward the American Joint Chiefs of Staff had conferred in the admiral's cabin. They were an oddly assorted bunch. Admiral Ernest J. King, chief of the U.S. Navy, would be sixty-five a few days later; his gaze was riveted on the Pacific theater of war. General Hap Arnold was a happy-go-lucky aviator, who spent much of the time penciling in a daily diary. General Marshall, the top U.S. soldier, was stern, authoritarian and incorruptible. Whatever their internal disputes, all were agreed on one thing: the need to defeat the British obstinacy about Overlord. The British, it seemed, wanted to back out both from Overlord and from the simultaneous landing by two divisions in southern France, a plan called Anvil. The British obviously had plans of their own—plans for operations in the Balkans, in the Greek islands, even in Norway. The Joint Chiefs had just received a discouraging message from the British refusing to place their heavy bomber squadrons under the American who would be appointed Supreme Commander for Overlord; that seemed to confirm that the British had gotten cold feet. Roosevelt's chief of staff, Admiral William D. Leahy, another of the *Iowa*'s distinguished passengers, suggested that in that case the Americans should abandon Overlord completely.

But Marshall's fear as the nine-hundred-foot-long battleship headed steadily eastward was that it was the British who might abandon Overlord. His planners had forecast that the British would try to claim that an invasion in the Balkans would knock out Germany even before May 1. Marshall urged Roosevelt to scotch Churchill's ambitions: "We have now over a million tons of supplies in England for Overlord. It would be going into reverse to undertake the Balkans, and prolong the war materially. . . . May I point out that commitments and preparations for Overlord extend as far west as the Rocky Mountains? The British might ditch Overlord at this time in order to undertake operations in a country with practically no communications." Just as Brooke had predicted, Marshall threatened: "We could say that, if they propose to do that, we will pull out and go into the Pacific with all our forces."

Roosevelt hardly heard him. He was toying with blue pencils and a map, sketching the proposed demarcation lines in Germany.

At Algiers, where they transferred to an airplane, they had been met by General Eisenhower. The theater commander was wearing his famous grin, but he saw little real cause for pleasure. He had reached the zenith of his military career and now he was packing, resigned to taking over Marshall's desk at the Pentagon. Everybody knew that Marshall had been chosen by Roosevelt to command Overlord. That was only right: he had done a splendid job as Chief of Staff, creating a mighty army since Pearl Harbor; he was entitled to some battle honors. History does not recall the names of even the greatest chiefs of staff.

Besides, Eisenhower was grateful to Marshall. It was he who had plucked him out of the Pentagon and sent him to London in June 1942. There Eisenhower had become the natural choice to lead the great invasions of 1942 and 1943—of North Africa, Sicily, and Italy. True, he had not had the thrill of combat; but he had had the more mature excitement of taking courageous decisions in the face of criticism, and of being proved right. He would miss that kind of urgency in Washington. His naval aide compared his mental attitude at this moment with that of a football quarterback who has been playing an excellent game and whose instincts rebel when the coach orders him to the sidelines just as the game is getting to fever pitch.

Eisenhower had boarded the President's airplane for the onward flight to Tunis. The "Big Boss" was supposed to be traveling secretly, though his fedora, the jaunty angle of his cigarette holder, and the famous Roosevelt profile would easily give him away.

The Joint Chiefs' plane had tactlessly been routed over the rugged Kasserine Pass, where German Field Marshal Rommel had humiliated American troops in a savage counterattack nine months before. The country was strewn with pillars and the ruins of Roman cities. At Tunis, someone said that Carthage had taken centuries to build, but Hap Arnold was unimpressed. "It took only eighteen months to build the Pentagon," he pointed out.

On the continuing flight, to Cairo, they traced the coastal terrains over which wars had raged since long before Christendom. It was along this 1,500-mile battlefield that Rommel and Montgomery had thrown punches at each other through desert heat and torrential rains. These soldiers of the New World looked down with fascination on the intricate patterns woven by modern combat—the splattered bomb craters, the tidy German trenches, the British foxholes, the minefield boxes that Rommel had laid out at El Alamein, and the barbed-wire tangles already half consumed by the greedy sand. At places they saw the enduring tracks of tanks, marking out dramatic geometries where sudden shifts of battle had forced the armor to wheel en masse, leaving behind a flotsam of fire-blackened vehicles and shattered guns, their succeeding layers of British, American, and Nazi war paint indicating how often they had changed hands. Once these machines of war had enthralled their beholders; now they were lifeless and oddly beautiful as they threw long shadows across the desert from the late autumn sun settling in the west.

At last the Nile Valley had greened beneath them. There were villages, there was flowing water, there were cities. They were checked into the Mena House hotel eight miles outside Cairo, opposite the ancient pyramids; the hotel residents had been evacuated, and around it a three-square-mile security zone set up, ringed with barbed-wire entanglements, antiaircraft guns, searchlights, pillboxes and gun emplacements. At the hotel the U.S. ambassador in London, John G. Winant, a quiet and cultivated man, informally briefed the newcomers. He courteously dismissed Marshall's fears that the British wanted to abandon Overlord. But, he said, they would oppose a binding deadline for the invasion. "The British feel," explained Winant, "that they are supreme on the sea, and that the British and Americans are supreme in the air—but that the Germans are still superior to both in ground operations. . . . As for the cross-Channel operations, the British are . . . impressed by the excellent Nazi communications running from east to west. And they doubt that by bombing alone it will be possible to prevent the Germans from bringing up sufficient reinforcements to put the issue gravely in doubt." Winant added: "The British are still behind the Overlord operation—but they wish to be sure that German resistance is properly softened before undertaking the actual landing operation."

In Cairo the Combined Chiefs of Staff had met. The CCS were the joint Anglo-American directors of the war strategy. Often they dined with Churchill and Roosevelt, who drove everywhere in a bullet-proof Packard surrounded by outriders and Jeep loads of soldiers armed with submachine guns. The only face unknown to the Americans was that of Admiral Sir Andrew Cunningham, the new First Sea Lord. The others—Sir Alan Brooke, Sir Charles Portal, Sir Hastings Ismay—were all as familiar as the white limestone of the pyramids a few hundred yards away.

At the meetings and the meals, the anticipated differences had surfaced. Churchill, as expected, was still set on entirely new operations in the eastern Mediterranean. He wanted to invade the Greek island of Rhodes in February, provided that Rome had fallen during January. He also wanted to bolster the Balkan guerrillas, who were tying down twenty enemy divisions. But where would they get the tank landing ships? These craft, large vessels with gates at the bow through which forty tanks could be disgorged directly onto a beach, would be urgently needed for Italy, India, southern France, and the Pacific. Above all, they would be needed for Overlord, and in the right place at the right time. At one meeting the Combined Chiefs almost came to blows when the British raised the possibility of diverting the LSTs, as they were known, from Burma. General "Vinegar Joe" Stilwell, who was also in attendance, wrote that Brooke got so nasty and Admiral King got so sore that King almost climbed over the table at Brooke. "God, he was mad!" wrote Stilwell. "I wish he had socked him." But Cairo was British-controlled territory, so Brooke was in the chair and he obtained order. To cap it all, the Americans—with what seemed to the British an unnecessary preoccupation over China—had invited Chinese generals to the meetings, and these were incapable of sagacious question or comment. Brooke became downright insulting to them. Mopping his brow after spending an entire session trying to extract any wisdom from them, he turned to General Marshall.

"That was a ghastly waste of time!" he fumed.

Marshall said laconically, "You're telling me!" Brooke thought the phrase unfortunate.

Above all, Churchill wanted to be rid of the May 1 deadline for Overlord. Marshall saw him, then told his colleagues: "It was the desire of the Prime Minister to postpone Overlord for five or six weeks in order to expedite operations in the Mediterranean." Churchill had put it thus: "I am desirous of supporting Overlord, but I also desire to avoid turning an Overlord into a tyrant."

Another familiar problem—that of the authority of the Supreme Commander—had taken on an added complexity. The leading candidate for the job, Marshall, had become larger than life among the military commanders. Roosevelt had wanted him to control the whole European theater, including the Mediterranean. Churchill had rejected that because of the British political implications. He insisted that the commander be appointed only for Overlord. Roosevelt knew he would have to give in on this. He also saw that this restriction would make the post somewhat smaller—no longer big enough for Marshall. It would be beneath Marshall, he believed, to accept only part of a theater. Thus it became likely that another general would have to get Overlord.

On Thanksgiving Day, November 25, Roosevelt invited the British over to his villa for the traditional turkey feast. He himself carved the birds. Then they all repaired to the big CCS conference room, a phonograph was wound up, and dance music trickled out of the horn. Sarah Churchill, the only woman present, was much in demand for dancing. Her father selected General "Pa" Watson, Roosevelt's military secretary, as his partner and waltzed him past FDR's sofa. But the Anglo-American staff meetings continued unfriendly. Hap Arnold recorded that the CCS meeting the next day "almost resulted in a brawl." Brooke admitted in his diary afterward having "the father and mother of a row" with Marshall. The rooms were hot and stuffy and tempers were running high, but the divergences seemed to be real and not just ephemeral.

Eisenhower had particularly disagreed with the British Mediterranean strategy. He suggested further operations toward the Po Valley in Italy and then along the Mediterranean coast to the west, into France, to pave the way for Anvil. "These will have a tremendous effect on the eventual success of Overlord," he said. "The British believe that if maximum forces can be applied in the Mediterranean, if Russia can continue her present advances, and if Pointblank [the air offensive] is maintained at full vigor, then Germany will be out of the war by spring. They are perfectly sincere in this belief: information from prisoners of war indicates that the German soldier's morale is undoubtedly declining. The soldier is being affected by letters from homes in the bombed cities."

This neat calculation left unresolved one glaring strategic deficit: the shortage of landing craft. It would be hard sledding, as Arnold put it. On November 27 they had flown on to Iran with the gulf between the British and Americans wider than ever.

Iran had been partitioned and garrisoned by Russian, British, and American forces. The locals looked on them as tourists. The Persian rugs and brassware on offer in the jabbering bazaar were four times as costly as in downtown New York.

As the British and American planes landed, Soviet security troops had swarmed over the Teheran airfield. The route from the airfield to the capital was lined with cavalrymen at fifty-yard intervals; the adjacent British and Soviet legations were ringed by British-Indian and Soviet police. For added security, Churchill prevailed on Roosevelt to move his residence from the American legation, three miles away, to the square, boxlike building inside the Soviet compound—a naive idea, because now every whisper could be monitored by the NKVD, the Russian secret police. But Churchill was crabby and ailing; he was coming down with pneumonia, and he had all but lost his voice.

The next day, Roosevelt met with his staff. The fate of Overlord was in the balance. If the British continued to insist on self-serving military digressions in the Mediterranean, the main chance in Europe might be lost. Churchill would be pained by later American descriptions of his role. Perhaps he had forgotten, or been too ill to recall. He would write in his memoirs, "It has become a legend in America that I strove to prevent . . . Overlord, and that I tried vainly to lure the Allies into some mass invasion of the Balkans, or a large-scale campaign in the Eastern Mediterranean, which would effectively kill it." Of course, the key words in this apologia were "mass" and "large-scale." But even the small operations that he had asked for would have used up the tank landing craft needed to make Overlord a success. Admiral Leahy saw this clearly. "We can do either of two things," he said. "Either undertake Overlord, or go after Italy and Rhodes." Roosevelt was still deeply suspicious of British motives at the eastern end of the Mediterranean. He observed, "We've got to realize that the British look upon the Mediterranean as an area under British domination." And in private, he told his son Elliott: "Trouble is, the Prime Minister is thinking too much of the *post*-war, and where England will be. He's scared of letting the Russians get too strong. Maybe the Russians *will* get strong in Europe. Whether that's bad depends on a whole lot of factors."

Stalin had arrived the day before; it was the first time he had set foot outside his country since the Revolution. He was dressed in an ill-fitting light-brown marshal's uniform with two red stripes down the trousers and, on his shoulders, outsize gold epaulets, each with a red star. He wore only one medal. With his bushy hair and iron-gray mustache, he had a magnetic, almost majestic quality, said one English officer. Not tall, he was soldierly and tough as his name—man of steel, in Russian —implied. He met with Roosevelt and Churchill—for the first time around one table—on November 28, in the Soviet legation. Between them, these three men were the masters of four hundred million human beings. But they were incapable at this moment of historic prose. "The President," noted General Sir Alan Brooke, "made a poor and not very helpful speech. From then onwards the conference went from bad to worse. . . . We sat for three-and-a-half hours and finished up the conference by confusing plans more than they ever have been before."

The next day, Stalin had raised the all-important question: "Who will command Overlord?" He himself laid no claim to any voice in the appointment, but he did want to know who it would be and he did insist on knowing the date—after all, the Allies expected a big offensive in the east simultaneous with the operation. Stalin was not prepared to tolerate any delay beyond May 1944. He feared further backsliding by the British and he probably wanted to discourage them from encroaching into the Balkans. As they parted, Stalin shot a look across the conference table at Churchill and hurled a challenge: "I wish to pose a very direct question to the Prime Minister about Overlord," he said. "Do the Prime Minister and the British staff really believe in Overlord?" Churchill equivocated but finally said he did.

Roosevelt was unimpressed by Churchill on this occasion. The British prime minister seemed peevish, unwell, and prejudiced. "Marshall," Roosevelt commented to his son, "has got to the point where he just looks at the Prime Minister as though he can't believe his ears. If there's one American general Winston can't abide, it's General Marshall. And needless to say, it's because Marshall's right." Like a distracted eagle, Churchill seemed to be swooping about the eastern end of the Mediterranean, looking for something to snatch, first settling on the Dodecanese Islands, then Rhodes, and finally concentrating his attention on Turkey—he wanted to get Turkey into the war on the Allied side, to serve as the air base for a British thrust against the Germans. Roosevelt would later relate to Secretary of War Henry Stimson how he had headed off Churchill time after time. "I fought hard for Overlord," he said. "With Stalin's help I finally won out."

For his part, Churchill was wounded by Roosevelt's unabashed conniving with Stalin. When he heard that the two men had conferred privately, he was apprehensive lest Roosevelt might be agitating against him. So he bearded the Soviet dictator in private and tried to reassure him. Stalin warned Churchill that the survival of the Soviet Union depended on Overlord. "If there are no operations in May 1944, then the Red Army will think that there will be no operations at all that year." His soldiers were already war weary. They would not hold on if Overlord were delayed. Perhaps he was deliberately exaggerating, but the prospect of Stalin coming to terms with Hitler was not a cheering one for the Western Powers.

The British prime minister hastened to assure Stalin that he had confidence in Overlord, but he added that he was worried because thirty or forty German divisions in France would suffice to throw the Allies out. "I am not afraid about getting on shore," Churchill said, "but about what will happen on the thirtieth, fortieth, or fiftieth day."

Meanwhile the British and American chiefs of staff had met at the British legation: three generals, three admirals, and an air chief marshal, commanding between them fifteen million troops. Once more the argument hinged on the landing craft. Marshall said that sixty-eight of the tank landing craft in the Mediterranean had been earmarked for

Overlord, but there would still be sufficient left behind to lift 27,000 troops and 1,500 vehicles. Sixty-eight craft represented three months' production, so if they did not get to England in time, Overlord would have to wait for three months. And that would rule it out altogether, because winter weather would be approaching. On November 30 they finally reached agreement: Overlord should be postponed to June 1. As usual, it was a compromise between several claims.

November 30 was Churchill's sixty-ninth birthday. He insisted that Stalin and Roosevelt dine at the British legation. It was one of the most memorable occasions in Churchill's life. He adored the tableau he had created: receiving Stalin and his immense armed guard, seating the despot on his left and Roosevelt on his right, the two of them obliged to beam goodwill at the British. Again Stalin asked, "Who will command Overlord?" Churchill nodded toward General Marshall but added that the President had not finally made up his mind.

There was joy and irritation during the dinner—joy for the Americans and irritation for the British. Following an American toast to Sir Alan Brooke, who had remarked that the British had suffered most during the war, Stalin, visibly angry, made scathing remarks about the general's anti-Russian sentiments. Brooke sat there beady-eyed and purpling, then rose and replied icily to Stalin: "You will remember that this morning, while we were discussing cover plans, Mr. Churchill said that 'in war truth must have an escort of lies.' . . . Well, Marshal, you have been misled by dummy tanks and dummy airplanes, and you have failed to observe those feelings of true friendship which I have for the Red Army."

Stalin had affected to be impressed by this tough reply. He stated that since this was a war of machines, and most of those machines were being produced by the United States, it was clear who was winning the war for the Allies. The Americans were delighted to see him take down the British, and Arnold wrote a flattering sketch of Stalin in his diary: "Fearless, brilliant mind, quick of thought and repartee, ruthless—a great leader, [with the] courage of his convictions as indicated by his half humorous, half scathing remarks about the British—the Prime Minister and Brooke." The American air force commander doubted that either had ever been talked to like that before.

Churchill had offered the last toast. Stalin tramped around the table clinking glasses with all the military men. He ignored the diplomats and civilians. "History was made, and how," wrote Arnold. There was no doubt that Stalin was an exceedingly shrewd statesman.

Waiting at his headquarters at Algiers for the President to return from Teheran and a second visit to Cairo, Eisenhower had been desolate and irritable. He was rattled by the impending disintegration of his battle-winning Mediterranean headquarters, with all its experience in land, sea, and air operations. And there were distractions from the home front too. When a letter came from his wife, Mamie, naively inviting him to go shopping for her, Eisenhower flared up. "Possibly it is difficult for you to understand," he wrote back, "that I cannot get time to go browsing around shops like a lot of others can." Returning to his headquarters on December 1 after a week's absence, he had pawed eagerly over the foot-deep pile of letters, looking for one from Mamie, but there was none. "I hope you're not reveling in Reno," he chided her. "But if you are not doing something equally drastic, what in the world is the matter with your writing hand?" In the same letter he cautiously reproached her: "I've heard the various rumors to which you refer concerning a possible change in my assignment. I know nothing about them—what is to happen should soon become evident, but I, for one, do not know what it is."

In fact he had already guessed how the cards were stacked: Marshall was to become Supreme Commander for Overlord, and he was to get Marshall's post. He was unenthusiastic about a desk job at the Pentagon. At dinner one evening in early December a member of his personal staff inquired whether they would be going with him to Washington. His face clouded. "No need," he snarled. "If I have to return to Washington, I'll be carried up to Arlington Cemetery within six months anyway."

He had cabled Marshall some weeks back asking to retain his chief of staff, Walter Bedell Smith, if he was moved elsewhere; there had been no reply. He was lonely and unashamedly homesick. He pined for Mamie and continued to worry because she hadn't written. It was eighteen months since he had seen her. On December 4, as he waited for Roosevelt to arrive, he wrote to her again: "I miss you terribly. What is going to happen as a result of all rumored changes in command, etc., I don't know. But no matter what does happen—I do hope I can have a visit with you before too long. I know I'm a changed person—

no one could go through what I've seen and not be different from what he was at the beginning. But in at least one way I'm certain of my reactions—I love you! I wish I could see you an hour to tell you how much!"

On December 2, the British and American leaders returned from Teheran to Cairo. For the next three days they and their staffs conferred. On December 3, the British were flabbergasted to learn that Roosevelt proposed to leave three days later. "With nothing settled," noted Brooke, "they propose to disappear into the blue and leave all the main points connected with this Conference unsettled." To Brooke it looked like the worst sharp practice he had seen. The outcome of the conferences was a defeat for the British. On December 6 the British and American chiefs of staff submitted their final report to Roosevelt and Churchill: "Overlord and Anvil are the supreme operations for 1944," they declared. "They must be carried out during May 1944. Nothing must be undertaken in any other part of the world which hazards the success of these two operations." It was an apparent end to Churchill's Balkan aspirations.

Many topics had been chewed over during those last few days, but only once did Roosevelt revert to the last remaining central issue when talking with Churchill: who would actually command Overlord? As they were driving out to the pyramids on December 6, Roosevelt almost casually mentioned that he had come to realize that he could not spare General Marshall. What would Churchill think, asked Roosevelt, if he appointed Eisenhower instead?

Marshall already knew of the decision. Two days earlier he had mentioned it to Hap Arnold, who penciled into his diary: "Marshall had lunch with President. He doesn't get Overlord, Ike does." Later Roosevelt described the Churchill luncheon to Henry Stimson. "You know," recalled the President, "Winston wanted Marshall to command Overlord." Stimson nodded. But, Roosevelt continued, he had reopened the issue with Marshall during their private luncheon and had left the choice up to him: would he prefer to remain Chief of Staff or to command Overlord? Marshall had tactfully declined to choose— this, he had replied, was a decision for the President himself to make. Roosevelt suspected that Eisenhower might not be suited to take Marshall's job at the Pentagon, since he knew next to nothing about the

Pacific and could probably not handle Congress either. So he made his choice—to keep Marshall in Washington.

It was a rare decision. It went against both Stalin's and Churchill's expressed wishes and the clear advice of both Stimson and Roosevelt's special assistant Harry Hopkins. It was less a preference for Eisenhower than a tribute to Marshall; the President had told Marshall: "I felt I could not sleep at night with you out of the country." Marshall was at that time sixty-three and the object of almost religious adulation by his generals. On the day in 1939 that Hitler had attacked Poland, Marshall had become the U.S. Army's Chief of Staff and a four-star general. At that time, the army and air corps together numbered less than 200,000 men; by the time the war ended he would have multiplied it to over eight million. He was a general of famed intellect, iron self-discipline, and a transparent honesty before which even an Eisenhower would pale. Yet his very aloofness brought problems. Roosevelt stood in awe of him, and found his inability to get on first name terms with Marshall an impediment to close relations. Roosevelt hinted, through an intermediary, that he would like to call him "George." Marshall discouraged it. "It would," he said, "be utterly out of character for me."

When Roosevelt told Churchill of his intention to name Eisenhower, Churchill had chomped on his cigar and nodded approval. By 8:10 P.M. that day the final report had been signed and settled. "Earliest approval of final report we have ever had," observed Hap Arnold contentedly in his diary. As the final meeting broke up, Marshall penned a message for Roosevelt to send to Stalin, answering the Russian premier's insistent query at Teheran: "The immediate appointment of General Eisenhower to command of Overlord operation has been decided upon. Roosevelt."

Eisenhower heard on December 6 that Roosevelt had returned from Cairo. He flew to Tunis on December 7, met the President's plane in midafternoon, and conducted him to a waiting car. Inside the car, Roosevelt turned to him: "Well, Ike, you are going to command Overlord."

CHAPTER THREE

Alibi in Washington

ON THE day after New Year's Day, 1944, the Secretary of War, Henry Stimson, returned from a rather lame horseback ride on the frozen ground around his Maryland estate to find a telephone message from General Marshall: Dwight Eisenhower, the new Supreme Allied Commander, had landed incognito at Washington. Before flying on westward to see his aged mother in Manhattan, Kansas, Eisenhower wanted to come and see the Secretary. Stimson readily agreed, and the time was set for the following afternoon.

Of the Secretary of War the scientist Vannevar Bush would say: "It's a singular thing, but the most forward-looking . . . of the military experts in Washington is a man seventy-five years old who was trained as a lawyer!" Fond of horseback riding and tennis, and a fanatical golfer who would put in nine holes on even the rainiest days, Stimson was more zestful than his age suggested. He loved to attend maneuvers at Fort Bragg, watching infantry regiments "attack" under the covering fire of 155s and 105s and to the rattle of machine guns. "War is the father of all things"—Adolf Hitler liked quoting this dictum, and it echoes from Stimson's private diaries too. It was natural for Eisenhower to wish to consult Stimson, who was not only the highest-ranking civilian in the military establishment but also a sagacious advisor.

Since Nazi agents might be watching, Eisenhower had to move around Washington furtively. The stars were taken off his uniform, he was driven in a plain car by a soldier in plain clothes, and he entered the new Pentagon building through a secret passage. He arrived at the Secretary's office at five P.M. Over tea, Stimson filled him in on developments in American artillery rockets—he had witnessed them in trials at Aberdeen Proving Ground a few days before—and warned him about the pitfalls of invasion without proper reconnaissance as evidenced by the marines' operation at Tarawa in the South Pacific. Stimson found Eisenhower "very much keyed up." Stimson described his attempts to get the President to moderate his uncompromising antagonism toward General de Gaulle and his French Committee of National Liberation. Eisenhower replied easily that he had de Gaulle eating out of his hand—the French leader had accepted all the American plans for the arming of French divisions in North Africa. Eisenhower felt that Roosevelt, who regarded de Gaulle as a grim and relentless power seeker, must reverse himself and virtually recognize de Gaulle's Committee as the present representative of France.

That night Eisenhower was guest of honor at a stag dinner thrown by Marshall at the Alibi Club, an eating place across the river in downtown Washington so exclusive that few people had even heard of it. Marshall frequently used it when he wanted to introduce his field commanders to congressional leaders and other prominent Americans. Eisenhower was grinning broadly as he and his host greeted the arriving guests. They included James F. Byrnes, associate justice of the Supreme Court, and three senators, as well as Stimson, his undersecretary Robert Patterson, and John J. McCloy, his assistant secretary. Also on hand were the influential financier and philanthropist Bernard Baruch and several generals, among them Hap Arnold, Brehon Somervell, and Joseph McNarney. They dined informally, seated around a large oval table, eating steamed oysters and tossing the excavated shells into large wooden bowls. While Eisenhower listened intently, Marshall encouraged each of the generals to outline his overseas operations. Joseph Collins, whose 25th Division had fought well on Guadalcanal and in

New Georgia, made a particularly fine impression. He was tough, wiry, with an Irishman's playful grin. Eisenhower then reported on the war in the Mediterranean. He talked for twenty-five minutes, after which everybody stood and drank toasts to him as well as to Marshall and Roosevelt.

A few days later at White Sulphur Springs in West Virginia, a rest haven established by the army, Eisenhower and his wife ran into Joe Collins and his wife; like the Eisenhowers they were staying in the white cottages amid a grove of ancient oaks. Eisenhower exclaimed, "Why, Joe! I didn't know you were down here. I understand you'll be coming over to join us." It was the first that Collins knew of his impending assignment to Europe. Eisenhower told him he would be a corps commander. Conscious of security regulations, they did not discuss the matter further, nor did they meet again until Collins reported to Eisenhower in England.

With Mamie, Eisenhower flew to Kansas and spent a day and a night with his brother Milton, and their eighty-two-year-old mother was driven over from the nearby cowboy town of Abilene to see them. The man who was soon to command the mightiest force of men on earth was returning to his roots before setting out on the great ordeal. Mamie was less entranced than he. Perhaps it was just that he was so wrapped up in what lay ahead; she sensed that his thoughts were too far from her. Whatever it was—perhaps having to do with rumors about her husband and the pretty British army girl who had become his chauffeur —something seemed to have come between them, and these few days were a strain for Eisenhower. He apologized in a letter after leaving her: "I find myself very glad I came home—even though things did seem to be a bit upsetting. I guess it was just because we'd been separated so long, and before we could really get acquainted again, I was on my way."

Back in Washington on January 10, he received a cable from Montgomery in London. The British general reported that he had closely examined the Overlord problem with the British naval and air commanders, and thought that the initial assault should be widened. Five divisions should be put on shore on the first tide. But Montgomery believed that this would be possible only if the landing craft earmarked for Anvil were released to Overlord. Anvil should be reduced to a bluff.

Eisenhower could almost hear the dry, clipped voice of Montgomery as he read the words: "If we do not get [the] Anvil craft, then I consider the chances of quick success are not good." Eisenhower was urged to express his own views to the Combined Chiefs of Staff. "Will you hurl yourself into the contest," Montgomery asked in closing, "and get us what we want."

Eisenhower replied that he would accept the abandonment of Anvil only as a last resort: "We must not lose sight of the advantages to Overlord which Anvil brings." He emphasized that it would be an important diversion of Nazi defenses. "Furthermore," he added, "there are certain strong considerations not purely military which have been brought to my attention here and which must be weighed." The Anvil operation had been suggested by the Russians, in fact, and the western leaders were too much in Stalin's debt to drop it without good reason.

Calling at the White House to pay his respects, Eisenhower found President Roosevelt was in bed, apparently with the flu. Eisenhower was ushered in to see the great man, who was propped up with pillows, drawing wearily on a cigarette in the famous long holder. The general was appalled at his haggard looks—he had deteriorated to a sallow shadow of the man who had breezed into Tunis from Cairo only five weeks before. The western world's two principal leaders were now both sick old men. Flicking ashes all over the bedspread, Roosevelt motioned the general to a chair and told him of his plans to carve up Germany after its defeat. "I favor taking northwest Germany for the United States," he announced.

Eisenhower was opposed to any such plan. From conversations he knew that the President visualized American forces remaining in Europe for a considerable period. No doubt the Russians would take all eastern Germany and the Balkans, and the British and Americans everything west of that line; Eisenhower hoped that the Allied zone would remain under one overall Allied commander.

Before noon he stepped in to see Henry Stimson again. He found quite a gathering in the Secretary's office: besides Stimson, there were several generals and the government scientist Dr. Vannevar Bush. An ordnance general had brought blueprints of a new tank on which a battery of rockets would be mounted, and another general described the plans for making the tank float, for use in invasions. Eisenhower had never seen anything like it. But then Bush told of the fears that the

Nazis were far ahead in rocket research and the possibility that the warheads might contain poison gases, or worse. Eisenhower wryly admitted: "You make me scared." He meant it. These fears of secret weapons of untold violence gradually invaded Eisenhower's consciousness and became waking nightmares.

The Germans were fighting doggedly in Italy and the Allies were making little progress. Eisenhower confidentially told Stimson that he had discussed the forthcoming seaborne invasion at Anzio in northern Italy with Winston Churchill. Stimson observed, "He [Churchill] is dead set upon making this offensive for political reasons." Eisenhower had powerful doubts about it. It would swallow up landing craft he badly needed for Overlord. But from Cairo, Churchill had been conveyed to Marrakesh to recover from his illness; and he was still languishing there and certainly did not relish returning to London with the present stalemate in the Italian campaign. He needed good news to tell the British people. He needed the rapid invasion of Anzio, because he needed Rome.

The generals discussed this infuriating sideshow again with Stimson that afternoon. The Secretary noted, "Of course, Churchill is banking on pulling off this operation quickly . . . [but] Overlord is already down to its lowest limit in landing craft."

To preserve secrecy, Eisenhower slunk out of Washington on January 13 with the furtiveness of a criminal with a price on his head.

Ten days later, in Nazi Germany, a stocky Japanese army officer with a permanent grin and a sword at his belt was shown into Adolf Hitler's bunker at Rastenburg, East Prussia. Hitler's mind might have been elsewhere. News had reached him that the Allies had that day landed in strength at Anzio, behind the German lines near Rome, and a desperate battle was at that instant raging to throw them back into the sea.

Hitler's visitor was General Hiroshi Oshima, the Emperor's ambassador to the Third Reich. He was one of the few people Hitler felt he could trust: Hitler always felt it safe to tell the Japanese his innermost thoughts, because Nazi cryptanalysts had reported that the Japanese machine codes were unbreakable, and because the Japanese were men of honor. They would not betray strategic confidences.

During the course of their long conversation, Hitler told him: "Now as for the question of the second front. No matter when it comes or at what point, I have made adequate preparations to meet it. In Finland we have seven divisions; in Norway twelve; in Denmark six; in France and the Low Countries sixty-two. . . . I have gotten together as many armored divisions as possible, including four SS divisions and the Hermann Göring Division. But how vast is that sea coast! It would be utterly impossible for me to prevent some sort of landing somewhere or other. . . . As for me," he continued, "I would just like to see the Anglo-Saxons come on and try to stage an invasion and establish a second front!"

"Does your Excellency have any idea where they may land?" Oshima inquired.

"Honestly," Hitler admitted, "I can only say that I don't know. The most effective area would be along the Straits of Dover, but to land there would require much preparation and the difficulties would be great. I don't think that the enemy will run such a risk."

He reminded the Japanese ambassador: "Of course, everything which I am telling you is said in the utmost confidence, but I can assure you that I have plenty of plans. . . . Besides, don't forget our coming retaliation against England. We are going to do it principally with rocket guns. Everything is now ready. . . . We also have ready two thousand *Schnellbomber,* fast bombers. Last night we carried out our first real bombing of London. With all these [means] I believe that we can gradually regain the initiative and, seizing our opportunities, turn once again against Russia."

After listening to Oshima for a while, he added, beaming with satisfaction: "I, for one, believe that this is the year that will decide who wins and who loses, and I have plans and calculations that will turn the tables by this fall."

From Berlin, Oshima sent to Tokyo a lengthy coded telegram reporting this dialogue. It was in six parts. Allied monitoring stations in India intercepted the telegram and passed it by radio to the secret center in Washington known as Magic, where experts pried out its secrets with captured codes and computers. Within seven days the entire text had been broken, translated into English, and circulated to a highly restricted circle.

From these Magic intercepts, the Pentagon knew that Hitler was planning some kind of secret attack on England. They knew that he was preparing every defensive measure to defeat the invasion. But these very intercepts—and those provided by the Ultra organization in England —would also be one of the most cogent secret weapons in Eisenhower's arsenal when the battle began. He could follow virtually every Nazi countermove before it began, and he could read of the effects of his own deception and campaign strategies.

CHAPTER FOUR

Stakes Incalculable

THE ROOMY C-54 brought Eisenhower in hops across the Atlantic—to dreamy blue Bermuda, to the Portuguese Azores, and then to Prestwick, Scotland. Fog mantled the whole of England, making further flying down to London impossible. A special train was waiting for him, with his own new private car, the "Bayonet." He cast an appreciative look around at the way that Colonel Sydney Bingham had furnished it, with its palatially paneled office, its ornate chairs lining one wall, and its sofa, desk, telephone, and table. Then he settled down for the journey south.

He had asked that nobody meet him in London. "I particularly desire that General Montgomery do not come to the train because of the practical certainty that he would be recognized," he had cabled ahead to General Omar N. Bradley, who for some months had been in London with the staff planning Overlord.

From the station, Eisenhower's British military assistant drove him to Mayfair, the most exclusive quarter of the city. His lodgings were to be a town house, Hayes Lodge, near Berkeley Square and only a couple of minutes' walk from his headquarters, a big red brick building fronting on Grosvenor Square. Hayes Lodge had been built by an eccentric old lady who lived in dread that things were going to get in at her; there were bars on every window, right up to the third floor. His assistant had ordered these iron gratings to be padlocked every night. But Eisenhower knew London, and guessed that a time might come when he would have to get out in a hurry, so he ordered the gratings above the ground floor left unlocked. The house had all the facilities he liked, including fireplaces: open fires were cheerful to look at and handy to throw cigarette butts into. Even at the Dorchester in 1942 he had had a real log fire. But he hoped not to be based here more than ten days, because he was going to move SHAEF—the Supreme Headquarters, Allied Expeditionary Force—to rural Sussex. Eisenhower hated cities—he hated any town larger than Abilene, the Kansas town he had grown up in, and Abilene was not large.

The burden on Eisenhower was great. No matter how he slaved, work just kept piling up on his desk. Moreover, he was having a recurrence of his gastric flare-ups, and they were worrisome at times. Like any man he had other worries too, such as how he was going to pay his taxes for 1944—he had just managed to clean up 1943 with all the cash he had left. "If I could give you an exact diary account of the past week," he would write to Mamie on January 23, "you'd get some idea of what a flea on a hot griddle really does!"

His office chief, Colonel Ernst R. "Tex" Lee, had used Eisenhower's B-17 Flying Fortress to fly the general's personal aides—his "official family," as he called his household staff—to England. The general was very glad to see them. At Christmas he had written to Mamie from Algiers, worried about whether he could keep them: "I don't know what I'm going to do with some of the people I've depended upon. For example, the darkies that live in my house with Mickey and the steward: if I have to live in a London hotel a while, these boys will be out of a job—yet I'll need them later." But he had been allowed to retain them. His British military assistant was Lieutenant Colonel James Gault, who had served with him since Sicily. Gault was a big Scots Guards officer, who wore a dress uniform so gaudy that one of the WAC drivers, Pearlie Hargrave, mistook him for a Russian. Harry C. Butcher, a former Columbia Broadcasting System official who was a trusted friend and had become the general's naval aide, would take care of the diary and household. Eisenhower had kept his batman, an Irish-American master sergeant, Michael J. McKeogh, who had been a bellhop at the Plaza Hotel until he was inducted into the army in March 1941. Mickey's father had died four years earlier; now he had found a substitute, and showed Eisenhower true affection throughout the war. From Africa also came his black kitchen hands—his "darkies"—and his tailor, Sergeant Michael Popp. He had brought Captain Mattie Pinnett as his personal stenographer ("I want a WAC officer for this job and she is completely satisfactory," he told Bedell Smith). Half a dozen other enlisted WACs completed the office. There was also one British woman—his "young chauffeuse," as FDR's secretary "Pa" Watson termed her; Kay Summersby had been assigned to him two years before, because the girls of the British transport service knew their way around London's intricate network of streets and squares better than the Americans.

More important than any of his household aides was his chief of staff, Walter Bedell Smith. Smith was the kind of manager and hatchet man who had to be able to fire without compunction an old friend who had failed. Personal heroism under actual fire was not a prerequisite for the position, however, which was just as well. In Sicily, General Patton had been puzzled to find Bedell Smith cowering behind a sheltering ridge; it turned out that an American 155-millimeter battery had just opened up and Smith, thinking it was an enemy salvo arriving, had leaped into a ditch and stayed there even when told it was safe. "When I got back," reminisced Patton, savoring the memory, "he was still pale, gray, and shaky."

Smith had been born in Indianapolis forty-nine years before. A childless, cold-blooded, stiff-faced major general with a wife described in one general's diary as "classy," he had served as secretary of the Joint Chiefs and then the Combined Chiefs until September 1942, when he joined Eisenhower in England. He was an officious person who made enemies faster than friends, but did not care. Eisenhower did not awe him. Asked for his opinion of Bedell Smith, Everett Hughes once used the word "tricky."

As soon as he had been designated Supreme Commander, Eisenhower had sent Bedell Smith ahead to London to investigate the planning work done by COSSAC, General Sir Frederick Morgan's invasion planning staff. Morgan, like Smith, was a staff officer. A man of great ability and "a straight shooter," he was considered to be pro-American; happily, his American chief of staff at COSSAC, General Ray W. Barker, demonstrated a corresponding understanding of the British mentality. At the beginning of their collaboration, Barker and Morgan had each removed a tunic button and secretly sewed them onto each other's uniforms—a symbol of fraternity. Morgan's staff employed about three hundred people at its headquarters, Norfolk House, a modern red brick building in the Georgian style standing in St. James's Square, just south of Piccadilly. Through its doors each morning streamed British, Americans, Canadians, and some South Africans—with orderlies, clerks, typists, mimeograph operators, mapmakers, and translators. In general, whether the COSSAC planners wore a "U.S." or a crown on their collar tabs made no difference. But there were minor operating differences. The Americans, for example, liked to begin work at nine A.M., while the British seldom showed up before ten. The Americans quit at five, the British at six.

Until Eisenhower's arrival, Barker and Morgan had improvised. They would typically start their day at a British ministry, then drive to Grosvenor Square for a discussion with the Americans, and then Freddie Morgan might say: "Well, I want to go to the War Office this morning to see Brooke." The two men worked hard and late, returning to Norfolk House at eight or eight-thirty P.M. with two or three other officers. They would trudge back to their billets at ten or eleven through the blacked-out streets, frequently being stopped along the way by one of the French streetwalkers who, Morgan remarked, had escaped the Continent, judging by their ages, many decades before Dunkirk.

Eisenhower now commenced to absorb Morgan's staff into his own headquarters, SHAEF. He set up an exhausting round of conferences with the British and American generals to find out what COSSAC had already done. On his first full day, January 16, he called in General Morgan, with the deputy theater commander General J.C.H. Lee and Omar Bradley, to discuss the COSSAC plan for Overlord. This plan provided for an initial assault on the French coastline by three divisions early in May, building up to a force of fifteen British and Canadian and twenty American divisions. Eisenhower had learned of it by chance during the summer and he agreed with Montgomery's stated view that the initial assault must be expanded to five or even six divisions. But that would not be easy, given the shortage of landing craft and of naval gunfire support.

Eisenhower had sent General Montgomery to London several weeks ahead to reconnoiter, and this had resulted in typical problems. Montgomery's customary public flourishes attracted unwanted attention to Norfolk House and caused the zealously security-conscious Morgan much heartburn. No sooner had Montgomery arrived than he announced to American troops that he was going to be the sole commander of the Allied ground forces: "I came home the other day from Italy," he said, in that curious clipped voice of his, "to take command of the British Army and the American Army of which General Eisenhower is the Supreme Commander. And he has put the First American Army under me for the battle." Publication of this boast was stopped only at the last moment by the censor. At a press conference the next day, Eisenhower was asked to confirm that Montgomery would be the ground commander in the forthcoming invasion. He suggested that the writers should not "go off on the end of a limb."

Churchill instructed his staff in embarrassment: "It would seem to be about time that the circular sent to generals and other high commanders about making speeches should be renewed."

The plan was for the ground forces to fight initially under the command of the 21st Army Group, a British headquarters to be commanded by Montgomery. The appointment of this spiky, self-obsessed general had been made by General Sir Alan Brooke against Eisenhower's expressed preferences. He had told Brooke five days after his own appointment that he preferred Alexander to Montgomery. But Brooke had his way with Churchill, and Montgomery got the job. Montgomery gratefully wrote on December 28 from Italy, "My dear Brookie, I must thank you for promoting me to command the armies in England. It is a big job and I will do my best to prove worthy of your selection. There is a terrible lot to do and not much time in which to do it. Immediately I arrive I will come and see you. . . ."

Montgomery was not widely beloved among his colleagues. "He was a tactless person," said an American staff officer, "who had no background. He was a sonofabitch. He had gotten ahead by being a greasy grind." Friendless, aloof, haughty, he was destined for the highest appointments that Britain's imperial armies could bestow. He was the antithesis of Eisenhower: cold, unmoved by feminine company, unorthodox in his dress, unforgiving to his subordinates. He surrounded himself with a claque of young and handsome staff officers; he craved glory and publicity. Inevitably he roused the ire of the West Point generals by his attitudes, his plummy voice, his arrogance, and his greed for power. One American army commander, offended by Montgomery's ill breeding, noted after a conference with him, "Monty gave me a five-cent [cigarette] lighter. Some one must have sent him a box of them." His rudeness was notorious. Once an American general asked to be taken to see Montgomery at his command post. The English aide attached to him, a bright young subaltern with a monocle, said: "General, I wish you wouldn't make that request of me. My boss is— you'll have to excuse me—a peculiar fellow, and if I go and make that request, he's liable to make you wait an hour before he sees you."

Even among the British the mere mention of Montgomery's name often brought a curl to the lips of otherwise restrained people. Lord Gort, governor of Malta, sneered to Bedell Smith: "In dealing with him one must remember that he is not *quite* a gentleman."

Montgomery had rocketed to media stardom during his long desert duel with the Afrika Korps. Before that he had been an obscure general who had not commanded a unit in action since Dunkirk. After his desert victory at El Alamein, he fought a series of slow battles; they were so methodical and ponderous that it seemed their main purpose was to preserve the popular impression of Montgomery's infallibility, even at the expense of allowing Rommel's army to escape. The truth was that his battles were often won by the British ability to muddle through—or as he himself put it, in writing to his War Minister in September 1943: "We do not always deserve to get away with it. We pull it off in the end which is the great thing."

He defeated the enemy armies less by tactics than by brute force— or what he called "administration." Unless he had his supply and maintenance organization ready, he would not move. Nor would he fight unless there was a good chance of success. "There must be no failures," he explained. He expected field commanders to have drive, moral courage, and the ability to act on verbal orders alone; they had to inspire their troops with confidence and wild enthusiasm. "They must enter the fight," he dictated, "with the light of battle in their eyes and definitely wanting to kill the enemy." His methods were controversial, but under his command the Eighth Army had distinguished itself all the way to Tunis. Now he had left the Eighth, at Eisenhower's behest, in Italy and had come to London to be the ground force commander during Overlord.

The son of a bishop, he never stopped sermonizing. "The wise commander," Montgomery had pontificated in one broadsheet, to which he gave wide distribution among British—and American—generals, "will see very few papers or letters. He will refuse to sit up late at night conducting the business of his army; he will be well advised to withdraw to his tent or caravan after dinner at night and have time for quiet thought and reflection."

To Montgomery, war was something of a game, which the "best team" won. His letters, his field orders, and his proclamations were full of sporting references and of sanctimonious quotations from the Scriptures. He was naturally arrogant. Once, at a dinner for the Overlord commanders, Montgomery announced, although only a guest, that he would not tolerate any smoking. War Office bureaucrats told of how very shallow Montgomery's mind was, and of how he used simple repetition to get his message across to the troops. "He would have been a success in the advertising world if he had not been a soldier," said Sir Eric Speed, Under Secretary of State for War, with evident distaste.

Remarks about Montgomery revealed a jealous and resentful undertow swirling beneath the professional reserve of the British high command. Air Chief Marshal Sir Arthur Tedder—who now became Eisenhower's deputy at SHAEF—drawled to an American general, "It is bad form for officers to criticize each other, so I shall!" He quoted the words used by Alexander about another general: "As a soldier, he is a good plain military cook." Tedder added: "The remark applies absolutely— to Montgomery. He is a little fellow of average ability who has had such a buildup that he thinks of himself as Napoleon. He is not."

Montgomery's foes, both Nazi and American, were not always so cutting. Under interrogation on May 5, 1945, German Field Marshal von Rundstedt would say that Montgomery was Britain's greatest general—"He has proved it in Libya, Tunisia, Italy and again since D-day." Probably his greatest American critic was George Patton, but even he had praise for Montgomery. After meeting him in 1943, Patton wrote this assessment: "Monty is a forceful, selfish man, but still a man. I think he is a far better leader than Alexander and that he will do just what he pleases, as Alex is afraid of him." In the privacy of his diary four months later Patton bragged: "I know I can outfight that little fart any time."

Each day Eisenhower walked the few minutes from Hayes Lodge to SHAEF headquarters in Grosvenor Square. In a sense he was occupying Marshall's desk after all, but not in the city that either he or Marshall had expected. Marshall's secretary Colonel Frank McCarthy had been so sure that his boss would get the job of Supreme Commander that he had already sent over Marshall's personal desk furniture and blotter from the Pentagon. Now it all had to go back.

Once or twice when he had been in London in 1942, Mamie, back in Washington, had told her husband's batman that she had a premonition that Eisenhower was going to be the Pershing of this war. Pershing had commanded the American Expeditionary Forces in Europe in World War I. Now that premonition was coming true.

Eisenhower's arrival in England had caused an upheaval. Although London was participating body and soul in the war, the involvement was mainly in corridors and clubs—officers and civilians meeting to discuss strategy. From Algiers, Eisenhower now brought the zing of an active theater commander. Cynical observers expected to see him fall flat on his face. Here the British were on their home ground, with Parliament, the Foreign Office, the War Office, and No. 10 Downing Street just around the corner. C. D. Jackson, the American executive in London who wrote privately to his boss, *Time* magazine owner Henry R. Luce, observed that the general's sudden appearance had put the cat among the pigeons: "A lot of people were planning, planning, planning, but the translation of those plans into action seemed to be fairly remote, with the inevitable psychological consequences. Now there is a new hustle and bustle, and the dawning of a sense that what is being put on paper really means something in terms of lives and logistics."

Promply upon arrival, Eisenhower looked up old friends—for the pleasure of it and for support. One was the First Sea Lord, Sir Andrew B. Cunningham. Many British commanders in North Africa had felt that Eisenhower lacked combat experience and thus was unsuitable to be Supreme Commander there. But ABC, as he was called, had gone out of his way as British naval commander in Algiers to make it clear that Eisenhower alone was in charge. There were two villas on the grounds of the St. George Hotel; Eisenhower had one, Cunningham the other, and their friendship had grown. They had often played Ping-Pong together, and found they were evenly matched. Eisenhower liked ABC's rough but human style.

The effort to blend British and American staffs into a smooth Allied team had begun out there in Algiers. It involved understanding. On one occasion, an American sentry who had killed a British marine by mistake had been sentenced to ten years for manslaughter. Eisenhower had feared that the British might think this too lenient, but Cunningham had counseled him: "One young life has been snuffed out; it would be a pity if another should be ruined." Eisenhower reduced the sentence to ninety days and sent the boy to the front to redeem himself.

The British admiral had celebrated the Fourth of July in 1943 by firing a forty-eight-gun salute, dressing ship, and offering other felicitations that clearly violated King's Regulations. Eisenhower felt flattered —until the admiral growled to him: "I am merely celebrating our success in getting rid of an entire nation of rebellious subjects." One of Cunningham's favorite expressions of disapproval was: "That's too velvet-arsed and Rolls-Royce." One evening ABC took his chief signals officer onto the terrace to be enraptured by the mouth-watering view of the bay of Algiers, and after a while he prompted the officer to comment: "Come on, man, what do you think of it?" The officer answered, "I was just thinking, Sir. Now I know what you mean by Rolls-Royce and velvet-arsed!"

This was the admiral who had succeeded Admiral Sir Dudley Pound as First Sea Lord of Britain's historic and still mighty navy in October 1943. One of his intelligence staff would later describe his startling countenance: "Not only was he of ruddy complexion with bright blue eyes, but at that time the lower lids of the eyes had become so lax that they turned over and lay down towards his cheekbones showing the red lining, exactly like the eyes of a bloodhound. Later he had these lids sewn up, I believe." Bloodhound or not, Admiral Cunningham remained an old sea dog. Cedric R. Price, a deputy secretary of the British Chiefs of Staff Committee, would assess him thus: "He was not quite the equal of his new colleagues intellectually: Alan Brooke and Portal were first-class staff officers as well as great commanders. Cunningham was a commander rather than a staff officer." Price added, "Like other great commanders—Montgomery, for example, with whom he had much in common—he found, 'direction of war by committee' irksome at first and quite foreign to his nature."

That day Eisenhower also spoke with the British chief of staff, Sir Alan Brooke. Brooke was not happy about Eisenhower's appointment —the job of Overlord commander had originally been promised to him. Now he had a bone to pick with Eisenhower. On New Year's Eve, Bedell Smith had pressed Brooke to transfer to England three of the best British staff officers in the Mediterranean—Humfrey Gale, J. F. Whiteley, and Kenneth Strong. Brooke courteously objected to this raid on the Mediterranean talent, and put Smith in his place. "I am responsible for the distribution of the staff on all fronts," he told him. "You can rely on me to take their various requirements into account. I will have no string-pulling." At this, the American general abruptly started toward the door, remarking: "You are not being helpful." Later Bedell Smith had to apologize to Eisenhower, who thought, as his aide Harry Butcher noted, that perhaps the war was getting on Smith's nerves. Butcher wrote, "I think it's his ulcer."

Bedell Smith's treatment of Sir Alan Brooke rang alarm bells in Eisenhower's mind. He called together 120 principal officers at Norfolk House the next morning and read them the riot act. He told them that he expected all thoughts and words indicative of an officer's nationality to be erased. And he laid down this demand: "Once we have made our plan, I want everybody to express their faith in it, no matter what controversies or misgivings you may have mentioned among yourselves when the plan was being formulated. Everyone has to exude confidence. Anybody showing less will not be doing his duty."

The implication was that offenders would be kicked off his staff. And they were. Once he heard an officer refer to another staff officer as "that British sonofabitch"; he ordered the man sent home, not for the noun but for the adjective.

During the first weeks in London, Eisenhower was under an additional strain. It was the strain that a man endures when trapped in a conflict between two women. He was caught between Mamie, the wife on whom he doted back in the United States, and Kay Summersby, the serene, willowy Irish girl in uniform who had been assigned to him as his driver. He bore the stress with dignity.

Mamie must have suspected. Summersby's role had been an open secret in Algiers and was now again in London. Her name figures in many diaries of visitors to Eisenhower, particularly in the unpublished diaries of his friend and deputy in Algiers, Everett Hughes. Well-meaning women friends may have inquired of Mamie how she felt about the attractive woman seen driving her husband around the capitals and battlefields of Europe. Mamie's annoyance crept out of her heart and drilled unwillingly into her letters to Eisenhower, and her hostile tone shook him. The whole affair must have affected his health; it certainly damaged his image. When "Pa" Watson referred to Kay Summersby as a "chauffeuse," there was as much play on the warmth implied in that word as on her ability to drive. General Montgomery, perhaps even more immune than most British officers to feminine allure, relished the situation. He wrote to Eisenhower in 1948 that he had learned that "your lady driver and secretary has written a book in the States" and asked in evident amusement for a copy. Eisenhower wrote back huffily: "So far as Mrs. Summersby's book is concerned I have not read it and do not know where it can be obtained. If I happen to run into a copy of this somewhere I will forward it to you."

Kay Summersby had migrated to England from an impoverished Ireland ten years earlier to work as a model and movie extra. At the time she was assigned to Eisenhower in June 1942, she was awaiting a divorce. She was with him in North Africa and became engaged to Colonel Robert R. Arnold of II Corps; the colonel duly showed up with her at Eisenhower's headquarters on January 8, 1943. But as the weeks passed, the staff noticed that it was their general who was going around with her. Some days they went to the front together. On others, they made up a bridge foursome with Butcher and Everett Hughes; they usually beat them. Hughes was a burly, grumpy general who lost no love on the army's women drivers, still less after one of them snapped at him: "We have been told to open car doors. You generals must cooperate." Nor were Summersby's driver colleagues pleased at her good fortune. "Elspeth Duncan comes to my room," jotted a bemused Hughes in his diary, "and cries over Kay and Ike. She foresees a scandal. Claims she is stooge for Kay. Wants to quit. I tell her to stick around. Maybe Kay will help Ike win the war." A few days later Hughes fired the overemotional Miss Duncan, noting: "I can't stand a woman driver. I want a man."

Many observers thought Eisenhower was carrying his interest in improving relations with the British too far. But Kay Summersby, thirty-four, flirtatious, and attractive, seemed different from the rest, and Hughes shared the general curiosity about their friendship. After a party at General Carl A. Spaatz's sumptuous Algiers villa with Eisenhower, Cunningham, and Mark Clark at the end of 1942, Hughes confided hazily to his diary that he had had three drinks too many and had sat around with Eisenhower after the party broke up. "Discussed Kay," he wrote, "I don't know whether Ike is alibi-ing or not. Says he wants to hold her hand, accompanies her to house, doesn't sleep with her. He doth protest too much, especially in view of the gal's reputation in London."

All this fruity speculation was squelched by Kay Summersby's announcement that her fiancé had applied to marry her and that Eisenhower had given written permission. Alas, two weeks before the planned June wedding the bridegroom-to-be became a colonel-that-was; with his death in action, Kay was back in Eisenhower's life.

She at once began to dominate the general. Once, when he and Butcher came to lunch, General Hughes mildly raised his eyebrows at the way his Supreme Commander was summoned from the table by his driver-secretary. On July 3, he noted that an Independence Day party was planned with Eisenhower, "but Kay is still broken up or down or something." Worried by how all this might end, Eisenhower's trusty friend Hughes quietly asked his own wife Kate to inquire whether Mamie would like to come out to North Africa; a few days later, on August 19, Kate replied: "Mamie will come if invited." No invitation went out.

The affair ran its natural course. By late 1943 Eisenhower's feelings for the woman were calmer. Indeed, as the clouds gathered over him that autumn of his seemingly inevitable return to the Pentagon to succeed General Marshall as Chief of Staff, there was one silver lining, an escape from her tender clutches. Nationality rules could not be waived in the Pentagon; as a British citizen, she could not work for him there. In October, Hughes made a note of Eisenhower's suggested solution to the tangle: "Ike wants me to take Kay with car thrown in." Hughes—who was more interested in the Packard end of the deal—added: "He doesn't want to be Chief of Staff of the U.S. Army." On October 14, Hughes threw a birthday party for Eisenhower and gave him a bottle of Benedictine, meaning it, as he noted, to sweeten Kay. (In his next letter to Mamie, Eisenhower gave a teasing picture of this party: Tex Lee "had Air Chief Marshal and Lady Tedder, Captain Briggs (!) a Wac in office of the chief of staff, Mrs. Kay Summersby my driver and secretary, Colonel Gault—a British officer I like a lot—Lee himself and one or two junior staff officers.") At dinner on November 10, Eisenhower placed Hughes next to Kay. Hughes deduced what his friend's motives were. "Guess Ike is about to turn over," he wrote in a reference to the imminent departure of the Supreme Commander to Washington.

Eisenhower's joy at his unexpected selection for Overlord was therefore tempered by a sudden, well-concealed chagrin, the realization that he had not gotten rid of Kay Summersby after all. The silver lining had a cloud: as he would once more be commanding an inter-Allied theater, she could reasonably expect to be transferred with him, and was.

At the year's end, when Eisenhower had gone to the United States for consultations at the Pentagon, there was apparently an encounter with Mamie at which the subject was aired. Whatever his passing feelings for Kay Summersby, he was still beholden to Mamie, and all his generals knew it. Once when Eisenhower had telephoned Patton and said, "My American Boss will visit you in the morning," Patton had cheekily replied—knowing full well Eisenhower meant General Marshall—"When did Mamie arrive?" (After that, Patton had pointedly noted in his diary: "Man cannot serve two masters.")

Mamie was something special to Eisenhower, and as soon as he left her again for London, he had begun pining for her; he sent her messages from along the route and by teletype as soon as he reached London. Her answer was to disappear. She had told him she was going to stay at Hot Springs, Arkansas, for two or three weeks and then go on to Texas. But in London there was a message saying that she would be staying at Little Rock instead. It was all rather vague and confusing. He felt punished by this uncertainty about her whereabouts, and for three weeks he worked in a complete state of bewilderment. He wrote to her all the same, ending one letter dolefully, "I love you so much, I'm very serious when I say, 'Please take care of yourself.' I miss you all the time and every day I look forward to the end of this war, so that I can come home to *you.*"

When he wrote to Mamie—in longhand, despite his aversion to using a pen—he was uninhibited, addressing Mamie as "darling," pledging his love to her and devising different ways of saying the same thing: "What a good looking, gorgeous gal you are—and how lucky I am!" But when he was under pressure and he had to dictate letters to a secretary, the typed letters became stiffer, beginning "Dear Mamie" and ending "As ever, your Ike." Typically, hearing that a courier was about to leave, he would pen a note to Mamie: "Please don't get impatient when you don't get letters. . . . Lord knows my letters are nothing—but I do love you so—as I'd like to be able to tell better and oftener but anyway it's true." Most of his letters were dutiful, affection-ate, and repetitive; they reflected the struggle to write about trivia while making decisions affecting the lives of a million men—decisions of which not even a ghost of an echo was allowed to enter the lines.

Fully aware that even his letters were screened by U.S. Army officers at the Bureau of Censorship, he searched for safe subjects. He wrote pages about Telek, his mischievous black Scottie which had been named after his home, Telegraph Cottage, and Kay: "My dog had a funny, harmless accident. He was in the front seat of the car and decided to crawl up into the open window of the door, to get a good view, I suppose. He lost his balance and had to leap for the ground. . . . I was sitting in the right rear seat and could see it all. His feet hit the ground nicely for a four point landing, but his forward motion started rolling him over and over—like a barrel going down hill. . . . When he finally scrambled to his feet he was thoroughly humiliated. His ears were down, his tail dragging and his coat covered with gray dust and gravel. . . . Took me a little time to restore his good humor."

On January 18, 1944, Winston Churchill returned from Marrakesh; two months had passed since he had left England for Cairo and Te-heran. The Chiefs of Staff met him at Paddington. Alan Brooke was relieved that Churchill had given up trying to run the war from Mo-rocco. What the general called "a three-cornered flow of telegrams in all directions" had resulted in utter confusion. The Prime Minister's physical condition was alarming. War Minister Sir James Grigg wrote that day, "Have just been to meet the P.M. He looks well, but shews signs of being an old man." Churchill was now in his seventieth year.

The next day his Chiefs of Staff held two meetings with him lasting four hours. "We accomplished nothing," fumed Brooke in his diary.

This was nothing new. Churchill was not easily trifled with in debates. He would smilingly say, "All I want is compliance with my wishes—after reasonable discussion." Overlord still unsettled him. He had been known to weep quite realistically whenever he thought it would benefit his cause, but he wept real tears at the thought of any loss of British life that could be avoided at the expense of foreigners. That was why he would have preferred to reinforce the guerrillas in the Balkans, in preference to Overlord. General Hap Arnold wrote in his private diary that, when the invasion was discussed, Churchill talked dolefully of "three hundred thousand dead British soldiers—floating in the Channel."

Little had happened to change his opinion since July 1943, when Brigadier General Albert C. Wedemeyer, fact-finding in London for the Pentagon, had warned the Joint Chiefs in Washington: "Concerning the Overlord operation, the Prime Minister is seeking every honorable avenue by which to escape the British commitment to such an operation." Impressed by this report, the Pentagon's staff planners suspected that the British aim still was to lure American resources into the Mediterranean. These men went so far as to prophesy in one document: "Overlord will not be launched in 1944." They dramatically concluded, "The remaining United States resources should be committed in the Pacific as rapidly as possible. The conclusion that the forces being built up in the United Kingdom will never be used for a military offensive against Western Europe, but are intended as a gigantic deception plan and an occupying force, is inescapable."

General Barker, Morgan's American colleague, was impressed by Churchill's pessimism. "He'd seen the destruction of a generation of young Englishmen," he said, "and at a briefing that we gave him at Norfolk House he shook his head, and said, 'I wake up at night and see the Channel floating with bodies of the cream of our youth.' He thought there might be a cheaper way of doing it, and he kept proposing operations in the Mediterranean—the underbelly."

This earlier British opposition to Overlord was a reason that Secretary Stimson had first suggested Marshall as commander of the operation, in a letter to Roosevelt during the summer; it would take a man of Marshall's stature to browbeat the Prime Minister and his Chiefs of Staff. Roosevelt's arbitrary change in favor of Eisenhower, at Cairo, stunned Stimson.

Now it would be Eisenhower's job to harness Churchill's imagination to Overlord, if the "Pacific first" admirals were not to have their way. He lunched with the Prime Minister on the twenty-first. Afterward, Eisenhower reported to Marshall that Churchill had seemed keen to support him, but that he had several times stated mental reservations —saying that although he was prepared to scrape the bottom of the barrel to increase the effort, the invasion would represent the crisis of the European war. "There is a very deep conviction here in all circles," Eisenhower told Marshall, "that we are approaching a tremendous crisis with stakes incalculable."

It still remained to unite the warring commanders. Eisenhower was not so naive as to assume that it would be easy to reconcile the British and American viewpoints. The Americans had now carried out several major amphibious invasions of their own in the Pacific, using massive naval gunfire to soften the beach defenses, yet the British did not seem inclined to throw their own naval guns into the initial Overlord assault. More significantly, they showed no willingness to place their strategic bombers under SHAEF command before the operation.

These were just some of the controversies outstanding at ten-thirty A.M., on January 21, as the commanders trooped into room 126 of Norfolk House for the first meeting to be called by Eisenhower as the Supreme Commander. It could have been the annual general meeting of some prosperous international corporation were it not for the well-tailored uniforms and for the gold braid stacked high up many a sleeve. And the air chief marshals, generals, and admirals were discussing the prospects of a hazardous operation on which hung the lives of a hundred thousand assault troops and the future of all Europe, not some company's sales figures. With Eisenhower sat his pipe-smoking, urbane deputy, Sir Arthur Tedder, and Chief of Staff Walter Bedell Smith. Facing them were the assembled British and American commanders in chief.

Montgomery jackknifed to his feet and announced right away that the present plan for him to lead off the assault on Hitler's Fortress Europe with three divisions was "just not on." He insisted on a minimum of five divisions plus one airborne division. Moreover, he sharply pointed out, the armies would have to capture Cherbourg quickly if they were not to become dependent for months on the two Mulberry harbors—gigantic prefabricated artificial harbors that were to be towed out and scuttled off the invasion beaches as temporary breakwaters. As Montgomery envisaged it: "It should be the task of the U.S. forces to capture Cherbourg and then to make a drive for the Loire ports and Brest, while in the meantime the British-Canadian forces would deal with the enemy main body approaching from the east and southeast." His proposal was that they gain control of the main road centers, then push armored formations between and beyond them and deploy them on suitable ground. "As at present planned," Montgomery announced bluntly, "I do not consider that Overlord is a sound operation of war."

Admiral Sir Bertram Ramsay, the Overlord naval commander, spoke next. Sixty, balding, and with the keen eyes of a painstaking staff officer, he was the architect of the Dunkirk evacuation in 1940, and he had been behind the planning of every seaborne invasion since North Africa. Son of a brigadier general, he had entered His Majesty's Navy at fifteen. There was little he did not know about transporting combat-ready armies into action across water. What he now voiced were doubts about those Mulberry harbors. He thought the idea of erecting them within seven days frankly fantastic. It would involve towing a million tons of material over the Channel, he reminded his colleagues, with some of the structures weighing six or seven thousand tons each. But the landing craft problem, he went on, was even more daunting. If Overlord was postponed to await the production of sufficient extra landing craft, then in his view the best time—from moon considerations alone—was early June.

That meant that they had only four months to complete their preparations. A million British and American troops had to be trained, equipped, briefed, fed, moved to their boats, embarked, and brought to the proper beaches on time. The weather had to be right for several days on end. And the stakes were, as Eisenhower put it, incalculable.

 CHAPTER FIVE

Patton Meets His Destiny

ON THE morning of January 26, 1944, a plane from Algiers arrived at Prestwick, Scotland. Shortly afterward, the phone rang on a secretary's desk at General Eisenhower's headquarters in London, and a squeaky, imperious voice announced: "This is Patton. Where in the hell do I live?"

The secretary passed the telephone to an aide, who notified Colonel Lee. Tex Lee said: "I'm afraid we will have to tell him."

There was bad news for Patton. Not only was his new command, the Third Army, going to have its headquarters in a drafty old English mansion in Cheshire, one of the wettest and dreariest of Midlands counties, but he himself was not going to be involved in planning the invasion, despite his expertise; nor would his army be leading the actual assault.

The apparition that walked into Eisenhower's offices in London later that day was dressed with the practiced nonchalance of an aristocrat who has been served by the finest tailors and most skilled valets all his life. He had a brick-red face, an imposing forehead, and silvery gray hair. He was a foul-mouthed "lion tamer"—as he called himself—a swaggering hothead who womanized ceaselessly and lived in dread of his wife's finding out. Born in California on November 11, 1895, he had served as aide to General Pershing in the punitive expedition to Mexico and it was there that he formed an intimate friendship with a former West Point classmate, Everett Hughes, whose unpublished personal diaries contain rare revelations of Patton's character. He looked fierce and aloof, yet Hughes noticed that Patton quite openly came to him for human company. "I feed him what he needs," Hughes wrote.

Patton's shrewd, expressive blue eyes had witnessed the birth of the American armored force in July 1940; he had been given command of the 2nd Armored Brigade, the fist of the 2nd Armored Division. He was good copy right from the start: he was pictured on the cover of *Life* magazine in July 1941 standing up in his tank turret wearing a helmet with a chin strap, rings on his fingers, and a pistol in a shoulder holster. Other photographs showed him in a glistening white belt with his cavalry boots polished to a gleam. In November 1942 he led the seaborne invasion of North Africa. After the Kasserine fiasco, in which the U.S. Army received its greatest humiliation at the hands of Rommel, Hughes advised Eisenhower to try giving to Patton command of II Corps in Tunisia. Patton conducted a brilliant Tunisian campaign, in which he considered himself sorely inhibited by the ponderous British generals, and was then given the Seventh Army for the seaborne invasion of Sicily.

His character was fiery, romantic, and unique. He himself was wealthy, flamboyant, and profane, and ashamed on all three counts, going to lengths to have these qualities expunged from early magazine biographies of him. "I do not believe that wealth acquired through the judicious selection of ancestors is in itself a mark of ability," he would explain. He compared himself favorably with Alexander the Great and other great warlords of world history. He was teasing, vulgar, witty, and arrogant. Patton had an incongruously high-pitched voice—it was as if a Greyhound bus or a Mack truck had been fitted with a bicycle's bulb horn, said one man. The voice was Caspar Milquetoast, while the figure was unmistakably Caesar. In it, he sang hymns and soldiers' ballads while beating time on the piano with a finger on which he wore a coiled-snake ring.

Patton had the fashionable prejudices of the California aristocracy against Mexicans and other local minorities. His overseas campaigns added a loathing of Arabs—"They have the same effect on me as a toad," he confessed in May 1943—and Sicilians. He told his staff that he could not understand how Arabs could share their hovels with the animals. Arriving in Sicily, he added that he could not understand how the animals could live with Sicilians in their yards. That was before he set eyes on the Polish Jews, he later scoffed. His wife shared his dislikes, describing one diplomatic advisor to Roosevelt, Adolf A. Berle, Jr., as "an objectionable little Jew with a strong accent."

One hatred outclassed these phobias: George Patton loathed the British. From what dark springs in what tenebrous corner of his warrior soul trickled forth this hatred? To be British and to win Patton's approval, a general had to be outstanding, and even then his admiration was temporary, qualified, and grudging. General Montgomery fascinated him. Patton wrote that he was "small, very alert, wonderfully conceited, and the best soldier—or so it seems—I have met in this war." But when he saw that Montgomery was reaping the glory and adulation that he craved for himself, the old hatred reemerged. On April 11, 1943, as he saw the fruits of victory in Tunisia going to Montgomery, Patton cried in his diary, "God damn all British and all so-called Americans who had their legs pulled by them. I will bet that Ike does nothing about it. I would rather be commanded by an Arab. I think less than nothing of Arabs."

Patton had found Eisenhower's kowtowing to the British insufferable. As early as August 1942, in London, he fumed in his diary: "It is very noticeable that most of the American officers here are pro-British, even Ike. . . . I am not, repeat not, pro-British." Among the Mediterranean commanders he found that he did not like General Alexander at all—a cold, distant figure, too quiet by far and altogether too unassuming, a fence-sitter who had not supported Patton in tactical arguments. "He has an exceptionally small head," remarked Patton. "That may explain things."

George Patton had little understanding of politics or strategy. Theoretically, wars are fought not for the glory of individual battlefield commanders but to achieve ends where politics have failed. Patton ignored this maxim. He had written in his private diary in April 1943: "Of course, being connected with the British is bad. So far, this war is being fought for the benefit of the British Empire and for post-war considerations. No one gives a damn about winning it for itself now."

He had gleaned much of his tactical wisdom from the German tank commanders. He had read a prophetic article about the employment of tanks in battle written by General Heinz Guderian in 1939 which confirmed what he thought about the pitfalls of employing large mechanized forces in battle. He had developed a dictum of his own: "The shorter the battle, the fewer men will be killed and hence the greater their self-confidence and enthusiasm. To produce a short battle, tanks must advance rapidly but not hastily. . . . Mobile forces should be used in large groups and [be] vigorously led. They must attempt the impossible and dare the unknown."

Patton was a soldier's soldier. He was a fine orator, and could capture his audience and hold its attention like few other commanders. He could put more fire into fighting men in five minutes than could any other officer. "Battle is the most magnificent competition in which a human being can indulge. It brings out all that is best; it removes all that is base." Thus spake George Patton to the 45th Division in June 1943. He impressed the young and simple soldiers by his command of classical military history. He could draw lessons from the Battle of Cannae (216 B.C.) as well as from the Battle of Cambrai twenty-one centuries later. A psychoanalyst peering into his mind would have been fascinated by his obsession with killing and with the saber. He was inventive and innovative, and pondered in the silence of his quarters on ways to improve the performance and fighting quality of his men and their equipment. Unabashed by the mockers, he designed a tanker's uniform—padded trousers, brass buttons, and football-type helmet— and modeled it himself for the newspapers. It was never adopted. He was ambitious beyond belief, and knew discreet ways of furthering those ambitions. Once he wrote to a lieutenant colonel on the staff of Lesley McNair, commander of the ground forces, with certain suggestions, diffidently adding that the colonel might like to mention them to McNair, "and not mention my name even in your sleep." Later, Patton would write letters that he knew might attract the army censor and be passed along, commending the U.S. Army's Chief of Staff, General

Marshall, as one of the greatest generals who had ever lived.

Like Rommel, he became attached to flying low over the battlefield in a light plane. Like Rommel, too, he understood publicity: he knew the value of a myth that struck fear into the enemy. He gave his 2nd Armored Division a nickname, "Hell on Wheels," and labeled it "the most powerful striking force the human mind has ever developed." He said that his tactics were "Hold 'em by the nose and kick 'em in the pants."

He was grotesquely confident. After a command post exercise in November 1942, he noted: "Compared to them I am a genius—I think I am." Safe within the privacy of his diary he would write ten weeks before the invasion of Sicily: "There must be one commander for ground, air, and sea. The trouble is, we lack leaders with sufficient strength of character. I could do it and possibly will. As I gain in experience, I do not think more of myself but less of others. Men, even so-called great men, are wonderfully weak and timid. They are too damned polite. War is very simple, direct and ruthless. It takes a simple and ruthless man to wage war." And six months later: "When I think of the greatness of my job and realize that I am what I am, I am amazed, but on reflection who is as good as I am? I know of no one."

George Patton feared no man, and only one woman: Beatrice, his wife. He wrote artlessly passionate letters to her. "It has been a long time since I saw you," he wrote in February 1944, "but the imprint of your lips on a recent letter looked pretty attractive . . . I love and miss you but this is no place for you." He was an active admirer of the fair sex—although his biographer Martin Blumenson would much later insist with exquisitely chosen words that he showed no serious interest in any woman "other than the members of his own family." Certainly a number of the WACs and Red Cross nurses who followed Patton and the other American commanders on their campaigns across northwestern Europe had cause to note their masculinity; indeed, when Patton talked about "gitting thar fustest with the mostest," he was not always referring to problems of military logistics.

His language was unique. He believed that he had to speak to men in words which they themselves used. "You can't run an army without profanity," he said. He professed to be religious and, like General Montgomery, often used the Lord's name for effect. It was perhaps a sincere conviction; at least he knew many hymns by heart. He was maudlin sometimes—he once cut a lock of hair from a friend's lifeless body to mail to his widow. And he was effortlessly insubordinate. Hearing a demolition charge go off, a veteran of Patton's campaigns wisecracked, "That's General Patton telling Ike something—in confidence."

Patton had a quality which Eisenhower defined an "extraordinary and ruthless driving power." He whipped on his corps, and then his army, as he would a polo pony, actually kicking scared soldiers *pour encourager les autres* in November 1942. But he himself was physically brave and knew the value of example on his men. Sometimes he would ignore the strafing attacks by enemy planes. If his column was stopped by a minefield, it was Patton—again like Rommel in North Africa—who got the attack moving by walking forward through the halted motor transport and tanks, and strolling across the strip mined by the enemy. He was confident that Destiny would not let him down.

In fact, fear disgusted him. When enemy shelling started, he timed his pulse, and if the rate had increased, he berated himself. He knew that a man would never hear the shell that killed him, so he trained his reflexes so that he did not bat an eyelash when the shells started coming over. He just kept right on talking as shells crumped down nearby—and enjoyed a sly pleasure as other officers winced. "One must be an actor," he wrote to Beatrice.

Like many an actor, he was pathologically vain, and if he feared anything at all, it was growing old—too old for combat overseas. He put on exaggerated displays of his own fitness and energy; he spent much time in his cabin when crossing the Atlantic to the North African landings running four hundred steps in place, holding onto a dresser. He had been a master of swordsmanship and a champion horseman. Although now fifty-nine, he kept fit by running along beaches, doing pull-ups, counting how often he could chin the bar. He despised obesity and was proud, as he several times wrote, that "I have not lost my girlish figure." He refused to drink—he found after a particularly bad fall playing polo in Hawaii that he was unable to hold liquor without becoming tearful, though he did not refuse the occasional champagne. He would not smoke. Whatever else he was, he was cultured, reading extensively in the classics and in military literature. (Strangely for a man so widely read, Patton regularly spelled many simple words wrong.) But he was also mercurial, unstable.

What had troubled General Eisenhower about Patton in the winter of 1943, and had persuaded him not to give him an army in the invasion of France, was a shocking incident that graphically displayed this instability. The facts were annihilating: on August 3, 1943, Patton, then commanding the Seventh Army in Sicily, had visited the 15th Evacuation Hospital and was going around among the battle casualties when he caught sight of an uninjured soldier, a twenty-six-year-old private from Mishawaka, Indiana. By this time Patton had inspected many hospitals full of grisly casualties—in one he saw a man with the top of his head sliced off; in others there were men with limbs blown away. According to the official report, he asked the private what he was doing among real battle casualties, and the man replied, "I get nervous, I just can't take it up there any longer." Patton shouted, "You're just a coward," and with a stream of oaths ordered him out. The man made no move, so Patton slapped his face with a glove, hoisted him to his feet by his collar, and kicked him out of the receiving tent.

A week after that, on August 10, there was another incident, this time at the 93rd Evacuation Hospital. After greeting half a dozen casualties with visible battle injuries, Patton dismissed without comment a patient who admitted only to a high fever. Then his eyes lit onto a private sitting in a huddle, shivering.

"It's my nerves," the man sobbed.

Patton yelled at him, "What did you say?"

"It's my nerves. I can't stand the shelling any more."

Patton retorted—according to the commanding officer's report two days later—"Your nerves, Hell. You're just a God damn coward, you yellow son of a bitch." He slapped the man. "Shut up that God damned crying. I won't have these brave men here who have been shot seeing a yellow bastard sitting here crying."

He then struck the man on the head. A nurse began weeping and had to be led away. Patton was yelling to the receiving officer, "Don't you admit this yellow bastard, there's nothing the matter with him. I won't have the hospitals cluttered up with these sons of bitches who haven't the guts to fight."

A crowd of nurses and patients had gathered outside from adjoining wards to see what the shouting was about. Patton turned to the soldier again, who was managing to sit at attention although shaking all over, and said: "You're going back to the front lines and you may get shot and killed, but you're going to fight. If you don't, I'll stand you up against a wall and have a firing squad kill you on purpose." Reaching for his pearl-handled revolver, he added: "I ought to shoot you myself, you God damn whimpering coward."

At first, his pals had hushed the scandal up. The corps commander to whom the first complaint went, Omar Bradley, filed it away. Patton's friend Everett Hughes, the deputy theater commander, also did nothing when Lieutenant Colonel Perrin H. Long of the Medical Corps told him about the incidents. But the whole of Sicily was soon buzzing with rumor, and newspapermen approached Eisenhower. Hughes noted in his voluminous diary: "Ike says that correspondents have some stories about Geo. they are dying to tell."

This was when Eisenhower made his biggest mistake: he persuaded them to keep the story under their hat. But he was exasperated, and sent a corps commander, John Lucas, over to warn Patton—if he did not stop wearing his pearl-handled revolvers and acting like a madman, he was doomed. He also wrote Patton a letter cussing him out. Patton's attitude was that he had done no wrong and had in fact saved the immortal souls of the enlisted men, and it was all Hughes could do to persuade him not to say so in his reply.

On September 1, Eisenhower directed Colonel Herbert S. Clarkson, the Inspector General of the North African theater, to go and investigate the incidents, while disguising his visit as a "morale survey." Clarkson interviewed junior officers and enlisted men, but took care that their superiors were out of earshot. He questioned them on their food, clothing, and cigarette rations and noted their complaints, only indirectly touching on the question of their opinions of their leaders. He found the troops seething with rumors and full of resentment. On September 16 he returned to Algiers and, aided by Hughes, wrote his report.

On Eisenhower's instructions, Patton apologized to the second man —but in bad grace. He lamented in his diary: "It is rather a commentary on justice when an Army commander has to soft-soap a skulker to placate the timidity of those above." He made a truculent speech to the assembled staffs of the two hospitals on August 22. ("You have all been witnesses of an incident that has turned out to be unfortunate," he had unrepentantly said.) At first Patton blustered to the Inspector General that he had put on a cold-blooded act to "cure" the two men;

then he contradicted this story—he had seen some badly wounded men, and the sight of these "neuro" cases "made me see red."

Colonel Clarkson's report had stated: "Many soldiers resent the use of profanity and vulgar expressions to individuals on the part of their appointed leaders. According to their own statements many soldiers have lost all respect for General Patton." And yet Clarkson had been impressed by one feature: the enlisted men who had served directly under Patton, for example in the 2nd Armored Division, were enthusiastic about him and considered him a great leader.

Clarkson sighed and told Hughes that he thought that Patton was through. But Hughes persuaded him otherwise. "Georgie is a bum," he said, "but he's a good army commander." Eventually Clarkson agreed. While these acts and others already committed by Patton in the Mediterranean theater had undoubtedly affected his standing as an officer and a gentleman, Clarkson recorded in his conclusions that Patton's standing as a brilliant tactical leader—one who in record time had brought off very complicated military maneuvers—was not affected, and that men would again be willing to follow him into battle.

On September 21, a month and a half after the slappings, Eisenhower lunched with Hughes and the rest of his personal staff and discussed the matter. The problem was that at least two reporters were known to have heard of the incidents; so Eisenhower was advised to tip off General Marshall about the scandal at once. Eisenhower disregarded this sound advice and decided to lock the report away in his safe instead. Hughes noted in his diary: "Ike seals and files Patton report." Hughes endorsed the document accordingly: "Read by Gen. Eisenhower . . . on 22 Sept 43. He directs the papers be placed in IGs [Inspector General's] secret files."

In November the bubble burst. One Sunday night the columnist Drew Pearson broadcast the news that George Patton had struck an enlisted man in the hospital. The rest of the press erupted. The New York *Sun* ran a three-column front-page story with Patton's picture under the caption: "Struck Soldier." His name was in every headline —but not the way he would have chosen. The Nazi radio broadcasting from Berlin—"When the hospital personnel interfered," it reported, "he pulled his pistol but was disarmed"—announced that Patton had been sacked. Eisenhower discussed the development with Colonel Arthur McChrystal, head of his censorship department. Hughes learned the outcome through the office grapevine, from a WAC who was his lady friend: "J.P. says McChrystal says Geo is thru." Eisenhower's press corps did what they could to save Patton: John Daly of CBS stated that Patton "made blanket apologies to his men, in some cases to thunderous ovations from his troops," and that Eisenhower considered the case closed. But it was not. General Joseph McNarney, Marshall's deputy, demanded a full explanation from Eisenhower. Bedell Smith drafted an answer which Hughes was able to intercept and have modified so that it did not take down his friend too much.

Patton said he was sorry in his own way to Eisenhower—who like many of his commanders had an inflatable ego. He wrote a two-page letter brazenly comparing Eisenhower's campaign in Africa with what he had just read in a book called *The Greatest Norman Conquest.* "There are many points in common with our operations," he said. "The Normans were very careful and meticulous planners. They always attacked. They were masters of landing operations, and they pursued a ruthless offensive in which the armored knights played practically the role of tanks." But all this was as nothing compared with Eisenhower's amazing feat of conquest, Patton innocently suggested. "One of the things for which the Normans are particularly lauded is the fact of the terrific chances they took with small forces," he went on. "Here again you have them beat. . . . I suppose what I have just written sounds like either bullshit or bootlick, but that is not the fact."

As the Overlord buildup continued, familiar faces vanished from the officers' messes; the big names continued to slip out of the Mediterranean theater and fly the long, circuitous route through Gibraltar to London. Late in 1943 President Roosevelt, on the way back from Teheran, had met Eisenhower and Mark Clark in Sicily; Patton was also there, very much downhearted. Eisenhower told him about Overlord. "You will have an army in that command," he promised. It pleased Patton no end. He could see his Seventh Army fighting in France already. But soon after that he was formally stripped of the army command. On January 2, Hughes summarized in his diary: "Patton has lost his Army, and is arriving at 1:15 to cry on my shoulder." When General Jacob Devers arrived in Algiers as the new theater commander three days later, he added his own verdict, talking with Hughes: "Georgie is done for. Patton's through."

By early 1944, as Patton moved to England to take up whatever command Eisenhower had for him in Overlord, he was clearly an emotionally unsettled man. In the aftermath of the slapping incident, what can only be described as acute paranoia had emerged in him. He persisted in the view that he was somehow above the law, that he had been unjustly criticized, and that the press was to blame for everything. Full of self-pity, he had told his wife in one letter that September, "One should wear chain mail to avoid the knife thrusts." And there were other disturbing characteristics in a general on whom five hundred thousand soldiers' lives depended: his flashes of euphoria, his moodiness, petulance, and childishness. Throughout his campaigns, he had nursed a secret but uncontrolled envy of his equals—generals like Mark Clark and Omar Bradley—and a desperate fear that they were overtaking him. He asked Beatrice to send every clipping she could about them, and cursed all their victories. He literally desired them dead. "I wish something would happen to Clark," he confided in his private diary on October 6, 1943.

Even more serious for an inter-Allied operation like Overlord were Patton's unblushingly anti-British sentiments. Ever since 1942 he had foamed at Eisenhower's subservience to the British. For a time in Tunisia his private diary became explosive with hatred against his commander in chief. "It appears to me," he wrote in April 1943, "that Ike is acting a part and knows he is damned near a Benedict Arnold, and . . . the British have got him completely fooled. In any case he is usually not telling the truth. He is nothing but a Popinjay—a stuffed doll. The British are running the show on the sea, on the land, and in the air. They . . . are playing us for suckers, not only in a military way but politically also. . . . [Omar] Bradley, Everett Hughes, General Rooks and I, and probably many more, feel that America is being sold. . . . I seriously talked to Hughes of asking to be relieved as a protest. Hughes says that he and I and some others must stick it out to save the pieces."

He was contemptuous of Britain's military ability. Although it had been fighting wars for centuries, he felt that its methods had not changed much. They were deadly slow. In Sicily, Patton had vented his fury in his diary: "We can go twice as fast as the British and hit harder, but to save British prestige the XXX Corps had to make the envelopment and now I think they are stuck. . . . Our method of attacking all

the time is better than the British system of stop, build up, and start."
This vehement anti-Britishness was why Eisenhower had hauled the far
younger Bradley up from below Patton and slotted him in above.
Bradley would command the leading assault army, and then command
the army group. (Besides, Bradley was one of George Marshall's pro-
tégés, and Eisenhower knew on which side his own bread was buttered.)

After Patton snapped to attention and threw a smart salute at Eisenhower in London on January 26, 1944, the Supreme Commander told
him he had been chosen ("tentatively, mind you") to command the
Third Army—Hodges's old outfit, due to arrive soon from America. Its
assignment would be to support Bradley's First Army. Bradley's men
would lead the way across the beaches and make the breakthrough—
just what Patton longed to do himself; then Patton's Third Army would
come along, in due course, and proceed from there. Patton did not
relish the prospect of "supporting" a former junior, but he kept quiet.
Encouraged by his silence, Eisenhower railed at him for not counting
to ten to avoid taking overhasty action. Patton reassured him that he
would take better care as to where he next threw a tantrum: "I certainly
won't choose a hospital."

Eisenhower invited him to dinner with him, Kay Summersby, his
naval aide Harry Butcher, his British ADC Jimmy Gaunt, and a WAC
captain. Patton accepted the invitation, and waspishly noted in his
diary afterward: "Ike very nasty and show-offish—he always is when
Kay is present—and criticized [General J.C.H.] Lee for his flamboyance which he—Ike—would give a million to possess." He himself put
on his most humble performance. An Eisenhower aide wrote that day,
"He is a master of flattery and succeeds in turning any difference of
views with Ike into a deferential acquiescence to the views of the
Supreme Commander." When the subject turned to history—of which
Patton had a genuine and expert knowledge—Patton assured his chief
that anybody would be foolish indeed to contest the rightness of his
views, "particularly as you are now the most powerful person in the
world." Eisenhower glowered, and knew no reply.

The tragicomic relationship that continued to grow between Patton
and Dwight D. Eisenhower was tortuous but infrangible. Eisenhower
had graduated from West Point six years after Patton and before North
Africa had been his junior in every way. He had never heard a shot fired
in anger. Patton considered him soft, but of course he did not say so.

"Ike is not as rugged mentally as I thought," concluded Patton in his diary, "he vacillates and is not a realist." Meeting Eisenhower in November 1942 at Gibraltar, Patton had observed sarcastically, "Ike lives in a cave in the middle of the Rock—in great danger." Eisenhower had a tendency, which Patton found obnoxious, to use foreign words like *flak,* and even British words like *petrol* and *tiffin* (lunch). He was no disciplinarian. Once he fretted to Patton, "The other day Kay and I were out riding and a soldier yahooed at us." Patton wrote with astonishment to Beatrice, "He told me he *glared* at the man!" "D. is a strange person," Patton had said in May 1943 in another letter to her. "I can't make him out but I begin to feel that he has an inferiority complex."

Nobody accused George Patton of that. He thought he was a genius. It was the English thinker John Stuart Mill, in his essay "On Liberty," who wrote that the border between genius and eccentricity is drawn precious fine. Unfortunately, Patton made it easy for Eisenhower to distinguish his eccentricity from his higher gifts. Once in mid-1943, as a mere corps commander writing to the Supreme Commander of the theater of war, he had addressed Eisenhower as "Sir Dwight." In this letter, Patton made sly digs at the British commanders' quaint habit of listing their honors after their name, while ostensibly complaining about Harry Butcher ("KC., CT., SS., SoB., etc.") for having mistakenly addressed him as commander of an armored division. Patton woundingly added: "I would further call your attention to the fact that he referred to you as a three-inch man (a three bottle man would have been all right) and cast some doubt as to your ability of becoming the first Father of the Country at your present age." Patton jocularly concluded: "While not wishing to push myself, I should be very happy to fulfill the duties of president of the court-martial court before which you will indubitably send him, or as his defense counsel. In either position, I can assure you of a conviction."

Patton was bemused, baffled, but in the final analysis still bewitched by Eisenhower. It was no mere play on Eisenhower's initials that prompted Patton repeatedly to write of him as "Divine Destiny." Eisenhower was his destiny—vacillating, feeble, infuriating, ungenerous, uncomplimentary, but still Supreme Allied Commander—and Patton was never allowed to forget it.

CHAPTER SIX

The Bomber Barons

IT HAD become the war of the strategic bomber. By 1944, fleets of these mighty creatures of armor plate and alloy, these marauders produced by the rival aircraft industries of Britain and the United States, were crowding the skies of Europe. Their very complexity threatened to dictate terms to their commanders.

The heavy bombers of the RAF Bomber Command had been nearly ten years in the designing. They had been developed for bludgeoning operations against city targets that were often many miles square. They were painted black, because they prowled the forests of the night. In them, Britain saw what the Elizabethans had once seen in Sir Francis Drake's great oak-walled galleons—the force with which Britain's will could be imposed on fractious foreigners. The Americans, however, starting later, had learned from British experience and disappointments and had boldly decided to fight their way into enemy air space by day, with their eyes wide open, so that they could identify their targets and bomb them with pickle-barrel precision and without wasteful spillage. Thus the American bomb groups were skilled in delivering rapier thrusts at smaller, clearly visible targets—ball-bearing factories and airplane engine plants and the like. This diversity of approach led to a rivalry between the two national commands and an unremitting strife between their generals. Each force belittled but silently admired the other. Each had its own larger-than-life commander. Each commander had his own ideas about how the war should be won.

From the moment of Eisenhower's arrival a struggle raged behind the scenes for control of the strategic bombers. The Cairo Conference in 1943 had directed that the bomber forces should make their highest strategic priority the "progressive destruction and dislocation of the German military, industrial and economic system, the destruction of vital elements of lines of communication, and the material reduction of German air combat strength by the successful prosecution of the Combined Bomber Offensive"—all this, it was emphasized, "as a prerequisite to Overlord." In response the RAF Bomber Command and the U.S. Army air forces had left the enemy's cities in blazing ruins, shaken by the thunder of late-detonating bombs, torn by the wail of sirens; the factories were rusting skeletons of Hitler's arms miracle. But now other target systems were emerging—such as Hitler's menacing secret weapons—and in November 1943 Churchill's Cabinet asked the Americans to attack their construction and launching sites with the same priority as fighter aircraft factories.

It was at this time that Sir Arthur T. Harris, the British bomber commander, had laid bare his soul in a secret message to Churchill, revealing the so-called bomber mentality at its most stark. He promised Churchill that his heavy bomber squadrons could win the war by demolishing the capital of Hitler's empire. "We can wreck Berlin from end to end," he wrote, "if the USAAF will come in on it. It will cost between 400–500 aircraft. It will cost Germany the war." In December he wrote to the Air Ministry boasting that his Lancaster night bombers alone could force Germany to surrender in three months—and that Overlord would thus be unnecessary. Others took a different view of the prospects of the bombing offensive, and thus the great clash between the warlords began.

Arthur Harris, a soft-spoken, unassuming, carrot-topped man, was known as "Butcher" Harris throughout the air force. Whether this name was a reflection on the slaughter inflicted by his RAF Bomber Command upon the enemy or upon his air crews was obscured in the smoke of history. Forty thousand of his airmen had been killed since the war began—more casualties than the entire British army to that point. He never visited his bomber stations, let alone flew on missions. He worked from an underground bunker near High Wycombe, a rustic town outside London noted for its fine beechwood chairs. His courage was of a different sort. He used to say that while a general risked his army once or twice a year, he, Harris, risked his entire front line every night, month after month; and his was the only force that could lose the war in one night.

As an air chief marshal he was equivalent to a four-star general, but he owed his clout to the rapport he had established with Churchill, who eagerly endorsed Harris's incendiary campaign against the cities—a two-year trail of nocturnal devastation that had spread over Germany's frontiers into the rest of Europe. No matter how forcefully another approach was urged upon him, Harris had always found ways of reverting to this, the role that his beloved bomber force had been designed for. And when in the autumn of 1944 he faced the bleak possibility that there would soon be no more point in it all, since the major enemy cities were largely in ruins, he recommended that he might just as well go on and take out the other cities. This proposal would meet with a pained rejection by the American Chiefs of Staff, who would point out that this would probably cost extra Allied lives, as well as the deaths of countless civilians.

Harris and his American counterpart, Lieutenant General Carl A. Spaatz, were two of a kind; both took it as an article of faith that the heavy bombers could make an invasion unnecessary. Spaatz commanded the U.S. Strategic Air Force; its Flying Fortresses and Liberators lifted by day off the scores of runways that had been laid out across the meadows of eastern and southern England. He had a face like a rusty nail. The elegantly tailored aristocrats among the army generals, like George Patton, scorned him as untidy and sometimes unshaven. When Eisenhower once ordered him to get his airmen to salute properly, Spaatz replied that he didn't care how his men saluted provided they did their jobs right. He cherished the workmanship of English gunsmiths—he purchased a custom-made 410 walking-stick gun—and was the kind of general who disliked being separated from his bourbon too long. He was a forceful poker player who regularly creamed Eisenhower's personal staff, seldom for less than six hundred dollars a head. He was not accustomed to mincing his language. He was the kind of general who hated to be seated behind a desk. In March 1943 he had flown a mission in the nose of a bomber that was heavily attacked— his tail gunner had shot down two enemy aircraft.

He hero-worshiped Eisenhower, and Eisenhower valued him: one year later, in February 1945, he would rate "Toohey" Spaatz, along with Omar Bradley, as the best of his officers and would call him an "experienced and able air commander; loyal and cooperative; modest and selfless." This mutual respect between them had been forged during the North African campaign when Spaatz, in England, had unselfishly handed over some of the Eighth's best crews to build the new Twelfth Air Force in North Africa. Spaatz knew the value of public relations. He assiduously collected damage photographs and press releases on American air raids—a term he deprecated; he regarded his operations as daily major battles—and sent albums of them to Arnold and Churchill and Stalin and His Majesty the King. He cultivated friendships with useful Americans like President Roosevelt's son Elliott, currently serving in a photographic reconnaissance squadron, and with powerful Englishmen as well.

Spaatz and Harris had the responsibility for their bomber forces, but they lacked the authority to throw their weight around as they wished they could. Just as a naval commander had been assigned for Overlord —Admiral Sir Bertram Ramsay—and just as General Montgomery would initially command all the ground forces in the invasion, so an air commander had been nominated, on the next rung below the Supreme Commander and his deputy. Sir Trafford Leigh-Mallory was the man whom the British had put forth for this task—to command the invasion air forces. This command, however, did not include the strategic bombers; they were a breed apart, by task and by virtue of the independence which their leaders had won for them. Leigh-Mallory nevertheless blithely began to campaign for authority over the strategic bomber forces too. And not surprisingly, both Spaatz and Harris declined to yield to him. For one thing, until now Leigh-Mallory had commanded only the RAF's Fighter Command. What would a mere

fighter commander know about the arcane business of strategic bombing? For another, he was known to have heretical views when it came
to what needed bombing.

Quite apart from all this, Leigh-Mallory was not an easy person to
get along with. He had been born in 1892 in Cheshire, son of a clergy-
man, and been given an exclusive education at Haileybury School and
Magdalene College, Cambridge. Round-faced, with a neat toothbrush
mustache and the soulful eyes of a well-fed spaniel, he had started
planning the air role in Overlord as soon as he moved into his new
headquarters at Stanmore, outside London. And his plans were at the
center of the bomber controversy. He proposed that the combined air
forces—including the strategic bombers—should pulverize the entire
French and Belgian railroad system for ninety days before the invasion.
To assist him in his planning he had staffed a research committee with
some of England's finest brains, including Solly Zuckerman, a professor
of anthropology who had earlier investigated the effects of bomb blast
on civilians by exploding bombs among captive goats. Now, for Leigh-
Mallory, Zuckerman turned to the theory of attacks on railroad systems. He concluded that they were like any other nervous system, and
that damage to any part would affect the whole. It all sounded a bit too
pat to the other bomber barons.

In desperation they appealed to Eisenhower and to his deputy, Sir
Arthur Tedder. Pipe-smoking, slim, urbane, and handsome, Air Chief
Marshal Tedder had until now commanded the Allied air forces in the
Mediterranean. He disliked the British army in general and General
Montgomery in particular—he had never forgiven Montgomery for
stealing all the credit for the victory of El Alamein from the desert air
force he commanded. At a dinner, Tedder was overheard speaking
ironically about the day "when the Army is up to date." Some soldiers
suspected that Tedder's real aim was to be Supreme Commander himself.

But Eisenhower liked him, and so did Spaatz. A happy friendship
had blossomed between the three in North Africa. It had been enriched
during 1943 by the presence of Tedder's girl friend in Algiers, Mrs.
Marie de Seton Black. A "big and bossy" Belgian blonde, she was
known to the whole staff as "Tops." When Tedder married her, it raised
eyebrows. Everett Hughes exclaimed in his diary, "What the hell!?"
Before they took leave of him to return to England, Hughes sat down

and wrote: "Tedder and Tops say that they are coming to tea and to say goodbye." He scornfully added her new designation: "Lady Tedder!!"

On January 11, 1944, Tedder flew to London to take up his post as Eisenhower's deputy Supreme Commander—the number 2 man in SHAEF. He offered two newspapermen a lift back to England in his plane, and one of them later gossiped about the flight to Basil Liddell Hart, the British military expert. In shocked tones in his diary, Liddell Hart noted his source's surprise when, just before their takeoff from North Africa, a three-ton truck arrived at the airfield with a mountain of goods—furnishings, wines, gastronomic delicacies, drums of olive oil —that the Tedders had bought and intended smuggling back to England, against all King's Regulations.

Tedder's arrival in London as Eisenhower's deputy in January 1944 generated big problems. It precipitated a feud that had been developing between the pro-Tedder and pro-Leigh-Mallory factions in the RAF. It must have become clear by then that it had been a mistake to appoint the unpopular Leigh-Mallory; Tedder, the amiable pipe-smoker, would have been a wiser choice, but now it was too late—he had been given a more exalted post, and the Leigh-Mallory job would have been a step down for him. Above the battle was the beaky, tall, chilly British air chief, Sir Charles Portal. The equivalent of Hap Arnold, he might have mediated in the fracas, but even he was far from being a free agent. He had to deal with the politicians and thus had to tread carefully. A quiet, unspectacular figure ensconced in offices at the Air Ministry building from which he seldom emerged, he maintained an Olympian impartiality.

General Spaatz was the first to develop a powerful dislike for Leigh-Mallory. After meeting him for the first time, Spaatz wrote in his diary, "[I] am not sure whether L.-M. has proper conception of air role." ("I distinctly did not have enough confidence in Leigh-Mallory's ability to handle the forces," Spaatz said in 1945, "to accept putting the strategic air forces under his command, except momentarily in the tactical battle.") What stunned Spaatz was the Air Chief Marshal's laconic statement that air supremacy might not be snatched from the Nazis until the very invasion itself. He wrote: "[Leigh-Mallory] apparently accepts possibility of not establishing air supremacy until landing starts."

This was a denial of everything deemed absolutely essential by all the

Overlord ground and naval commanders for the success of the operation. Montgomery had written in a 1943 pamphlet, *Notes on High
Command,* "The first and basic principle is that you must win the air
battle before you embark on the land, or sea, battle." Eisenhower, too,
recognized the strategic imperative: on no account must the Nazi air
force be in a position to interfere.

As for the bombing strategy to be followed, the mission given Spaatz
by Washington was clear. "Overlord and Anvil," General Hap Arnold
had told him, "will not be possible unless the German Air Force is
destroyed. Therefore, my personal message to you—this is a *must*—is
to destroy the enemy air forces wherever you find them, in the air, on
the ground and in the factories."

Arnold was worried about well-documented evidence that the Nazi
air force was actually growing in defensive strength, despite the crushing Combined Bomber Offensive. He shared Spaatz's belief that the
strategic bombers should continue to smash the Nazi air force's power
base, its aircraft and arms factories. Spaatz scowled at any academic
proposal to switch those bombers to any other target system—be they
cities, railroads, or the vaunted Nazi secret weapons. He knew that his
bombers—with their famed ability to hit precise targets like bridges and
gun emplacements by day—would inevitably be asked to carry the
burden of the Overlord air offensive. But to switch the bombers now
to pre-Overlord bombing, he passionately believed, would be a mistake.
In fact, Spaatz would be consumed by secret skepticism about the whole
invasion plan until the very eve that it was launched. From experience
in North Africa he doubted that the GIs would storm across minefields
—and Spaatz knew that the beaches would be mined far more heavily
than those in Africa. He asked whether Overlord was really necessary:
could those invasion armies do anything which the Combined Bomber
Offensive, with its hail of fire and bombs upon Germany's cities, could
not?

Bedell Smith, for one, was eager to see the Nazi rocket weapon sites
thoroughly blasted. As Eisenhower's chief of staff, he pleaded with him
to move SHAEF headquarters out of London. He was "mortally
afraid," as one of Eisenhower's aides noted with amusement, "of the
rocket bombs which he thinks will be released on London in the near
future." Eisenhower professed unconcern; he did not expect the rocket

attack for some weeks, he said. But on mature reflection he agreed that the move might be prudent—he gave as his reason that a city did not provide the best of atmospheres for a staff to work in. His headquarters would transfer as soon as possible to Bushy Park, a suburb just thirty minutes west of central London. He hoped too that by bringing everybody into one compound, if not under one roof, a harmonious command could be rapidly synthesized.

With Kay Summersby at the wheel, he drove out to reconnoiter Bushy Park in his bulletproof Daimler, which he referred to as his Al Capone car. General Spaatz, who had been using Bushy Park as his headquarters, met him and poured out his troubles—his worries about the future command setup, his shuddering dislike of Leigh-Mallory, his fears that the wrong targets were being assigned to his precious heavy bombers. Spaatz showed him a cable of protest that he was drafting to send to Hap Arnold. He had talked the previous day with Portal, Harris, and Leigh-Mallory and had told them that there must be only one air commander under Eisenhower—and that he himself would willingly serve under Tedder, but not under Leigh-Mallory. Eisenhower put a hand on Spaatz's shoulder. "I suggest you soft-pedal the necessity for an overall air commander at this time," he said. "What we have to assure is *operational* control by a single air commander at the proper time for Overlord."

This question, the control of the RAF strategic bombers, was one of the toughest that Eisenhower faced: would he get it or not? The British bomber force amounted to about 1,300 heavy bombers. Control was due to pass to Eisenhower in time for Overlord, and he was not prepared to compromise on this issue. He commented to his private staff: "We now have a much larger air force in the U.K. than even the British. We have thrown all *our* air force into the Supreme Command and I cannot face our Joint Chiefs if the British hold back this important striking force." He had naively hoped that having his British friend Tedder as his deputy would oil the wheels in any conflict with the RAF.

At first it seemed that it would be smooth going. When Bedell Smith had arrived in London in mid-January, he had related that Churchill had assured him in Marrakesh that all operational aircraft would come under Eisenhower's control. But as soon as Churchill returned to London, the British Air Ministry evidently persuaded him to change his mind.

The issue finally reached the conference table on January 21, at the first SHAEF meeting in London. Leigh-Mallory blandly stated his views. "Pointblank," he declared, using the code name of the Combined Bomber Offensive, "has already resulted in a fall of German fighter production to some six hundred a month, instead of the one thousand to fifteen hundred for which the enemy had planned. Nevertheless, it is unlikely that the decisive battle in the air will take place until the day of our assault; we will fight for air superiority then, and we are likely to achieve it."

Spaatz once again was shocked that Leigh-Mallory was making so light of what must by any account seem a major admission of failure. If, after all their combat and bombing operations, the Luftwaffe would still throng the skies on D-day, something was horribly amiss.

Leigh-Mallory proceeded to explain his plan. The Allied air forces would start bombing the rail network about two months before the invasion, continuing until—as Montgomery had requested—the entire railroad system within 150 miles of the invasion area was paralyzed. The Luftwaffe, he reiterated, would have to be destroyed in the actual air battles on invasion day; he would provide one fighter squadron as a canopy over each assault division, and commit twelve more squadrons after ten A.M., when he expected the Luftwaffe to arrive in force over the invasion area.

Spaatz was glum as he assessed the implications of Leigh-Mallory's plan. "If time [of Overlord] is as now contemplated," he reflected sadly in that day's diary, "there will be no opportunity to carry out any air operations of sufficient intensity to justify the theory [of Spaatz and Harris] that Germany can be knocked out by air power [alone]."

Late that very night the Luftwaffe demonstrated that Germany was still a long way from having been knocked out. Its bombers raided London in unusual force, the first heavy raid for two years. It was Hitler's personal answer to Harris's saturation bombing of Berlin. The British government scoffed and dubbed this and the raids that followed during the next nights the "Baby Blitz," but to those who had not been through the real thing, this was real enough. It was fearsome. A private shelter had been allocated to Eisenhower's staff, an old wine cellar in a house built two centuries before by Lord Clive, several blocks from Hayes Lodge. The shelter had bedrooms for the Supreme Commander and Harry Butcher, electric heaters, and a kitchen. Eisenhower learned that the shelter was run by the Oxford Group, a pacifist organization, and thought of looking for an alternative. He surmised that the pacifists would not approve of him as tenant—after all, he did now command the largest war-waging force ever known.

With the Baby Blitz, the plan to move the SHAEF staff out of London suddenly seemed more urgent, but for the time being Eisenhower remained at Hayes Lodge. An overlarge mansion, Castle Coombe—a few hundred yards away from Bushy Park—had been assigned to him, but he turned it over to Tedder and Tops to set up their new home in. He chose to stay instead in Telegraph Cottage; he had fond memories of living there in 1942. The elderly cottage was built on high ground at Kingston, about ten miles south of London, and was once a link in a semaphore network. It had three bedrooms and a kitchen with a coal stove. On January 28, Butcher wrote in a letter: "In a few days we will move again, back to our old cottage, but we'll keep a place in town [Hayes Lodge] for the times when Ike has to stay overnight." He continued with a comment on the wartime atmosphere in London: "They have sat on their fannies for so long and have never seen any action, that they look like putty and seem far removed from reality. The only thing that puts them back into the war is the occasional air raid, and while we had a good one recently it didn't touch first base of what we had in the Mediterranean. The papers shrilled and screamed about it. . . ."

While the argument over the strategic bombers swelled in volume, Eisenhower continued his round of duties. He dined with the Prime Minister and the King, and took his train to inspect troops in southeastern England. The journeys sapped his strength badly. The weather was raw and blustery, but the reverence displayed for him by the soldiers everywhere inspired him. When he went to a London playhouse one Sunday in February for the final performance of *This Is the Army,* the GI audience gave him a standing ovation. General J.C.H. Lee—the bald, self-important American commander was seated in the box just below him, escorting Lady Mountbatten—thought that the cheering must be for him and rose to acknowledge it.

Each week seemed more crowded than the one before. Eisenhower did not feel too good—he had taken no exercise for eight months and now chain-smoked through the day. The cold he had caught in November was dragging on. The London fogs did not help. He believed that he had built up defenses against his unceasing pressures and responsibilities, and he had tried to clear his brain only for essentials by delegating the right people to the right jobs. But at the back of his mind was the worry about Mamie's recent irritability. She was now in Texas. He sent her a Valentine card with a hasty letter—the writing of which was interrupted six times by callers. "Take care of yourself, my sweet," he wrote. "Maybe on next Valentine's Day I can crack your ribs instead of hurting your eyes with a scrawl like this." Sometimes, he told Mamie artlessly, he looked at the Red Cross girls and wished that she was in London too.

The air issue, still unresolved, overshadowed all else. On February 12, top-ranking American couriers—Rear Admiral Charles M. Cooke, Jr., and Major General John E. Hull—arrived from Washington with a highly secret letter from Marshall about the thorny problem of air command, and became embroiled in disputes on other matters. Fresh material for conflict was uncovered with each staff conference, it seemed. The Americans, with their superior experience of amphibious landings in the Pacific, were growing nervous at weaknesses they detected in the invasion plan. They were unimpressed by the meager naval bombardment that was planned to precede the invasion assault. Eisenhower asked for at least six more battleships. Admiral Cooke cabled Admiral King, the U.S. Navy's commander, knowing that he would find a willing ear: "I am very dubious about the strength of naval gunfire support now tentatively planned for Overlord which appears to be about one fourth of that used at Kwajalein. . . . It is my opinion that chances of success of operation are too low."

In mid-February two more officers arrived from Washington with a brain wave of Hap Arnold's, a plan to use four airborne divisions exclusively in a strategic role: they should stage a mass landing near Paris, around Dreux and Evreux, with the object of drawing off Nazi panzer divisions from the beachhead battle. Eisenhower's experts had to tell them that at the present state of play this entire airborne force would probably be wiped out; it would have no artillery support at all. Montgomery lectured the visitors. "A commander," he said, "has first to decide what he wishes to do, and then he has to concentrate all his resources to carry out that object." And Omar Bradley defined what that was: "The main object . . . must be to seize Cherbourg as soon as possible." That was where the airborne forces must go. Eisenhower then drew a scathing comparison with the Churchill-inspired Anzio landings: "In spite of the fact that we have been pouring into Anzio from three to five thousand tons a day and have increased the strength to some one hundred and fifty thousand men, that force has not succeeded in joining up with the main body. Moreover, it must be apparent that without direct access to the sea the troops we have put into Anzio could not have survived." He suggested that Arnold should ponder how long his "airhead" would survive many miles from the nearest harbor, surrounded by hostile panzer divisions. The embarrassingly naive proposal was evidence to Eisenhower of the lack of realism being displayed by those who were far removed from the operational scene.

Everybody at SHAEF knew that the invasion battle was going to be touch-and-go. For many weeks the conferences were haunted by the fear that if Hitler continued to reinforce his mobile strength in France, Overlord might have to be called off altogether. The main invasion effort would then have to be switched to the Mediterranean and southern France. That was another reason to continue planning Anvil—if they were blocked in northern France, southern France would become crucial as an invasion site. Bedell Smith suggested that they postpone until, say, April 1 any decision on whether to bring the tank and infantry landing ships up from the Mediterranean. "The present German strength, which includes twelve mobile divisions," said Smith at a staff conference, pointing to the invasion sector, "has already reached the critical point." In a scrambler telephone hookup to the Pentagon, he was cruelly frank. "My personal view is that Anvil . . . is not going to have any material effect on Overlord during the first fifteen to thirty days. On the other hand, we may find that we cannot do any Overlord. The buffer of German divisions confronting us across the Channel is just now approaching the absolute maximum that we can handle. Do you see what I mean?"

"Exactly," said the voice at the Pentagon end.

"It might become necessary for us to shift our center of gravity back to the Mediterranean," said Smith.

On February 12, Eisenhower presented his Overlord command plan to the air chiefs. Quite simply, it required all the participating aircraft to be placed under the control of Leigh-Mallory. The plan aroused fierce antagonism from the slighted recalcitrants, particularly Harris and Spaatz, and during the following week they won the support of Churchill, Brooke, Portal, and Arnold—a formidable lineup against Leigh-Mallory and Eisenhower.

Leigh-Mallory's feud with Spaatz blazed out into the open a few days later. Early on the morning that the British officer was to present his air plan for the Overlord campaign to the British and American air commanders at Stanmore, his headquarters, Spaatz drove to see Eisenhower. He was not in a cooperative mood, and noted afterward, "Discussed L.-M. with Eisenhower and told him my feelings in the matter are that I have no confidence in Leigh-Mallory's ability to handle the job and that I view with alarm any setup which places the Strategic Air Force under his control."

At the conference itself, Spaatz found himself heavily outnumbered by the British air marshals. Leigh-Mallory launched straight into his theory: basically, his plan was to shift bombing emphasis from the defeat of the German air force to the Overlord campaign early in March; he proposed to pulverize the railroads from the invasion coast all the way back to western Germany. In his view, the enemy air force would fight to defend them.

Spaatz disagreed: "Suppose they don't fight? Then I've got to have the latitude to attack anything else that will make the German air force fight. Otherwise I'm not going to be able to accomplish my primary task —the destruction of the German air force."

The British commander insisted that as of March 1, Spaatz's Strategic Air Force would come under his operational orders. Spaatz choked back his anger. He snapped: "I can not agree to limit my targets. I must be able to bomb whatever I find to be necessary to make the enemy fighters fight!"

Leigh-Mallory, his spaniel eyes doleful, said, "The landing of our ground troops on the Continent will make the fighters fight."

"That will be entirely too late!" Spaatz shouted. "We've got to weaken the German air force fatally before the landing, if the landing's going to stand a reasonable chance of success."

Now Butcher Harris waded in, fists swinging. He declared that Leigh-Mallory's whole plan was based on a fallacy. "I don't believe that the rail communications throughout this whole area can be sufficiently interrupted by air attack to impede military movements."

Leigh-Mallory insisted that his experts supported him, and he invited Professor Zuckerman to back him up. The scientist agreed; in fact he agreed at great length.

Harris disagreed, somewhat more curtly. He now claimed that the precision of his bomber command's new target-finding devices was overestimated. They really wouldn't be much good, he insisted—fallaciously, as it later proved—against compact, Overlord-type targets. Again he contemptuously dismissed Leigh-Mallory's calculations. "They're quite unrealistic," he sniffed. Spaatz nodded happily. Harris raised his voice. "I'll give a written guarantee," he said, "that this proposed plan for interrupting the railroad communications will not succeed. And that the army will then blame us, the air forces, for their failure."

Eisenhower was embarrassed by Spaatz's hostility to Leigh-Mallory. Spaatz saw Eisenhower a few days later and wrote triumphantly in his diary: "He tried subtly to sell Leigh-Mallory [to me], saying that after talking with him this morning he felt that maybe proper credit had not been given to the man's intelligence. I told him that my views had not and would not change." Spaatz continued his campaign. When he saw the draft of a news release stating that his Ninth Air Force was under Leigh-Mallory's control as "Air Commander-in-Chief," his telephone sizzled with angry calls to Tedder and Harris, and the statement was deleted. When Eisenhower asked him how, then, the setup could be made to work with Leigh-Mallory in his present position, Spaatz replied bluntly that it was impossible.

On February 22, Tedder, upset, wrote confidentially to the chief of air staff, Portal: "I am more and more being forced to the unfortunate conclusion that the two strategic forces are determined not to play. Spaatz has made it abundantly clear that he will not accept orders, or even coordination, from Leigh-Mallory, and the only sign of activity from Harris's representatives has been a series of adjustments to the records of their past bombing statistics, with the evident intention of demonstrating that they are quite unequipped and untrained to do anything except mass fire-raising on very large targets."

Eisenhower was fed up with all the wrangling, but it went on and on. Tedder composed a committee to draw up an acceptable air plan. The British dominated the committee, and dug their heels in. At two meetings Eisenhower spoke to the Prime Minister quite sharply. "If the

unhelpful British attitude continues," he said, "then I will go home."
At the second meeting—a dinner with Churchill on February 28 that
lasted until one-thirty A.M.—the matter came to a head. Churchill was
obviously deeply upset at the prospect of Leigh-Mallory—a former
fighter commander—commanding the strategic bombers; probably
Harris had coached him. Eisenhower begged him to wait until Tedder's
committee had issued a directive—and to give it a chance to work.
Churchill sulked, but said he would agree to whatever arrangement
Eisenhower and Portal found satisfactory.

"He seemed very impatient," Eisenhower afterward told Tedder,
"but I told him that if I needed any help, which I did not anticipate,
I'd come to him promptly." He begged Tedder to hurry the conferences
and planning to a final answer. "Otherwise," warned Eisenhower, "the
P.M. will be in this thing with both feet."

On Leap Year's Day there was a heated meeting between Churchill,
Eisenhower, and Portal. Eisenhower told Marshall later: "The Prime
Minister was quite violent in his objections to considering Leigh-Mallory as the overall Air Commander in Chief. . . . His query was, 'Why
did we give you Tedder?' and my answer was merely, 'Why?'"

Eisenhower was baffled at the hatred of the British for Leigh-Mallory, whom they had themselves selected for the post. Exhausted, he
gave in to the solution put forward by Churchill—that the deputy
Supreme Commander, Tedder, should add to his present duties the
command of the Overlord air effort. Leigh-Mallory would keep his
post, but he would have to take orders from Tedder. Eisenhower des-
perately hoped that this arrangement would prevent Churchill and his
Chiefs of Staff from bypassing him and issuing conflicting orders direct
to the bomber squadrons when the pre-Overlord campaign began—the
thought of the potential for chaos gave his organized brain the shivers.
"Just when I think I have the problem licked," he lamented to his staff
a few days later, "someone else's feelings are hurt and I have another
problem to settle."

On March 5, Eisenhower finally transferred SHAEF headquarters
from 20 Grosvenor Square to Bushy Park. It was a series of Quonset
huts in a small private estate in the outskirts of London. Henceforth
he would divide his time between here and 47 Grosvenor Square, where
he still had responsibilities as war theater commander—he wore two

caps. By Jeep the drive took half an hour. It led from Hyde Park Corner through London's outskirts and down increasingly narrow country roads. At the entrance to a tree-shaded lane, a burly white-helmeted MP (or "snowdrop") checked identification papers. The asphalt drive wound past the garages, cut across a small lawn, and vanished under a huge camouflage net. Eisenhower's offices were in a one-story brick building with a tin roof. The floor creaked, the linoleum was buckling, the paint was flaking off the walls. But from it, he was to command the raising of the biggest military force in history.

Each day Eisenhower arrived early, stepped through the big outer office where four assistants sat, passed the door leading to Bedell Smith's room, and shut himself into his own twenty-foot-square domain. He would throw a switch and the newfangled fluorescent tubes overhead would flicker on, casting their light over his big walnut desk and the bare walls, which had none of the maps usually decorating commanders' offices. Then he would light his first cigarette of the day. Elsewhere under this net were the offices of Ramsay, Tedder, and Spaatz. Eisenhower insisted that British and American officers work side by side at Bushy Park, with no distinction. A visiting officer of Henry Stimson's staff was struck by the complete integration at SHAEF. British and Americans shared every office except for Eisenhower's and Bedell Smith's.

One of the first people to visit him at Bushy Park, on the day after SHAEF moved in, was General Patton. He was shown in while Eisenhower was on the telephone to Tedder. "Now, listen, Arthur," Eisenhower was shouting, "I am tired of dealing with a lot of prima donnas. By God, you tell that bunch that if they can't get together and stop quarreling like children, I will tell the Prime Minister to get someone else to run this damn war. I'll quit." Patton was quite impressed.

That day, Eisenhower lunched with Churchill and spent valuable hours thrashing over the air command row. Gradually he was getting his way with his plan to have an *overall* air commander for Overlord —including the RAF sections that Churchill had wanted to hold back. That commander would of course be Tedder. Later that day Churchill sent for Portal and talked alone with him. The upshot was a draft paper which Portal sent to Eisenhower the next day agreeing that, between dates to be laid down by the CCS, the entire strategic bomber force should be at Eisenhower's operational disposal. It stipulated, however, that the British chiefs should have certain reserve powers to use their own force "for the purpose of meeting other contingencies." Portal assured Eisenhower that this was not to be taken as a reflection on their confidence in him or in Tedder. After haggling with Tedder, Portal sent Eisenhower a modified version. Eisenhower pinned a note to it: "Exactly what we want."

Eisenhower told his staff that the question of air command had been settled, "providing that the air commanders themselves do not fall out and begin fighting among themselves." Even now messages flowed back and forth between London and Washington, and a fresh conflict threatened: would Eisenhower "supervise" or "command" all the air forces during the critical period of Overlord?

Eisenhower's patience with the British was expended, and he recommended to Marshall using language that left no room for later British backsliding. On March 22, he pledged to his diary: "If a satisfactory answer is not reached, I am going to take drastic action and inform the Combined Chiefs of Staff that unless the matter is settled at once I will request relief from this Command." However, the British Chiefs of Staff met that morning and assured him the word *direction* was acceptable to them if it was to him. In his diary he scribbled: "Amen!"

Time was running short. An acceptable general bombing plan would have to be worked out. Even now there were still big differences in outlook. General Spaatz was continuing to hold out for a vast endeavor of precision bombing, starting immediately. He was now proposing that the strategic bombers be thrown against enemy gasoline, fighter aircraft, and ball-bearing production, followed by rubber and bomber production. He estimated that with two weeks' good weather, his planes could flatten these targets. Then they could switch to tactical support for Overlord.

That was his plan, and he found dissent intolerable. On March 24, on the eve of the conference that was to decide Overlord bombing policy, Spaatz slammed into Leigh-Mallory's plan to attack the enemy's rail transportation. He pointed to an intelligence estimate that the Germans would need fewer than eighty trains a day running into the battle area; this was so little compared with their available rail capacity that, as he put it, "the proposed attack on transportation will be a misdirection of effort." Spaatz insisted that all the strategic air forces must attack a target system that the Germans would be bound to commit their fighter squadrons to defend—so that fighters could be destroyed and thus removed as a threat to the invasion. That crucial target, he declared, was oil. "We believe," said Spaatz, "that they will defend oil to their last fighter plane." Fourteen synthetic oil plants, he pointed out, produced eighty percent of all Hitler's synthetic gasoline and oil. He simply would have to send up fighters to protect them, whereas any fourteen rail yards, targets of about the same size, were only a fraction of the Nazi railroad potential.

Tedder disagreed. While he conceded that the oil plan would ultimately have grave effects on the whole German war effort, he doubted that the synthetic plants were as easy as Spaatz had suggested to reach, find, attack, and destroy in the short time available before Overlord. Besides, what part could Harris's night bombers play in it, let alone the fighter-bombers of the tactical airforce?

It was a finely balanced debate. Tension grew as the rival air commanders arrived at the British Air Ministry building on March 25 with bulging portfolios of statistics, damage photographs, and analyses of projected results. Which target system, oil or transportation, would force the Nazi fighter squadrons into combat and self-destruction? Portal presided. First Tedder had his say, then Portal, who pointed out that even if the Germans managed to get only a trickle of supplies through the undamaged part of the rail network, these and the supplies already stockpiled would make the Leigh-Mallory plan less worthwhile. The experts suggested that it was near impossible to cut rail lines for more than a day or two.

A broad grin spread across Spaatz's face. He rubbed his stubbled chin, convinced that the transportation plan had been licked. Only a few days previously, he had told Eisenhower of Leigh-Mallory's pessimistic words: "You won't get control over the German air force until the invasion starts—because that is where the big air battles are going to be." Spaatz had warned: "Ike, if the air battles take place when your invasion takes place, then that will be too late—you're not going to succeed. We've got to get control of the air *first.*"

On that occasion Eisenhower had agreed. But now he changed his mind. The grin faded from Spaatz's rumpled features as Eisenhower stated not once but repeatedly during the conference that everything he had read had convinced him that Leigh-Mallory's transportation plan was the logical way for the air forces to contribute to the land battle during the first vital weeks.

In vain Spaatz expatiated upon his rival oil plan. A Ministry of Economic Warfare expert pointed out that the Nazis undoubtedly had big oil stockpiles in the west for just this event, so no amount of damage to the refineries could sabotage their short-term defense against Overlord. As for Butcher Harris, he consented reluctantly to carry out attacks on the railroad centers, but wanted to continue his attacks on German cities. He agreed that he would guide his attacks as far as possible over transportation targets but he warned General Eisenhower that the effect would be largely fortuitous.

Only at the end did Sir Charles Portal equably mention one factor that would shortly overshadow all others in this debate: the French civilian casualties that the transportation plan would inflict. They could not send heavy bombers in to attack railroad yards without strewing death over wide areas. Portal came up with a remedy: they would drop leaflets giving everybody within one mile of such targets warning to clear out immediately. That notion seemed to salve all consciences. The outcome, refereed by Eisenhower next day, was a victory for the transportation plan. The oil plan would take too long to bite.

Thus this extraordinarily tortuous argument came to an end, leaving a tangled and intricate command structure between Eisenhower and the bomber squadrons. From the end of March 1944 he began informally exercising command of the air. In mid-April he took over officially, for the duration of Overlord. Henceforth he, his deputy Tedder, and General Spaatz kept in such close personal touch that little could go wrong; but as Spaatz admitted later, if one of this trio had been hit by heart failure, if might have cost the Allies the war. "In other words," said Spaatz, "from an organizational point of view it was lousy." And General Frederick Morgan would later say: "It will, I think, be a considerable time before anybody will be able to set down in the form of an organizational diagram the channels through which General Eisenhower's orders reached his aircraft."

CHAPTER SEVEN

Eyes and Ears

LATE WINTER was particularly bleak in England that year—wet, raw. The American invasion troops, living in barracks and Quonset huts up and down the countryside, were restless, boisterous, waiting to hit whatever beaches their Supreme Commander ordained. Many were still arriving from the States. They detrucked and stood in line in the drizzle, cold and edgy. They talked about the German MG-34 "burp" gun in the same voices they once had used back home when talking about the latest Fords and Chevrolets. They developed their proficiency with the 30-caliber machine gun, bazookas, and mortars. They practiced the techniques of reducing field fortifications with grenades, flamethrowers, and bangalore torpedoes. They tended to tune in to German radio stations, because the reception was better than that on the American Forces Network. Deprived of magazines and newspapers, they talked about war, women, and home—the only topics in their young lives. "We're like the f——ing air corps," said one grizzled GI to the man behind him in the chow line. "After twenty-five missions they get sent home. We get to go home too—after twenty-five invasions!"

Evenings, the young GIs shined up and walked a couple of miles to the local movie theater, or strained the profanity out of their language and boogie-woogied with the British girls at the town hall, or stood around street corners ogling, or ambled into the Red Cross Donut Dugout—usually a converted store with Ping-Pong, reading tables, and attractive young women in crisp uniforms.

One American staff officer, concerned about morale, put on the uniform of a private and lived among the troops for a day. He found that the main thing that troubled them was not knowing where the invasion was to be. "Christ," one doughboy said, "I don't mind fighting this goddam war, but I wish to hell they'd tell me something about it. Has anybody got a map of France?"

But England was full of generals who knew precisely when and where these young men would soon make history.

Major General Joseph Collins kissed his wife and daughter goodbye in the United States at the end of January and flew to Europe. It was early on February 2 when his train pulled into London. From his billet in the luxurious Dorchester Hotel in Park Lane he walked at once to Grosvenor Square and reported to Eisenhower and Bradley. Collins had come a long way in more than one sense. His grandparents had left Ireland in the 1860s and gone to New Orleans; his father had found work as a delivery boy and had married the boss's daughter. Joe, tenth of eleven children, had grown up barefoot in Louisiana's sticky blue clay, and owed much of his skill in arithmetic to a blind man who had taught him about courage as well. He had studied hard, and added merit to a West Point class which in due course turned out other fine generals, such as Mark Clark and Matthew Ridgway. Posted in 1933 to the Philippines, Collins had helped plan the islands' defense and had met many leading commanders, among them Douglas MacArthur and Dwight D. Eisenhower.

In London, Eisenhower and Omar Bradley keenly grilled Collins about his combat achievements at Guadalcanal in the Pacific. Collins dismissed them as merely an application of the infantryman's maxim: hit the high ground. "He talks our language," Bradley later remarked to Eisenhower. Eisenhower decided he could trust the scrappy little general with one of the two American corps that would attack the beaches on D-day. It would be Collins's mission to land on the Cherbourg peninsula and capture the crucial port as rapidly as possible. (The other corps would be commanded by Major General Leonard T. Gerow. "Gee" Gerow had had no real experience at modern combat and was not renowned for brilliance, but he was a warm personal friend of Eisenhower.) Collins went off to his command post, a Tudor mansion at Braemore, a little village of thatched cottages south of the cathedral city of Salisbury.

Then in London there appeared another sort of major general altogether—a big, handsome, saturnine fellow with a slightly wicked sense of humor and a somewhat jaded manner. It was Eisenhower's buddy and Patton's old West Point classmate Everett S. Hughes. He was one of the inner circle of men who were never far from Eisenhower. Eisenhower had been pining for Hughes ever since arriving in London, and had written to Mamie in February, "I do miss Everett, wish I still had him." When Jake Devers, Eisenhower's successor in North Africa, declared Hughes surplus—he was said to be too cold toward enlisted personnel—Eisenhower's eyes had lit up and he had cabled the Pentagon at once: "I can use General Hughes very advantageously in this Theater."

Hughes agreed to come although he hated leaving Algiers. He hated it because it would mean leaving his girl friend, referred to in his diary as "J.P." The night after he heard of his impending transfer, he dreamed that his wife had come in unexpectedly and that J.P. had had to "run like hell down the back stairs"; he guiltily wrote this down next day. That morning he asked her if she wanted to go to England with him and she said yes. He said goodbye to Mary June Cooper, George Patton's lady friend, who had not yet received a similar invitation to travel, and left Africa by C-54 on February 20. Hughes arrived in London the next day and sent a cable to his wife: "Glad to see the old gang." The gang was glad to see him too. He was the indispensable sort of person who knew how to obtain the unobtainable. He could, for example, lay his hands on fifteen cases of whiskey at a time, and since Eisenhower's stocks of Director's Reserve always seemed to be in need of replenishment, Hughes had a lot of clout in the Supreme Commander's hard-drinking entourage. It took all kinds to make a war.

Hughes had been born in Ipswich, South Dakota, fifty-eight years before. He had served with the field artillery, first in the punitive expedition into Mexico in 1916 and then in France. He was five years older than Eisenhower, his career no longer ascending—the perfect man for the job Eisenhower wanted him for. The Supreme Commander called Hughes to see him on February 21, and disclosed to him that while ostensibly he waş to become Patton's chief of staff, in fact he was to act as Eisenhower's "eyes and ears." Hughes's eyes and ears were highly developed; he never missed a trick and liked to jot things down. He packed diaries with a scratchy, barely legible handwriting which thwarted historians from the moment they were deposited in the Library of Congress after his death in 1957.

Hughes made a good inspector. He had taken an inquisitive interest in most of the women on Eisenhower's staff and had noted indelicately a year earlier, in October 1942: "I suspect from the females that Ike is taking [to North Africa] that Butch has his eye on a bit of —— for the CG [commanding general]." Eisenhower in fact soon had his Irish driver, Kay Summersby, and thereafter displayed only distaste for what he regarded as the promiscuous Women's Army Corps. Indeed, so exercised did Eisenhower become that he cussed out the WACs in a speech in August 1943, accusing them of unsoldierly comportment and admonishing them either to mend their ways or to quit; forty-one obliged and went home. Eisenhower was possibly the origin of the scurrilous definition of a WAC that found its way into Hughes's diary: "A double-breasted GI with built-in foxhole."

The theater headquarters was full of Everett Hughes's old friends, but the deputy theater commander was not one of them. Major General J.C.H. Lee buttonholed Hughes at once and urged him to move his office out to Bushy Park. Hughes surmised that Lee did not want him snooping around at Grosvenor Square. Lee was an oppressively religious man, who after the war would become a lay brother in a monastic order. As a general he invoked the Lord's name whenever it seemed advantageous. "We could never have made the grade alone," Lee later would reminisce: "We thanked the dear Lord every day for having learned to put our faith in Him and to start each morning at His altar whereon we laid our problems." Lee kept up a vast correspondence, employing eight secretaries. He had put together a special train of a dozen coaches for his journeys around England; Eisenhower thought this overpretentious and referred privately to Lee in less than glowing terms. On March 14, he explained to Hughes that he was sore because Lee was planning and issuing orders without consulting him. But Lee could get away with it: he had powerful backers in Washington. He could afford his grandiose, bullying manner.

Lee became a Lieutenant General on March 5, ranking above Bedell Smith; as deputy theater commander he came right after Eisenhower in the Overlord pecking order, and that irked Bedell Smith even more. Smith griped to Hughes that Lee's promotion had been forced on Eisenhower. A few days later Smith complained that General Bradley had called him, and not Lee, about a bulldozer. Hughes suggested, "Probably Bradley didn't want to talk to Lee?" Reporting back from an inspection trip on April 5, Hughes warned Eisenhower of "an apparent disinclination of commanders to discuss full and frankly with either you or General Lee matters about which there is some doubt or question." On April 20, after a visit to Ashchurch, where acres of artillery and trucks were piling up for the operations ahead, Hughes observed: "Too much heel-clicking. Too much spit and polish. Too much Lee for me." For much of his information, Hughes relied on the Red Cross hangers-on and camp followers. "Marjorie M. doesn't treat Ike or Bedell Smith," he wrote cryptically. "Gave [me a] fine thumbnail sketch of both of them." Soon after his arrival he dined with Eisenhower and Kay and mentioned that Butcher and Butcher's Red Cross girl had invited him to dinner the next day; Eisenhower warned him not to talk shop in front of the girl.

Security was Eisenhower's bugbear. If somebody talked out of turn, not even a general's stars would save him. Too many people knew about Overlord already—the time and place. By mid-May no fewer than 549 officers assigned to SHAEF headquarters alone would have the vital information. Some men could not keep the secret. On April 18, General Edwin Sibert, Bradley's G-2—intelligence officer—was eating in the public dining room at Claridge's when Major General Henry Miller, of the Ninth Air Force, began arguing with a Red Cross woman and, "obviously intoxicated," according to Sibert, named the target date for Overlord three times, in a voice loud enough to be heard even by the waiters. Sibert sent a handwritten report to Bradley, Bradley passed it to Eisenhower, and Eisenhower hot-footed to Spaatz. Spaatz had Miller arrested. It was the end of his career. He was busted to lieutenant colonel and sent home in disgrace.

The date and location of Overlord were vital state secrets, and a complex plan of the utmost secrecy, Fortitude, had been devised to protect them. It involved Bradley and—unwittingly—Patton. On February 28, Hughes visited Bradley's headquarters in a women's college outside Bristol for a briefing. Omar Bradley had rough-hewn features, was modest and retiring, and had simple, homespun tastes. Once Eisenhower treated him to a gourmet luncheon, serving up a feast of fresh oysters specially flown over from Washington, with oyster soup, raw oysters on the half shell, and fried oysters, followed by bouillabaisse. Bradley went green and murmured inoffensively, "I can't touch oysters." The staff rustled up some peanut butter and navy beans instead.

For all that, however, Bradley was not to be underestimated. He had a keen mind. He wore two hats. He commanded both the First Army and also the army group headquarters that would be transferred to France once the beachhead expanded enough to accommodate all four armies. The second of these hats was a secret; at present the public knew only that he commanded the U.S. First Army. Bradley told Hughes that, to fool the Germans, the word was being spread around that it was Patton who was commanding the American army group. This was in line with a further cover plan designed to persuade the Germans even after D-day that Overlord was merely a feint and that a big army was still waiting in England to mount the "real" invasion elsewhere. The presence of this spurious army group in eastern England was being faked by truck movements, newspaper leaks, and radio traffic. To the Germans it would seem natural that a soldier of Patton's stature would command this force in the "real" assault. This deception plan was labeled Fortitude.

A fine snow drifted down over London's sooty buildings, mantling their scars under its cloak as Hughes moved to a billet in Grosvenor House, not far from Grosvenor Square. It cost him six guineas, or about twenty-five dollars a week. He made a mental note to move to somewhere cheaper. His first action, once ensconced, was to ask Patton to come and see him.

The friendship between Patton and Hughes had been deep and intimate. They had much in common—they had been in the same class at West Point and shared many interests, including girl friends like J.P., who was the wife of a GI taken prisoner by the Japanese in the Philippines. Hughes had employed her on his staff in Algiers. On June 23, 1943, Hughes smugly recorded in his diary, "Patton fell for J.P."

After Patton's arrival in England late in January, he had gone to Scotland to welcome the advance party of his new Third Army as it disembarked from the *Queen Mary,* and then he had begun its training program. Because he talked too much, his superiors had not made him privy to the secret of the Fortitude deception plan. He had been told that nobody—but nobody—must know that he, the famous George Patton, was here in England. After a few weeks, of course, he was touring American army camps like an election candidate, with a loud-speaker van, addressing the assembled troops but begging them not to mention his name. He was seen at the theater and was cheered by the audience and loved it. Every speech contained some such words as, "I am still a secret and not to be mentioned."

And then one day Patton learned that he and his Third Army would eventually come under the command of Omar Bradley. It was galling. As recently as Sicily he had been giving orders to Bradley, whom he considered "a man of great mediocrity." In Tunisia and in Sicily, Bradley's name had been entered in Patton's diary in terms of the utmost disapproval. "On the other hand," Patton wrote with irony, "Bradley has many of the attributes which are considered desirable in a general. He wears glasses, has a strong jaw, talks profoundly and says little, and is a shooting companion of the Chief of Staff." But Patton had only himself to blame for this reversal in his fortunes. Eisenhower considered him a fine battle commander but a tactless and untrust-worthy roughneck. So leary of Patton was Eisenhower that he did not make him privy to the Ultra secret either—the extraordinary fact that most of the Nazi military messages were being intercepted and decoded by the Allies. When Bradley would come to him in August with an "intuition" about a probable German counterattack, Patton could only offer skepticism, and then marvel when the intuition came true.

Patton tried to behave. After a visit to Montgomery's headquarters in a school in West London to talk over invasion plans with him, Patton made a surprisingly admiring remark: "Monty . . . is an actor but not a fool." Later he was even more restrained about Montgomery, evading direct reply when McCloy, McNarney, and Lee pressed him for his opinion. "I prefer not to answer," he said at first, but then he ventured: "I think he's too cautious, he won't take calculated risks." His real views on Eisenhower he kept to himself, but he went out of his way to sprinkle flattery around the periphery at SHAEF like fertilizer around a rose bush. "Ike," gushed Patton to Harry Butcher, "is on the threshold of becoming the greatest general of all time—including Napoleon."

Patton was struggling to be tactful, but it was uphill work. Of dire necessity he was sycophantic to Eisenhower's austere, hatched-faced chief of staff Bedell Smith in particular, and it was distasteful. Hughes and the influential general Theodore Roosevelt tried to figure out how to cut down the growing anti-Patton brigade. "Teddy" Roosevelt was a good soldier, no yes-man even to his illustrious relative. ("Franklin won't be reelected," he snorted. "The country is rising against the Democrats. It doesn't know what it wants, but it does know what it *doesn't* want!") One day Hughes noticed that a bad infection had developed on Patton's lip, but Patton lightheartedly dismissed it. In his diary Patton jocularly reflected: "After all the ass kissing I have to do, no wonder I have a sore lip." Hughes was his only true friend and confidant. On March 1, Patton shared lunch with him and their mutual friend, J.P. Afterward they all went out to buy Patton a dog. He selected the ugliest bull terrier he could find and called him Willie. Hughes hoped Willie would cheer up Georgie. He was concerned about the growing opposition to Patton, and about Patton's morale.

For Patton was in a complex mental state. He considered himself vastly superior to any of Eisenhower's other commanders, yet he was not being called on at any stage in the Overlord planning. He was not even sure what the role of his Third Army would be. The prevailing view was that dramatic cross-country tank thrusts like those by the German commanders Guderian and Rommel were no longer possible. That was certainly the British view. A few days later Basil Liddell Hart, the British military expert, was introduced to Patton. The bony British officer talked with enthusiasm about the methods used by William Tecumseh Sherman in the Georgia and Carolina campaigns of the American Civil War—stripping his forces of impedimenta to quicken the pace, cutting loose from communications, and getting forward fast. He urged Patton, once in the field, to swerve past the enemy opposition, reach into their rear, unnerve them, and unhinge their position. Patton, who ordinarily would have thunderously agreed, replied dismissively that he believed the campaign would be a repetition of the slow fighting of 1918.

On March 16, Patton drove up to London to attend a big reception given by Eisenhower at Claridge's. He noticed that Montgomery and

Brooke were absent, and suspected that Montgomery chose to be absent because he could not bear to be second fiddle. Patton did not like what he learned that day about Overlord, and he said so the next day when he called on Everett Hughes, bringing J.P., to help finish off some expensive new liquor that had cost Hughes five dollars a bottle. The day after that, Hughes lunched with Patton and listened to him talk about the suit he had ordered in Savile Row and badmouth the plan again.

By now the military muscle of the United States was reaching out across the globe. More than three and a half million U.S. troops were overseas. Canadian troops were also flowing across the Atlantic, nearly a hundred thousand of them, and their First Canadian Army would also face command problems in England. Until November 1943, they were led by Lieutenant General Andrew G. L. McNaughton, a man of strong will who had little esteem for Montgomery ("We did not like one another," he noted in his diary; years later he spoke of efforts by Montgomery "to destroy my military prestige in order that he might gain control of the Canadian forces for himself") and by General Sir Bernard Paget, the commander of the British 21st Army Group. Paget believed that McNaughton was not fit to command an army in battle: he was "too much absorbed on the technical side at the expense of training and command." He sent for McNaughton and told him this. McNaughton did not take it lying down. "I am still commanding the First Army," he shot back, "and as such I have direct access to the Prime Minister of Canada, and I intend to report the incident in full detail. I think some heads may fall." But the head that fell was his own. The usual lie was released to the press, announcing that he had asked to be relieved because of a physical disability, and a successor was appointed. For a while the British tried to put one of their own generals in command of the Canadian army—claiming an obscure precedent— but the Canadian prime minister, William Lyon Mackenzie King, re- belled, and Lieutenant General Henry Crerar landed the job.

Crerar had commanded the Canadian I Corps in Italy. He had seen a lot of Montgomery while down there, and they were firm friends. "He has his peculiarities, like most of us," he wrote to another general, "but I would never question his abilities as a military commander." A quiet and little-known man, he had none of Montgomery's flash or Patton's flamboyance. He once said: "The most valuable form of courage is that of a man who knows what fear is and who, recognizing that it is compounded of selfishness and ignorance, succeeds in repressing and controlling it."

Throughout the late winter and into spring the martial preparations continued. One maneuver followed another. Off hours, the fraternizing with the British women continued as well—fast and rewarding, although a Canadian brigadier got a letter from his wife which indicated her displeasure at his taking one lass, a Miss Ruth Maunsell, to dances. "As usual she is right, and I shall in future go alone to dances," he wrote in his diary, capitulating sorrowfully, "if at all."

Eisenhower wrote on April 4: "As the big day approaches tension grows and everybody gets more and more on edge. This time, because of the stakes involved, the atmosphere is probably more electric than ever before. In this particular venture, we are not merely risking a tactical defeat; we are putting the whole works on one number. A sense of humor and a great faith, or else a complete lack of imagination, are essential to sanity."

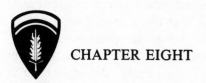

CHAPTER EIGHT

George, You Talk Too Much

THE OLD paranoia was gripping Patton again as he waited for D-day —the belief that "They" were out to stop him, to gag him, to deprive him of the power, prestige, and applause to which he was entitled. In Patton's writings, "They" seemed to include most other generals, many newspapermen, several congressmen, the entire British nation, and most of Eisenhower's staff. The paranoia was fed by friends and relatives who assured him that if he, and not Mark Clark, were calling the shots in Italy, then Rome would have fallen long ago. He felt hurt and insulted at not commanding one of the armies that would hit the fighting beaches on D-day. But he could understand the decision. "I have a feeling," he wrote in mid-April 1944, "probably unfounded, that neither Monty or Bradley are too anxious for me to have a command. If they knew what little respect I had for the fighting ability of either of them, they would be even less anxious for me to show them up."

An entirely new reproach was about to hit him. The subject was the alleged maltreatment of enemy prisoners by troops under his command. In those pre-Nuremberg years, the subject was treated lightly by American headquarters. Even the punctilious Eisenhower, writing to George Marshall in 1943, had described the problem of what to do with a surfeit of prisoners as an embarrassment for which West Point had not adequately prepared its officers. Then he had added words to this effect: "Too bad we couldn't have killed more." By the early 1970s, when Eisenhower's *Papers* were published, attitudes had changed and the infelicitous remark was deleted on War Department insistence. If it had been Patton who uttered those words, his peers would have dismissed them as pure Patton bellicosity. But simpler soldiers were drilled to convert words to deeds, and when Patton did utter such a thing, it was nearly his undoing.

In March 1944 a War Department investigator arrived in London, called briefly at SHAEF, then went up to Cheshire to see Patton: he had been accused of ordering his troops in Sicily in July 1943 to take no prisoners.

The killings were, like the slapping incidents that followed a month later, the talk of Sicily. They were by no means isolated atrocities. British war correspondent Alexander Clifford saw GIs of the 45th Division mow down a truckload of German prisoners with a heavy machine gun as they climbed out onto the tarmac of Comiso airfield, killing all but two or three. Then he saw them kill sixty Italian prisoners the same way. Clark Lee, an American war correspondent, reported further incidents. There were still more killings by the same division: on July 14, near Gela, Sergeant Barry West of C Company was ordered by superiors to take thirty-six prisoners to the rear, but he became apprehensive as dusk approached, and machine-gunned them at the roadside; that same day near Buttera airfield a young U.S. Army captain, Jerry Compton, smoked out forty-three snipers, most of them in regulation combat uniform, lined them up against a barn, and machine-gunned them to death. Bradley, as Patton's corps commander, got the horrible news immediately and hurried over to report the captain's crime to Patton—he had shot the prisoners down in "cold blood and also in ranks, an even greater error," as Patton sarcastically quoted Bradley in his diary. Patton suggested it was probably an exaggeration.

But they had to avoid an outcry in the press. "Tell the officer," he told Bradley, "to certify that the men were snipers, or had attempted to escape, or something." Matter-of factly he recorded the incident in his diary, adding, "Anyhow they are dead, so nothing can be done about it." Bradley, to his credit, investigated further. He told Patton on August 9 that the two men must be court-martialed. Patton made no comment. In their defense, the men pleaded that Patton had given orders to kill prisoners in his speech just before their division, the 45th, had sailed for Sicily.

On March 30, 1944, eight months after the crime, the officer from the War Department was ushered into Patton's office at Peover Hall, and took down his statement. It cannot have been on oath. At any rate, Patton denied having given any such oral orders. Deprived of their defense, both men were convicted, but returned for the duration to their units; they were killed in action.

In London, a few days after making his denial, Patton dined with Eisenhower, Bradley, and Bedell Smith. He found himself disliking Bradley. "He does all the getting along," noted Patton later, "and does it to his own advantage." It probably irked him even now that Bradley had come up smelling like roses after the episode of the murdered prisoners. Eisenhower quietly rebuked Patton but gave him the extreme unction. "George," he said, "you talk too much."

Hitler's generals were also talking too much. And the Axis diplomats who hovered around them were reporting their secrets to their own capitals. And Magic was eavesdropping on all of them. As Eisenhower was saying those words to Patton, his intelligence staffs at Bushy Park, having analyzed the intercepts, were conveying a fact that lost none of its urgency by reason of its simplicity: Hitler was staking everything on defeating Overlord, as the prelude to negotiating acceptable peace terms with the United States, Britain, and the Soviet Union.

The intercepts also spoke of the recent blitz on London as the "first step in a campaign of retaliation." It was virtually certain now that Hitler was preparing some kind of secret weapon—an activity that was diverting bombing, intelligence, photographic reconnaissance, and secret agent effort from Overlord. The rash of launching sites for the mysterious weapons—some sort of flying vehicles for explosives—was spreading over northwestern France. Experts pored over the stereo photos, trying to deduce the nature of the seven giant bunkers being excavated and concreted at frantic pace near Calais and Cherbourg. They were baffling in their enormity. At Siracourt, what had at first been thought to be two narrow buildings were seen now to be concrete walls twenty-five feet thick and covered with an immense concrete roof. This one building had swallowed a hundred thousand cubic yards of concrete and a million man-hours. As for the rocket weapons, if they were rockets, it was estimated that they could send up to 4,320 tons of explosives to hit London in the space of twenty-four hours. Moreover, Ultra intercepts of radio reports on the test launchings revealed that the weapon was getting more accurate, that ninety-five percent of the test launchings were successful, and that sixty percent of the operational version would probably reach London.

But Magic intercepts had crumbs of comfort. The Nazis were grossly exaggerating the strength under Eisenhower: "Germany estimates that from seventy-five to eighty-five Allied divisions have been assembled in Great Britain for the second front," reported Ambassador Oshima late in February.

If the Nazis thought the thirty-nine divisions actually available for Overlord were but half of the total Allied force, they would withhold large portions of their own forces to defend against the putative (and nonexistent) other half. Magic also revealed an important shift in Hitler's defense strategy. The Japanese dispatch from Berlin had continued: "As a result of studying the problem, and because of recommendations made by Marshal Rommel, the Germans have now decided that the coastal lines must be held at all costs and that the enemy must not be permitted to set foot on the Continent." Sure enough, on March 11 Magic intercepted another Japanese message: "The German Army has recently begun the construction of obstacles in the water in order to strengthen the defense of the coast." Contact mines on piles and sharp-pointed iron stakes were being driven into the seabed and obstacles were submerged in a swathe up to two hundred yards offshore in order to sink landing craft. This news was frustrating to Montgomery, who would command the landing troops. The longer the invasion was delayed, the more formidable the beach defenses would become. But through planning and inspiration, he felt confident, he would once again hurl back his old foe Rommel.

When Bernard Montgomery was a wiry little boy, he had been a prefect at an ancient school, St. Paul's, in West Kensington. He had captained the Rugby first fifteen and had been a member of the school's cricket and swimming teams. When he grew to general's estate, and was pronounced commander of the 21st Army Group, he was pleased to find that St. Paul's was serving as the army group's headquarters. As a boy, he had never entered the High Master's room; "I had to become a Commander in Chief to do so," he would write. Now the room was his own sanctum. To the scene of his boyhood tribulations, then, the hero of El Alamein returned in pomp and glory. Better still: he could bring the mightiest statesmen and generals in the world and lecture to them in his old school hall.

On April 7, he called to that beamed and paneled lecture hall every general who would be in Overlord, down to division level. He peremptorily summoned politicians and top civil servants too. They arrived early that morning from their comfortable homes and their luxury hotels and their headquarters. There were so many cars that many were assigned parking lots half a mile away; it was a chastening experience for a lieutenant general to park his Buick or Plymouth and walk several blocks to the conference; as one amused Canadian officer put it, "Only the Very High Priced Helps' cars were allowed to the front door." A large relief map of Normandy, showing all the landing beaches, was displayed on a tilted platform on the floor of the hall. Montgomery had held a similar conference in North Africa to review his campaign up to the Mareth line. General J.C.H. Lee would write the next day to Stimson: "In both cases he had a large model on the floor of the conference room, as well as well-drawn maps to reveal the plan and the progress of the operation, including logistics and especially supply."

As the generals shuffled into their allotted places in the semicircular tiers of chairs around the tilted map, Montgomery clapped his bony hands for silence and opened the proceedings. He then embarked on a two-hour portrayal of his plan, in which, oddly, Patton was the only army commander to be mentioned by name. Perhaps there still lingered in Montgomery some of the envious irritation, bordering on admiration, from Sicily. He was certainly displeased with Bradley. When they had planned the meeting, Bradley had strongly resisted Montgomery's wish to mark the map with phase lines showing the positions to be reached by certain dates; Bradley was damned if he was going to be forced to commit himself to reaching prescribed objectives on a tight timetable. It wasn't realistic. Montgomery had tut-tutted and said well-all-right-old-chap; nonetheless, he had gone right ahead and marked out just such green, yellow, and black phase lines on the tilted map. The armies were to reach the green line in the first twenty days after the landing. "We will fight continuously until we get it," Montgomery said. After fifteen or twenty more days they were to have reached the yellow line, while the ultimate target line, denoting D-day plus ninety, was shown in black.

"This is an Allied operation," Montgomery announced, "being carried out by British and American forces with the forces of our other Allies cooperating. It is a great Allied team and none of us could do any good without the others. The Supreme Commander, or captain of the team, is General Eisenhower." He continued, "The present enemy situation in the west will be known to you. The present number of identified enemy divisions is fifty-five, of which eight are panzer or panzer grenadier. What the situation will be by D-day is not certain. . . . Since Rommel toured the 'Atlantic Wall,' the enemy has been stiffening up his coastal crust, generally strengthening his defenses, and redistributing his armored reserve."

For an hour he strutted around the miniaturized beaches, hills, and streams in his trim, well-tailored uniform, barking out details of the terrain in his furry, educated voice and poking around with a long pointer. "Rommel," he announced, "is likely to hold his mobile divisions back from the coast until he is certain where our main effort is being made. He will then concentrate them quickly and strike a hard blow; his static divisions will endeavor to hold on defensively to important ground and act as pivots to the counterattack." Montgomery expected Rommel to bring in six panzer divisions by D plus five. A lot would depend on whether Rommel realized that this was the main invasion by then or not. By that day, all being well, Montgomery would have landed fifteen divisions, and about three days later Rommel might well begin an offensive to "rope off" the invaders—to stop their expansion from the beachhead area.

Montgomery smiled stiffly. "Some of us here know Rommel well," he said. "He is a determined commander and likes to hurl his armor into the battle. But according to what we know of the chain of command, the armored divisions are being kept directly under Rundstedt and delay may be caused before they are released to Rommel. This fact may help us, and quarrels may arise between the two of them."

Lest this seem a low-value card to stake such an operation on, Montgomery reminded the generals that the air forces would do all they could to embarrass Rommel. "But," he warned, "the enemy buildup can become *considerable* from D plus four onwards; obviously, therefore, we must put all our energies into the fight and get such a good situation in the first few days that the enemy can do nothing against us."

But first they had to get ashore, and Montgomery expressed anxiety about the obstacles now beginning to bristle along the Normandy beaches. Although no underwater obstacles had yet been sighted in the Overlord area, tens of thousands of Rommel's troops were known to be erecting heavy steel obstacles just above the point on the beaches where the landing craft would touch down. The infantry could get around them, but landing craft on later tides might hit them. Rommel was also flooding the routes inland from the beaches, and blocking them with minefields, craters, and demolitions.

Montgomery had hatched a clever plan to fool Rommel. He was aware from reading months of intercepts that the Germans regarded the British as stronger in combat than the Americans. Therefore the serious breakout threat would be expected from the British sector of the bridgehead, while the Americans would be likely more or less to hold the fort at their end. Well, let them think that! He would attract the German panzer divisions to the British end, he would feint repeatedly with his British left, then swing a powerful right hook at Rommel from the American end, just where he would not be anticipating it. The plan involved risks, of course. More painful for Montgomery, it would undoubtedly invite ignorant criticism—there would be those who would not understand that at first he would be just feinting. He would be accused of dragging his feet. But if it would win the battle, he was prepared to pay that price.

Viewed in retrospect—in the light of later controversy—Montgomery's remarks were significant in that they confirmed that at this early stage he was definitely planning for the British Second Army on the left (commanded now by his friend Sir Miles Dempsey) to make a feint—to develop operations to the south and southeast, moving toward Falaise; it would have no intention of moving much farther, but the Germans could mistake it for a serious drive toward Paris. The effect would be to attract and stall enemy reinforcements from the east. And the effect of that, in turn, would be to protect the eastern flank of Bradley's First Army—which would be delivering the right hook against the unsuspecting Germans.

Montgomery also defined Patton's role in quite limited terms: Patton's task would be to clear Brittany and capture its ports, then to cover the southern flank of the lodgement while Bradley's First Army swung northeastward toward Paris. It was quite clear that Montgomery was going well out of his way to make sure there would be scant glory for his old rival.

After Montgomery sat down, Dempsey and his corps commander Crocker outlined their plans. They stood diffidently on the floor below the tilted map while a junior officer pointed out key features. Joe Collins, whose troops were to land on the extreme right flank, spoke last. There was nothing diffident about him. He did as Montgomery had done—he climbed up onto the map and actually stood on it, freely brandishing the pointer himself. As he resumed his seat, Bedell Smith, sitting behind him, chuckled. "Joe," he whispered, "done in the best tradition of Fort Benning!"

After Admiral Ramsay and Air Chief Marshal Leigh-Mallory had described their plans, Montgomery lifted the no-smoking ban. On this cue, Winston Churchill walked in clutching a cigar. He looked stooped and older than many of them expected. He lowered himself into a chair to hear Montgomery's summing up. According to the version General Lee gave to Stimson, Montgomery stressed three points: "First, implicit confidence in the operation so that commanders through all echelons and the men themselves will feel it; second, the importance of exploitation once the defense crust has been broken through; and third, the vital need of the soldiers' seizing airfields for the airmen."

For ten minutes Churchill then spoke himself. "It was timely," wrote Lee, "because Mr. Churchill left no doubt whatever in anybody's mind regarding his attitude, agreeing fully with what General Montgomery had said about confidence. He inferred that last year and the year before he did not believe in the operation, but now he was sure that the time was ripe, that the commanders are experienced, that the men, equipment and craft are available. He gave us a really inspiring talk." Even Patton was impressed. "The Prime Minister," he wrote in his diary, "made the last talk and the best. He said, 'Remember that this is an invasion, not a creation of a fortified beachhead.' "

Churchill wished them all good luck. His last few sentences were spoken with considerable apparent emotion. Those who knew him intimately were less impressed. The Secretary for War, Sir James Grigg, wrote of his anxiety about the invasion preparations and added, "It is made much worse by a conviction that Winston is a very old man, that his two illnesses have taken away a good deal of his power of decision. There is therefore a good deal of manoeuvering and dirty work going on, particularly on the part of [Lord] Beaverbrook and [Brendan] Bracken. . . ."

For over a week, Churchill had been laboring under one of the ugliest Cabinet squabbles he could recall—about the proposal to make violent bombing attacks on French transportation targets. Just when the whole plan had seemed settled, shocked voices had been raised against it. "The Cabinet today," Churchill had to write to Eisenhower on April 3, "took rather a grave and on the whole an adverse view of the proposal to bomb so many French railway centres, in view of the fact that scores of thousands of French civilians, men, women and children would lose their lives or be injured. Considering that they are all our friends, this might be held to be an act of very great severity, bringing much hatred on the Allied Air Forces."

Eisenhower had lost track of the day of the week. The weeks were endless inspection trips, a sea of young and eager faces milling around him, anxious to see the Supreme Commander before they sailed to that unknown beach of an unknown country. His nerves were wearing thin, his hands ached from writing, drafting, signing, and from shaking hands. In mid-April he wrote to Mamie in soft lead pencil because his hand had just gotten too crippled to write with anything else. At Bushy Park he found letters from anxious mothers pleading for their boys to be sent home—he had to refuse them all. But the basic brutality of it did not leave him unaffected. "It is a terribly sad business," he wrote privately, "to total up the casualties each day—even in an air war—and to realize how many youngsters are gone forever. A man must develop a veneer of callousness . . . but he can never escape a recognition of the fact that back home the news brings anguish and suffering to families all over the country. Mothers, fathers, brothers, sisters, wives and friends must have a difficult time preserving any comforting philosophy and retaining any belief in the eternal rightness of things. War demands real toughness of fiber—not only in the soldiers that must endure, but in the homes that must sacrifice their best."

Problems were arising even at this late stage. The naval gunfire program had been increased. American naval officers thought that the British were skimping. Admiral Alan G. Kirk, the senior American naval commander during Overlord, privately griped to Everett Hughes on April 15: "The British are not putting any good ships into the fight. They are being anchored up in Scapa Flow. The U.S. is putting three battleships, four cruisers and twenty destroyers into the fight."

The whole Overlord decision would hinge on the weather. Eisenhower began asking his meteorological officer, Group Captain James Stagg, to present after each of their commanders' conferences a consensus weather forecast for the rest of the week, just to test their reliability.

The final date would have to be decided at the last moment. On March 6, a datum line had been defined for the invasion, June 1. Future documents identified the invasion date in terms of this "Y-day" plus four. Secrecy became an obsession. A new supergrade of classification, Bigot, was attached to documents mentioning Overlord or Neptune, the operation's other code name.

When Eisenhower thought of security, he thought of Patton. He was still reluctant to let the press announce Patton's presence in England, fearing some fresh incident. But Bedell Smith and the SHAEF public relations staff persuaded him, arguing that some unscrupulous columnist might otherwise write that Eisenhower was unwilling to let the American public know that Patton, object of so much contumely and dismay, was to exercise a command in Overlord. Late in April, Eisenhower softened.

Almost at once he had cause to regret it. Patton opened his big mouth again and there was hell to pay. On April 25, he made a few remarks at the opening of a ladies' welcome club for American soldiers. The scene was the Third Army's local market town of Knutsford. At first he instinctively declined the invitation actually to speak; but then temptation bettered him, he blushed, and accepted, prefacing his remarks with the by now routine words that he was "not there officially." Fifty women listened as Patton twitted them about the value of such clubs. Then, enlarging on his theme, Patton said, "It is the evident destiny of the British and Americans"—he paused, and added *sotto voce,* "and of course the Russians"—"to rule the world." He crossed his fingers for his obligatory white lie, because in truth he found English females unattractive: "As soon as our soldiers meet and know the English ladies and write home and tell our women how truly lovely you are, the sooner the American ladies will get jealous and force this war to a quick termination." A vote of thanks was proposed, and a British colonel, Thomas Blatherwick, seconded it at a length that had Patton shuffling his boots impatiently.

The remarks about ruling the world nearly cost Patton his Third Army command. A British agency released the story—somehow omitting the words "and the Russians"—calling it Patton's "first public address." SHAEF's public relations staff tried frantically to get "and the Russians" included in the dispatch, but it was too late. There was a storm in Congress. A Washington editorial called Patton "Chief Foot-in-Mouth." More ominously, a priority telegram arrived at SHAEF headquarters from Marshall. "We were just about to get confirmation of the permanent makes," said Marshall—referring to the latest list of officers up for Senate approval as permanent major generals, including Bedell Smith and Patton. "This I fear has killed them all." Bedell Smith almost fainted when he read the cable. He telephoned Patton, heatedly saying that his "unfortunate remarks" had probably cost them *both* their promotions. Patton, shaken, wrote to Hughes that it smelled "strongly of having been a frame-up." That was quite possible, as the Ministry of Information may have used this means of leaking his name to the press in type big enough for even the dumbest Abwehr agent to read. The cover story was, of course, that Patton was commanding an army group, preparing to invade France—but near Calais. Patton was badly frightened. He wrote to his daughter Ruth, "Jesus suffered only one night but I have had months and months of it, and the cross is not yet in sight."

Eisenhower was out of London when the Patton bomb burst. He had left by train on the evening of Patton's speech, taking with him Tedder and Bradley to watch a big invasion rehearsal. In January, the government had evacuated an area about five miles deep and fronting some three miles on the coast at Slapton Sands to enable new weapons to be tried out against real targets. It was that part of Devonshire between Dartmouth and Plymouth, along the southwestern coastline of England that looks like a ballet dancer's leg extending toward America. As the British and American ships trained in U.S. Shore Fire Control procedure, the empty farmsteads of the former village of Slapton Sands crumbled under naval gunfire and heavy bombing. The newly developed amphibious tanks crawled about the beaches; these were medium tanks to which canvas collars had been fitted so that they would in theory float. Here too Eisenhower saw the new rocket-firing planes called Typhoons, an astounding British war invention; they dived on their targets at four hundred miles an hour and released a missile which accelerated into the target at supersonic speed.

The invasion exercise began out in Lyme Bay, with Raymond O. "Tubby" Barton's 4th Division, which had not seen combat yet, landing from the sea on beaches remarkably like the real thing in Normandy. They had shallow water behind them and high ground commanding the beach. American engineers had copied the bunkers and pillboxes along the shore. It was the first time that the ships had turned up in force for such an exercise. Shortcomings immediately became evident. The battle fleet had to stand twelve miles off the coast, because Ramsay had told Bradley that the Nazi shore batteries had a range of thirty thousand yards. So the little landing craft had to plow the last twelve miles to the beach alone. After a heavy naval bombardment, there was an unconscionable postponement in H-hour, the moment of invasion, while twenty-one LSTs, twenty-eight LCIs (landing craft infantry), sixty-five LCTs (landing craft tank), fourteen miscellaneous, and ninety-two small landing craft laden with infantry milled around waiting for the signal to go in. Harry Butcher, watching from an LCT, wrote: "If there had been enemy fire, the tanks would have been easy targets, as indeed would have been the landing craft." He came away feeling depressed.

The young American officers had appeared as green as the growing corn. "They seem to regard the war as one grand maneuver in which they are having a happy time," Butcher noted. The full colonels were fat, gray, and elderly, many wearing the First World War's rainbow ribbon. As the "Bayonet" clackety-clacked across the countryside that evening, carrying Eisenhower and his staff back toward London, there was a disconsolate post mortem. Eisenhower was baffled about H-hour having been postponed, particularly without his being informed. Gee Gerow agreed with him. "Never change the time once it is set," he said, "because too much confusion arises."

Tedder made a calculation and said that the strategic bombers would have to go in with split-second timing on the real day if they were to put down a mass carpet of bombs on the beaches, while the assault craft packed with storm troops waited 1,500 yards offshore. The boats would have to land, he pointed out, within one or two minutes of the ordained times. But the bombing was vital, and any short-falling bombs might detonate underwater mines and blow up landing craft. Gerow was not happy when he thought about those underwater mines, and he feared the underwater obstacles most of all: the inanimate beasts tethered in the deep to gouge the bottoms out of his landing craft while they were still hundreds of yards offshore. The photographs showed the steel hedgehogs clearly, but the question was, had the Nazis used seventy-five-pound or hundred-pound railroad rails to make them? Army bulldozers could not bend the latter. He was worried too about the cliff on his right flank, with gun emplacements. Eisenhower tried to cheer him up: he reminded Gerow that backing him would be the greatest firepower ever assembled on the face of this earth. "I'm not pessimistic," the corps commander replied. "Merely realistic."

Back at Bushy Park that evening, April 28, Eisenhower rounded off a long, hard day at his desk. Outside, his chief of staff was chatting with Commander Butcher when there was shocking news. Nazi E-boats had sneaked in among a convoy of seven American LSTs carrying engineer support troops during the big invasion exercise and had torpedoed two of them off Lyme Bay. Casualties were heavy. Bedell Smith jabbed the intercom button and dictated the bad news to Eisenhower. "This reduces our reserve of LSTs for the big show to two," he said. Eisenhower's voice was edgy: "Get off a cable to the Combined Chiefs, advising them of the loss." He meant the loss of LSTs, not the loss of the men. The telegram to Washington read, "Details not available but first report is that two LSTs were sunk and one damaged but arrived in harbor. Three hundred to four hundred casualties probable." It was actually worse than that. Of more than a thousand men in the two LSTs that were sunk, 503 were drowned.

Now too Eisenhower read Marshall's priority telegram about Patton's indelicate remarks. Eisenhower panicked and made no attempt to learn the facts before cabling Marshall to the effect that the episode raised doubts as to "the wisdom of retaining him in high command despite his demonstrated capacity in battle leadership." He had worked with Patton closely for one and a half years, he said, but doubted he would ever completely overcome his "lifelong habit of posing." Twice he slid the buck to Marshall, cravenly angling for Patton's recall; twice Marshall pushed it back across the Atlantic to Eisenhower, saying that he had the responsibility for Overlord. He hinted at the unmistakable fact "that Patton is the only available Army commander for his present assignment who has had actual experience in fighting Rommel and in extensive landing operations followed by a rapid campaign of exploitation." Churchill took a more robust line. He grunted that he could see nothing wrong in Patton's remarks: "Patton simply told the truth."

On May 1, Patton was summoned like a miscreant schoolboy before the Supreme Commander. "George," Eisenhower said, motioning the general to a chair, "you have gotten yourself into a very serious fix."

Patton stopped him right there. "Your job is more important than mine," he said deferentially. "So if in trying to save me you are hurting yourself—throw me out!"

Eisenhower quoted Marshall: Patton's serious mistakes had shaken the confidence of the country and the War Department. "General Marshall even harked back to the Kent Lambert incident," he added.

Patton thought, *Certainly a forgiving s.o.b!* He recalled the case well: Colonel Kent G. Lambert had commanded part of the 1st Armored Division at the entry into Bizerte, Tunisia, the first successful attack by American armor in the war. But then he had written to his wife about secret matters, sending the letter by a friend to avoid army censors, whom he cursed in the letter. It was intercepted. Nothing could save Lambert. Patton had often sent letters home by friends, but for the record he reprimanded Lambert: "Had it not been for your stupid act I would congratulate you for your magnificent performance, but I repeat, no magnificent performance as a soldier can get by in the face of stupidity." Privately, he had asked Everett Hughes (who had noted, "I may have to bust L.") to destroy the evidence, adding perhaps prophetically: "Men like Lambert will not survive this war, and it is too bad to lose them for trivial reasons." George Marshall had, however, taken an unmerciful view. When Eisenhower had recommended Lambert's promotion to general a few days later, he refused.

Patton refused to be cowed by Eisenhower, however. At last he had the Supreme Commander's ear, and he might as well give him his advice—even if unsolicited—about Overlord. It was a British plan, expanded by Monty from three divisions to five. Patton urged now that there should be three separate attacks on at least a ninety-mile front. "I am not threatening," he began, "but I want to tell you that this attack is badly planned and on too narrow a front. It may well result in an Anzio, especially if I am not there."

Eisenhower shrugged: "Hell, don't I know it, but what can I do?" Perhaps he was just referring to the shortage of landing craft—which would be even tighter now that the LSTs had been sunk at Slapton Sands. But Patton took it differently and observed in his diary that that seemed to be one hell of a remark for a Supreme Commander to make. Two days later Eisenhower cabled Patton: "I have decided to keep you," he said. "Go ahead and train your Army."

Patton was going to be indispensable, and both generals knew it.

CHAPTER NINE

Gathering the Reins

As SPRING came there seemed to be more and more to do and less and less time to do it. Few officers in London did not have their minds on the coming summer and its dominating event: the assault on the coasts of Hitler's Europe. The tension grew as the immovable date—foreordained by times and tides and the moon and Josef Stalin—approached: the invasion of France must take place early in June.

By May southern England was blossoming. Telegraph Cottage was surrounded by fruit trees, lilacs, and chestnuts; its gardens were quilted with beds of azure and red. There were even cuckoos popping in the trees, which delighted Eisenhower, who had heard them before only in clocks. He still smiled sometimes, but his cigarette smoking now exceeded the three packs a day he had earlier allowed himself. His staff could feel their muscles getting tighter, like those of a man about to go into the dock on trial for his life. The eyes of the world would be on Overlord, not just on the day it happened, but for centuries to come. A triumphant success for this venture would be hung on one man's name. But so would a bloody failure.

The Americans were in the west of England, the British in the east. The GIs willingly pitched in and did what they could to ease relations with the villagers. In one village they helped rebuild a bombed church. The dedication ceremony was broadcast live to the United States—which was unfortunate, since the bishop observed how grateful they all were for the "succour from America." Soldiers, sailors, airmen strolled around London, enjoying the last few weeks before the biggest moment of their lives. Harry Butcher passed the time by writing to his wife in California: "The best day of my week is Sunday afternoon, when I listen to the Hyde Park lecturers, the crackpots, Communists, Socialists, Capitalists, and just plain preachers. One is tops. He is a one-man brain trust and answers all questions. . . . 'What is the relationship between celery and rhubarb? Is celery merely anemic rhubarb, or is rhubarb merely bloodshot celery?' This guy goes on and on, said he got to be regular lecturer with a soap box assigned to him regularly after years of understudy as a heckler. . . . Has an old felt hat and wears pince nez spectacles which dangle from the end of his nose. Says he is the only bright and sensible lecturer on the grounds: the others think they know what they're talking about, but he knows he doesn't."

The whole of southern England had become an armed camp. Almost every day brought fresh units from the United States and Canada. The troops overran Britain and northern Ireland, and a million tons of crated supplies filled every warehouse, every dockside, every quarry, mine, and tunnel; stacks of crates spilled along the country lanes and roadsides. During May, 160 shiploads flowed to England for Overlord. At one point thirty-eight ammunition ships rode the swells off northern harbors, waiting to unload. The southern ports were clotted with invasion craft.

Everett Hughes had spent late April and early May 1944 inspecting field divisions as Eisenhower's unofficial eyes and ears. Sometimes he went out to the heavy bomber airfields and watched missions being flown to Germany. Eisenhower was responsive to his suggestions: that key commanders should be confirmed in their positions, because any insecurity about their future tended to make for yes-men; that promotions among combat troops had to be attended to; that the orders Eisenhower was issuing were too detailed. He drove down to Taunton to see the V Corps boxing matches, inspected the 4th Division at

Tiverton, lunched with the 29th Division at Tavistock. Some days he got home tired as hell.

Hughes found that security was not always tight, though the British tried hard. One day he went to Weymouth to observe the small boats and troops of the 1st Division practicing embarking. A rotund British army major approached Hughes and importantly demanded to seè his papers.

"Who are you?" Hughes asked, unruffled.

"Port security."

"Can you prove it?"

The man pulled out a bright red ID card. Hughes scrutinized it. "I'm sorry," he said, "but I don't recognize any of the signatures on the card. And incidentally, who are all those men sitting there on the dockside, in nondescript uniforms? And who are those hundreds of people watching from that building back there?"

The British officer shrugged his shoulders. "I don't know, sir. But we're working on that."

"I'll tell you what I'll do," Hughes said, loving every minute of this deviltry. "When you find out who those men are, then I'll let you see my papers." And then he loped away.

Eisenhower, too, conducted frequent inspections. He seemed to want to see every man in person, to look him in the eye and wish him Godspeed. He was never happier than when mingling with his troops. "Our soldiers are wonderful," he had written some months earlier. "It always seems to me that the closer to the front, the better the morale and the less grumbling. No one knows how I like to roam around among them—I am always cheered up by a day with the actual fighters." Homesick for the golden plains of Kansas, he never gave up hope of meeting a boy from Abilene whenever he stopped and talked to GIs. Often he found men from Kansas, and once a soldier who lived near Abilene, but never one from the town itself.

His mind was on the future—after Overlord, after this war. It was on distant beaches, and the sun—he wanted to fly to the four corners of the earth, he wrote Mamie, with no schedule, and no regard for time: Baghdad, Rangoon, Sydney, Tahiti—all those places he had heard of. Of course, if he had to head an army of occupation, he could always invite Mamie to Germany. He would prefer, however, to retire and rattle around the world with her. "Of course," he added, perhaps toying with the fantasy of incorporating Kay Summersby into this idyllic future, "I'd have to write some to make enough for expenses, but we could drag along a secretary to whom I could dictate an hour or so a day—which ought to pay hotel bills. What do you think of it?"

There is no record of what Mamie—or Kay Summersby—thought about that gingerly advanced notion, but Mamie had evidently continued to hear rumors, because in her first letter on her arrival back in Washington after her travels in the south, she finished with a dark comment: "Such tales I've heard since returning." That caused Eisenhower hastily to respond with protestations of innocence. "I know that people at home always think of an army in the field as living a life of night clubs, gaiety and loose morals," he began disingenuously. "So far as I can see . . . the American forces here are living cleaner and more nearly normal lives than they did in Louisiana, California, etcetera, when we were in large encampments. Ninety-nine percent of officers and men are too busy to have any time for anything else.

"In the larger cities such as London," he conceded, "there are undoubtedly numbers of officers and men that are living loosely; but it is also true that the pictures painted by gossip are grossly exaggerated. So far as the group around me is concerned, I know that the principal concern is work—and their habits are above reproach."

Whatever the nature of his habits, his devotion to work was indisputable. The first week in May gave Eisenhower not one minute's respite. Conference followed conference. On May 6, a cold and rainy morning, he wrote Mamie to confess an illicit prospect: "Tomorrow morning I think I'll sleep very late—or if I don't sleep, I'll at least stay in bed until 9:30 or 10:00. I have a new Western I *must* read."

Two days later, he called his eighteenth meeting to decide on H-hour —which would vary according to the particular day picked as D-day. Admiral Sir Bertram Ramsay—who as the Overlord naval commander corresponded to Montgomery for the ground forces and Leigh-Mallory for the air—said that June 4 had been dropped, but that June 5 or 6 was possible. Eisenhower told Harry Butcher afterward that he wished he could have his friend ABC Cunningham again as invasion naval commander; he wasn't fond of Ramsay. Later, the Supreme Commander lunched alone with the Prime Minister. Churchill looked fit, and as they parted he said, with tears skidding down one fat cheek: "I am in this thing with you to the end. And if it fails we will go down together."

At Supreme Headquarters, Eisenhower and Bedell Smith seemed to have much of their time consumed with the most mundane matters: the amounts being paid for rugs, billets, and a thousand other things; the situation in Park West garage; which generals were sleeping with which WAC drivers. Hughes noticed that Brigadier General Henry B. Sayler, the chief ordnance officer, was looking tired, and wrote in his diary: "H.S. has his chauffeuress (?) back, and looked red eyed."

Eisenhower had to see to the printing of huge sums of French money. On May 11, he had to send a message to the Combined Chiefs of Staff about how much toilet paper and disinfectant would be needed for French refugees during the first ninety days of Overlord: "Requirement for estimated numbers of refugees for whom provisions should be made totals: Latrine paper nine five million sheets, Cresol 18,700 gallons based on British army scale of five sheets of paper per person per day and one gallon Cresol per one thousand persons per day." The War Office replied regretfully that the paper would not be available in the United Kingdom until after mid-July.

The frustrating thing was that many decisions that should have been military—like the Overlord decision itself—were ultimately in the hands of political leaders. Hughes noted: "Will D-day be a political or a military decision? Apparently Joe [Stalin] has been promised something."

Forward planners at the Pentagon were acutely aware of the graver problems that would confront Eisenhower later in his campaign. One in particular, the manpower problem, worried both Marshall and Stimson. By no means would Eisenhower have numerical superiority over the Germans; the Germans would have an estimated fifty-six divisions defending France, the Allies barely more even by the end of the summer. Stimson moreover drew attention to the high average age of American troops. He pointed out that German morale was high, and that they already had a strategic reserve estimated at eleven divisions, compared with only fourteen divisions remaining as a strategic reserve in the United States once the Overlord divisions had been committed. If the Russian offensive slackened as their supply lines lengthened or if Hitler voluntarily shortened his overall front line, he could substantially increase his reserve. The Americans would have put most of their strength in the shopwindow, and the Germans, Stimson thought, would be bound to perceive this American manpower weakness. "There [would be] nothing . . ." he wrote, "to make [the Germans] feel the futility of fighting hard for a stalemate." Stimson was dreadfully afraid that there would be a stalemate in France in the autumn like the deadlock at that moment in Italy.

There was another fear. During May, Stimson's War Department tried to assess Hitler's secret weapon preparations. A department report speculated on the nature of the weapon and described the countermeasures so far taken. The document was half an inch thick, marked Top Secret, and impressively bound in black, but it contained little hard information. Nobody knew for certain what the weapon would be— pilotless aircraft or long-range rocket—or where it was being manufactured. Some kind of missiles had been photographed from a great altitude at Peenemünde, on the Baltic coast. Launching sites were still being built in France. The report warned: "The number of newly discovered 'modified ski' sites increases daily." Nearly thirty had already been found.

It was this kind of knowledge that abraded stamina. It was all such a colossal strain. Bedell Smith invited Commander Butcher to lunch at his home on May 11 and confessed that preparing Overlord had worn him down. He was fed up and was hoping to quit the army after the war was over. "He said he had no misgivings about our troops getting ashore," wrote Butcher, "but [he] gave me the alarming prediction, confidentially, that our chances of holding the beachhead, particularly after the Germans get their buildup, is only fifty-fifty." Smith had added that the chance was worth taking.

The strain was telling on Eisenhower too. Butcher noticed that he looked worn and tired, older now than at any time. No matter, however, how Eisenhower himself felt; he was responsible for the morale of his men. With Overlord drawing closer, the time had come to stoke the necessary fires in the hearts of the combat troops—to make the character of their Nazi enemies absolutely clear to them, as Eisenhower put it in a circular to his top commanders—and to stress the absolute need for crushing them. The troops had to be encouraged. They must be reminded that they had defeated this same enemy before and that they could do it again. Just as the Red Army had its commissars, just as Hitler had National Socialist Leadership officers to indoctrinate the Wehrmacht troops, so Eisenhower now directed that each regiment have an "orientation officer" to make sure that each company of troops got suitable propaganda briefings. Eisenhower's own headquarters would furnish "News Maps" and "Army Talks" for this purpose, supplemented by material printed in *Yank* and *Stars & Stripes* and broadcast over the American Forces Network.

As it happened, Everett Hughes was waging a surreptitious propaganda campaign of his own, against the man he loved to hate, Walter Bedell Smith. The sniping had gone on for some time. Hughes had once advised Eisenhower: "Don't let Beedle needle you." Asked by General Wedemeyer for his opinion of Bedell Smith, Hughes used the word "tricky."

Hughes was fascinated by Smith's way with women. Hughes noted in January 1943: "During early days of expedition a ship with five WAACs, thirty navy nurses, 200 English nurses was torpedoed. Bedell flew to Oran, took over the WAACs; the five were promoted to captains at $2,000 p.a., the nurses got nothing except English battledress." Later in 1943, Hughes twittered, Smith had gotten into "some personal entanglement" with a Nurse Wilbur, who "returned a Chief Nurse." Eisenhower wanted to fire the nurse, but Hughes protested that Eisenhower should not become involved in Smith's personal activities.

As the months passed, Hughes's amusement over Smith became mixed with disdain. At the height of an investigation of the misuse of American government money, Hughes learned that official funds were being spent in the most curious ways. He had visited a gunsmith and what he learned there bothered him: "When Geo and I visited Purdey's gun shop the other day we found a beautiful gun being made for Bedell Smith. On the side we found two carbines presented by Beedle." Smith, in other words, had actually sold U.S. government weapons in order to pay for the fancy shotgun being made for him. Hughes went on to make references to gifts from Smith to Purdey and his family, and then recalled his favorite Bedell Smith quote, from a previous incident: "The photos are expensive—I'll charge them to my entertainment allowance."

On May 15 the senior Allied commanders assembled again at St. Paul's School for a final review of Overlord planning. Never before had so much rank been pulled together under one roof for an operational briefing. King George VI was present, as were Winston Churchill and Field Marshal Jan Christiaan Smuts, Prime Minister of South Africa. All the Allied heavyweights were on hand, including Eisenhower, Bradley, Patton, and Montgomery with his two army commanders, Sir Miles Dempsey and Henry D. Crerar, the quiet Canadian. Up on the stage was a scale map of the entire Normandy invasion coast. It was marked to show the beaches that each of the two invading armies was to hit.

Eisenhower called the hall to attention: "We're going to have a briefing on the invasion of France." He asked them all to iron out any disagreements still remaining between the three services.

As the ground commander, Montgomery talked first. He had prepared his performance. They were facing sixty German divisions in France, he announced, including ten panzer divisions. "Last February," he said, "Rommel took command from Holland to the Loire. It is now clear that his intention is to deny any penetration; Overlord is to be defeated on the beaches. To this end, Rommel has thickened up the coastal crust, increased the number of infantry divisions not committed to beach defense and allotted them in a lay-back role to seal off any break in the coastal crust, [and] redistributed his armored reserve." He went over the probable sequence of events, the rate at which Rommel's panzer divisions could appear. By dusk on D plus one, Rommel might have nine infantry and panzer divisions confronting the invaders, and when the overriding menace became obvious the next day he might start thirteen *more* divisions moving to the Overlord area. He could launch a full-scale counterattack by all ten panzer divisions at any time after D plus six.

Montgomery did not spare his admiration for his feared adversary. "Rommel is an energetic and determined commander; he has made a world of difference since he took over. He is best at the spoiling attack; his forte is disruption; he is too impulsive for the set-piece battle. He will do his level best to 'Dunkirk' us—not to fight the armored battle on ground of his own choosing, but to avoid it altogether by preventing our tanks landing, by using his own tanks well forward." He predicted that Rommel would try to hold Caen and Carentan and become obsessed with the nodal point, Bayeux. If Rommel succeeded, said Montgomery in his dry, nasal voice, "we would be awkwardly placed."

It seemed a grim picture. The unknown nature of the beach obstacles emplaced to foil landing craft, and the chaos that must reign after a sea voyage to a strange coast, added to the menace. But then Montgomery presented his solutions. "We must then rely on the violence of our assault, our great weight of supporting fire from the sea and air, [on our] simplicity, [and on our] robust mentality. . . . We must blast our way on shore and get a good lodgement before the enemy can bring sufficient reserves up to turn us out. Armored columns must penetrate deep inland, and quickly, on D-day; this will upset the enemy plans and tend to hold him off while we build up strength. We must gain space rapidly, and peg out claims well inland."

After that, Montgomery called on Bradley and Dempsey and they talked. Admiral Ramsay described the difficulties of getting the troops ashore. Leigh-Mallory and Sir Arthur Harris also spoke—the latter still arguing, even at this late hour, in favor of bombing as a substitute for invasion. Later he would write to Eisenhower lamenting the diversion of his planes from the bombing of inland cities to the preparing for and supporting of Overlord. "You will recall my statement . . . at St. Paul's School," he wrote, "that five months' virtual freedom from bombing would enable Germany to restore in full her essential war production."

Patton did not speak—he was not considered important enough; he nevertheless was "resplendent," according to one witness. The few words the King spoke were painful to Patton because of His Majesty's efforts not to stammer. On first meeting the King, Patton had privately summed him up as "just a grade above a moron, poor little fellow." At lunch Patton sat opposite Churchill, "who asked me," he wrote in his diary, "whether I remembered him, and when I said I did, he immediately ordered me a glass of whiskey." Patton was impressed by Churchill's fighting language. Eisenhower got the same impression. "I am hardening toward this enterprise," Churchill told him. Now even Churchill's doubts were dispelled. He could smell victory in the air.

After lunch the party broke up. It had all reminded General Sir Hastings Ismay, who was there, of King Henry's speech before Agincourt, as suggested by Shakespeare's *Henry V:*

> . . . he which hath no stomach to this fight,
> Let him depart; his passport shall be made,
> And crowns for convoy put into his purse.

Among those who had not been invited to St. Paul's was Everett Hughes. He was annoyed. "All the brass hats meet today to go over the final plans," he complained to his diary. "Wish I had been invited. I am certainly on the fringes." He began to suspect that the war had passed him by.

Pique, perhaps, was the reason for his next action. On May 16, he broached the subject of that shotgun to Bedell "and he gets mad," Hughes noted triumphantly. So his suspicions had been right! Later that day he jotted a fuller entry: "Beedle gets mad and blames Patton when I mention seeing the shotgun. See my memo on the subject." The next day, Hughes tattled to Henry Sayler about the shotgun. "I like it," Hughes chortled afterward. "He thinks I should keep mum on the subject. Maybe I'd better wait until I.G. [the Inspector General] has finished his investigation re billets. Sayler says Beedle was issued two carbines which he *lost* and then paid for."

Mother's Day came and went without Eisenhower even knowing it. That was the darned thing about this island, he wrote Mamie: the British had never even mentioned Mother's Day. He had kept thinking it was a Sunday in June, and now he had to write a letter to Mamie telling her how sorry he was he'd overlooked it.

Several days after the Saint Paul's School conference, Lieutenant General William Simpson, newly arrived in England, called on Eisenhower. The Supreme Commander greeted him warmly and asked: "What army have you got?"

Simpson replied, "The Eighth Army."

"My goodness," exclaimed Eisenhower, "we can't duplicate the famous British Eighth Army. I am going to send a message to General Marshall and recommend a change."

The next day he called Simpson up and said, "You are now the Ninth Army instead of the Eighth." Eisenhower was learning to take Montgomery's vanity into account.

Montgomery was now busy touring the field armies for a second time. He wrote to his political boss, Sir James Grigg, the War Secretary, on May 21: "This time I am speaking my final words to the senior officers—down to the lieutenant-colonel level inclusive. This is a big job and will take about ten days in all; but it will, I feel sure, pay a good dividend, and I have always done it. I thought it might interest you to have a copy of what I say." In his speech, he talked about the past—about how Britain had had to wait while the United States developed its strength enough to help Britain fight back—about the present situation, the prospects, and the immediate task. The text was always the same. He would end up by stressing his main points, one of which was Allied solidarity. "We are a great team of Allies, British and American," he would say grandly. "There must be throughout this team a friendly spirit; we must have confidence in each other. As a British general I regard it as an honor to serve under American command; General Eisenhower is captain of the team and I am proud to serve under him. And I regard it as a great honor to have American troops serving under my command."

In the last week of May, Eisenhower had to cancel two planned inspection trips of his own because he had so much important work left unfinished at headquarters. He felt as if he were living on a network of high-tension wires. He was unashamedly homesick and his dog was still in quarantine. ("He was really all I had here," he assured Mamie.) He was frantic with fatigue. He wrote to Mamie one day and by the next he could not for the life of him recall if he had written that morning or several days before. "I get twisted as to time," he told her. His left eye was sore and angry, and he had had a ringing in one ear for a month now.

On May 26 he issued stern orders to Montgomery, Bradley, and the other commanders, reminding them of their duty not to inflict wanton destruction on the historical monuments of Europe. He had the example of Cassino in mind, where the air force had blasted the ancient monastery to pieces in the mistaken belief that the Nazis were using it as a vantage point. That accomplished, he lunched with the royal family at Buckingham Palace. He found that Queen Elizabeth radiated personality, while King George was quiet and introverted except for once pointing out that the Supreme Allied Commander's napkin had dropped to the floor.

The twentieth meeting of the Overlord commanders was held at Southwick House, under Tedder, on May 29. It dealt with the need for the American airborne divisions to assist in the beach landings, whatever the casualty rate that Leigh-Mallory gloomily predicted. They also discussed the time restrictions on the mass bombing that would go in on the beaches minutes before the troops hit them. The weather that day was warm and clear, and the Americans feared from their own home experience that rain and wind must follow.

The next day, at noon, Eisenhower called together in the auditorium at Bushy Park the one thousand men and women who had worked there at SHAEF headquarters. They had made the plans, he said, and made them well. Now it was up to the combat troops. After the invasion, the SHAEF staff would inevitably be split up—some staying at Bushy Park, some going with him the next day to his advance command post at Portsmouth, others to the Continent with him.

On May 31, at the eleven A.M. air meeting held at Leigh-Mallory's headquarters at Stanmore to discuss the next days' targets, Eisenhower told the bomber commanders to go ahead and saturate the Overlord area now. Later they were discussing the elimination of some tough Nazi radio-jamming stations that protected the Normandy beaches. Harris turned to an officer and said: "Why can't we take on one of those objectives tonight?" Eisenhower overheard the remark and was pleased at this new evidence of cooperation. Harris, after all, had been so difficult on the matter of Overlord support. Once Eisenhower had confided to the Canadian general Henry Crerar: "I'm like the driver of a team of four skittish horses whose job it is to keep them all pulling in the same direction." Maybe he at last had learned to drive those horses.

CHAPTER TEN

Ends and Means

ONE TUESDAY morning in April, Eisenhower stood at the airfield at Upper Dunmow, a two hours' drive north of London, watching thirty-nine B-26s dispatched at twenty-second intervals to blast the French railroad marshaling yards at Charleroi. Then he went on to Debden airfield to watch the 4th Fighter Group operating. After the briefing there, he spoke about the coming invasion and said that the fighter pilots were spearheading the great trinity of land, sea, and air forces, each of which must do its share. At Bassingbourn airfield he hung around, hoping to see its B-17s return from an attack on Germany, but there was a delay—and later that evening Spaatz got the grim news by telephone that he had lost sixty-four more bombers and sixteen fighters that day.

Toohey Spaatz was getting the air battles that he craved, but they were not all turning out as he wanted. "There is a lot more life in the Luftwaffe than previous optimistic reports would indicate," wrote Harry Butcher. Most of the damage now was from antiaircraft fire. The flak bursts were so thick that one pilot said he had the feeling he could

122

step out and walk on them. Even Hap Arnold—a man of perpetual exuberance—could see grim morale problems ahead. He told the Joint Chiefs that the massive likelihood of death was beginning to affect his crews—the loss rate was currently eighty-five percent of the total force over a tour of twenty-five sorties. From the Magic intercepts, Washington gleaned hard hints that Hitler would soon have a jet-propelled fighter squadron in use. The Japanese military attaché in Berlin confided to Tokyo: "I have it from someone in the Messerschmitt Company—this source is particularly secret—that such a plane is now undergoing tests . . . and that the one at the Messerschmitt Company is practically completed."

Eisenhower reported to Marshall: "We are seizing every opportunity to force the Luftwaffe to fight. When our penetrations go very deep we have to pay a good price, but Spaatz's crowd is taking a big toll of the enemy, and once we get a really good operation against about three or four important targets east of Berlin we won't have to go that far for a long time."

When State Department officials called on Eisenhower on April 25, both the Supreme Commander and Bedell Smith spoke in worried tones of the importance of getting some definition of the term "unconditional surrender," which was what the Allied leaders had insisted upon at the Casablanca Conference in January 1943. Morale in the German air force had actually improved in recent months, they said, in spite of heavy losses—they were fighting harder partly because they believed they had no alternative but to fight or die. Eisenhower and Bedell Smith considered it vital to be able to tell the German military, at some stage, that they would not be annihilated. Otherwise the Allies would face a desperate foe who would fight their battles to the bitter end. The diplomats replied: "This question has been raised three times with the President and . . . he has not been willing to authorize any step in the direction of defining or interpreting Unconditional Surrender."

By mid-April 1944 the new air command had effectively been under Eisenhower for two weeks, and seemed to be working well. But Leigh-Mallory's plans were still the ones in favor, and the American air force generals were still dubious about their wisdom. Doubts were voiced about bombing the beach defenses, because the bomb craters would present even worse obstacles to the invasion troops. More fundamentally, Spaatz believed that his bombers had only about three more months in which to smash Hitler's war industries—after that, by all accounts, Hitler would have his new jet-propelled fighter in service. With the remarkable H2X radar, Spaatz's bombers could attack in all weathers; with fighter cover they could still roam to all vital targets in Germany. The German jets would alter that. If there must be a seaborne invasion, argued Spaatz as late as this, then why not an effortless invasion of Norway, which would have the acquisition of airfields in Sweden as a bonus? The three U.S. bomber forces—the 8th, 15th and 9th—could then smash into Germany from all four sides. (In the next war, he explicitly wrote, the key to the domination of Europe and the Soviet Union would be air bases in Sweden and Norway.) "If this were done," he said to another general, "the . . . Overlord operation could be eliminated. It might take somewhat longer, but it would be surer; whereas the proposed cross-Channel operation is highly dangerous, and the outcome is extremely uncertain. A failure of Overlord will have repercussions which may well undo all of the efforts of the strategic bombing effort to date."

Until Eisenhower and Tedder took over command of the air forces on April 15, four priorities had been assigned to the strategic bombers: (1) the German air force; (2) the enemy's communications; (3) the coastal gun sites; and (4) the secret weapons sites. All were top priority.

On that day there was a meeting of air commanders in Tedder's office. Tedder removed his pipe from his mouth and declared that a new directive had now been "agreed on" for the use of the strategic bombers. Everyone knew what that meant: high priority for Leigh-Mallory's transportation plan. There was a hubbub of opposition: he was denounced by Portal's deputy, Air Vice Marshal Sir Norman Bottomley: "No directive has been agreed on by Portal, largely because it has not been cleared by the Prime Minister for political reasons." This, then, had become a major factor in the controversy: the high rate of civilian casualties that would be inflicted on the French, Belgian, and Dutch civilian populations if the strategic bombers were turned loose on their transportation centers.

Tedder, brazening it out, announced that transportation attacks had been cleared for the next seven days and that nineteen specific targets in France had been assigned to Spaatz. Spaatz retorted that since he was primarily expected to destroy the German air force and neutralize the secret weapons (Crossbow) sites, he had little hope of inflicting serious damage on the nineteen transportation targets. Tedder said: "That is the price we've got to pay if the Crossbow sites are to be neutralized."

On April 19, Tedder, reflecting a growing panic about Hitler's secret weapons, ruled that they were to get immediate top priority for attack, "even over [the] German air force," as Spaatz noted with disbelief. He called on Eisenhower to protest. This was a violation of all strategic principles, he said; it effectively gave the initiative to Hitler. They were reacting to his alleged threat instead of taking action themselves. By now the exhausted Eisenhower had lapsed into that most bankrupt of leadership techniques—responding to the most recent claimant to his attention; he gave Spaatz permission for two days of visual bombing against the oil targets which he had been demanding, just to ascertain whether this would force the Germans to send up fighters in strength: "[We] must find some way to force them into the air so that the strength of the German air force can continue to be decreased by knocking them down in the air," Spaatz said in summary.

His anger had been roused by the nonchalant admission at an Air Ministry press conference on April 12 that the German fighter strength had actually increased by three hundred since November. He complained to Portal that such statements would seriously affect the morale of his crews, who had devoted the last year to wearing down the Luftwaffe. Air Minister Sir Archibald Sinclair wrote a groveling apology to Spaatz. What nobody liked to admit was that, despite everything, the Germans were rapidly expanding their mighty fighter aircraft industry. Spaatz felt badly hurt by it, and told three top U.S. newspaper correspondents over lunch on April 17: "The great tribute to the Eighth Air Force is that they have sustained the greatest losses of any other air force operating during this war, and have survived. Our crews must be made to know and believe that these losses have been worthwhile."

Two days later Spaatz drove over to Ridgewell air base. His bomber crews there were badly shaken. Spaatz could see that both commanders and men now believed they had been misled about the imminence of "the defeat of the German fighter force." Lunching with Spaatz the next day, the commander of one of the battered bomb groups cast an eye over the joint press release that Spaatz proposed to issue and handed it back with the words, "General, it will be hard to make the crews believe anything just now. They're dubious of anything they read."

The American air force was experimenting with secret weapons of its own. A week later, Everett Hughes drove from London to an air base where the bombers were taking off on a mission to test a secret weapon. He arrived in time to glimpse the weapons as the planes took off past the tower—five-hundred-pound winged bombs that would be released twenty miles outside the target area and glide the remaining distance. Their final accuracy was not great—they could fall anywhere at all in a zone about ten miles by ten. Hughes was an old-fashioned general, and he was disturbed about what he had seen. In his notes he used the word *barbaric*. He hurried back to London and confronted Eisenhower. "The Air Force has always prided itself on its pinpoint bombing," he said. "Yet here they are planning to use bombs which can be dropped several miles from the target with the hope that *some* of them will sail the rest of the way—and to hell with what they hit or where they go!" Eisenhower made no comment, and Hughes left in dismay.

The increasing operations against non-German targets brought out an unsuspected moralistic streak in the Allied high command. Spaatz, for example, informed Eisenhower that he wanted to develop an air plan for Overlord that would not result in civilian casualties. There had recently been American air raids against French and Belgian rail centers—and a series by the daylight bombers of Spaatz against Balkan capitals like Bucharest, Budapest, and Sofia—and Spaatz was troubled about them. He spoke to the sagacious U.S. ambassador in London, John Winant, telling him of his concern about the bombing of non-German towns and villages. Afterward, Winant sent a telegram to Roosevelt pointing out—they were probably Spaatz's arguments—that the Soviet air force bombed only military objectives, and that Europe would take a long time forgetting what the British and American air forces were doing. As for the French casualties, Winant warned the President: "Last week [Robert] Sherwood [of the Office of War Information] stated that *we* are being blamed for some unknown reason for the casualties and destruction produced last month in France by British night bombing." Winant too was upset by the destruction and the mass killing contemplated, but as he had told Spaatz over lunch, he shared Eisenhower's belief: "If it is necessary for winning the war more quickly, it must be done." The end justified the means. Nonetheless, all of them were happy that it was Eisenhower who had taken the decision and not they.

Eisenhower was restless about the slaughter of French civilians all the same, and was grateful when, at his conference on April 24, Leigh-Mallory somberly assured him: "Available reports indicate the reaction to date is apparently not unfavorable to the Allies." One can only speculate on Leigh-Mallory's sources for these comforting reports. The records now show that most Belgians and French were furious, but they were impotent to stop the campaign. On April 29, Paul-Henri Spaak, the foreign minister of the exiled Belgian government, protested a recent American raid that had devastated one of the most densely populated areas of Belgium, causing enormous casualties. The French also made vociferous protests. The British Chiefs of Staff shifted uneasily as the clamor mounted. Eisenhower, having made his decision, stood by it.

Now the buck-passing began in earnest. On April 28, Churchill sent for Eisenhower and told him the Cabinet was in uproar about the bombing of the French railroad system. Eisenhower told him firmly that the British Chiefs of Staff would have to send their views to him through the Combined Chiefs in Washington, to whom alone, he insisted, he was answerable. Military necessity, he said, dictated the bombing of the French transportation areas. Eisenhower told Marshall the next day, "The British government has been trying to induce me to change my bombing program against the transportation systems, so as to avoid the killing of any Frenchmen. I have stuck to my guns because there is no other way in which tremendous air force can help us, during the preparatory period, to get ashore and stay there. The Prime Minister talked to me about bombing 'bases, troop concentrations and dumps.' The fact is," Eisenhower told Marshall, "that any large [military] concentrations are [located] by battalion in large villages. Any immediate attempt to bomb the German troop units throughout France would probably kill four Frenchmen for every German."

The results of the transportation bombing appeared controversial. An intelligence report on May 1 said that the damage was being quickly repaired. "Enemy military traffic," the report warned, "is not at present being appreciably hindered, and the weight of dislocation is falling primarily on French civilian traffic." But at his seventeenth Overlord conference, that same day, the Supreme Commander announced that the bombing of the rail centers would continue.

Churchill still professed to be unhappy. He slid the buck across the Atlantic to Roosevelt. On May 7, he appealed to the President: "The War Cabinet share my apprehensions of the bad effect which will be produced upon the French civilian population by these slaughters, all taking place so long before 'Overlord' D-day. They may easily bring about a great revulsion in French feeling towards their approaching liberation." The pressure on Marshall grew too. On May 5 the French Committee of National Liberation sent a memorandum of protest from Algiers, but got no answer. On May 16, Marshall was notified that Lieutenant General Marie Emile Béthouart, de Gaulle's chief of general staff, had written to express his anger at the continued killing of his fellow countrymen. Marshall pushed the problem back to Eisenhower, and he was man enough to accept it for a while. But even he found a way to step neatly out of the dilemma of conscience. He passed it to his hatchet man, Bedell Smith, and left London late on May 16, to visit units in Northern Ireland. Bedell Smith tackled the French military mission in London. To his surprise, General Pierre Koenig, the mission's chief, was cold-blooded, almost complacent, about the killing. "This is war," expatiated Koenig, "and it must be expected that people will be killed. We would take twice the anticipated loss to be rid of the Germans."

Smith, who was not exactly a bleeding heart himself, was nevertheless amazed at Koenig's sangfroid. It was easy for the French general ensconced in London, at the giving end, to volunteer these lives; perhaps, thought Smith, it was just as well that Koenig's fellow countrymen, who had to take the brunt of the strategic bomber offensive, could not be asked their view.

After the war, the British and Americans took pains to play down the suffering the bombing had caused. Some very low figures were included in their official histories. But in a letter written on May 29, Field Marshal Rommel, in charge of the entire defense zone, gave a different picture. "The French are suffering badly," he wrote. "Three thousand dead among their population in the last forty-eight hours alone." The campaign did yield one bonus that neither Eisenhower nor Leigh-Mallory had included in their computations. In anticipation of the invasion the Germans had prepared forty thousand extra hospital beds throughout northern France, with twenty-eight thousand more standing by in Paris and Brussels, in addition to twenty thousand in southern Germany, to handle the combat casualties that would occur during the first six weeks of the campaign. But by the day that Overlord actually began, every one of these beds was filled with French victims of the pre-Overlord bombing campaign.

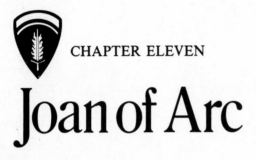

CHAPTER ELEVEN

Joan of Arc

BY 1944, it had become a war being fought not only by but also between the Great Powers, and to some degree for their own interests and aggrandizement. The minor powers, on whose behalf the mighty had once taken up arms, were thrust aside and forgotten. Poland was permitted to fight on, with one corps doing gallant deeds in Italy and gradually bleeding away to insignificance. Czechoslovakia was in Hitler's sullen hegemony. France was an interloper, whose inconvenience was magnified by every action of its self-appointed and autocratic representative in Algiers.

Charles André Joseph Marie de Gaulle knew how to play off both ends against the middle. Britain and America viewed each other's dealings with him mistrustfully. In May 1943, when American official censors eavesdropped on Churchill's secret conversations with Anthony Eden about the latest intolerable deeds of this Frenchman whom Churchill contemptuously dubbed "Joan of Arc," it reassured the State Department to hear the British Prime Minister exclaim in angry, upset tones, "He owes everything to us," and to urge Eden: "You must strike now. . . . We cannot allow our affairs to be compromised."

President Roosevelt saw no need to fret over France's sovereignty. Voyaging to the Cairo Conference aboard the *Iowa* in November 1943, he revealed to his Joint Chiefs of Staff his intention of expanding America's domains at French expense. Let postwar France keep its Syria and Lebanon, but it must lose its other colonies like Indochina; and Dakar, said Roosevelt in secret to his military advisors, must become an American outpost on the coast of West Africa. De Gaulle expected the Americans to equip several Free French divisions for him, but Admiral Leahy predicted only trouble if America complied. "If de Gaulle gets into France with, say, ten well-equipped divisions, he can readily take charge of the government of France by force."

One thing was clear to the Allies: once they had liberated France, de Gaulle would try to establish a personal dictatorship there. Over the years, Gaullist officers had gradually monopolized the highest posts in the army. His closest advisors, said one report, had a definite "führer" complex in speaking of him. American intelligence obtained articles he had written for the *Revue Militaire Française* in 1930 and 1931, two years before Hitler's seizure of power, in which de Gaulle said that France needed a master who would lead the country with a strong and paternal hand. Roosevelt was a campaigner for democracy, and he had no intention of foisting a dictatorship onto any liberated nation. He was absolutely unwilling to let de Gaulle's resistance movement take responsibility for setting up the provisional government in liberated France. Feelings were running high, but in Washington the opposition was intractable.

De Gaulle had wandered the vaulted corridors of Westminster ever since France's defeat in 1940. A gangling specter, tall and stubborn, he was the most formidable thorn in the Allied flesh. He had been born at Lille in 1890; he had graduated from St. Cyr Military Academy, taught history there after the First World War and become the youngest major general during the second. He had fled France in June 1940 and resumed the battle from London with the famous dictum: "France has lost a battle, but France has not lost the war." Since November 1943 he had been sole president of the French Committee of National Liberation established at Algiers.

In England, de Gaulle demonstrated his concept of paternalism. From Carlton Gardens, the London headquarters of the Fighting

French, bizarre rumors began to seep. Respectable Frenchmen who had been smuggled out of Europe through de Gaulle's escape system, but who had political differences with him, were reportedly subjected to harsh physical and psychological persuasion. They were obliged to capitulate. "It was the price of my ticket," said one, a former high government official.

The ugly business finally surfaced, to a degree, for Britain was a country were the law still ruled, though not over de Gaulle. A French soldier escaped the Gaullist secret service headquarters at 10 Duke Street—not three minutes from the American headquarters—and had the audacity to prosecute de Gaulle for detaining and torturing him when he refused to talk about his work for the British secret service. In Britain the High Court is of adamantine independence and there was no way to quash the embarrassing writ which it proceeded to issue. De Gaulle, however, refused to attend the High Court, denying its jurisdiction over him. No one knew what to do, so nothing was done, and things went on as before at Carlton Gardens and at Duke Street. Both before and after the liberation of France, according to further evidence, the secret service organization of André Dewavrin used brutality to enforce the oath-taking and pledging of personal allegiance to General de Gaulle that was required. Frenchmen in Britain who were reluctant to join de Gaulle were deported to a remote French colony and "quietly dropped from view," as a source phrased it in a report to the American government. But the problem for the other Allies was that perhaps as many as ninety percent of the French people looked up to him as a symbol of resistance.

De Gaulle had ridden to power and prestige on a wave of French bitterness and hatred of the Anglo-Saxons. He blamed France's humiliating defeat in 1940 on Roosevelt's lack of support. He was surrounded by anti-American advisors. His radio stations and newspapers campaigned against U.S. policy; virulent anti-American feelings were inculcated in the French troops training even now in England. He hated the British, and was reported to have said in a secret speech to his parachutists on February 4, 1943, "Although it is now necessary for the French to make pro-English propaganda, fundamentally the British, like the Germans, are hereditary enemies of the French; it is the Russians who will win the war from the military point of view and the French should flatter them and obtain whatever gains may be possible from their difficulties with the Anglo-Saxons; finally, after gaining control of France I will not stand in the way of allowing the Russians to occupy Germany temporarily."

Churchill was no fool, and realized the damage de Gaulle was doing to Anglo-American relations and to the war effort. In January 1943 he had advised de Gaulle that the British did not regard him as indispensable; and he asked Anthony Eden to "knock him about pretty hard" for his own good. In May 1943 Churchill cabled London, while visiting Washington, to ask whether it would not be best to eliminate de Gaulle altogether as a political figure.

It seems possible that somebody *had* tried to eliminate de Gaulle altogether, the month before. He was to fly from London to Glasgow to decorate sailors of the Free French navy. His personal plane was a Wellington Mark IA bomber, placed at his disposal and maintained by the British government. Since the runway at Hendon airfield, north of London, was short and there was a railroad embankment at its end, a pilot would routinely rev up his engines to full power with the wheel brakes on, then would raise the tail by applying the elevator controls, release the brakes, and zoom down the airstrip. On this particular occasion, at 10:05 A.M. on April 21, 1943, the pilot of the de Gaulle plane had begun this routine when the tail suddenly dropped. The elevator control had gone dead: it was loose in his hands. The pilot halted the aircraft just in time. De Gaulle and his party were helped out of the plane, while the pilot—Flight Lieutenant Peter Loat, DFC —climbed into the tail. He found that the elevator control rod had parted. He summoned the airport security officer, a wing commander, who checked the controls and allowed Loat to select another plane. Loat chose a Hudson trainer and flew de Gaulle and his party to Glasgow. The fractured control rod was sent to the Royal Aeronautical Establishment at Farnborough. Experts there found that the metal rod had been cut through with acid.

Flight Lieutenant Loat, along with one of his British passengers, Lieutenant William Bonaparte Wyse, were solemnly instructed by their superiors that German saboteurs must have been responsible. (In fact, incidents of German aircraft sabotage are unknown, and the Abwehr —German intelligence—had a rather quaint rule forbidding political assassinations.) De Gaulle evidently did not have confidence in the "German sabotage" explanation at the time; he returned to London by train.

Loat and Wyse confirmed to this author that they were assured it was sabotage. De Gaulle's French aide, François Charles-Roux, told the author he recalled having been asked to leave the plane but says that he was not informed of sabotage. When questioned by this author in 1967 about the incident, General de Gaulle claimed he "had no memories of it." Diplomacy may have drawn a tactful veil across his memory; he certainly never flew by plane in Britain again.

While hammering wedges ever deeper into the Anglo-American alliance, de Gaulle had veered ever closer to the Soviet Union. To an astonished colleague he announced in May 1943 that he no longer had confidence in the Anglo-Saxons and that he would base his policy in the future on Russia and Germany. In the summer of 1943, Churchill issued a confidential warning to the press that de Gaulle could not be considered a trustworthy friend of Great Britain.

Roosevelt wrote to Churchill on June 17, 1943, "I am fed up with de Gaulle and the secret personal and political machinations of that Committee in the last few days indicates that there is no possibility of our working with de Gaulle. . . . I am absolutely convinced that he has been and is now injuring our war effort and that he is a very dangerous threat to us."

By this time de Gaulle had become transmogrified from soldier into politician, and admitted it quite openly in talks with diplomats. "The war is as good as over," he told the American consul at Rabat, Morocco, in August 1943. His methods of consolidating his position were reprehensible. The State Department learned that de Gaulle's London headquarters saw to it that officials in France taking a too "independent"—or anti-Gaullist—line were betrayed to the Gestapo. In consequence, for two years the Allies refused to give him advance information on military operations since it was inevitably leaked.

Eisenhower had long been asking the Combined Chiefs for a directive that would permit him to encourage resistance movements within France. He was planning to land Allied agents to foment resistance and sabotage, and to encourage passive resistance by the population once Overlord began. But a member of the French underground who had left

France in mid-April 1944 warned Eisenhower not to expect the French railwaymen to help the invasion effort. As Butcher put it in the diary he kept for Eisenhower, "They are completely cowed by the Germans."

Eisenhower believed that the invasion would need the support of the French Resistance and that, in return, Resistance leaders could be permitted to set up the initial civil administrations in the occupied— or "liberated"—areas. Thus the cooperation of de Gaulle and his French Committee of National Liberation was vital. But de Gaulle had few friends in Washington. Roosevelt became mulish whenever the name was mentioned. Secretary of State Cordell Hull also distrusted the Frenchman. In January 1944, Henry Stimson noted to himself: "The British and Churchill are having conferences with de Gaulle abroad, and they may work out a formula—which we haven't yet done." His own deputy, John McCloy, was worried and felt that the Allies were losing ground to de Gaulle's ambitions.

The matter was discussed at a U.S. Cabinet meeting in February. Roosevelt suggested they leave the details of recognition of the French Committee to Eisenhower himself. Basic to the dilemma was the reluctance to recognize de Gaulle's Committee as the government of France. "After thinking it over," noted Stimson on the last day of the month, "it seemed to me to present a situation much like what would be the case, if in the earlier frontier days, one of the western states had gotten into the hands of disorderly elements of such strength that it had been necessary to call in the United States Army to restore order." Clearly, the Allied armies occupying France would at first have to rely on a great variety of local vigilante committees to advise on the selection of proper interim sheriffs. But that would enrage de Gaulle and his cronies. If only they were not so power hungry.

In March, Stimson gave Roosevelt a proposed directive to Eisenhower on future relations with de Gaulle. In effect, it told the Supreme Commander to do what he thought best. Roosevelt eventually signed it but Churchill did not, and there the matter rested for many painful months. In London, the American magazine executive C. D. Jackson wrote: "All circles seem to be agreed that the President's behavior toward the French is pretty outrageous and can only lead to trouble, if not disaster. The French themselves here are so much more realistic and understanding and generally decent than the French in North Africa, that one cannot compensate one's own bitterness over U.S.

foreign policy by getting peeved at the Frogs—which it was possible to do in North Africa."

De Gaulle had moved his headquarters to Algiers in 1943 after the Allied invasion of North Africa. He appointed, as head of the French military mission in London, General Pierre Koenig, hero of the siege of Bir Hacheim. Eisenhower and Bedell Smith considered him congenial and professional. In mid-April, Smith called in Koenig and told him that Eisenhower intended to deal with him without waiting any longer for a directive from Washington. Eisenhower considered the collaboration and assistance of the French military authorities essential, and there were many questions of civil affairs which also had to be discussed immediately, including public health, legal questions, and financial matters—a supplementary franc currency would have to be printed in Washington, as there would not be enough currency in the occupied zones. Besides, Eisenhower counted on the influence of the French Committee of National Liberation to reconcile the French people to the necessity of his pre-Overlord bombing campaign. (There were, however, as has been seen, bitter protests from Algiers.) Eisenhower had no confidence in the FCNL. But he told officials privately that his principle was: "If you can't lick 'em, join 'em." On May 8, a month before D-day, anxious to tie up arrangements for coordinated action by French resistance groups, he pressed the Combined Chiefs of Staff for permission to tell Koenig personally and under pledge of secrecy "the name of the country in which the main attack will take place"—a reasonable suggestion, since the country happened to be France—"and the month for which it is scheduled."

De Gaulle's being in Algiers, however, posed a severe problem. Koenig would need to communicate these crucial matters to his superior, for his permission. Yet, for security reasons, the British had now forbidden the French mission in London to communicate in code with Algiers. The British felt that any information on Overlord that reached Algiers would soon reach Paris too—and since the French Resistance was heavily infiltrated by the Nazi secret service, it would also reach Berlin. Eisenhower proposed a solution: invite de Gaulle to return to London. In London he could be dealt with directly—and kept under surveillance. Churchill, though uneasy about having the difficult Frenchman in his backyard once again, came to agree. On May 13 he telephoned Bedell Smith and said that he was prepared to invite de

Gaulle to London—but that the general must promise to stay in England until after Overlord began, and could not communicate at all with his Committee back in Algiers. Smith was horrified at the thought of setting these conditions: he knew de Gaulle would indignantly refuse. The proposal would only compound the hard feelings and hurt the effort at cooperation.

Churchill, buffeted, now reversed himself. "If General de Gaulle were invited to this country now," he told a Cabinet meeting, "he would almost certainly be accompanied by some staff officers and would demand to be allowed to exchange telegrams freely with Algiers. He would almost certainly regard a refusal of this request as an insult and an aspersion on his honor." Still no invitation.

Thus when the last weeks before the invasion arrived, General de Gaulle, in the opinion of most of his nominal Allies, was still acting like a spoiled brat. In mid-May, he informed a cheering French National Committee assembly in Algiers that its name was henceforth changed to the "Provisional Government of the French Republic." This was a fresh slap in the face for democracy and the Americans—no one for a moment expected the Provisional Government to be the least bit provisional. Roosevelt's uncompromising policy toward this obstreperous general gained authority, and Eisenhower's more lenient policy was doomed. Roosevelt reminded Eisenhower of the wording of the Atlantic Charter that both Roosevelt and Churchill had signed in 1941—its insistence on the right of all peoples to "free determination." No group outside France had the right to dominate the French people as de Gaulle was proposing to do. Roosevelt sent a message to Churchill stressing this point. Frenchmen who supported neither Vichy nor de Gaulle sent word to Eisenhower, by agents, declaring that the prospect of a Gaullist regime terrified them. They feared that de Gaulle would exterminate them, ostensibly for collaborating with the Nazis, but actually to clear the path for his autocracy. The argument was not lost upon Eisenhower. In March he had lunched with Churchill, who had told him that the Gaullists in Algiers had gone mad, executing Frenchmen who had actually assisted the Allied landings in North Africa. Sickened at heart, Eisenhower had sighed to Butcher: "I get so weary of these things."

As the date of Overlord approached, however, French cooperation became ever more necessary and the French potential for compromising the security of Overlord diminished. On the last day of the any-thing-but-merry month of May, Churchill invited de Gaulle to come. He must have promptly regretted it. In London, the French general obstructed with even more virtuosity than he had in Algiers. A State Department secret summary indicted him for deliberately embarrassing the British and Americans by his persistent fractiousness, to the point where they had no option but to recognize his Provisional Government. "That such action on his part is crippling our military effort at this critical time," read the analysis, "apparently causes him little concern; on the contrary, he is callously using our military needs as levers to obtain his objective." Typical of his noncooperation was his refusal to broadcast on D-day to the French people in support of Eisenhower. "It was a means," reported an American agent on the FCNL, "of disas-sociating himself from the Allied effort." Moreover, on the eve of D-day, de Gaulle demanded that Eisenhower's staff eliminate one pas-sage from the Supreme Commander's forthcoming broadcast to the French people. This was the sentence, "When France is liberated from her oppressors, you yourselves will choose your representatives, and the government under which you wish to live."

There was no prize for divining precisely why de Gaulle objected to this concept. But the speech had already been recorded by Eisenhower in full, and when Bedell Smith telephoned him about this last-minute rumpus after lunch on June 5, Eisenhower replied, "To hell with him. Say that if he doesn't come through, we'll deal with someone else."

Then he said, "We'll announce that de Gaulle is in London and can be expected to broadcast during the day."

After a moment's pause, he added, "I've played some poker myself."

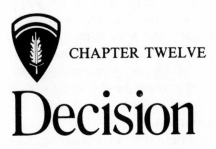

CHAPTER TWELVE

Decision

JUNE ARRIVED with storms and gales over the Channel. Through the narrow lanes of southwestern England the truck convoys wound their way to the hards where the LSTs were waiting. Close to the coast, all the roads became one-way. In a sense, that was symbolic, because the morale of the men was high and they had no thought of going back. The convoys were marshaled in reverse order, so that the last truck to be loaded now would be the first to hit the beaches. Counterintelligence agents screened everybody going on board. Seasick pills were issued— a mild sedative.

As D-day approached, the commanders had moved to advanced command posts in the vicinity of Southwick House, an old mansion near Portsmouth. Eisenhower had had his trailer brought up from Africa. It had all the conveniences, including a bathroom with shower, electric hot water, and a comfortable bed. It was like a bungalow on wheels. His command post, "Shipmate," was a nickel-plated trailer parked in a woods nearby. The rest of the staff lived in tents and worked in other trailers. Meteorologists in Quonset huts penciled on charts and surveyed the skies.

From June 1 to 5, agonizing decisions had beset Eisenhower at every commanders' meeting. The weather was turning unstable. A worrying depression was looming over Iceland, conditions were suddenly poor for air operations. Ugly clouds formed and high winds whipped the English Channel. Nevertheless, on June 2 he had ordered the slower bombarding ships to sail. The next day the weather forecast was still bad. Kay Summersby observed in her diary that he was "very depressed." Eisenhower kept postponing a final decision—to invade or not to invade. His chief meteorological officer, Group Captain Stagg, was cautious. Montgomery was eager. After the nine-thirty P.M. meeting on June 3, he wrote in his diary: "My own view is that if the sea is calm enough for the navy to take us there, then we must go; the air forces have had very good weather for all its [sic] preparatory operations and we must accept the fact that it may not be able to do so well on D-day." Eisenhower felt the burden of decision more keenly, and postponed a final decision until four-thirty A.M.

The next morning was very chilly, and the clouds were lowering. Kay Summersby noted: "No change in the weather." Thousands of craft had already put to sea; now they had to be recalled. At the special commanders' meeting, Tedder said that the weather was too bad for air support. Ramsay equivocated. Montgomery again was all for going. Eisenhower once more refused to take the risk. He drove back to his trailer and spent the morning with the Sunday newspapers and the latest Western. The harbors began filling up again with returning ships. Nobody bothered to inform Spaatz that the invasion had been postponed, although Leigh-Mallory had promised to telephone him in person should there be such a delay.

Early on the morning of June 3, General Bradley had driven down to Plymouth from his headquarters in Bristol and met General Collins, whose VII Corps was to land on "Utah" beach, near Carentan. A barge took them to the cruiser *Augusta,* the command ship of Rear Admiral Kirk. Bradley was cool, logical, measured, and sure of himself.

George Patton had gone down to Portsmouth too. He seemed more composed and was tanned and slimmer. Colonel W.H.S. Wright, sent to England by Secretary Stimson to report on D-day, had carefully observed Patton with Omar Bradley for one long evening at Bristol. "He gives the impression of a man biding his time," reported Wright, "but ready to bust loose and raise hell at the proper moment."

Patton and Bradley took afternoon tea—an agreeable English cus-
tom—with Bernard Montgomery at Portsmouth. While they were with
him, Montgomery telephoned London to dissuade Churchill from coming down on Sunday, June 4. "If Winnie comes," Montgomery explained to Patton tautly, "he'll not only be a great bore but also may
well attract undue attention here. Why in hell doesn't he go and smoke
his cigar at Dover Castle and be seen with the Lord Mayor? It would
fix the Germans' attention to Calais." Montgomery's chief of staff,
Frederick de Guingand, Patton wrote later, "is very clever but is extremely nervous and continuously twists his long, black oily hair into
little pigtails about the size of a match." Montgomery brought out a
betting book and wrote down a wager with Patton: "General Patton
bets General Montgomery a level £100 that the armed forces of Great
Britain will be involved in another war in Europe within ten years of
the cessation of the present hostilities."

Afterward, Montgomery toasted the four army commanders. Patton
raised his glass as well. "As the oldest army commander present," he
said, "I would like to propose a toast to the health of General Montgomery and express our satisfaction in serving under him." It was a lie,
but, he added in his diary, no lightning bolt descended to chastise him.
He added: "I have a better impression of Monty than I had." It would
not last long.

The final air planning meeting had been held at Leigh-Mallory's
headquarters on June 3. Odors of the months-old disputes still lingered
on, like wraiths of cordite smoke across a stilled battlefield. The day
before, Eisenhower had approved Leigh-Mallory's ruthless plan to
flatten by bombing all the routes through the French towns and villages
along which enemy reinforcements might move. Leigh-Mallory, pointing out that one road and four rail bridges across the river Seine were
still intact, called for the big bombers. Spaatz would have none of
it. His face crinkling with anger, he shouted that air supremacy still
had not been achieved. U.S. Major General Hoyt S. Vandenberg,
Leigh-Mallory's new deputy, noted afterward with tactful understatement: "General Spaatz brought up the question of the German air
force. . . ."

A fierce argument broke out. Leigh-Mallory refused to change his
very rigid program for air operations after the initial assault phase.

Tedder was now wholly on Spaatz's side: "By attacking road centers, we are wasting our effort," he said. The objectives the night before D-day would be the bridges in the city of Caen just behind the British landing beaches. Loss of French civilian life was going to be awesome. To appease the consciences of the others, Leigh-Mallory proposed they drop warning leaflets by the light of parachute flares during the night, but Spaatz objected because of security problems. The decision was to permit only radio warnings to the specific target towns one hour before the final bombing run began.

Vandenberg wrote in his diary afterward: "A slightly acrimonious air pervaded as the meeting was adjourned, however without changing the C-in-C's [Leigh-Mallory's] plans." Spaatz came to plead with Vandenberg: "You've got to press Tedder and you must freely express your views to Ike when he comes to [Bushy Park] this afternoon."

Spaatz lunched with Leigh-Mallory and Butcher Harris. Harris spluttered with rage about a newspaper statement by Spaatz that the U.S. Strategic Air Forces had dropped more tons of bombs during May than the RAF Bomber Command. He protested: "You've included the tonnage dropped by your bombers based in Italy under the Mediterranean air force!"

Spaatz replied coolly that he was entitled to, since both air forces came under him.

"If I included the RAF bomber forces based in Italy," roared Harris, "I could increase our figure too."

Spaatz was unrepentant. "If you think that the few Wellingtons based in Italy can give you a substantial tonnage increase," he scoffed, "then I suggest you get them brought under Bomber Command!"

As a final shot before Overlord, Leigh-Mallory wrote to Eisenhower predicting that the airborne operations in the Cherbourg peninsula would be a complete failure and would result in the loss of three-quarters of the troops. Eisenhower discounted the air chief marshal's gloomy prediction. They were a vital ingredient of the success of the landings on Utah beach, and Eisenhower insisted on retaining them.

Winston Churchill had been lurking around the area since Friday, in his special train, hoping for the thrill of seeing soldiers loading for the invasion. But his timing was wrong; he arrived at the wrong loading places at the wrong times—which caused him to become, in the word of his aide Commander C. R. Thompson, "peevish." Churchill went to see Eisenhower instead, his caravan of motorcycle outriders and cars flooding into the general's compound unexpectedly, his men replenishing their gas tanks and raiding the Americans' dwindling stocks of Scotch. Churchill told Eisenhower that they were bringing de Gaulle over to see him on Sunday, June 4. Thompson added in an aside to Butcher, "And you can keep him."

Sure enough, on Sunday, June 4, at three-thirty P.M., Churchill, Smuts, and de Gaulle arrived to see Eisenhower. The Frenchman had arrived that day from Algiers. Churchill had telephoned Eisenhower and said it was vital to get de Gaulle to broadcast something to the French. Kay Summersby wrote: "De Gaulle is very difficult, sees only his own point of view. He has been informed of target for D-day."

On the afternoon of June 4 the weather outlook was improving. That evening Montgomery and Eisenhower met again. Things were continuing to improve, and they all agreed to return at four the next morning. Vandenberg put a call through to Spaatz around midnight and told him he would call him again early in the morning, as soon as the decision had been taken.

The night gave way to dawn, windy and cold, with a fine drizzle. There was a conference aboard the *Ancon*, the command ship of Admiral John L. Hall. On hand were Generals Bradley, Huebner, whose 1st Division was to land on "Omaha" beach, next to Utah, and Gerow, the easygoing commander of V Corps, and Admiral Kirk, chief of the American naval task force. The conferees agreed that the troops could not be cooped up on board ship for another two weeks, and made a recommendation to go ahead on June 6. Kirk drafted a message to Eisenhower. Similar messages were sent to Eisenhower by Collins's VII Corps and by the British.

At four A.M. Eisenhower arrived at Southwick House, followed by Montgomery in baggy corduroys and sweatshirt. Dazzling in dark blue and gold, Admiral Ramsay announced, "Admiral Kirk must be told within the next half hour if Overlord is to take place on Tuesday." The meteorologist announced with his trace of Scottish accent: "I think we have found a gleam of hope for you, sir." A clear spell of about twenty-four hours was possible from late on June 5. There was a brief babble of questions from the air and naval commanders, each pursuing his own interests. Then a silence lasting for five minutes, while Eisenhower sat on the sofa before the immense bookcase. After that his face cleared, and he said without a trace of tension: "Well, we'll go!"

It was not an easy decision. Kay Summersby wrote: "D-day has now been decided on. E. has listened to all the advice of his commanders, weather experts, etc. He alone is the one to say—we will go. As E. came out of the conference he told me the date of D-day." Bedell Smith would write a few months later: "This was the most vital decision of all. . . . I never realized before the loneliness and isolation of a commander at a time when such a momentous decision has to be taken by him, with full knowledge that failure or success rests on his *individual* judgment."

It was about 4:15 A.M. when the order went out. Eisenhower thoughtfully penciled a few lines—he did it now because if things went wrong, he would have his hands too full to write a communiqué. "Our landings in the Cherbourg-Havre area have failed to gain a satisfactory foothold and the troops have been withdrawn," he began. He licked the pencil and crossed out the last words. "I have withdrawn the troops," he wrote instead. "My decision to attack at this time and place was based upon the best information available. The troops, the air and the Navy did all that bravery and devotion to duty could do. If any blame or fault attaches to the attempt it is mine alone."

Later that day Kay Summersby drove him down to South Parade Pier in Southsea. He wanted to see the troops embarking. The Americans were, unfortunately, embarking elsewhere. But there were many shouts of "Good old Ike!"

Thus the invasion fleet sailed, this time for certain. At six P.M., Eisenhower left Portsmouth to pay a surprise visit to three airfields around Newbury where grotesquely blacked-up paratroopers of General Maxwell Taylor's 101st Airborne Division were getting ready to board their planes. The stars on his car were covered, but when he was recognized, the clamor was tremendous. He liked that. He stepped over packs, guns, and equipment and chatted with the men. He recalled Leigh-Mallory's written prediction, the day before, that more than three quarters of these airborne troops would be immediate casualties. But their operations on the Cherbourg peninsula were vital for the success of the Utah beach, and Eisenhower had gone on record, too— ordering the jump to go ahead. In her diary, Kay Summersby described the scene on the loading airfields: "General Taylor was about the last person to get aboard his ship. E. walked with him to the door of the C-47. By this time it was getting quite dark. We returned to 101st headquarters with several members of the staff, had some coffee and then proceeded to climb on the roof of the building to watch the aircraft circling over the field getting into formation. It was one of the most impressive sights that anyone could wish to see, visibility was perfect, all the stars were gleaming. E. stayed for about half an hour. We then started the drive back to our C.P., getting back about 12:45 A.M."

It was nearly four A.M., Washington time. Henry Stimson rolled over in bed and fumbled in the semidarkness for the radio. As the filaments glowed, a voice rose from the loudspeaker, that of a radio journalist who had flown in with the first wave of parachute troops and watched them jump. Stimson was thrilled—it was actually happening. For him it was something of a personal triumph. He had argued for Overlord ever since Churchill's first visit to America right after Pearl Harbor in 1941; in fact, it had been at the top of his agenda for that meeting, and he had pushed it ever since. It was Stimson who, after visiting England in July 1943, had advised Roosevelt to press for American overall command.

For an hour the old man listened to the dramatic dispatches, then switched off and pulled up the blankets to his chin again. He was satisfied.

CHAPTER THIRTEEN

Invasion

AFTER THOSE years, months, weeks of brain-splitting deliberation and dispute, all of it plagued by a flux between raging ego and dogged self-sacrifice, the generals had actually managed to do it—to get two hundred thousand fallible human beings into their boats and planes on schedule, and setting out across the English Channel. Whatever might happen thereafter, this in itself was an achievement.

Eisenhower, on D-day, had thirty-nine divisions at his disposal for Overlord. His air forces could throw eight thousand bombers at the enemy. The navies prepared for him by Admiral Ramsay had 284 warships, including seven battleships, twenty-three cruisers, and more than four thousand landing craft and ships. But his most precious asset were the men: on land, sea, and air there were nearly three million of them, ready to do his bidding. An unimaginably vast military force was about to bear down upon one tiny point of seacoast. All the threads were coming together, about to be pushed through five needle eyes—beaches in Normandy called Sword and Juno and Gold and Omaha and Utah. Soon history would learn whose passionately held views of this and that—the transportation plan, the five-division front, all the rest of it—had been justified.

There, already returning from their missions, were the bombers that Spaatz and Harris had husbanded so jealously, streaming back over England's cliffs, passing the troop-laden gliders being towed in the opposite direction, toward France. There were the LSTs, the vital landing ships that Churchill had coveted for his far-flung military adventures, expeditions into the Balkans and Dodecanese: great lumbering ships big enough to bear other, smaller landing craft with tanks or other vehicles. And there were the British battleships, well offshore, dutifully pounding away as if they were the whole of His Majesty's Navy and not just a fraction of the force that could have been made available.

But where was the Supreme Commander himself? He was passing time at his command post near Portsmouth, sitting in his trailer office with Kay Summersby, reading a Western and drinking one coffee after another. Between pages, he wondered about the West Point parade at which his son, Lieutenant John D. Eisenhower, was graduating in a few hours' time. Three days before, on June 3, he had written to Mamie, "Darling . . . There's nothing I would not have given to have been with you and J. on June 6, but c'est la guerre!" He wondered if Mamie had understood the hint. Kay was writing in her diary: "The next few hours are very trying for E., he has done everything in his power to ensure success and all he can do now is to wait for reports to come in." As for Montgomery, he had spent the day puttering in his garden at his headquarters near Portsmouth. He had issued his "Personal Message from the C-in-C to be read out to all troops." In it, Montgomery hopefully suggested that the Allied combined forces constituted "one great Allied team." They should pray that "the Lord Mighty in Battle" —of whose good offices Montgomery had frequently made use before —would go forth with them.

The politician-generals, the manager-generals, and the planning generals had done their work. Now the battle's triumph or defeat devolved on the combat commanders, who would put their lives on the line along with their men. One such was an American brigadier general named Norman D. Cota. He was the assistant division commander of the 29th Infantry Division. At two P.M. the previous day, June 5, he had called his staff together in the wardroom of the U.S.S. *Charles Carroll* and warned them: "This is different from any of the other exercises that you've had so far. The little discrepancies that we tried to correct on Slapton Sands are going to be magnified and are going to give way to incidents that you might at first view as chaotic. . . . You're going to find confusion. The landing craft aren't going in on schedule, and people are going to be landed in the wrong places. Some won't be landed at all. . . . We must improvise, carry on, not lose our heads." Norman Cota was to be proven prophetic.

The rattle of chains through hawsepipes and the splash of anchors plunging into the dark waters of the English Channel were so loud that, aboard the U.S.S. *Bayfield,* Rear Admiral Don P. Moon and General Joseph Collins exchanged glances. They were a full twelve miles off the French coast, but it seemed impossible to them, edgy as they were, that the noise would not alert the German defenses on Utah beach. Collins and Moon had shifted their command posts to the ship four days before. Collins, looking at his friend, again found himself worrying about him. Don Moon was a man of great charm, but he had worked so much overtime on the loading and landing tables, on communications and other details, and delegated so few responsibilities to his staff, that he had become a nervous wreck. Collins had noticed the admiral's exaggerated fears about everything. "He is the first Admiral I've ever met," Collins said in a letter to his wife, "who wears rubbers on a mere rainy day." Don Moon had already had a tough war. He had served in the escort of the tragic and harrowing convoy to Russia, PQ 17. A few weeks after D-day the accumulated strain would overwhelm him and he would take his own life. Collins forced the concern for Moon from his mind. His troops would hit Utah beach at H-hour, six-thirty A.M., about one hour after the first light—in four hours. The tide would be low by then, enabling combat teams to go in first and demolish Rommel's exposed beach obstacles.

A rumble in the sky ahead of them swelled to thunder as squadrons of American transport planes returning from the French mainland swept past at almost masthead level. They had dropped their paratroopers over vital targets in the rear of the enemy defenses: behind Utah beach. Collins knew that in the Sicily landings, twenty planes like these had been shot down by jittery antiaircraft gunners—and a shiver of apprehension ran up his spine. But the guns were still and the planes passed safely by.

Fifty feet below ground in the Citadel, the operational intelligence center in London, to the rear of the ancient Admiralty building, Lieutenant H. McMicking was on night watch in room 40, the Admiralty's submarine tracking room. At about three A.M. the door opened. The visitor was wearing a reefer jacket and sea boots over his pajamas. The face was unmistakable—it was ABC Cunningham, the First Sea Lord. The pink-eyed apparition loped over to the chart table and asked the lieutenant how the landing was proceeding. He was obviously too concerned to sleep. McMicking replied, "There are still three hours to go before the landing craft are due to reach the beaches."

"I'll be back later," said the admiral.

It was getting lighter. Rolling only slightly in the twenty-foot Channel waves stood the American troopship U.S.S. *Charles Carroll.* Its infantry were from one of General Cota's regiments, the 116th. They were already waiting in twenty small landing craft, LCVPs, suspended from the davits high above the water. At five-twenty the ship's loudspeakers clattered: "Away all boats!" The davit winches whirred and the boats began to descend. For tense moments it seemed likely that the waves would smash the little boats against the ship's sides; then they were afloat and their screws bit the water, and they churned and boiled off into the darkness, toward the rendezvous areas and Omaha beach —a long, soaking-wet ride through heavy seas. Already more LCVPs were gathering around the troopship to take on the second wave of infantry. Officers and men clambered down the rough, wet cargo nets and leaped into the landing craft, which bucked like wild horses in the swell.

Three miles offshore the howitzers of the 116th were being loaded into amphibious trucks called DUKWs. Waves began slopping over them and starboard and aft. Eleven of these craft foundered and sank before reaching shore, losing their guns and men.

Aboard the *Bayfield,* Collins trained his field glasses on that other American beach, Utah. The long, thin lines of landing craft ferrying frightened infantrymen toward the enemy looked awfully frail. Immense convoys stretched across Collins's horizon—visible to him only by their barrage balloons. The shoreline was a stripe of purple in the haze.

Seventeen warships of the naval task force began slinging shells into the German gun batteries and strongpoints that had been located in advance by daylight reconnaissance. As the landing craft covered the last few hundred yards to the beaches, this naval bombardment was lifted and moved to targets farther inland, and army artillery mounted in the tank landing ships in the rear assault waves opened fire as well. Hundreds of missiles howled toward the beaches from rocket ships— seven hundred from each of them. Even General Collins, who had seen a lot of war, was stirred. He gripped the rails of the *Bayfield,* awed by the distant fourteen-inch naval guns belching yellow flames and by the greasy black gunsmoke rolling across the entire invasion area. He couldn't help wondering how many of the shells were hitting the enemy and how many his own men.

At eight minutes before six, as the hundreds of small landing craft bore down on the beaches, the bombing of the German coastal batteries began. From twelve miles away, Collins could not hear a sound, but he could see the bomb flashes rippling along the coastline. Far away to his right he could see the silent glitter of antiaircraft fire. Palely silhouetted against the flashes were the ghostly outlines of other troop transports, of landing craft, and of landing ships crammed with machines and men waiting to tumble onto the beaches of occupied Europe.

The British landing beaches extended from Bayeux to the Orne River. They were taken at low cost by their three divisions.

Utah beach, at the base of the Cherbourg peninsula, was also taken with negligible resistance. After the bombers, waves of rocket-firing craft went in and subdued the opposition. Losses of men and materiel were small. Since Utah beach was sheltered from the wind, the seas were smooth and nearly all the amphibious tanks landed and supported the infantry well.

At Omaha beach, west of Bayeux, the American troops were stumbling into a nightmare. Three things went frighteningly wrong, for which the generals had not planned: clouds prevented aerial bombardment; surf wrecked the landing operations; and an unexpected extra German division lay in wait.

One thing alone eventually saved the day here, and that was generalship, particularly the bravery and coolheadedness of one man. Norman Cota, an expert in amphibious assaults and infantry warfare, had decided that he probably would die that day anyhow, and that if he survived he would be a hero, but that either way he would put his mission first. He and his brigade headquarters hit Omaha beach with the lead infantry elements at about seven A.M. Omaha beach would rank with Saratoga, the Alamo, Gettysburg, and Château-Thierry as a great display of American fortitude and determination. "Dutch" Cota provided the fire and heart that finally got the troops off that ill-fated beach.

The general plan had been for naval and air bombardment to destroy the defenses and cover the approach of the assault craft. Then a wave of tanks would be landed to storm the enemy beach defenses and to cover the combat demolition parties while they cleared lanes through the beach obstacles. Then waves of infantry, artillery, and trucks would be fed through the lanes, up the beach, and up the gap through the 150-foot cliffs—called exits—and out onto the roads behind the beach.

As Cota's LCVP neared the beach, which was emerging through the mists at three miles' visibility, he saw a long band of beach obstacles and stakes that ran parallel to the shore. He was stunned. They had not been cleared—the engineers of the 146th Special Underwater Demolition Battalion had been landed two thousand yards east of the right place. Sixteen lanes should have been cleared through the obstacles, but the demolition teams had cleared only five, and of those, four were inadequately marked, so that only one was in use for any time. There was extreme difficulty getting anyone and anything ashore. An infantry landing craft beached, but before its ramps had lowered, flames engulfed it. A shell fragment had hit the flamethrower strapped to a soldier waiting to go down the ramp. The craft burned and crackled like a firework as crates of 20 mm Oerlikon ammunition were found by the inferno. One LCVP, attempting to surge past a stake with a mine wired to it, crashed three or four times against it, and the mine dislodged. The coxswain gunned his engine once more, cleared the obstacle, and dropped the ramp. Mortar fire was whistling down, and Nebelwerfer rockets exploded into spade-sized fragments that severed men in half.

A Ranger company commander, Captain John Raaen, was second out of his LCA (landing craft assault). He splashed ashore with water barely over his boots, thrilled at the cacophony of rifle and artillery fire he heard—until he realized two things: the gunfire was coming *at* him, not from his side; and nobody had yet left the beach. Bullets ripped the saltwater puddle ahead of him. He pointed to a low wooden seawall and yelled, "Ranger headquarters, there!" He ran over to his radio operator, but the man was lying on the rocks cringing with fear. Instead of shouting at the man, Raaen calmly asked him to help him out of his lifebelt, and the man forgot his fear and said: "Sure, captain." He stood up, cut it off, and went about his task.

Raaen could see General Cota standing amid the fire. He walked up and down the beach, giving his men an example. Raaen wrote afterward: "It was rough. Hundreds of machine guns emptied their belts on a beach that was about two miles long. A thousand riflemen faced us from prepared positions, and there were mortars and howitzers galore. There was a terribly steep hill behind the beach, about 150 feet high, and it was there that Jerry was emplaced. The Navy did a wonderful job," he added. "The Air Corps might have instead done better if they had landed their planes on the beach and chased the enemy out with bayonets, but no other way. But even so, it was just plain hell on that beach. An infantry battalion was to hit before us and clean out the hills behind that beach. They didn't succeed, they were cut to pieces in the water, and when we arrived on the beach they lay there on that narrow strip of sand, behind the sea wall."

The tanks were supposed to have gone in first. Around five-thirty A.M. a navy officer on Omaha saw the first wave of DD tanks approaching after launching from LCTS three thousand yards offshore. The DD tank was a British development—the tank was cupped in an inflated well of heavy canvas through which two propellor shafts protruded, enabling it to swim ashore. But the heavy seas at wind-whipped Omaha were swamping the DDs. The officers observed that they were "maneuvering with great difficulty and first one and then finally all of the DD tanks were seen to founder." All but two of these tanks vanished beneath the waves. The second battalion of DD tanks was released much closer to the shore; they almost immediately touched ground and climbed onto the beach.

The enemy defenses were still very alive. A German division about which intelligence knew nothing, the 352nd Infantry, had arrived in the area. Thus Cota's men faced two regiments on this beach, twelve times as many men.

Cota saw the orange diamond on the back of the Rangers' helmets and called to them: "You men are Rangers. I know you won't let me down." The five hundred men of that Ranger battalion went over the top and up that fortified hill.

About eighteen of the surviving DD tanks were facing inland at hundred-yard intervals, firing at enemy positions. Two tanks were blazing, hit by several rounds of well-aimed 88 fire from the concrete bunker near the Vierville-sur-Mer exit. Cota could see that the tanks were fighting for dear life. Twenty-one of the fifty-one medium tanks that had landed were knocked out on the beach. One tank commander, Lieutenant Colonel John S. Upham, dismounted from his tank and shouted at the crews to let a tankdozer through the exit, and was hit in the shoulder by machine gun fire; he would lie there, unnoticed, for the next fourteen hours. Machine gun fire was splashing and ricocheting in the water. Concealed artillery was hurling down accurate gunfire. Guns in one strongpoint were holding their fire until each landing craft touched down on the beaches; then they placed one round near it, followed by another well-aimed round three seconds later. Some craft were hit by four shells. Many were blazing.

An hour after H-hour the troops were crowded hard against the wooden seawall, lying on the banks of pebbles washed up against it, units higgledy-piggledy, pinned down by rifle and machine gun fire.

Colonel Charles H. Canham reconnoitered to the left, and was shot in the wrist. General Cota went to the right, walking upright and apparently unconcerned along the beach. He directed the placing of a Browning machine gun nest on top of the seawall. Then he supervised the blowing of the barbed wire fence. Then he sent troops to break through to the base of the bluffs, under cover of smoke from burning grass. Every moment he expected to be his last, but each time the deadly round chose another target. The first man sent to break through was hit by heavy machine gun fire, screamed "Medico, I'm hit, help me," and died with the word "Mama" on his lips. Cota himself went next and the rest followed him unharmed. They dropped thankfully into slit trenches dug by the enemy.

But now two-inch mortar shells began dropping on them. Two men were killed three feet away from Cota. He found that most of his radio equipment had been knocked out—it seemed that the soldiers staggering under the heavy backpack SCR 300 radio sets had been singled out by the enemy riflemen. These German riflemen, lonely, desperate figures who probably knew this was their last day on earth, still fought from foxholes on the bluffs. Far away, Cota could see American riflemen closing in on one foxhole—as they approached, the German rose from his hole and hurled a grenade. The soldiers hit the ground and let it explode. Then they closed in and slew him.

Working his way up the bluff, Cota saw a single GI marching five German prisoners ahead of him at gunpoint, their hands in the air. This was the enemy, visible at last, and a ripple of interest stirred in Cota's soldiers. But just as the little group approached the beach exit, the two front prisoners crumpled under German machine gun fire. The GI ran for cover. Two of the three surviving Germans dropped to their knees, and the third German was hit by the next burst full in the chest.

Ten thousand yards off Omaha beach, V Corps commander Gee Gerow could not see what was going on very well, even with high-powered glasses. There was ground haze, and fires had been started ashore by the bombardment. His command ship, the *Ancon,* was staying that far offshore, because of the German artillery thought to be located at Pointe du Hoc (later they found out there was none there). Just below decks there was a relief map of the French shore, and in front of it was a long desk at which sat the operations officer. Markers were placed on this relief map as messages came in. The messages reaching General Gerow and Admiral Hall were not satisfactory—all very discouraging. Hall and Gerow became very nervous and ordered Colonel Henry Matchett ashore to get a firsthand report of the landing. He took the admiral's gig. It was about ten A.M., three hours after the landing, when he got to the beach. Everywhere were dead bodies and destruction. He found General Cota—they had served as captains in the army together. They sheltered behind a tank and talked for a little while. Then he saw the American troops beginning to rise up over the crest of the hill, and he talked to a wounded soldier who had been carried out on a stretcher. Colonel Matchett said, "Soldier, where'd they get you?" He said, "Sir, they got me in both legs, but I'm going to get out of it and I'll be back with the outfit." That was the kind of spirit that Matchett reported to Admiral Hall and General Gerow later that afternoon.

From a thousand yards offshore a warship had begun hurling shells at the German emplacement still blocking the Vierville-sur-Mer beach exit. Cota and his men worked their way past it and found themselves on the village main street. The asphalt surface bucked and heaved as the shells landed, and several of his group were jolted off their feet. But still the Germans kept firing. Acrid cordite smoke and dust from the shattered concrete hung in the air.

This was Omaha beach:

Engineer troops were calmly eating K rations while the dead and the dying lay around them.

A sailor from a shot-up LCT stopped Cota's aide John Shea and asked: "How in hell do you work one of these?" He was holding a jammed rifle. Shea told him to take a rifle from one of those men who would not be needing a rifle any more. The crewman went away. "This is just the goddam thing I wanted to avoid by joining the navy," he said, "fighting as a goddam foot soldier."

Major Stanley Bach, the liaison between Cota's headquarters and the 1st Infantry Division, pulled an envelope out of his pocket, tore it open, and began scribbling minute-by-minute notes on its clean inside. Soon he tore up another envelope and began a second sheet. "11:30," he wrote. "Mortar, rifle, 88 and machine gun fire so heavy on beach, it's either get to ridge in back of beach or be killed. . . . Noon," he wrote. "Beach high tide, bodies floating. Many dead Americans on beach at HWM [high-water mark]. . . . 12:15: Heavy mortar and 88 fire started on beach from E end to W end—series of five shells in spots. Direct hit on Sherman tank, men out like rats—those alive. . . . 12:30: LCT hit two mines, came on in—hit third, disintegrated and rear end sank. At burst of shell two Navy men went flying through the air into water . . . never came up. . . . 14:40: More mortar fire and more men hit. LCVP unload five loads of men, they lie down on beach, mortar fire kills five of them, rest up and run fox holes we left couple of hours ago." At four-fifty: "Established CP [command post] and saw first time the 1st Division friends who were quiet, fighting men—gave me heart." At five P.M.: "Prisoners began to come up road—a sorry looking bunch in comparison to our well-fed and equipped men." As dusk fell, the major scribbled on yet another envelope this postscript: "I've seen movies, assault training demonstrations and actual battle but nothing can approach the scenes on the beach from 11:30 to 14:00 hours—men being killed like flies from unseen gun positions. Navy can't hit em, air cover can't see em—so infantry had to dig em out."

Norman Cota penetrated inland on this day, D-day, to a point the American front line as a whole would not reach until two days later.

He would get a Silver Star and the Distinguished Service Cross from the Americans, the Distinguished Service Order, the second highest British medal, from Montgomery, and a "hell of a bawling out" too—from the army commander, Bradley—for getting too far out in front. His men had proved what one of them wrote a few days later, that they would "go through hell for him."

At 5:15 P.M., General Huebner, commanding the 1st Division, left the *Ancon* and established his headquarters on the beach. The action here had diminished now to the occasional artillery round or mortar fire. Thus the grisly day ended. A dog snapped and barked at a foot patrol as it set off along the Vierville promenade. It had been the pet of a German strongpoint that had been blasted off the map.

The invasion had gone well, despite inevitable flaws. Some of the paratroopers had landed in the darkness far from their target zones. The big German gun battery at Marcouf had not been silenced. The assault waves of the 4th Division had hit beaches two thousand yards too far south. The paratroopers of the 82nd Airborne Division were widely scattered. The 101st Airborne Division also was scattered. It took three days to assemble its men and lost most of its parachuted artillery; its assistant division commander, a brigadier general, was killed when his glider crashed into a hedgerow. These hedges were to prove a serious impediment. Mud walls thrown up between the patch-work fields, matted with the roots of saplings cut back from time to time for firewood, the hedgerows were almost impassable even for the Allied tanks.

Aboard the *Bayfield,* Admiral Don Moon had become so alarmed at the loss of some ships through mines and gunfire, and in particular at a disturbing report from a lieutenant sent ashore by his intelligence officer to check beach conditions, that he had proposed calling off further landing operations. Joe Collins, the VII Corps commander, had put his foot down and persuaded his friend—who had tactical command of the Utah task force until such time as VII Corps established its foothold ashore—to change his mind.

More or less at H-hour, Air Marshal Leigh-Mallory telephoned Eisenhower's command post. Harry Butcher, clad in flannel pajamas and a woolen bathrobe, ran to the tent and took the call on the green scrambler phone. Leigh-Mallory's news was good: he had been wrong about his warning. Only twenty-one of the more than eight hundred fifty C-47s of the airborne divisions were missing. The British had lost only eight of their four hundred. And only three Luftwaffe fighter planes had been sighted so far. Leigh-Mallory sounded hearty. It looked as though the Luftwaffe had been duped by the radar tricks and lured away to the Calais end of the Channel. Butcher found Eisenhower in his trailer, hunched over his new Western, and he told him. The Supreme Commander was relieved, but tried not to show it.

At eight A.M., Eisenhower was at his command post and was getting further reports. Kay Summersby noted: "The landings on the beaches are going according to schedule, except on General Gerow's beach, very heavy artillery fire making landings impossible."

Gerow, on Omaha, was calling pretty urgently for bomber support. Eisenhower wondered what Montgomery's headquarters was doing about it. Gerow was one of Eisenhower's best army friends. He considered the general one of the finest commanders and always knew that he would make good. In him, he would assess some months later, he saw a "good fighter, balanced, calm, excellent planner—always optimistic, selfless, a leader." Well, Gee would need those qualities today. Later, the Supreme Commander visited the army group headquarters. Montgomery was in his usual sweater, pottering around the garden. Eisenhower's aides could not help noticing that while they themselves had old-fashioned British telephone sets with magnetic hand wheels, Montgomery's headquarters had smart American-style equipment.

Gerow's urgent request had still not reached Leigh-Mallory's air headquarters by the time his six P.M. air conference on target selection began. There was no information at all from the two American landing beaches. His American deputy, General Hoyt S. Vandenberg, blamed this failure on Leigh-Mallory's dismissal of virtually all the American staff "except for those used," as he put it, "as messenger boys." Vandenberg's temper rose over dinner with other American air force generals. "I propose," he said, "we go right over and that I as deputy commander of the AEAF forcibly express my disapproval at the way things are being handled." At the RAF headquarters at Uxbridge, he demanded brusquely: "I want to see the requests for Tac R [tactical reconnaissance missions] that have come in during the day." This established that until about five P.M., none had come in. Vandenberg marched into the advanced battle room and pointed out that whereas all three British beaches had clearly defined information on them as to the approximate position of the front lines, there was not one single mark on either of the American beaches.

Vandenberg was speechless about this lack of information. Shortly an American general told him that a very late report had now come in from Omaha stating that they were held up by mortar fire on the beaches and did not know where it was coming from. Vandenberg declared: "This has been known since at least noon. In my opinion insufficient reconnaissance has been sent to find out what the difficulties were and to direct fighter bomber squadrons to deal with the mortar fire." He then, to use his own words in his diary, "stormed into [Leigh-Mallory's] headquarters," found a British air vice marshal, pointed out the lack of any information on his map, and sharply criticized the handling—that Leigh-Mallory should have insisted on more reconnaissance. The RAF officer replied, "We're holding a meeting in about fifteen minutes' time to . . . attempt remedial action." By that time it was nearly ten P.M. Vandenberg retorted: "In my opinion this action is being taken ten hours too late."

That afternoon Eisenhower still had no news from Gerow and V Corps on Omaha beach. He was getting worried about the silence, and he wished he were running the army group himself. He returned to his trailer and pondered. Once he looked at his watch. At that instant, on the parade ground at West Point, three thousand miles away, Mamie must be watching young John's graduation.

Over at army group headquarters, Montgomery's anxiety for news was well controlled: "As the morning wore on," he would write nonchalantly, "it was clear that we were ashore, and that all was going well as far as we knew." Later that evening, he decided that his place was in Normandy. At nine-thirty P.M. he sailed in a destroyer to the far shore.

The First Army's headquarters staff was still on the U.S.S. *Achenar.* They had shipped their first casualties on board at eight P.M.—an officer from the 1st Division and several enlisted men. But the waves tossed the craft about, and it took an agonizing hour to bring on one man from an LCI using a breeches buoy. An hour later the ship moved to within four miles of Omaha beach. They could see the angry flashes of fire from the cliffs above the beach, even without field glasses. From the American battleships *Texas, Nevada,* and *Arkansas,* the French cruisers *Montcalm* and *Georges Leygues,* and a motley fleet of other warships, shells were being hurled at the beach—at the cliff tops, the enemy's rear, and the town of Port-en-Bessin. The town, marking the boundary between the two invading armies, was ablaze.

By evening the 1st Infantry had its command post set up on Omaha beach and Gerow could take his headquarters ashore. Around dusk, Colonel Henry Matchett and other officers also went ashore on Omaha beach to stay. By dawn, a short telephone line, less than a mile long, had been run between Matchett's headquarters and General Huebner's 1st Division headquarters. At daylight the telephone rang. A voice said, "Henry, this is Hueb." It was General Huebner. The voice added, "We're being attacked all along our front by infantry and tanks." Matchett thought, "Oh Lord, we're going to be back in the Atlantic in no time flat now." He reported it to the corps commander, General Gerow, and they ordered the cooks and other support personnel to be sent up to the front line. As it turned out, they weren't being attacked by infantry and tanks. Somebody had just heard trucks going by, and had made the false report.

Along Omaha beach, the first night, medical facilities were using the cover of the darkness to perform their grim tasks. Blankets were taken from the wounded who had died and handed to those who still could use them. Many dead and dying had been collected from the beaches and from the ground before the bluffs and taken to the promenade. Some of the wounded had scooped out shallow trenches to escape the shells falling at ten-second intervals along the beach; those who then died rested in graves they had dug for themselves. Several infantry landing craft were still burning, and anybody silhouetted against the flames was fired on by Germans still holding out along the crest.

More than nine thousand men were casualties on this first day, probably one third of them killed. The 82nd Airborne Division lost 1,259 men that day and the 101st Airborne, 1,240 men. On Utah beach, the 4th Division lost 197, while on Omaha beach the chaos was so great that the casualties to Huebner's 1st Division and one regiment of Norman Cota's 29th Division can only be guessed at, as well over two thousand. On Gold beach the 50th Northumbrians lost 413 men, and on Juno beach the 3rd Canadian lost 961; on Sword, the 3rd British Infantry Division lost 630 men, and the 6th British Airborne Division lost some eight hundred men in the first two days' fighting, with about a thousand men missing from the airborne drop.

By the morning of June 7 at Omaha, the dead of both sides had been pretty well cleared away. Temporary cemeteries had been established. Groups of corpses were being gathered in the rear; few had yet been buried. There were more urgent things to do.

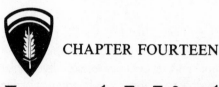

CHAPTER FOURTEEN

Lord Mighty in Battle

ON JUNE 7, 1944, one day after D-day, General Montgomery set out for France. He was to command the ground forces, both British and American, until the beachhead was big enough to receive a Canadian army on the left and Patton's army on the right. From this moment on, Montgomery was never far from the headlines; he was the center of controversy, too, raging disputes that would severely burden the harried Supreme Commander and at times threaten to cloud all other issues. For Montgomery was a vain, self-centered, troublesome general.

Bernard Law Montgomery was born in Northern Ireland in November 1887 but had spent his formative years in Tasmania; his father had become bishop there when the son was two. When he returned to England for school, it was with memories of the harsh household regime imposed by his mother: sweets were prohibited; lessons began

161

at seven-thirty A.M. in a schoolroom built outside the house. At school, Montgomery displayed team spirit only when he himself was the captain. As a mere team member he was a nuisance; and as at school, so he would remain in the Allied hierarchy. At the Royal Military College, Sandhurst, he was something of a bully. The ringleader of a gang who set fire to a cadet, he was reduced to the rank of gentleman cadet as punishment. There were many who later disputed his entitlement to that word, gentleman, but nobody disputed his claim to personal courage. He won the Distinguished Service Order as a subaltern in a bayonet charge at the first annihilating battle of Ypres in World War I, and was badly injured there.

He was an unorthodox army officer, with little respect for the War Office. At his lectures he forbade his listeners not only to smoke but to cough. He was austere, dedicated, and eccentric, especially about money. He once leased military property to a fairground owner in order to raise funds for garrison amenities. His generosity was of the most painless kind. When a cancer hospital sent him an appeal for aid, Montgomery sent back a check for twenty-five pounds—drawn on the Army Comforts Fund. On another occasion he sent a youth organization a check drawn on the Eighth Army Benevolent Fund.

In 1927 he married Betty Carver, widow of an exceedingly rich officer killed at Gallipoli. The marriage was ideal: he commanded, she obeyed. Montgomery would return home in the middle of one of her bridge parties and loudly announce in the drawing room: "Six P.M. is long enough for any such party to go on. You all ought to pack up and go home to your husbands." She would meekly comply. Her brother, "Hobo" Hobart, an army specialist in armored warfare, resented the marriage of this loud and domineering officer to his quiet and gentle sister, but the couple were inseparable, and were parted only by her untimely death after being stung by a bee. It was said that he never fully recovered from the loss.

The general who had defeated Rommel in Africa was afraid of no man, and to prove it, he firmly and frequently put Churchill in his place. Three weeks before D-day, when Churchill came to Southwick House intending to argue the loading of the landing craft, Montgomery gave him the typical treatment. The punctilious general was prepared to overlook Churchill's dishabille—he had arrived wearing his denim boiler suit—but not his interference. In his study, he tackled the Prime

Minister. "I understand, sir," he said, "that you want to discuss with my staff the proportion of soldiers to vehicles landing on the beaches. . . . I cannot allow you to do so. My staff advises me and I give the final decision. They then do what I tell them. That final decision has been given. In any case I could never allow you to harass my staff at this time and possibly shake their confidence in me. . . . You can argue with me but not my staff." An awkward silence followed. Then he led the Prime Minister into the next room to meet his staff. Churchill knew he was on a bad wicket. He huffed to the officers: "I wasn't allowed to have any discussion with you gentlemen." Later he wrote a few hopeful, suitably admiring lines in Montgomery's autograph book: "On the verge of the greatest Adventure with which these pages have dealt, I record my confidence that all will be well and that the organisation and equipment of the Army will be worthy of the valour of the soldiers and genius of their chief."

Small wonder that Eisenhower was not happy to have the prickly, overbearing Montgomery imposed on him. But British leadership of the ground forces, at the start, was inevitable. The initial assault waves were predominantly British, and Eisenhower's own appointment had been a bitter pill for British self-esteem. Eisenhower had told Sir Alan Brooke at that time that he would prefer General Alexander. Brooke suspected that Eisenhower feared he would not know how to handle the volatile Montgomery. But Brooke got his way, and Montgomery got the post —he was the general with the battle-winning experience.

For that very reason the troops trusted him, and he loved to be among them. In the prelude to Overlord, he inspected two or three parades of ten thousand men every day. Here too his unorthodox methods raised eyebrows among fellow officers. He would order the men drawn up in a hollow square. Then the ranks were faced inward, and he walked slowly between them, so that each man could see him at close range. "The men 'stood easy' throughout so that they could lean and twist and look at me all the time if they wished to," he would write, "and most did."

As Montgomery's fortunes rose and fell, so opinion about him shifted, like loose cargo below decks in a storm-lashed ship—often threatening to sink him permanently but never quite succeeding. Generally the higher up the military hierarchy, the more outspoken were his critics. Ordinary soldiers adored him; junior officers admired him.

Captain John Walsh, ADC to the commander of VII Corps, set down his impressions of Montgomery in a letter: "He is most charming and every inch a soldier, though there aren't many inches to him—he is rather short. He was wearing a very well-tailored battledress uniform —gleaming with decorations and the famous black beret." The loftier staffs disliked him, as much for the grime and odor of battle that hung about him as for the obvious self-confidence and disdain of them that he effused. Arriving at St. Paul's School to take over the headquarters of the 21st Army Group in January 1944, he had found little that he liked about it. He had decided to inject new blood, and brought his own battle-trained officers from Italy. His chief of staff, Francis de Guingand, an amusing, wine-loving general with a slightly slick image, set up a new staff, and their predecessors were elbowed aside. Some found shelter in SHAEF, where they stirred the anti-Montgomery undercurrents already generated by General Sir Frederick Morgan, who was displeased at the alterations made to his COSSAC plan by this upstart from Italy. Other disgruntled staff officers filled the armchairs of the clubs and coined sour jokes in cricketing vernacular, to the effect that "the Gentlemen are out and the Players are just going in to bat." The ousted generals sat back and waited for Montgomery to make his first mistake.

As Montgomery was heading for France, to set foot on French soil for the first time since Dunkirk, a fast minelayer, HMS *Apollo,* churned out of Portsmouth naval dockyard with General Eisenhower aboard. As misfortune had it, the ship ran aground on a submerged sandbank and Eisenhower had to transfer to Admiral Ramsay's flagship. Off the embattled beaches of Normandy that afternoon, they met Montgomery's ship and he came aboard to confer. Then Eisenhower returned to England. Later, Montgomery signaled to him, "General situation very good," but added, "Caen still held by enemy." The next morning, as Montgomery's destroyer edged in close to the beach at his insistence, it also slithered up onto a sandbar. Montgomery, cheerfully unaware of the reason for the halt, sent his young aide up to the bridge to inquire if they were not then going any closer to the shore. The destroyer captain was not happy to be asked. Montgomery, told by the aide that they were aground, said: "Splendid. Then the captain has got as close in as he possibly can. Now, what about a boat to put me on shore?"

In his first week ashore, Montgomery prepared his assault on Caen, the hinge he needed for his pivoting movement. The first attempt was to be a thrust by the 7th Armoured Division. Montgomery had originally wanted to land the 1st Airborne Division within range of the 7th Armoured's artillery, in the Villers-Bocage area. But Leigh-Mallory vetoed that suggestion. Montgomery was furious, and it showed in the letter he penned on June 12 to his chief of staff, General de Guingand, who was still in England. "The real point," he wrote, "is that L.M. sitting in his office cannot possibly know the local battle form here; and therefore he must not refuse my demands unless he first comes over to see me; he could fly here in a Mosquito in half an hour, talk for an hour, and be back in England in half an hour. Obviously he is a gutless bugger, who refuses to take a chance and plays for safety on all occasions. I have no use for him."

The 7th Armoured jumped off, after repeated delays, the next day. The attack was halted two days later, and only the artillery support given by the neighboring American V Corps enabled the British to extricate themselves from encirclement. And so Caen, which was supposed to have been captured on the first day, remained uncaptured the first week.

Unabashed, Montgomery had been issuing overoptimistic battlefront dispatches, and, encouraged by them, a plague of Allied leaders zoomed toward Normandy, eager to taste the thrills of victory. As early as June 9, Churchill had begun pestering Eisenhower for permission to make the crossing. He saw his chance when the American Joint Chiefs of Staff also hurried across the Atlantic.

When the august visitors arrived in England, the British housed them in a Henry VIII mansion about forty minutes from London. Churchill and the Joint Chiefs went to see Eisenhower at Bushy Park. The Prime Minister told the Americans that Stalin had sent word that he would shortly start his own great offensive on the eastern front. Churchill agreed with the Chiefs that they must all visit the Normandy beachhead. To this end, his special train would pick them up and he would give them dinner aboard it. The Americans, not familiar with British railroads, arrived on the platform on time, to find no train. For forty minutes the locals were entertained by the view of George Marshall and Hap Arnold—commanders between them of eleven million men—sitting on a railroad bench, while Admiral King paced back and forth, looking at his watch.

Omar Bradley met them at Omaha beach. Jeeps took them up the path over the bluff that the 29th Infantry Division had finally stormed on D-day after hours of crisis—a path along which would march in single file by early August half a million GIs. At the cliff-top landing strip, hospital planes were being loaded with casualties for evacuation. Everywhere there was evidence of the war: shattered buildings, shell holes, bomb craters, and a few indomitable Frenchmen trudging back through the dust to the ruins of their homes.

Over at the British end of the beachhead, Montgomery was aghast at Churchill's arrival with Sir Alan Brooke and the rest. They were thirsting for evidence of triumphs which he could not substantiate. "The P.M.," he wrote, "[was] very obedient and I pushed him away at 1500 hrs and would not let him go beyond my H.Q." However, Churchill had smooth-talked him into allowing His Majesty himself to come over in a few days' time, resulting in a frantic letter from Montgomery to his chief of staff: "Whatever date is settled, keep anyone else away on that day, i.e., warn Eisenhower off if he proposes to come the same day. I cannot deal with more than one VIP—and [I] told the P.M. today he must not come again just yet." To his War Office superior, Sir James Grigg, he explained, "It is not a good time for important people to go sight-seeing and visiting forward areas; I have made this clear to the P.M. My Corps and Divisional generals are fighting hard and I do not want their eyes taken off the ball."

There was small wonder that Montgomery was crabby. He was now planning to delay his next attack on Caen. Eisenhower expressed concern—he was anxious that the Germans be kept off balance and that the Allied drive should not falter. But Montgomery wanted to tidy up his "administrative tail," as he called it. He wanted to get all his supplies forward before jumping off.

He had now persuaded Leigh-Mallory to visit him after all. The meeting took place on June 14. Leigh-Mallory offered to throw the strategic bomber forces in to blast a path for the British army forward into Caen. His proposal created an uproar among the bomber commanders. At two P.M. the next day Leigh-Mallory's American deputy, General Vandenberg, was telephoned by his senior staff officer, General Frederic Smith, his voice hoarse with rage about the news. Vandenberg shared Smith's indignation. So did General Spaatz, who found this plan unedifying. "Fourteen half-baked Nazi divisions," as he called them in his diary, would thus contain the striking power of the American and British air forces in one narrow beachhead. He told Eisenhower that he was perfectly willing to provide his B-17 Fortresses for supply drops to resistance groups fighting in southern France, and when Eisenhower tactlessly touched on the need to exercise his "full imagination" and recognize the need to help the ground forces, Spaatz rasped, "Complete lack of imagination exists in the minds of the army command, particularly Leigh-Mallory and Montgomery. They visualize the best use of tremendous air potential in plowing up several square miles of terrain in front of the ground forces to obtain a few miles of advance. Our forces now are far superior to the Germans opposing us, both in men and materiel." And he added: "The only thing necessary to move forward is sufficient guts on the part of the ground commanders." At six P.M. General Smith telephoned Vandenberg with the word that, with the help of Tedder and Air Chief Marshal Sir Arthur Coningham —commander of the RAF's Second Tactical Air Force—this plan had been killed. Vandenberg noted in his diary with relief: "Spaatz, who had been worried, is now calm."

Two days later Spaatz voiced the same protest to Tedder. He told him: "The American people would greatly resent tying up of tremendous air power provided to plow up fields in front of an army reluctant to advance. . . . I thought the time had been reached when our strategic air forces should be given a general directive for the employment of the major portion of their power, primarily against Germany, with sufficient force held back to act as a 'fire brigade' for the ground forces." Tedder agreed to put this up to Ike, but he said he was reluctant to move too rapidly in this direction.

Escorted by thirteen P-47 Thunderbolts, Eisenhower and Tedder flew over on June 15 to the British sector. Eisenhower took his son along. John Eisenhower had graduated from West Point on D-day. His father had looked forward to seeing John for weeks. "I'll burst with pride!" he had predicted in one letter to Mamie. On the day John actually arrived, he had written: "I'm really as excited as a bride—but luckily I have so much to do I haven't time to get nervous!"

They drove along a dusty road near the landing strip to a gateway leading to a tented encampment just inside which a sign ordered: "Keep to the Left." This was unmistakably the British headquarters. Montgomery had not stayed to meet him, but had left to see Bradley. Eisenhower swallowed his annoyance, and went on to Sir Miles Dempsey's army headquarters nearby. As Montgomery's aide drove them to Bayeux, he told Eisenhower about a speech which de Gaulle had delivered there yesterday—he had declared that the French were now, "with the aid of the Allies," reconquering their lost territory. The Supreme Commander choked, and his son feared for his blood pressure.

Scottish infantry was moving up into the line. Eisenhower eagerly scanned their faces for indications that they recognized him. His son was lost in thoughts of his own. "I saw absolutely no evidence of German abuse of the population," he recorded the next day. The countryside was a picture of prosperity. "The people, though not hostile, were a long ways from enthusiastic." His father remarked that they did not even look up as the convoys of warriors roared past.

They were back at Montgomery's camp in time for tea. Eisenhower told Montgomery that he was annoyed at the confusion concerning the responsibility for tactical air operations. "I soon straightened this problem out," he told Kay Summersby that evening.

Back at Telegraph Cottage he organized a little party just for John, Kay, and a couple of other members of his private household. He was worried about his boy. John seemed too quiet, and he was hard for his father to see into. "He has gone with me everywhere," he confessed to Mamie, "but it is difficult to tell when he is pleased." But he was amused to see that John had taken a shine to Kay Summersby. A few days later he ingenuously informed Mamie, "Johnny seems to be having a good time. My driver, you know, is British, and has been taking him here and there." He added, "I think he is going out too for an afternoon drive." John, meanwhile, was writing down his impressions of the British sector of Normandy. It had seemed most unwarlike, he wrote, with hardly any damage and no enemy dead visible. To John Eisenhower, even London looked more like a war zone than the British beachhead.

War-zone London soon became more horrific than anyone expected.

As Eisenhower flew back that evening, something sinister began happening along the southeastern coast. The air raid sirens began to scream on the cliff tops at Dover, where Canadian divisions were waiting endlessly for their army to be fed into Normandy. The Canadians tumbled out into the open and saw red Bofors tracers fountaining into the air a few miles along the coast. Almost at once the Dover rocket batteries opened up, and as spent shell fragments rained down through the bushes the soldiers spotted a bright light moving in fast toward them across the night sky, coming from across the Channel, with searchlights triangulating it. It was a missile of some sort and it filled the air with a throaty rumble as it passed over, like an idling engine but a thousand times louder. More approached and passed overhead. As dawn came, Spitfire squadrons were scrambled to shoot the flying missiles down, but aiming machine guns at point-blank range into a warhead containing a ton of high explosive was a risky sport—the Canadians saw one Spitfire blown up that day.

The Joint Chiefs had retired to bed early on June 15 at their Tudor mansion. An air-raid alarm sounded just before midnight. Hap Arnold, commander in chief of the world's mightiest air force, heard but ignored it. At five-thirty A.M. he had a bomber commander's dream. He dreamed that he was hearing explosions—earthshaking tremors followed by the rustle of falling glass. He rolled over and opened one eye. After a quarter of an hour there was a bang that shook the whole building. In the space of minutes there were several more. Was Goering's bomber force back in business—or was this something more sinister? Arnold's mind began flicking back through the possibilities. Around six A.M. he heard, or rather felt, a loud, throbbing engine sound like an organ's diapason note approaching. The sound vanished right overhead; now what did that signify? Seconds later a terrific explosion lifted him out of bed. He picked himself up off the floor, dressed, and went down for breakfast. Marshall, King, and the others joined him soon after, grim faced. The explosions were coming at five-minute intervals, some distant, some very close; it was like being under an immense, slow-motion artillery barrage.

At 9:10 A.M. a phone call told Arnold that the bang that had thrown him out of bed was a missile that had nose-dived out of the clouds with a dead engine, then leveled off and started a slow turn before detonating about a mile and a half away. The first big attack by Hitler's secret weapon was just beginning. Three hundred had been launched at London—twenty-foot flying bombs powered by a ramjet engine out of which streaked a flame as long as the bomb itself. Two hundred had already impacted in and around London. Arnold tried to read cablegrams but his mind was not on them. At nine-thirty the all clear sounded; he sent for his car and drove over to see what remained of the flying bomb.

It had landed a hundred yards from a small village. The mighty blast of one ton of aluminized explosive had smashed every window and pushed in roofs like straw; trees had been gusted away and about two hundred villagers injured, many badly. Around the crater lay remains —pressed steel sections bolted together. Arnold guessed it had had a wingspan of about twenty-six feet. His expert eye spotted a wrecked gyro compass lying among a tangle of flexible control cables, insulated tubing, and a myriad of finger-sized dry batteries. One of the wing fragments showed traces of antiaircraft fire; but without a pilot aboard to worry, the plane had just kept on course.

Arnold was not an ignorant man. Settling back into his plane bound for North Africa that night, he guessed that these missiles probably cost about two thousand man-hours each to make, or about six hundred dollars. His thumbnail calculations indicated a nightmarish possibility: if the Nazis could launch them every one or two minutes and had forty-eight launchers serviceable, then they could hurl fourteen *thousand* of these bombs at London every day. He took out his notebook. "That will," he wrote in his notebook, "cause consternation, concern, and finally break the normal routine of life even in Britain and dislocate the war effort. No one can predict where they will hit—you can hear them coming with a swishing noise—they are hard to dodge. One went over General Eisenhower's headquarters while we were there."

Eisenhower himself was shattered by the onset of the new weapon. Already alarmed by the slowdown of the Allied advance in Normandy, he overreacted to every stimulus that indicated Hitler might be regaining the initiative. Moreover, Bushy Park lay right beneath the flight path of these pernicious missiles as they approached from their catapults in France. The first air-raid alert lasted all day. He still had John with him, and after supper the two of them settled down to watch a movie of the Overlord assault landings, but it was interrupted by that organ note, and more flying bombs came across. At first he too took it calmly. When the siren howled again at one A.M. he stayed in bed with his book. "I prefer to stay here," he told Butcher. "I don't want to shuttle back and forth to the shelter all night." A colossal blast a short distance away dispelled this insouciance. He fled to the shelter with John and the rest of his household, camping on the cold concrete floor. When he awakened the next day he was cursing Hitler for his secret weapons, and clutching his head because of the fumes from the newly painted shelter.

The public reaction to the weapon that the Nazis now named the V-1 was fury. After four years of war, the British were now distinctly rattled by the weapon. "The V-1s are unsporting," was how a Canadian summed up British feelings in his diary. Eisenhower asked Bedell Smith to investigate whether SHAEF could move to Portsmouth, out of the way of the flying bombs. But communications were the problem.

The War Cabinet was in no less a panic. Just as Eisenhower was preparing on June 19 to leave for Portsmouth—intending to cross to France—Churchill shuffled in, "very much concerned regarding Cross-bow," as Kay Summersby observed. He detained Eisenhower for a ninety-minute conference and asked him to give the secret-weapon launching sites priority over everything except the urgent requirements of battle—until "we can be certain that we have definitely got the upper hand of this particular menace." The weapon was fraying nerves. "Most of the people I know," wrote Butcher, "are semi-dazed from loss of sleep and have the jitters, which they show when doors bang or the sounds of motors from motorcycles to aircraft are heard." Ninety-five percent of all bombs had fallen within twelve miles of Streatham, an inner London suburb, which was only five miles away. Unbeknown to Eisenhower, British Intelligence now authorized methods of duping the Germans into aiming their V-1s short. By chance, Bushy Park would be in the center of the shortfall area. So the rate of fire built up. From seven P.M. on June 19 to one A.M. the next morning there were twenty-five violent, earthshaking explosions. There seemed to be no defense.

The V-1 alerts left everybody at SHAEF red-eyed and irritable. John told Everett Hughes, "Dad is tired." The weather was rainy and cold—Hughes checked his diary and found there had only been three warm days so far that year, and he knew of at least one SHAEF general who went to bed with a hot-water bottle.

The weather gave Montgomery an excuse. By now his big offensive toward Caen should have restarted, but once again he postponed the date. Eisenhower was getting impatient. On June 18 he had reassured Montgomery: "I have been putting a lot of steam behind phasing up fighting units and ammunition at the expense of all other types of personnel and stores." But he added encouragingly, "I can well understand that you have needed to accumulate reasonable amounts of artillery ammunition but I am in high hopes that once the attack starts it will have a momentum that will carry it a long ways."

The skies lowered and storms began lashing the Channel—the worst in twenty years, said Group Captain Stagg, who reminded Eisenhower that if he had postponed D-day from June 6, it would have had to be retimed right in the middle of these storms. On the same date, Montgomery issued a new directive, M-502, to the two army commanders, Omar Bradley and Sir Miles Dempsey. It called for the capture of Caen and Cherbourg by June 24. "Caen is really the key to Cherbourg," he lectured them. "Its capture will release forces which are now locked up in ensuring that our left flank holds secure."

Montgomery made a plea to Eisenhower in a handwritten covering letter. "We shall be fighting hard for the next two weeks or so, and I would be most grateful for your help in keeping visitors away. I shall have to grip the battle tightly as it is very important at this stage to make it go the way we want, and not to let it get untidy, and not to lay ourselves open to a counter blow. I shall have no time for visitors." Whether he meant Eisenhower himself or he was thinking of General de Gaulle—who had come to France a few days earlier—is open to speculation. The next day detailed examination of the problem revealed to Montgomery that Dempsey, the British commander, would have a tougher job than he had thought, because Ultra revealed German reinforcements moving into position. Further delay was inevitable.

Montgomery ate humble pie. He wrote Eisenhower an apologetic letter in his big, schoolboy pen-and-ink handwriting. "Bad weather and other things have caused delays in Divisions arriving here, and marrying up with their vehicles, etc., and becoming operative. Operations have begun in a small way on Second Army front; they become more intensive on 22 June and on 23 June I shall put VIII Corps through in a blitz attack, supported by great air power as at El Hamma."

For the Canadian II Corps, still waiting near Dover to cross into the bridgehead, the delays were frustrating and tinged with tragedy. It was no secret that there was already serious congestion in the beachhead. Early on June 20 Samuel Gamble, a staff officer of II Canadian Corps, got the telephone call that many officers now dreaded—his wife Margaret had been killed by a V-1 at seven P.M. the night before. Gamble was in a daze. He had only just come back that morning from their house at Walton-on-Thames.

The Canadian generals' plight was not enviable. Five days after they should already have crossed to Normandy, General Guy Simonds—the II Corps commander—and his eight brigadiers and colonels were still huddled under a tarpaulin on the deck on their freighter rocking in the high seas off Sheerness, complete with bedrolls and cooking stoves. On June 24 the Canadian army commander, Henry Crerar, went on ahead to confer with Montgomery, then sent for Simonds. The yellow-brown of the airstrip B2 showed vividly across the green of the country surrounding Bayeux, as Simonds landed the next midday in Normandy. The bitter news was that Montgomery had decided that only one division should cross from England at that time. "He has apparently decided," wrote Simonds's chief of staff in his diary, "to fight the eastern end of the bridgehead with one army instead of two. . . . First Canadian Army headquarters is disappointed of course, but on straight tactical considerations it is undoubtedly a logical decision. . . . It is a position several rungs down the ladder from that which General McNaughton had in mind when he conceived, gave birth to, and brought up to at least adolescence our First Canadian Army of five divisions and two armoured brigades." The truth was that the British sector was still so constricted that there was just no room for a Canadian army in it.

Montgomery talked his way out of his difficulties in his own florid style. On June 24 he wrote to Eisenhower with fulsome praise for the GI. "Having now had American soldiers under me in battle," he enthused, "I realise what wonderful chaps they are; they are singleminded in their wish to see things through, and their bravery in battle is very fine. I have now moved my Tac HQ into the American Zone so I am seeing a good deal of them. I am absolutely devoted to them." It almost seemed as though his tune had changed. He even wrote, "When are you coming over to see me?" In truth, he knew full well that Eisenhower —who was desperate to discuss the threatening stalemate—had no hope of getting over the storm-tossed Channel. But Montgomery, given the fact that he had still not made much progress, was obliged to be affable.

The temptation to use the heavy bombers to help the stalled British infantry was growing. On June 21 there was more talk about it. Vandenberg still doubted whether the heavies would perform any useful function other than to dig up the ground in front of the lines. The trend now was to use the tactical air forces. Hostility over Leigh-Mallory still boiled in American breasts. He seemed deliberately to belittle the American squadrons' efforts. When an excellent film was prepared by the 8th Fighter Command, showing the results being obtained by the American fighters against ground targets, he refused to see it. Nevertheless, Spaatz urged Vandenberg to tread softly with his criticisms of the powerful British air chief marshal. "Lunched with General Spaatz," wrote Vandenberg, "at which time he cautioned me to be very careful not to create the incident which, in his opinion, was desired by the RAF to start the disintegration of this can of worms." The debate about bombing boiled on.

Montgomery kept cool. He believed that, provided the troops used the equipment properly and their tactics were good, there should be no difficulty in defeating the Germans. He informed Grigg of this on June 24. "It has come to my notice," wrote Montgomery, "that reports are circulating about the value of British equipment, tanks, etc., compared to the Germans'. We cannot have anything of that sort at this time. We have got a good lodgement area, we have built up our strength, and tomorrow we leap on the enemy. Anything that undermines confidence and morale must be stamped on ruthlessly."

Montgomery had cause to use these words. British troop morale was suffering under German fire. A battalion of the 49th Division had fallen apart completely under fairly heavy mortar and shell fire. After two weeks only twelve of its officers remained—the commanding officer and every rank above corporal in the battalion headquarters had been wiped out, and two companies had lost every officer except one. Three quarters of the men reacted hysterically when shelling began or when comrades were killed or wounded; the hysteria was spreading, and some young soldiers succumbed to it even when their own artillery opened fire. Discipline had collapsed—the NCOs and officers had taken off their badges of rank. The battalion commander, a lieutenant colonel, reported to Montgomery: "I have twice had to stand at the end of a track and draw my revolver on retreating men. . . . Three days running a Major has been killed . . . because I have ordered him to help me in effect stop them running during mortar concentrations." And then he said: "I refused to throw away any more good lives." His opinion, he emphasized, was shared by two fellow commanders.

Montgomery wrote to the War Office that he had withdrawn the battalion as unfit for battle. He appended a handwritten note: "I consider the C.O. displays a defeatist mentality and is not a 'proper chap.' " Montgomery badly needed a great victory to restore his army's confidence in him.

On June 25 the British XXX Corps' limited advance at last began in the Caen sector. The next morning General Dempsey drove forward in his Jeep, wearing a raincoat and red hat, trying to look nonchalant. His main blitz by VIII Corps had commenced that morning, with the 11th Armoured and 15th Infantry divisions and with 675 guns supporting his attack. "Once it starts," Montgomery had confidently promised in a telegram to Eisenhower, "I will continue battling on eastern flank until one of us cracks and it will not be us." He reiterated his basic strategy: "If we can pull the enemy onto Second Army it will make it easier for First Army when it attacks southward." The next news, late on July 26, foreshadowed doom. "Attacks of Second Army went in today," read Montgomery's message. "Weather very bad with heavy rain and low cloud. . . . Fighting will go on all day and all night and I am prepared to have a showdown with enemy in my eastern flank for as long as he likes." But Montgomery, whether through tardiness or necessity, had waited so long before jumping off that now two more panzer divisions were facing him, and the Nazis had had time to dig in. After fierce fighting, Dempsey's attack was stopped along the line from Villers-Bocage to Caen. A simultaneous 3rd Division attack north of Caen on June 27 was also halted. Despite this, Montgomery wrote a reassuring letter to Brooke: "My general broad plan is maturing. . . . All the decent enemy stuff and his panzer and Panzer SS divisions are coming in on the Second Army front—according to plan. That has made it much easier for the First U.S. Army to do its task."

Montgomery was entitled to his self-satisfaction, for in truth his plan was working. All that his critics saw, however, was Caen—that city was still firmly in enemy hands; therefore he had "failed." But he had not failed. One of the main aims of Fortitude—the grand deception plan— was to dupe the Germans after D-day into believing that he intended to make his main thrust through Caen, in the British sector, directly toward Paris. They thus would be obliged to devote forces to await this thrust. The real breakout would then follow in the other, American sector. Much of the highest-level SHAEF planning had gone into abetting this deception. Montgomery had often stated this aim, and had tried to explain it at Eisenhower's commanders' conferences ever since March. On March 10, for instance, he had snappily described his real intention as being "to maintain a very firm left wing to bar the progress of enemy formations advancing from the eastward." So there was no excuse for the top American generals not to have grasped it by then, and still less for the British officers attached to SHAEF—like Tedder and Morgan.

Still, very soon after D-day an outcry began. It was as if Fortitude had succeeded in duping the Allies along with the Germans. It was charged that because Montgomery had failed to capture Caen in one bound, as he had hoped, therefore his *whole* strategy was in collapse. It was not. But even long after the war, the same voices continued with their criticism. Walter Bedell Smith, never one of Montgomery's supporters, would write, "It was clear that our advance was not going to take place as originally planned on the east flank, and that a breakthrough would have to be accomplished on our right in order to loosen up the whole front, and establish mobile warfare." He would claim that on June 24, Eisenhower, visiting Omar Bradley in the Cherbourg peninsula, had "already made up his mind . . . to break out into the open on our right." This decision had been made by Montgomery months before D-day.

Montgomery was partially to blame for the controversy. When the battle was joined, he smoothly glossed over his setbacks, insisting that "everything had gone according to plan." And he overemphasized the main aspects of the plan in order to mask his failure in its lesser ambitions. He would claim, for instance, in a lecture to the Royal United Services Institution in October 1945, that the Normandy operations had developed precisely as in the general plan he had given out to the generals in London in March. "Once ashore and firmly established," he said, "my plan was to threaten to break out on the eastern flank—that is in the Caen sector; by this threat to draw the main enemy reserves into that sector, to fight them there and keep them there, using the British and Canadian armies for the purpose. Having got the main enemy reserves committed on the *eastern* flank, my plan was to make the breakout on the *western* flank, using for this task the American armies under General Bradley, and pivoting on Caen; this attack was to be delivered southwards down to the Loire and then to proceed eastwards in a wide sweep up to the Seine about Paris."

The archives substantiate this. However, from the army's outline plan for Overlord, the Ground Force Plans, the SHAEF battle map of June 4, and the 21st Army Group's own map showing the phase lines to be reached, it is clear that Montgomery had in fact assigned to the British and Canadian armies a somewhat more aggressive mission. They were to advance inland *across* the Caen–Saint-Lô road and, by D-day plus fourteen, June 20, secure a bridgehead *beyond* Caen roomy enough to develop airfield sites as quickly as possible. In this effort, in effect to take the whole city of Caen, he would indeed fail for two months.

Although Omar Bradley's First Army still came technically under Montgomery's overall control, nobody credited the British general with the success that the American troops now achieved in Cherbourg. By June 24 all three American divisions of Joe Collins's VII Corps had pierced the outer defenses and begun converging on Cherbourg. When Bradley visited Collins the next day, he showed him Montgomery's imperious directive M-502.

"Joe, you'll love this," he cackled. "Monty has just announced that Caen is the key to Cherbourg!"

Collins grinned and said, "Brad, let's wire him to send us the key!"

Eisenhower wrote to Bradley that day, "I most earnestly hope that you get Cherbourg tomorrow. As quickly as you have done so we must rush the preparations for the attack to the southward with all possible speed. The enemy is building up and we must not allow him to seal us up in the northern half of the Peninsula. The Second Army attack started this morning and enemy reinforcements should be attracted in that general direction. This gives us an opportunity that may not obtain very long." Bradley replied later in the day that he hoped to have Cherbourg cleaned out by the end of the month, although it would give the troops practically no rest. As Hughes flew out of the area in a C-47 on June 27, a white flag was already flying over Cherbourg's arsenal. He too had urged Bradley to step up his next offensive southward from the peninsula, but the army commander was not optimistic.

Back in England, Hughes drove out to SHAEF to see Eisenhower and gave him a letter from Bradley postponing his jump-off until July 1. Shortly afterwards, another letter came, postponing the offensive yet another two days. "I am very anxious," Bradley had written, "that when we hit the enemy this time we will hit him with such power that we can keep going and cause him a major disaster. I want to keep going without any appreciable halt until we turn the corner at the base of the peninsula."

Eisenhower sighed. "Sometimes," he told Hughes, "I wish I had George Patton over there."

Dwight D. Eisenhower and Bernard L. Montgomery.

The Eisenhower–Montgomery relationship ranged from friendship to fury. Eisenhower maddened Montgomery with his indecision and strategic shallowness. Montgomery tormented Eisenhower with aloofness and relentless power-seeking. At right, the D–day entry in Montgomery's autograph book.

The armed forces of the Allies landed in France on 6 June 1944. The H.Q. of the Supreme Comd and his C's-in-C were at Portsmouth.

Supreme Comd. *Dwight D Eisenhower*

Naval C-in-C *B H Ramsay*

Army C-in-C *B. L. Montgomery* General

Air C-in-C *T Leigh-Mallory*

Tactical Air Forces *a Cunningham*

The initial operations were very successful and a good lodgement area was soon got.

Above, the Supreme Commander and his invasion chiefs at a press conference just after his arrival in England. Front row (from left): Arthur Tedder, Eisenhower, and Montgomery. Back row: Omar Bradley, Bertram Ramsay, Trafford Leigh-Mallory, and Walter Bedell Smith. Sir Arthur Tedder, at right, Eisenhower's principal deputy at SHAEF, supported him passionately against Montgomery's every thrust.

Winston Churchill used tears and tantrums to get his way with Eisenhower, to no avail.

So great was the dignity and moral authority of George C. Marshall, chief of staff of the U.S. Army (shown here under a portrait of his predecessor, John Pershing), that the job of Supreme Commander was considered too small for him. Even President Roosevelt did not dare call him by his first name. Other American titans were (on facing page, clockwise from upper left): Army Air Force generals Hoyt Vandenberg and Carl Spaatz, Ernest King of the Navy, and the Army's "Hap" Arnold. They commanded eleven million men.

His Majesty's commanders: On this page, Henry Crerar of Canada (top); Andrew "ABC" Cunningham (lower left); and Miles Dempsey. On facing page, Alan Brooke (top); Henry "Jumbo" Wilson (lower left); and Trafford Leigh–Mallory.

November, 1944: Eisenhower visits his field commanders (from left): Leonard "Gee" Gerow, Eisenhower, Norman Cota, and Omar Bradley. On facing page, Bradley pins the Distinguished Service Cross on Cota for bravery at Omaha Beach. At upper right, Courtney Hodges. At bottom, Brehon Somervell (left) and Jacob Devers.

Front–line generals Troy Middleton (left) and Joe Collins.

Arthur "Butcher" Harris (above, left) and "Toohey" Spaatz were, respectively, the leading British and American advocates of heavy bombing. Between them they laid waste to Europe, attempting to destroy both the enemy's morale and his ability to fight. Much against their wishes, their bombers were sometimes used to blast a path for ground troops. During one such raid, miscalculations by James Doolittle (right) and other air commanders led to the bombing of American troops and many lost lives.

Everett Hughes (facing page, at top) was Eisenhower's "eyes and ears" and kept a secret, extremely candid diary. Its villain was Hughes's personal bête-noire, deputy theater commander J.C.H. Lee (shown, at bottom, at a British celebration honoring the American Merchant Marine). Its hero was Hughes's close friend George S. Patton, Jr. (shown, above, being congratulated by Eisenhower for raising the siege at Bastogne).

Patton did little to hide his fervent dislike of the British. The object of his scorn in this case was Louis Mountbatten.

CHAPTER FIFTEEN

Anything May Happen

THE FIGHTING on the Cherbourg peninsula ended, but at fearsome cost. The ground was bomb-cratered and shell-blasted; little green remained. Scattered among the crazily tilted Nazi bunkers was the debris of battle—shell casings, shredded clothing, cartridge belts. On the last day of June, Omar Bradley toured Pointe du Hoc with his taciturn deputy, General Courtney Hodges. Hodges wrote, "There was still present the sweet, cloying smell of the dead." He saw a helmet lying on the path 150 yards behind the main forts and picked it up—it had belonged to a soldier of the 2nd Battalion. A bullet had drilled neatly through the front and splayed the steel on emerging at the back. The inside was still damp. Four thousand young Americans had already been killed since D-day.

179

For two weeks, the rains streaked down in long, endless slivers, needling the gray mud of Normandy, loosening the surface, turning the fields into morasses, enlarging the inundations that Rommel had prepared during his months of wait for the invaders. Rain or no rain, mud or no mud, somehow the British and American armies had to move southeast, to reach the flat terrain around Falaise and Argentan. Only from there could they unroll their massive superiority in armor toward Paris.

As the fighting in the Normandy beachhead slowed toward a deadlock, the mood in England blackened. One man's mood was blacker than the rest—George Patton's. He felt left behind. As the thunder of war sounded distantly from across the Channel, he was disconsolate. Eisenhower was on English soil too, but at least he could hop on a destroyer and visit the battlefields when he wanted. Patton could not. He had put on his shoulder holster on D-day, to get into the invasion mood, but they'd all gone off to war, leaving him to sit around his headquarters at Peover, Cheshire, feeling like a slacker.

On June 18, two weeks after D-day, he came down to London for Sunday dinner with Everett Hughes and J.P., and he cooked them all an omelet, which J.P. served to them. It had too many peas in it. It was a doleful dinner in any case. That morning a V-1 flying bomb had cut out over the Guards' Chapel on the edge of Saint James's Park and killed two hundred officers and men worshiping inside. Among them was a colonel on Patton's staff.

The V-1s bothered Patton less than they did Hughes or Eisenhower. He wrote to his wife, Beatrice, "I think they have only nuisance value." There were limits, however. The next day Hughes lunched again with Patton. Before he could raise the fork to his lips, a buzz bomb impacted not far away. There was a cascade of broken glass as its one-ton warhead detonated, and a great pall of smoke rose outside the window. Hughes, trembling, noticed that Patton had not flickered an eyelid. He had trained himself, of course. "I'm going back to the country," the Third Army commander said all the same. "I'm afraid of being killed —that is, except on the battlefield."

That same day, Patton saw the British military expert Liddell Hart, and baldly commented that while the British had so far failed to gain any of their objectives around Caen, the Americans were overrunning the Cherbourg peninsula. Liddell Hart pointed out that the British had surely absorbed the Nazi strength at the critical moment, enabling the Americans to do their overrunning. Patton then asserted that more Germans were facing the Americans. Liddell Hart, who knew the facts —four panzer divisions were being engaged by the British against one by the Americans—again courteously disagreed. In his diary that night he wrote: "It struck me as curious that he should express such slighting comparisons between the American and British effort to anyone with whom he had quite a short acquaintance."

A few days later Eisenhower invited Patton, still morose, to join him for an inspection tour in Cornwall. Patton thought Eisenhower quite clever in his approach to the men, but his speeches were too familiar for Patton's taste; he used the first person too often. "It is the style of an office-seeker," Patton noted suspiciously in his diary, "rather than of a soldier." He wanted to get over to France. He had been in purgatory too long. The months of waiting had seemed endless. Was he to get no chance to redeem himself after the disgrace and humiliation heaped on him since Sicily? Now the press was not even allowed to mention his name. He, George Patton, would change all that.

Late in June he was directed to begin moving his army toward its Channel embarkation port. At last! Driving at twenty miles per hour, spaced at sixty-yard intervals, making regulation halts for ten minutes every two hours, his truck convoys wound their way down to wait at the embarkation areas. It would not be long now before the orders arrived that he had been waiting for so long—to take his Third Army headquarters to France. The date had been revealed to him—July 6, D plus thirty.

The menace of the V-1s towered over every other topic now. On June 29, one of Eisenhower's staff wrote in his diary, "Ordered not to write home about the buzz bombs, which are coming over in increasing numbers." Life in London was punctuated into time quanta, day and night, by the sirens as each vicious V-1 droned in. "Too many bombs," Hughes wrote, sick with fatigue, "122 yesterday." There was probably worse to come, he knew. An eighteen-year-old German prisoner told interrogators hair-raising stories about the "V-2"—he said that it was a rocket capable of blasting an area of ten square miles, and that it was "Germany's last hope of preventing defeat."

Once again the maddened London crowds had taken to the subway tunnels—not to travel, but to sleep. In February 1944, crowds like these had panicked on the staircase at an East End subway station when antiaircraft guns had suddenly opened fire outside; two hundred people had been trampled to death. Now it was the V-1s, and the subways were back in the rooming house business. In some places three tiers of bunks had been stacked against the walls.

It simply wasn't Hughes's sort of city any more. He dropped in at the Ritz, the Dorchester, and Claridge's, but all the bars were closed by nine-thirty. The streets were empty by nine.

General Eisenhower was pretty depressed too. He had a long talk on June 30 with his deputy, Tedder, who had just spent a day in the beachhead. Days of gales had whipped up high seas. The artificial harbor, Mulberry A, had been wrecked and abandoned. In consequence, the buildup of troops and supplies was falling far behind schedule. Furthermore, though it was now D plus twenty-four, none of Montgomery's objectives had been reached. Eisenhower and Tedder were both disappointed by the slow progress. Montgomery should by now have captured some twenty-seven airfields from which sixty-two squadrons of Allied planes could have begun operating. The reality was sadly different. After Tedder left, Eisenhower told Kay Summersby, "Monty is expecting a heavy counterattack, but is confident that he can defeat it. Meanwhile—he is just waiting." She wrote in her diary, "Bradley's attack to South postponed." Omar Bradley's breakout at the root of the Cherbourg peninsula should have started on June 22, but the country was unyielding, the troops were tired and wet, and ammunition shortages and storms were bogging down the operations even more.

A painful period for the generals was beginning. Allied newspapers had started pinning the unforgiving word *stalemate* to the battle. Despite the smashing of Europe's railroad system and road bridges, German reinforcements were arriving from the Russian front. The nightmare of trench warfare like the World War I charnel house began to loom.

There was a personal reason for Eisenhower's gloom, as he set out on July 1 for the battlefields himself. He had just sent his own B-17 Fortress back to the United States with young John, and on an impulse he had filled its empty spaces by sending his staff, including Kay Summersby, on furlough. On another impulse, he arranged for her to call on Mamie, explaining disarmingly in a letter, "Mrs. Summersby is going to try to find Mrs. Arnold (mother of her late fiancé). . . . All are counting on having a good time for the week the plane will be in the United States."

From the air, all of Normandy seemed awash to Eisenhower, and as his plane sloshed to a standstill, he saw his impression had not been wrong. It had been raining ever since the violent storms subsided. Omar Bradley was at the airstrip to meet him, and they drove to Bradley's headquarters near Grandcamp-les-Bains, where Eisenhower was to spend the night. Bradley had set up his First Army command a mile from the coast in an apple orchard that had been badly mauled by naval shelling. The Rangers had passed that way too, and thirty-two bodies had been removed from the orchard when his advance party moved in. In the lane bordering the command post were four abandoned German 155s and stacks of their ammunition.

Hodges, his deputy, and Charles Corlett, the XIX Corps commander, were waiting there, and so was the dashing Elwood "Pete" Quesada, who at thirty-five was already a brigadier general and commander of the Ninth Fighter Command. Before dinner, Bradley pulled out the maps and explained his forthcoming infantry attack. It had taken Bradley several days following the fall of Cherbourg to regroup. The landings on the beaches had been planned and practiced in every detail but, oddly, nobody had had any idea that the terrain beyond the beaches would be as tough as this. The Cotentin peninsula was lush with woods and marshy meadows, a patchwork of tiny fields boxed in by impenetrable hedgerows as tall as three men standing on each other's shoulders. To reach a good jump-off ground for the main American tank assault, the infantry was obliged to chew slowly southward through the swamps and *bocage* country—a defender's paradise.

Eisenhower stayed with Bradley during the first five days of these infantry attacks, which began on the day he arrived. It was dogged, close-shouldered fighting, and called for high leadership qualities in the small-unit commanders. He pulled on his soft garrison cap when he set out to visit the troops. He was that kind of person. He would not wear a helmet—he did not want his GIs to think that he imagined he was in a battle, when he knew that he was not.

With Bradley, he called on Montgomery. The rumor was that Montgomery had been so slow in launching his attack that the enemy had had time to dig in. Montgomery was claiming to have destroyed three hundred German tanks—but the scuttlebutt was that the enemy tanks were proving almost impregnable, and that newspaper stories being filed from the front about British and American tank inferiority were being censored by Montgomery. Eisenhower was eager to learn the truth. He found Montgomery and his young officers returning from church. The British commander's two puppies—Rommel and Hitler—were scampering disrespectfully in the grass around two captured vehicles, new Nazi Panther and Tiger tanks. Montgomery confirmed the bad news. Neither the Allied antitank guns nor the Sherman tank's gun could pierce the Panther or the Tiger. Eisenhower sent a long telegram to Bedell Smith, ordering an investigation.

Eisenhower watched Bradley's infantry lumber off at first light, but the guts were not in the attack. The skies seemed only inches above the muddy ground. The rain poured down endlessly. From atop a former enemy flak tower, he scanned the assault terrain that extended south toward Saint-Lô—swamps, minefields, machine gun positions, and more swamps. None of SHAEF's planning had prepared the ground troops for this. The enemy could not have picked better country. The single and double hedgerows concealed deadly machine gun and mortar positions, and the Germans had built a whole series of defensive lines while Bradley's troops had been thrusting north to Cherbourg.

Back at Bradley's headquarters Pete Quesada, the youthful fighter commander, climbed into a Jeep and told Eisenhower, "I'm flying down toward Paris [to] see if we can't dig up a fight!"

Eisenhower's eyes sparkled. "I'll go down with you!" he said.

"Sure," Quesada said, "we have a Mustang with the tank taken out."

Bradley did not look too pleased about this escapade, so Eisenhower called out to him: "All right, Brad, I'm not going to fly to Berlin." And off he went in Quesada's plane, in company with the whole 365th Fighter Squadron. In fact, Quesada flew little more than halfway to Paris before deciding to turn back.

When Eisenhower returned, he learned that the infantry attack was failing. The Germans knew it too—they arrogantly sent back captured American medical personnel with a note saying that the Americans would probably be needing them more than they did. Eisenhower left the beachhead and flew back to England. He was not happy about the progress that either the British or the Americans were making. "I've ploughed through rain and mud and seen lots and lots of troops," Eisenhower wrote to Mamie. Later in the same letter, he assured her, "Sometimes I miss you so much I could do anything except act sanely. There is no-one else but you, so far as I'm concerned."

George Patton—still in England—was growing more and more impatient. The Americans were bogging down, just as the British had around Caen. Patton observed resignedly that if Bradley played safe, if he kept on attacking down successive phase lines to the south, "we will die of old age before we finish." On July 4, tiring of waiting for the call to France, he breezed into London to meet a beautiful young woman who had arrived from Boston.

Her name was Jean Gordon, and she was Patton's niece, the child of Beatrice Patton's invalid half-sister. She had lost her father when very young and had subsequently vacationed from school with the Pattons. Over the years she had become exceedingly close to Patton, and he adored her. She was charming, clever, and sensitive. Now she had enlisted as a Red Cross "doughnut girl" and managed to get to Europe to be with her Uncle Georgie. She was about as old as his own daughter.

Patton found her stunning in her uniform. He later murmured to Everett Hughes that he didn't want her presence known in London. Hughes, already a repository of many buddies' secrets, kept mum. Jean Gordon was the first of several young women who joined their American generals on the battlefields. In England and later in Europe, she would become Patton's constant table companion when he entertained important visitors. The two of them would converse animatedly with each other in fluent French, to the confusion of those around them. Hughes could not help wondering what the relationship was.

Patton was among those called to see Eisenhower when he returned from France on July 5. To Patton he seemed cheerful but "a little fed up with Monty's lack of drive." Eisenhower was toying with the idea of taking personal command of the ground battle, but he was still vacillating. "He cannot bring himself to take the plunge," observed Patton in his diary. Hearing now from the Supreme Commander that eventually four American armies would operate in France—three under Bradley (including Patton's own) and one small American army under Montgomery—Patton privately expressed puzzlement: "Why an American Army has to go with Montgomery, I do not see, except to save the face of the little monkey."

His own usefulness in England—as a decoy—was over. His imminent departure to the battlefields would leave a residual problem for the deception planners. While hitherto Fortitude had duped the Nazis into expecting Patton to be at the head of a major new invasion in the Calais area, the time was coming when Patton's presence in Normandy would become known to the enemy. A plausible new commander would have to be found for the fictitious army group that Patton had been "commanding" in England, as part of the cover plan. Eisenhower asked Marshall to designate General Lesley J. McNair himself, commander of the army ground forces.

On July 6, the man of destiny finally arrived in France. His plane swung to a halt on the airstrip on Omaha beach. He stepped out, climbed into a Jeep, and stood up in it while troops swarmed all around him. There was a single pistol in a holster but no other obvious concessions to his Buck Rogers image. "I'm proud to be here to fight beside you," Patton announced. "Now let's cut the guts out of those Krauts and get the hell on to Berlin."

He was General Hodges' guest for drinks, and spent the night with General Bradley. His tent shook from the firing of American artillery all around, and he could not sleep. He had forgotten how noisy war was. His bulldog Willie did not like it at all, and trotted out of the tent several times to have a look. "As a matter of fact, so did I," confessed Patton in a letter to his wife.

The next day he and Bradley went over to lunch with their commander, Montgomery. Afterward they went into the British general's war tent and, as Patton wrote, "Montgomery went to great length explaining why the British had done nothing." Bradley was uncomfortable in Montgomery's presence, Patton observed; but soon Bradley would get out from under Montgomery. He would take command of one of the two army groups that would fight henceforth. Montgomery would have the other one.

It amused Patton to see how Montgomery tried to get Bradley to agree not to let Patton start operating until Avranches, on the coast, had been captured. Bradley declined to rise to the bait. He wanted Patton moving just as soon as possible.

On his way back to Bradley's headquarters, Patton marveled at the prosperity of the Normandy countryside. As they drove, he privately savored the fact that neither the French, nor the Germans, nor the rest of the world yet knew that he was in France and about to begin one of the most dashing campaigns of his career.

That same day Bradley had to admit to Eisenhower in a letter: "I am still disappointed at the slow rate of our progress but everyone concerned informs me that we are running against very carefully prepared positions and are walking into some pretty good troops. However, I feel that as soon as we can break this crust and get out of these bottle-necks, our progress should be much more rapid. In any case," he consoled the Supreme Commander, "we are busy killing Germans."

Montgomery had also written to Eisenhower on the subject of progress. When Eisenhower had returned to London on July 5, he had found the long letter. In it, Montgomery boasted of his success in attracting panzer divisions to the British sector, enabling the Americans to take Cherbourg and now to regroup undisturbed. "All this is good," Montgomery observed. "It is on the western flank that territorial gains are essential at this stage, as we require space on that side for the development of our administration"—an astonishingly blinkered view of the prospects of an American breakout, which caused even Eisenhower, who was no strategic genius, to underline the words "development of our administration" on his copy.

Eisenhower's staff was astounded at the subtle shift of emphasis displayed in Montgomery's letter—from his earlier ambition to capture Caen, to this new, more modest desire just to hold the British sector firmly. "In Monty's previous directive he seemed to be all out to capture Caen," observed Butcher in his diary, "which he still doesn't have." Eisenhower was furious to see Montgomery once against calling for air support before he would advance. The next day he called Tedder and Air Marshal Sir Arthur Coningham to a conference. Coningham (who, for some odd reason, had been nicknamed "Mary," just as Admiral Harold Stark had been dubbed "Betty"; they even signed themselves in this fashion when writing to their fellow commanders) was annoyed. "The army," he said, "does not seem prepared to fight its own battles." Tedder echoed these sarcastic words.

Encouraged by them, Eisenhower vented his smoldering anger in a letter to the British commander on July 7—a letter that in effect directed Montgomery to pull his finger out, if the Allied forces were not to find themselves corralled into the beachhead. "Dear Monty," Eisen-hower wrote. "When we began this operation we demanded from the air that they obtain air superiority and that they delay the arrival of enemy reinforcements in the Neptune area. Both of these things have been done. In the meantime, in spite of storms and hard luck, our ground build-up has proceeded rapidly and on the British side we are approaching the limit of our available resources. Very soon, also, we will be approaching the limit in the capacity of the ports now in our possession to receive and maintain American troops. Thereafter it is possible for the enemy to increase his relative strength; actually he seems to be doing this already. These things," continued Eisenhower, "make it necessary to examine every single possibility with a view to expanding our beachhead and getting more room for maneuvering so as to use our forces before the enemy can obtain substantial equality in such things as infantry, tanks and artillery. On the left we need depth and elbow room and at least enough territory to protect the Sword beach from enemy fire. We should, by all means, secure suitable air fields. On the right we need to obtain additional small ports that are available on the north side of the Brittany coast and to break out into the open where our present superiority can be used.

"It appears to me," added Eisenhower, "that we must use all possible energy in a determined effort to prevent a stalemate." He admonished Montgomery for having limited the weight of the British attacks to only two or three divisions so far, when a fully coordinated attack by the entire Second Army might well put the left flank in motion: "We have not yet attempted a major full-dress attack on the left flank supported by everything we could bring to bear." It was his sternest criticism of his ground forces commander yet.

Rather tactlessly under the circumstances, but meaning to be enter-taining, the Secretary for War, Sir James Grigg, sent to his friend Montgomery a copy of a letter written by a Briton who had fought at Agincourt. It was a dispatch from Sir John of Assheton, who was the Seneschal of Bayeux, Governor of Haye du Puits and Bailiff of Coutances in 1419, to Henry V, "oure Souverain Lord the King, moste hegh and Myghty Prince, moste dowtewyse and soverayne Lorde." Once Montgomery's aides had decoded the Old English, they found that the document indicated that the British siege of Caen in 1417 had taken only a month, an embarrassing comparison. Montgomery had already been stalled at Caen for longer than that.

On July 8, Montgomery replied to Eisenhower's complaint—at equal length. That day his renewed assault on Caen had begun, so he began confidently: "I am, myself, quite happy about the situation. I have been working throughout on a very definite plan, and I now begin to see daylight." He recalled that when Bradley's recent advance ran into its atrocious terrain and weather problems, Montgomery as ground forces commander had decided "to set his eastern flank alight, and to put the wind up the enemy by seizing Caen." Montgomery added that Sir Miles Dempsey, commander of the British Second Army, had just launched an attack aimed at securing Caen. It was going very well, Montgomery said, and the armor of VIII Corps would join the fray in two days' time. Montgomery reassured Eisenhower, in the lecturing tone of an experienced combat commander wearily justifying himself to a younger man who, frankly, doubts his word: "Of one thing you can be quite sure —there will be no stalemate."

Air Chief Marshal Tedder did not share his faith. Asked what he thought of Dempsey's operations, he scornfully dismissed them with two words: "Company exercises." And when Sir Charles Portal returned from a visit to Montgomery, he agreed with Tedder. "The problem is Montgomery," he said. "He can't be either removed or moved to action."

The next night a coded message arrived from Montgomery. By four-thirty A.M. it had been decoded. "Operations on eastern flank have proceeded entirely according to plan," it read, "and will continue without a halt. VIII British Corps joins in tomorrow. Have ordered Second Army to operate southwards with left flank on Orne. . . . All this will help to expedite affairs on western flank. Have had good conference with Bradley today and he will crack ahead hard tomorrow."

Eisenhower felt he had to reply. He commented pointedly on the fact that, despite Montgomery's promise to contain the panzer forces at the Caen end, "It is unfortunate that before Bradley's attack to the southward could get into full swing, some of the Panzer elements had time to shift to his front." This accusation baffled Montgomery, because Ultra showed clearly that between July 1 and 4 all the panzer divisions except for one weak division had been successfully attracted to the British sector and were still there.

From his waiting position in the wings of these great battles, George Patton watched the fighting but failed as yet to grasp the strategy of Montgomery's tactics—seesaw from right to left, dislodging the enemy defenses. In fact, it pained Patton to see how the American commanders lowered themselves—as he regarded it—before the British. "Neither Ike nor Brad has the stuff," he commented in his diary on July 12. "Ike is bound hand and foot by the British and does not know it. Poor fool. We actually have no Supreme Commander—no one who can take hold and say that this shall be done and that shall not be done. It is [a] very unfortunate situation to which I see no solution."

He was as irritated as Eisenhower by the delays, but for his own reasons. His army was still assembling but had no mission. The American sector was still too narrow to accommodate them. "Brad says he will put me in as soon as he can," he noted impatiently on July 14. "He could do it now with much benefit to himself, if he had any backbone. Of course, Monty does not want me as [he] fears I will steal the show, which I will."

And then Patton wrote, "Sometimes I get desperate over the future. Bradley and Hodges [Bradley's understudy in the First Army] are such nothings. Their one virtue is that they get along by doing nothing. I could break through in three days if I commanded. They try to push all along the front and have no power anywhere."

The British commanders in the field, it is plain, understood Montgomery's strategy. On the day before his operation began at Caen, July 7, General Dempsey briefed the five corps commanders and told them explicitly that his Second Army's task was "to draw onto itself and contain [a] maximum number of German divisions, to hold [the] present front and when opportunity offers to get Caen." This, he continued, would enable Bradley to restart his major offensive southward from the Cherbourg peninsula.

That evening, 460 four-engined bombers thundered over the troops on their way overhead to "liberating" Caen, as one Canadian officer put it. They poured 2,300 tons of bombs into the city and its obstinate defenders. On July 8 the ground attack began.

All such attacks now had to be as sparing of British blood as possible, because Montgomery had just received a warning from the adjutant general, Ronald Adam, that he could no longer rely on drafts from England to replace his casualties; there simply were no more British reserves. This was why Montgomery had decided to use his armored divisions instead of infantry for the main Caen attack. The tanks went in the next day but made little headway. General Crerar, the Canadian army commander, watched the attack from a convenient church tower, and went forward the next day to inspect the battlefield. "The Boche had fought very hard indeed," he wrote on the day after that, "many groups battling it out to the end. It is extraordinary what a dozen years of high-power indoctrination can do to men. Monty told me two stories yesterday concerning German prisoners in British hospitals which, he said, were authentic. One concerned a German prisoner who was about to be given a blood transfusion in order to save his life, but refused it as the blood was British. He died. The other concerned a dying German who was told of his state and asked which particular brand of chaplain he would like to have with him. He replied that his priest was the Führer and refused, whatsoever, any religious assistance."

By July 10, Montgomery's troops had captured only part of Caen. The Nazis were still holding the larger part of the city, on the far side of the river.

Over in the American sector, on July 8, Hughes visited the new but as yet idle Third Army headquarters in the Cherbourg peninsula. Tension here was mounting as they awaited the call to battle. Hughes and Patton dined together, then Patton invited him to stay for the night and gave him a sleeping bag; Hughes "got all balled up in the bag with rubber mattress and blankets."

The next day was Sunday. Hughes was up at seven A.M. and borrowed George's razor. Before going off to the local Catholic chapel for a field mass, Patton talked to Hughes about Jean Gordon. In a mood which Hughes divined as more boastful than repentant, his friend told him: "She's been mine for twelve years." That answered the curious question that had been at the back of Hughes's mind.

The next day, July 10, a new directive arrived from Montgomery, addressed to Bradley and Dempsey and also to Patton and Crerar, whose Third U.S. and First Canadian armies were both about to enter the field. Patton was not pleased to read the document's final paragraph. "Subsequently," Montgomery declared, "all operations in Brittany will come under the direction and control of Third U.S. Army, which Army will have the task of clearing the whole of the Brittany peninsula."

There were clearly no laurels to be earned in clearing the Brittany peninsula, which was below and well away from the present scene of action and by no means on the glory road to Paris. Evidently Montgomery had no intention of letting General Patton repeat the humiliation of Sicily, when he had overtaken him around the other side of the island and reached Messina first.

In England, the V-1s seemed to be following Eisenhower around. No sooner had he fled from Bushy Park to SHAEF Forward at Portsmouth, than the Germans switched their target too. Kay Summersby, who had returned from the United States, noted on July 11: "Large number of Buzzers at Portsmouth last night. E. came up to Main [Bushy Park] today for three conferences." And Eisenhower himself wrote privately to Mamie from Bushy Park that day: "It seems to me I'm a flea on a hot griddle. . . . Ask Johnny how promptly I duck to the shelter when the Buzzers come around! (There goes the warning—now we'll see whether I get an 'imminent' warning!)"

During her visit to America, Kay Summersby had not impressed Mamie as a lady of presence or sagacity, according to Mrs. Robert M. Littlejohn, wife of Eisenhower's quartermaster general, who was with Mamie at the time and who wrote her husband about the meeting of the two women. Apparently, the army grapevine was atwitter, and Kate Hughes kept Everett well apprised. "Enjoyed Kate's comments on Kay's trip home," Hughes wrote in his diary on July 15. "Kay not enjoying it. John [Eisenhower] has to leave Mamie to entertain Kay. Must tell Butch. . . . Kate says that Kay came with papers asking to be a WAC." (Eisenhower swung her a commission as a second lieutenant a few months later.)

Eisenhower, unaware of all the whispering, carried on. He talked with Hughes about the problems besetting Bradley. Bradley's biggest complaint was over the supply system. This gave Hughes the opportunity to sound off against his old nemesis General J.C.H. Lee and Lee's organization. Hughes was scathing about the slowness of clearing the port of Cherbourg. He had witnessed scenes reminiscent of the WPA make-work projects created during the Depression—"men picking up leaves and branches off road." The harbor was still stitched with mines of every type.

This was all part of the continuing feud between Hughes, Lee, and Bedell Smith. In early June, Smith was still fulminating against inspector generals (meaning Hughes) who, as Hughes put it, "delve too much into his affairs." On June 22, Hughes evidently chanced on yet another expenses scandal involving Smith: "[I] read [an] invoice," he noted, "for that general's belt about which I have heard so much." Six days later Hughes added: "I[nspector] G[eneral] said Bedell don't like the way he has been investigated. I can see that."

Now Bedell Smith, tit for tat, gave Hughes an unsavory job. He ordered him to reorganize the whole European Theater of Operations (ETO). As the sympathetic J.P. said, "It seems rather late in the day to be figuring out how ETO is to be organized."

Hughes, never one not to put an adverse situation to good use, drafted a plan: it would eliminate the supply services and the deputy theater commander, none other than Lee. Smith happily okayed the plan. At the beachhead, the sharp-eared Hughes had found evidence of Lee's strange methods. In an inspection report on June 16, Hughes warned about Lee's habit of sending a planeload of presents to the field commanders before asking if they were satisfied with his supply arrangements. "When we arrived at General Bradley's headquarters," reported Hughes, "General Lee opened the conversation by asking if the presents had arrived. . . . Due to the fact that he had just received a nice present, [Bradley] did not want to take [the] offensive [against Lee]."

When Bradley came to see Montgomery on July 10, the American First Army commander frankly admitted that his own breakout effort had failed. Montgomery reassured him: "Take all the time you need. We will go on hitting, drawing the German strength onto ourselves and away from your front."

It was after this conference that Dempsey suggested to Montgomery that their whole strategy should now be changed—that the British Second Army should be assigned the breakout role, at Caen. Montgomery was tempted, but eventually he refused to agree to such a drastic change of plan. He did, however, approve of Goodwood, Dempsey's plan for a massive thrust by all three British armored divisions—a mighty, earth-trembling force of over seven hundred tanks—that would break through Caen after a path had been cleared by the strategic bomber force. After the air bombardment, II Canadian Corps infantry would push forward on the right and I British Corps infantry on the left, creating a breach in the defenses through which the three armored divisions of O'Connor's VIII Corps would debouch into the open countryside.

The air force commanders were reluctant to agree this time, since they felt that Montgomery had not properly exploited their most recent bombing effort on Caen; but Montgomery painted a rosy picture of the prospects of Goodwood. He asked Eisenhower to order the entire weight of the air power to be thrown into support of his land battle. "My whole eastern flank will burst into flames on Saturday," he wrote. "The operation on Monday may have far-reaching results."

This time Eisenhower liked the idea of saturation-bombing the enemy defenders—perhaps a half-mile area could be wiped out. "The infantry," he told Butcher, "could then practically walk through." After consulting Tedder, he sent Montgomery a radio message assuring him of the maximum air support that the weather would permit. The next day, Eisenhower enthusiastically assured him: "With respect to the plan, I am confident that it will reap a harvest from all the sowing you have been doing during the past week." Meanwhile, he wrote a fawning letter to Butcher Harris, praising his recent performance at Caen and saying: "We could not possibly get along without you."

For once, Tedder too was enthusiastic. "Have spoken [to] Eisenhower," he informed Montgomery. "In particular [I] can assure you that all the air forces will be full out to support your far-reaching and decisive plan."

In his ensuing orders and directives, Montgomery was perhaps purposefully vague about what the tanks should do when and if the breakthrough was achieved. Would they halt again, or would they keep going straight on to Paris? "I have decided," he wrote to Sir Alan Brooke, on July 14, "that the time has come to have a real 'show down' . . . and to loose a corps of armoured divisions in to the open country about the Caen-Falaise road. We shall be operating from a very firm and secure base. The possibilities are immense; with 700 tanks loosed to the SE of Caen, and armoured cars operating far ahead, anything may happen. . . ."

"Anything may happen!" He wrote the words again later in the same letter—but added that he would certainly do nothing foolish which might open his army to a German comeback. Moreover, he sent his military assistant to London to reassure the War Office. This lieutenant colonel said explicitly: "Having broken out in country southeast of Caen he [Montgomery] has no intention of rushing madly eastwards, and getting Second Army on the eastern flank so extended that that flank might cease to be secure." To make himself even more plain, the colonel added: "All the activities on the eastern flank are designed to help the [American] forces in the west while insuring that a firm [English and Canadian] bastion is kept in the east."

That all his operations were designed to break the logjam for Bradley's army became evident from the letter which Montgomery wrote on the same day to Alan Brooke about the American sector, where Bradley's First Army was plugging down toward the Périers–Saint-Lô road. "Once it can get a footing on the road," predicted Montgomery, "it will be able to deliver a real blitz attack. . . . The time has arrived to deliver terrific blows designed to write off and eliminate the bulk of the enemy's holding troops. I doubt if he can collect more troops to rope us off again *in the west,* and it is in the west," he again emphasized, "that I want territory."

Eisenhower's letter to Montgomery, dated July 14, yet again showed that he still had not fully grasped Montgomery's simple strategy. "I am sure, also," he wrote, "that when this thing is started you can count on Bradley to keep his troops fighting like the very devil, twenty-four hours a day, to provide the opportunity your armored corps will need, and to make the victory complete." Montgomery's strategy was the reverse, though: to give Bradley the main chance while he preoccupied the enemy with Caen.

True, General Dempsey, the Second Army commander, had bold ambitions. While Montgomery's grand plan called for a tactical breakthrough at Caen, Dempsey aspired to a strategic breakthrough. His intention was to make his first move at dawn on July 16, on one flank of the city, then spring O'Connor's VIII Corps armor on the Germans two days later—in Operation Goodwood—after the defenses had been neutralized by fragmentation and high-explosive bombs. That would set the whole British army into motion across the open Falaise plain, toward Paris.

It sounded infallible, almost easy. For several days, however, Montgomery delayed the attack—driving Eisenhower to mounting irritation which he expressed to his deputy, Tedder. The British air chief marshal already had found grounds to dislike Montgomery. On July 13, Hughes, who was on close terms with Lady Tedder, wrote: "Tops says that Tedder is going to Churchill to complain about Montgomery. She says things are not moving fast enough, that Monty is backed by the P.M. and out of control, that Tedder is sick of the whole situation, [and] that *she* wants me to talk to Tedder. I refuse. I cannot tell a Britisher what I think. Perhaps I should tell Ike as C in C. But now I think not." Afterward, in a separate notebook, Hughes carefully reminded himself: "Tops' visit. When the ladies get into the higher realms of politics, war is dangerous."

In the middle of all these agitations, a big, well-furnished plane landed at Newquay, near Land's End, bringing the American Secretary of War, Henry Stimson. He was coming at Roosevelt's behest, to investigate the rumors of growing friction between the British and American commanders over Montgomery's strategy. He was accommodated on an eight-thousand-acre estate near the small village of Abbott's Ann. The manor, Red Rice, near Andover, had been mentioned in the Domesday Book—Rede Ric was Anglo-Saxon for a council chamber. The manor's staff were lined up in the drive for Stimson's arrival. The manor hall, some eighty by forty feet, was hung with ancient paintings.

On July 13 Eisenhower arrived and conferred with Stimson for over an hour in the manor's Yellow Room. Stimson made detailed notes. Eisenhower told him confidentially that he thought that Churchill was now favorably disposed—"loyal" was the word that Eisenhower used —to Anvil, the landing next month in southern France, and would become increasingly so if that operation proved successful. "The P.M.," said Eisenhower, "always likes to back the winner." He warned Stimson of the risk that if Anvil stumbled, Churchill might want to "prance off on something else." Then Stimson went off to tour the battlefield.

The American sector was checkmated, but the British end was the scene of hectic preparations. It was now the eve of Goodwood. Montgomery wired Eisenhower: "Grateful if you will issue orders that the whole weight of the air power is to be available on that day to support my land battle." Eisenhower issued the orders, and his personal staff group left Bushy Park for their command post outside Portsmouth.

Eisenhower was quiet and feeling in fact rather depressed. The V-1 menace had become a nightmare.

He was feeling ill, too. Butcher asked if he still had the ringing in his ears, and he nodded. Eisenhower suspected that the ringing was caused by high blood pressure, but he feared that if some specialist came, the news would get back to Washington and count against him. He preferred the ringing noise. They arrived at Portsmouth in time for dinner. Eisenhower hollered for old-fashioned Army-style baked beans. Montgomery's attack was due to begin the next day.

Never, that summer, were higher expectations pinned to one battle than to Goodwood—this mighty tank drive whereby Montgomery planned to regain the initiative at Caen. A lot would depend on the timber of O'Connor's three armored division commanders. Of the three, one was led by a man thought to be brave as a lion with lots of dash but little brain. Another was too cautious, while the third was no great thruster either. O'Connor himself climbed into a Jeep to go forward into battle—an odd choice for an armored corps commander, who should surely have ridden a tank himself.

Goodwood exploded into action at five-thirty A.M. on July 18. At the first light, 1,599 heavy bombers went in, supported by medium and light bombers, and laid down their carpets of bombs—7,700 tons of high explosive—along the path of the VIII Corps tank advance and upon more distant targets believed to be sheltering German defenders. It was the most violent air attack in support of ground armies ever attempted. In a rising crescendo, the big field guns joined in, together with the armament of the British warships still in range of Caen.

The German defenders were dazed, battered, and broken by the blasting from the air and sea and ground. But still they clung to their positions. They crawled out of the wreckage, righted their overturned guns, started up the surviving tanks, and fought back. By midday, British and Canadian losses were mounting again, and the British tanks were stopped.

Nonetheless a code message timed 7:40 P.M. arrived for Eisenhower during the night, in which Montgomery, declaring himself well satisfied, claimed that he had definitely caught the enemy off balance. The three British armored divisions, he proclaimed, were "now operating in the open country to the south and southwest of Caen." That was not true. The truth was that, as dusk had fallen, the German lines were still holding—and the Germans had destroyed or disabled 186 of Montgomery's tanks.

The next day VIII Corps resumed the struggle, baffled by the German tenacity. Sixty-five more tanks were lost. In a personal letter to Sir James Grigg on July 19, Montgomery again concealed the scale of his reverse: "We have got off to a very good start in the battle on the eastern flank," he claimed, "but there is still much to be done and the German is fighting well and hard; the great thing is to 'write off' enemy personnel and equipment so as to weaken his war potential—and this we will do."

The following day he called off the VIII Corps attack. Montgomery's Operation Goodwood had failed. Bradley commiserated. "We must grin and bear it," he said. But for Montgomery it was becoming increasingly difficult to grin.

CHAPTER SIXTEEN

Headaches

As SUPREME Commander, General Eisenhower was plagued not only by the political issues of fighting a coalition war and the need to balance national against strategic interests, not just by the rivalry between the army commanders and their conflicting solutions to tactical problems, not just by the shortages and the weather; there were at times fierce, often wholly unexpected problems that threatened to overshadow all else.

The first of these headaches that summer was a horrific revelation, a waking nightmare for both British and American combat troops. They had found that their guns were incapable of penetrating the frontal armor of the enemy's Panther and Tiger tanks. This was no small problem. From Ultra, the Germans were known by late June to have eighty Tigers and 250 Panthers—as well as 350 of the older Mark IV tanks—facing the beachhead. There was a danger, as General de Guingand termed it in a letter, of a "Panther and Tiger complex" gripping the invasion troops.

The infantry would have denied that word *complex*. For them the

Panther, a forty-five-ton low-slung colossus, was a very real terror—
snorting eighty-eight-millimeter shells and spraying heavy machine gun
bullets as it came lumbering down streets and across fields toward them,
deflecting their answering fire like a rhinoceros shaking off a shower of
pebbles. If the Panther remained buttoned up, there was nothing the
ground troops could do but scramble to get out of its way.

The superiority of the Nazi tanks was nothing new to the Allied
commanders. It had been reported by tank crews in the Anzio beachhead. C. L. Sulzberger of the *New York Times* had tried to expose the
scandal: that the Sherman tank's armor was inferior to the Tiger tank's,
that its gun was outranged by the guns of the Mark IV special and the
Tiger, and that the new German antitank gun had twice the muzzle
velocity of the best American weapon. Instead of demanding instant
corrective action by the American ordnance authorities, General Devers, the American theater commander in Italy, instead ordered it
against correspondent Sulzberger.

This urge to muzzle serious criticism appeared to be a common
characteristic among top commanders. Montgomery acted identically
when similar unrest began almost simultaneously in the British sector.
Reports began reaching him from the liaison officers attached to corps
and division staffs, voicing doubts about the quality of British equipment. His reply was to pen a note on June 23 to his chief of staff. "Such
reports," he wrote, "must on no account go on; they are highly suspect
and must be most carefully vetted." The reports nevertheless got to the
War Office, and that evening Sir James Grigg telephoned de Guingand
to say that he anticipated trouble in the Guards Armoured Division
regarding the "inadequacy of our tanks compared with the Germans."
The next day de Guingand wrote to Montgomery reporting on the
tank-gun problem: "War Office are doing everything possible to remedy
the situation." Montgomery then wrote to his army commander, Sir
Miles Dempsey: "At a time like this, with large forces employed and
great issues at stake, we must be very careful that morale and confidence are maintained at the highest level. Alarmist reports, written by
officers with no responsibility and little battle experience, could do a
great deal of harm. There will therefore be no reports, except those
made through the accepted channels of command." That, like Devers's,
was Montgomery's solution to the problem.

There was no doubt that in Normandy, as at Anzio, the Americans were finding that their weapons were inferior. Their bazooka had so little punch that GIs were being trained in the use of captured German Panzerfaust bazookas, which could punch through thick armorplate at considerable distances. For the Americans too, however, the most serious headache was the superiority of the Panther, a tank in which Hitler had vested high hopes ever since first personally issuing the specifications for it three years before. It had frontal armor that was four inches thick. Maurice Rose, who would take over in August as commander of the experienced 3rd Armored Division, confirmed to Eisenhower that the American M4 and M4A3 tanks were inferior to the Mark V and Panther. The inferiority was outweighed only by better American artillery, air support, and maneuvering and by better American gunnery. "I have," wrote Rose, "personally observed on a number of occasions the projectiles fired by our 75 and 76mm guns bouncing off the front plate of Mark V tanks at ranges of about 600 yards."

He attached a file of statements to his report to Eisenhower. Among them was one from an American tank battalion commander, Lieutenant Colonel E. W. Blanchard, who stated: "The only Panthers I have seen not knocked out by our artillery or our air, were either abandoned by their crews or had been been hit by our tanks at very close ranges. ... Discounting our air and supporting artillery, we defeat the German tanks by our weight in sheer numbers of tanks and men." A staff sergeant agreed: "I have fired at 150 yards at a Panther, 6 rounds—4 APs and 2 HEs, without a penetration." A tank commander with nine months' combat experience added his voice: "Jerry armament will knock out an M4 as far as they can see it." Then there was Private John A. Danforth, of E company, a gunner for nine months who had had two tanks shot out from under him. "I think we don't have enough gun," he said. "The people who build tanks I don't think know the power of the Jerry gun. I have seen a Jerry gun fire through two buildings, penetrate an M4 tank, and go through another building."

There was no answer. The enemy tanks could be attacked only indirectly—by bombing the factories that built them, the refineries that supplied their gasoline, the cities that housed the next of kin of the tank crews. For the rest of the war, the Allied soldiers had to face the terrifying sight of the Panther bearing down on them inexorably, knowing that, except in special circumstances, it would be likely to have its deadly way with them.

Another kind of headache was that inflicted upon Eisenhower by the Free French. On June 13 he was notified that, without consulting him, London had arranged for General de Gaulle to visit Normandy the next day—he would cross in a French destroyer. There were those on Eisenhower's staff who professed to be surprised that de Gaulle was not planning to walk across the wave tops. Bedell Smith informed the British War Cabinet that, since they had approved de Gaulle's visit, Eisenhower would raise no objection. But the Supreme Commander would, he said, insist that the Frenchman confine himself to the British beachhead; further, Eisenhower was adamant that de Gaulle refrain from making any statement whatever while in France.

De Gaulle was smarting under the American reluctance to recognize his Committee as the new French government. In retaliation, the temperamental general had stepped up his harassments. The American government had printed special French currency—with the acquiescence of de Gaulle's representative in Washington. De Gaulle now publicly branded that money "counterfeit." He had already refused to allow five hundred liaison officers specially trained by the British to accompany the Overlord forces. He finally picked twenty to go, but they turned out to be Gaullists, who would attempt to sabotage Eisenhower's efforts to set up a neutral civil administration and who refused to issue the supplementary francs. Nazi propaganda capitalized on this and broadcast warnings to the French that shopkeepers were being instructed by Resistance leaders not to accept the "Washington francs."

Then de Gaulle implied in a press interview that Eisenhower was going to administer France as a conquered enemy territory. Marshall, still in London, advised the State Department, "General Eisenhower deeply resents de Gaulle's statements."

"It's as bad," Stimson wrote, "as if he were trying to steal our ammunition on the battlefield or turn our guns against us." He said much the same to Roosevelt. "Four years ago, when a would-be dictator stabbed a neighboring nation in the back, you spoke vigorously and strongly. Today on a smaller scale a leader who is supposedly an ally of ours has virtually stabbed our troops in the back on the beachhead of France."

That was tough language. But de Gaulle's behavior was considered outrageous, particularly since he had begun angling for an invitation to Washington. Roosevelt was not eager to have him come, because de

Gaulle was hard to deal with and Roosevelt was not prepared to make any concessions. A very important issue was at stake. Back in March, Roosevelt had signed a directive authorizing Eisenhower to negotiate civil administration in France with the Resistance leaders he found there, not necessarily de Gaulle people. But Churchill had not so far honored his promise to sign it too. Evidently Anthony Eden, his foreign secretary, was preventing him.

Visiting London, the Joint Chiefs encountered de Gaulle in person. Admiral Leahy noted on June 13: "As a matter of fact the persistent effort of General de Gaulle to have us impose him upon the French people has been a continuing annoyance, and many of his actions, such as the removal of General Giraud from command of the Army, have adversely affected our military effort."

Marshall, King, and Arnold sent the President a worried telegram. The next day Secretary Stimson telephoned General Marshall in London. The general used blistering language about de Gaulle and Foreign Secretary Anthony Eden. Eden, said Marshall, was fighting Churchill tooth and claw over de Gaulle—and Eden, he added, was a man of real power. Marshall warned Stimson that Eden was playing with fire. If the American public ever found out about how the French were being obstructionist while American boys were dying on the beaches, then America would probably ditch France for good and revert to isolationism. Stimson showed the dictaphone transcript of Marshall's warning to the British ambassador in Washington, Lord Halifax. Halifax agreed to send Eden a message warning about the damage he was doing to Anglo-American relations by supporting de Gaulle.

Marshall personally gave de Gaulle a dressing down and brought him into line enough for de Gaulle's visit to Washington to go ahead. Marshall also spoke frankly to Eden at a house party at Chequers, Churchill's official country house. "Eden was trying to push Churchill into the recognition of de Gaulle," wrote Stimson later, giving Marshall's version, "and finally Marshall broke loose. He said he couldn't talk politics but he said he knew more about the Army and he knew more about the people of the United States than Eden and that, if Eden went on in this way and the things that had happened from de Gaulle's course came out in the press in full, how he had attacked our money and how he had refused to send over men who had been trained for the very purpose of helping us in the invasion, it would make a wave of indignation in the United States which would swamp the whole damn British Foreign Office." Stimson added: "Eden got very angry, his face flushed, and he finally left the room and went upstairs and stayed away from the rest of the conference."

The final insult came a few days later. It was learned that de Gaulle was sending his own military officers into France to take over the civil and military administration in his name. Rouen had already fallen into his hands in this way. He announced in London that their activities would not come under Allied supervision. A State Department official exploded that this was incredible. "The regions in question are not tranquil back areas many miles from the front," he wrote on June 17. "They are zones of most active and fierce combat fighting where American and British boys are dying and where military considerations are and must for some time remain paramount."

Exactly one month after D-day, General Charles de Gaulle flew to Washington. He was received at the White House, and he charmed more than one of his most obstinate critics by his unquestionable leadership qualities. On the invitations which he sent out for a reception, he styled himself: "Président du Gouvernement Provisoire de la République Française"—which was a rather shabby way to office.

That summer, Eisenhower's troops were facing problems with the French on another level, as his armies became the occupiers of France.

From the first the invaders were amazed at the behavior of the French populace. "The attitude of the French," John Eisenhower had written in a report after touring the British sector, "was sobering indeed. Instead of bursting with enthusiasm they seemed not only indifferent but sullen. There was considerable cause for wondering whether these people wished to be 'liberated.' "

As for that, on June 13 SHAEF had directed: "General Eisenhower desires that in all future communiqués, the word 'liberated' be used instead of the word 'captured' when referring to locations in France." To the French, the distinction was sometimes a narrow one. Towns and villages in the beachhead area were subjected to crushing bombardment by Allied battleships and raids by thousands of Allied heavy bombers. The air raid on Caen on the afternoon of D-day had killed 2,500 people, including families bringing children for their first communion in the city's famous twin-spired cathedral. Peasants and villagers were machine-gunned and strafed. Montgomery candidly wrote on June 14 to Brooke: "I see SHAEF communique said yesterday that the town [Carentan] had been liberated. Actually it has been completely flattened and there is hardly a house intact; all the civilians have fled. It is a queer sort of liberation." He visited the Cherbourg peninsula and scoffed, in a handwritten—and therefore uninhibited—top secret letter to de Guingand on June 23: "Montebourg and Valognes have been 'liberated' in the best 21 Army Group style, i.e. they are both completely destroyed!! I think Valognes probably wins; it is worse than Ypres in the last war."

Small wonder, then, as Eisenhower and the Joint Chiefs toured Normandy on June 12, not all of the French civilians they encountered were rejoicing. "The majority waved," wrote Eisenhower's British aide, Colonel Gault, "whilst others looked somewhat dazed. This is only natural when you realize that they had been subjected not only to bombing but naval gunfire in the assault. . . . I think the average man and housewife were more interested in collecting what few belongings were left from their destroyed houses." He added in confusion, "The people looked well-fed and the children healthy and well-dressed." A Canadian colonel touring the British sector on June 26 entered in his diary his own impressions of the French civilians: "They were well fed, neatly dressed and glad to see us, but waiting until they are sure we're there for keeps before showing their relief or pleasure to any degree."

This had been the suspicion of many Allied visitors to post-Overlord France: the French—at least in Normandy—were none too pleased to be invaded. Things had apparently not been so bad before the Allies came. Arriving in Normandy with Churchill on June 12, Sir Alan Brooke had written: "I was astonished to see how little affected the country had been by the German occupation and five years of war. All the crops were good, the country fairly clear of weeds, and plenty of fat cattle, horses, chickens etc." Churchill nudged him and said in his own vivid phrase: "We are surrounded by fat cattle lying in luscious pastures with their paws crossed!" Brooke observed in his diary, with displeasure: "The French population did not seem in any way pleased to see us arrive as a victorious army to liberate France. They had been quite content as they were, and we were bringing war and desolation to their country."

Eisenhower had no difficulty squaring his conscience. He blamed the misery and destruction squarely on the enemy. He hated the Germans with an intensity equaled only by Bedell Smith, whose Prussian ancestors had come to America one generation after Eisenhower's own German forebears. Once, after driving back through Saint-Lô—the city was now just a mass of rubble—Eisenhower would write to Mamie, "Some of the larger towns in our path of advance have been pulverized. Saint-Lô and Caen especially. I always feel sad when I face the necessity of destroying the homes of my friends! The German is a beast."

The French emigrés and politicians, like de Gaulle and Koenig, were willing to inflict any injury to evict the German invaders. But less sophisticated French folk saw only the Allied battleships and bombers and tanks, pounding their towns into ruins. In a reflexive act of self-preservation, many of them seized arms to aid Rommel's army against the death-dealing newcomers; some of them were perhaps reacting to a hereditary historical resentment against the foreigners from across the Channel who centuries ago had come over to maraud that part of France. Montgomery had to cable Brooke an advance warning about Churchill's planned visit on June 12: "Roads *not* 100 per cent safe owing to enemy snipers including women." General Arnold, who also visited Normandy that day, took a dim view of the French. "Some snipers," he wrote in his diary, "one a French woman, who was shot. French surely a poor, sickly looking lot. Doubt if they have the courage, determination, love for freedom to ever regain position as a first-rate power." The *francs-tireurs* posed an awkward military problem throughout June, and a public relations one as well, and toward the month's end General de Guingand would write, "SHAEF are very keen on putting out a denial that the French have been sniping our troops, as they consider it very desirable from the political point of view to do this."

A crueler problem soon arose to test relations between the liberated and the liberators. It sprang from the very brutality of the war itself, a violence spawned by violence. The American troops had taken a beating at Omaha beach, and after that they had not always abided by the rules. For instance, they often took no prisoners. Clarence Huebner, whose 1st Division had suffered badly in storming Omaha, said on June 25 to General Hodges—"with his mouth curling into a smile," as Hodges noted approvingly in his diary—that his men refused to take prisoners. "Could have taken four yesterday easily, but preferred to kill them," said Huebner.

A number of the combat troops in Normandy carried their battle psychosis over into the rear areas. Foreigners were foreigners, to many of them, whether French or German or Italian. An ordeal began for the French who had stayed behind in Normandy to welcome their liberators. They were liable to be vandalized, robbed, raped, murdered. Indeed, the behavior of GIs throughout liberated Europe was causing apprehension in Washington. The Joint Chiefs reviewed a report from Rome too that conditions now were worse than when the Germans had been there; said Admiral Leahy: "A situation which a United States official can so describe should not be permitted to develop." Eisenhower, his desk already crowded with tactical and administrative problems, found the whole business tedious. It involved him in endless sessions with the theater judge advocate, Brigadier General Edward C. Betts. It began just three days after D-day, when he was confronted with the cases of two blacks sentenced for rape and murder. It was a delicate problem, one that loomed ever larger for the Americans, threatening to damage their image as the world's peacemakers, the bringers of law and order to Nazi-ravaged Europe. Liddell Hart, visiting Caen later, would note, "Most Frenchmen speak of the correctness of the German Army's behaviour. They seem particularly impressed that German soldiers were shot for incivility to women and compare this with the American troops' bad behaviour towards women."

After the capture of Cherbourg the embattled armies had moved off, leaving in their wake a wrecked French countryside and a flotsam of heartbreak. In Cherbourg itself, the first big city entered by combat troops, riots broke out as bored GIs used their firearms indiscriminately against the French. "Unfortunately," said the official report of Normandy Base Section, "from the American angle, this created an unfavorable impression on the civilian population." Military police battalions had to be assigned early in August 1944, the situation being partially cured only by a complete withdrawal of arms and placing all bars off limits to U.S. troops. "Unfortunately most of these undisciplined acts were caused by colored troops," the report continued, "and great efforts were made to bring this situation under control." During September and October the violence increased. "The victims of the crime could not be brought back to life," the report said, "but the assailant could be punished. To prove to the civil population we were doing everything possible to bring about justice, executions were held at or near the scene of the crimes. The immediate family of the victim and civic officials of the towns were present to see the execution."

On August 1, Eisenhower telephoned Betts for a complete report on the number of death sentences passed on American troops: "I'm especially anxious to see the numbers as between white and colored troops," he said. But in the British sector too there were problems, and on August 10, Montgomery had to write to all three army commanders —Bradley, Dempsey, and Crerar—ordering them to stamp out looting of French property which was becoming rife not only in the forward battle area but also well outside, where the objects taken had no military use whatsoever.

By the autumn, GI morale was breaking down in the face of the wet, the unhoped-for German resistance, the lack of furloughs, and the bad personnel replacement system. The discipline of even some of the finest U.S. units was cracking. The death sentences that Eisenhower now had to review multiplied—Betts brought him the dossiers once a week and laid them on his desk to read and sign. On November 5, Kay Summersby, worried, recorded: "General Betts reports that disciplinary conditions in the army are becoming bad. Many cases of rape, murder and pillage are causing complaints by the French, Dutch, etc. E. is assigning several officers to make a complete investigation and report personally to him. . . . E. discussed with Bedell at length the discipline of our troops, the chief of staff has had a report which substantiated Betts' report." The next day Bedell Smith was again called in. "E. discussed with him the discipline of the 101st and 82nd Airborne Divisions. It is bad, numerous cases of rape, looting. Strong measures will have to be taken. E. suggests that there should be a public hanging, particularly in the case of rape." Previous executions had been inside army stockades. For the Supreme Commander to suggest making an example of the celebrated U.S. airborne divisions by a humiliating public spectacle of a sort seldom seen since the nineteenth century was an indication of the urgency of the problem.

The problem persisted. When Major General LeRoy Lutes arrived a month later to inspect the theater for Brehon Somervell, he wrote in his diary, "The French now grumble . . . that the Americans are a more drunken and disorderly lot than the Germans and hope to see the day when they are liberated from the Americans." He added that the Allied propaganda about the Germans was evidently untrue. "I am informed the Germans did not loot either residences, stores, or museums. In fact the people claimed that they were meticulously treated by the Army of Occupation." By the time the campaign in Europe ended, Betts would have noted that there was a definite correlation between the number of rapes and murders committed by GIs during any given period and the general combat activity of that period. "From the initial landing in June 1944 to the middle of July the crime trend corresponded to the gradual increase in the number of troops," Betts would report. "However, following the St. Lo breakthrough at the end of July a sharp rise in the number of cases occurred, followed by a rapid decline after the stabilization of the battlefront. . . . From the breakthrough at the Ruhr River in February 1945 until the cessation of hostilities, the trend again shows a sudden sharp rise hardly proportionate to the number of troops engaged." At one stage there were over five hundred instances of rape per month.

In all, 454 GIs were sentenced to death by courts-martial. Many got off the hook, but seventy were executed—all except one for nonmilitary offenses like rape and murder. The exception was case CM ET0 5555, better known as *United States* v. *Slovic*; Private Eddie Slovic became on January 31, 1945, the only American soldier in the war to be shot for desertion.

CHAPTER SEVENTEEN

Rain Check

ON JULY 20, members of Hitler's general staff tried to assassinate him. He survived and issued an immediate order to the regiment launching the V-1s—his "revenge weapons." They were to double the missile attack on London so that nobody should get the idea that he was weakening.

In London that night, Everett Hughes was kept awake until five A.M. by the deafening organ note of approaching flying bombs. Eisenhower too was troubled, even though he had a bomb-proof dugout at his command post near Portsmouth, which he allowed favored generals to sleep in much as Hughes had parceled out crates of whiskey to his favored friends in Africa. On July 21, he wrote Mamie: "Bombs, bombs, bombs!"

Ever since early July, Omar Bradley's slogging battle through the sopping *bocage* country had made little headway. It was very tough going. German resistance was strong, and no amount of force or boldness seemed to make a difference. The U.S. First Army had suffered 62,000 casualties, including nearly eleven thousand dead. The bodies were piling up in long rows in the open in the cemeteries, awaiting interment by black burial squads. That was what stalemate meant. On about July 10 Bradley told General Collins that he had an idea for breaking it. His plan was to blast a path for Collins's VII Corps through the enemy line with a saturation bombing attack. This raised some eyebrows among Bradley's staff, because the British had recently tried similar tactics (this was well before Goodwood) and found that their tanks ran afoul of the resulting bomb craters. Collins agreed to take a chance on it.

Thus the birth of operation Cobra. The final field orders were dated July 20. They provided for the commitment of four infantry and two armored divisions to the ground attack, supported by an immense American air effort. What Bradley did not tell Collins during these days of planning—no doubt in the interest of security—was that to the north, General George S. Patton was waiting with a powerful force that would be used to exploit any breach torn in the German lines. But Bradley did hint at it, confiding to Collins: "Joe, if this thing goes as it should, we should be in Avranches in a week."

Bradley and his tactical air commander, Pete Quesada, flew to England to discuss the bombing with the allied air commanders. Leigh-Mallory promised a total force of 2,246 aircraft. General Vandenberg wanted the heavy bombers to fly right over the American lines, perpendicular to the wide patch they were to obliterate, and Leigh-Mallory would not hear of this. "No, the bomb approach will be done parallel," he insisted. The parallel approach, with the bombers flying along the battle line, never over their own troops, seemed to some to make more sense: otherwise the bombing might creep back and hit the American lines. But the Americans knew from experience that *lateral* dispersion was the greater danger. Once the target area was blotted out by smoke and dust, the bombardiers would tend to lose track of the battle lines and the planes could stray over their own men. Vandenberg spoke out against parallel. "It worries hell out of me," he said. But Leigh-Mallory seemed to carry the day.

In detail, Bradley's plan was to pummel a rectangle seven thousand yards wide and five thousand yards deep with two thousand bomb loads, trampling a blood-red carpet through the German lines. The nearest edge would be about two thousand yards from the forward American troop positions. Through this gap would storm three divisions of infantry. They would buttress its sides against counterattack, and then two armored divisions, side by side, would roar south through the gap—and on into open France. It sounded workable, but the weather, secrecy, timing, and bombing accuracy would have to be perfect. And those four seldom were.

James Doolittle, renowned for leading a bombing raid on Tokyo soon after Pearl Harbor, was the commander of the Eighth Air Force. He took it upon himself to defy Leigh-Mallory's wishes as to the bombing method. He decided to attack this oblong target area broadside—perpendicular—so as to race his huge force across it in the minimum possible time. Besides, he too believed that the likeliest bombing error would come from lateral dispersion, because the aiming point would be obliterated almost at once by smoke. Bradley agreed to accept the risk that went with a perpendicular approach run but evidently kept this disquieting information from Collins. The attack was scheduled for July 19. Bad weather caused delays.

Tedder was gunning for Montgomery, and the failure of Goodwood had given him the ammunition he needed. That evening he telephoned Eisenhower and reported a dismaying fact that he had just learned— Montgomery, instead of pressing the attack, had in effect stopped the armor from pushing on. Eisenhower had been at Portsmouth when Montgomery's optimistic messages about Goodwood had come in. Kay Summersby had noted his reactions: "So far big attack on British side progressing well." She had added, "E. just wants Monty to keep pressing forward." His pleasure at Montgomery's exuberant reports faded to anger now as Tedder told him the truth. Goodwood had been stalled by the Germans. From stall to stalemate was not a long difference.

Poor Montgomery. On July 18, in the midst of his travail, a message had arrived for him from Winston Churchill saying that he wanted to visit. Montgomery had shot a peremptory message to Eisenhower saying that he did not want the Prime Minister to come over. He knew his attack was not going well, and he did not need formidable witnesses.

At noon on the eighteenth, Kay Summersby drove Eisenhower over to meet Henry Stimson, who had spent the previous day touring American troops in Cherbourg. Back at Eisenhower's command post, they all lunched pleasantly together—Bedell Smith had caught some trout the day before—then conferred for half an hour.

From Stimson's unpublished notes it is evident that his visit had an important underlying purpose. In this presidential election year, he had to find ways of meeting the popular conviction in the United States that America was being called on to suffer disproportionate losses and even to fight solely or predominantly for British interests. He himself, once in Europe, had quickly noticed American disenchantment over the British effort and apprehension as to the plan to place the prospective Ninth American Army under Montgomery's command. Both Bradley and Eisenhower, he found, were restive about this but were exercising patience and forbearance. They were looking forward to Montgomery's coming attack as a test and guide for the future. Stimson noted, "I told [Eisenhower] that this was no Anglophobia criticism of British but a real problem arising out of British limitation of strength." He spoke too of "the public relations problem in US which might arise from that, in a presidential year." Stimson advised Eisenhower to move his command post to the Cherbourg peninsula as soon as possible, to forestall domestic criticism of Montgomery's preponderant role.

Late that day Eisenhower learned that the British tanks in Goodwood had hit a screen of antitank weapons that had stopped them cold with heavy casualties. Montgomery covered his tracks with a dramatic press conference at which he announced that 156,000 Germans had been killed or wounded since D-day. He did not mention that he had taken only 2,500 prisoners in his operation Goodwood, or that he had advanced only seven miles at a cost of a thousand tons of bombs per mile. The fact was, however, that Goodwood had failed, and Montgomery needed a goat. On July 19, he sent another personal message, Eyes Only for General Eisenhower. Butcher deciphered it: "Am anxious to discuss some points with you and in particular the air set-up. Could you come and see me tomorrow morning 20th July? Grateful if you would come alone." The implication was that Montgomery did not want Tedder or other senior airmen in the party. "Message from Monty," recorded Kay Summersby faithfully in her pocket diary. "Wants to see E. alone. . . . The Germans counter attacked today."

Eisenhower replied at 11:15 A.M.: "Will come to see you Thursday morning weather permitting."

At 11:30 P.M. that evening, aide Jimmy Gault called Butcher out of a poker game and said another code message had come from Montgomery. "Would you mind staying up to decipher it," he asked, "as I've got to get up early to go with the boss, and you can sleep. And besides, the ATS officer who will help isn't bad to look at." It took Butcher until two A.M. to decipher the message. Montgomery was reporting that Bradley's big attack, Cobra, was off until July 21, because of the weather. Butcher read it to Eisenhower in his dugout. Eisenhower said he was still going to France, and went back to sleep.

The day before, Churchill had telephoned Eisenhower to pester him for information regarding Goodwood and to plead again for permission to visit the beachhead. Eisenhower told his personal staff about Churchill's row with Montgomery concerning the visit. Churchill was "much upset because of limitations placed upon his movements," observed Summersby. Eisenhower had made inquiries and informed the Prime Minister's bodyguard, Commander Thompson, that if Churchill wished he could go to Cherbourg under the auspices of General J.C.H. Lee's Com Z organization, then drive to Omaha beach, and then reembark and sail along the British beaches (at a safe distance from Montgomery). He had meant the advice kindly, but the result was a furious telephone call from Churchill. Eisenhower—who had hoped to get away to France himself if the weather permitted—found himself listening to a long petulant wrangle and then receiving by dispatch rider a letter from Churchill insisting that he was going to fly over the next day and drive around the Cherbourg peninsula and visit "several of these alleged rocket launching strips." Churchill hastened to say: "I have no intention of visiting General Montgomery's Headquarters, and he should not concern himself about me in any way." He added peevishly: "With hundreds of war correspondents moving about freely, this cannot I think be considered an unreasonable request from the head of the Government who is also Minister of Defence. If however General Montgomery disputes about it in any way, the matter will be taken up officially, because I have both a right and a duty to acquaint myself with the facts on the spot."

The pressure of events had told on Eisenhower. SHAEF's medical chief gave him a checkup with special attention to the ringing in the ears, and found high blood pressure. The bad weather, the frustratingly slow battle, his own inability to participate in field decisions, and what Butcher called "his inward but generally unspoken criticism of Monty for being so cautious"—all had contributed stress. Eisenhower looked forward to getting out of England the next day and crossing to the comparative calm of the Normandy battlefield.

Tedder was seething. He had—wrongly—understood Montgomery's plan as being to break through at Caen and head his armies straight on to Paris. According to Butcher, Tedder telephoned an "I told you so" to the Supreme Commander and an angry hint. The British Chiefs of Staff, he said, "would support any recommendation" which Eisenhower might care to make. The purport was plain: that if Eisenhower should want to get rid of this tedious ground commander for failing to "go places" with his muscular three-armored-division offensive, he would not run into trouble higher up.

Eisenhower did not take Tedder up on that but remarked to him: "Monty apparently wants the air to pulverize every inch of the enemy's ground before he will attack or continue one." Eisenhower knew how to swear, and used real profanity when roused. Now he used some words as adjectives that were not adjectives at all. After that he turned in to bed early, and did not wake until a siren sounded a flying bomb alert the next morning at seven.

Tedder followed up his sally with a letter: "An overwhelming air bombardment opened the door, but there was no immediate determined deep penetration whilst the door remained open and we are now little beyond the farthest bomb craters. It is clear that there was no intention of making this operation the decisive one which you so clearly intended."

Eisenhower now instructed Montgomery that, more than ever, it was important to be aggressive throughout the front. (The influence of Stimson's remarks about domestic opinion was obvious.) "The recent advances near Caen have partially eliminated the necessity for a defensive attitude," he suggested, "so I feel that you should insist that Dempsey keep up the strength of his attack. Right now we have the ground and air strength and the stores to support major assaults by both armies simultaneously. As Bradley's attack starts, Dempsey's should be intensified, certainly until he gains the space and airfields we need on that flank. . . . The enemy has no immediately available major reserves," he pointed out. "We do not need to fear, at this moment, a great counter offensive."

The spirit of Anglo-American harmony, so often preached by Eisenhower, was fast evaporating in his own headquarters. His staff even discussed who might succeed Montgomery. Then the realization dawned that Montgomery—or Chief Big Wind, as Butcher termed him —was a survivor and had a sixty-forty chance of surviving this defeat too. Eisenhower might well find that Montgomery had ordered his advancing tanks to stop and dig in, to frustrate a German counterattack. Of Eisenhower's effort to pin down Montgomery's failure, Butcher aptly observed: "Ike is like a blind dog in a meat house—he can smell it but he can't find it."

The afternoon of July 20, Eisenhower took off in his comfortable B-25 to see Montgomery. En route he dropped by Bradley's headquarters and consulted Bradley, Gerow, and Collins about Cobra. Then he drove over to Montgomery. The contrast between the fighting form, the drive, and the enthusiasm of the Americans and the caution of Montgomery was open and aggravating. He flew back to England late that evening and spent the night at Telegraph Cottage. Kay Summersby recorded his remarks: "Monty seems quite satisfied regarding his progress, says it is up to Bradley to go ahead. E. is *not* pleased at progress made."

The next morning, while she went to fetch their terrier Telek from quarantine, a thirty minutes' drive away, Eisenhower conferred with Tedder at the cottage. They had learned of the bomb attack made the previous day on Hitler's life. Tedder was bitter. "Montgomery's failure to take action earlier has lost us the opportunity offered by the bomb attempt," he told Eisenhower. He admonished the Supreme Commander: "You've got to act at once!" Eisenhower agreed and promised to write to Montgomery.

Another letter! That made Tedder fume. He warned Eisenhower that if he continued to give Montgomery his unqualified support, then the Americans would think he had sold them out. He decided to state his views in writing to the British Chiefs of Staff.

At Bedell Smith's staff conference that morning, Tedder asked him how soon the V-1 launching bases in the Pas-de-Calais would be overrun. Smith offered little comfort. The group was shocked to see Tedder —normally a calm, pipe-smoking, undemonstrative little man—become enraged. "Then we must change our leaders for men who *will* get us there!" he retorted.

Eisenhower wrote his new letter to Montgomery. Tedder glimpsed it that afternoon and swooned—it was all milk and water again. "A few days ago," a rueful Eisenhower had written to Montgomery, "when armored divisions of Second Army, assisted by tremendous air attack, broke through the enemy's forward lines, I was extremely hopeful and optimistic. I thought that at last we had him and were going to roll him up. That did not come about." He demanded now that Dempsey attack continuously to open up terrain for airfields and gain space on the eastern flank. He realized that Montgomery was short of reinforcements, but he hinted strongly that he felt that the British and Canadians were not pulling their weight. "Eventually," he wrote, "the American ground strength will necessarily be much greater than the British. But while we have equality in size we must go forward shoulder to shoulder with honors and sacrifices equally shared."

On reading this mild letter, Tedder snapped to a member of his staff: "It is not strong enough. Montgomery can evade it. It contains no *order.*"

Montgomery's directive dated that same day, July 21, reiterated the policy of "holding our left." But the next day he evidently realized the seriousness of Eisenhower's complaints and replied in a hurt tone: "There is not and never has been any intention to stop offensive operations on the eastern flank." He tried to worm his way out of his plight. He had never meant to restrict offensive operations by Dempsey, he said. He had been regrouping. "Does above assure you that we see eye to eye on the main military problem?" he asked.

"Bombs really bad last night and this A.M.," scribbled a sleepless Hughes on July 21. And Kay Summersby added up that day's total: "We have been to the shelter twenty-five times today, one of the worst days in London." Tempers were raveling. Hughes went to see Eisenhower with Colonel Royal B. Lord, his deputy chief of staff, to protest the letter Eisenhower had now written about the reorganization of the European theater. "Lord and I couldn't talk him out of it," recorded Hughes angrily afterward, "but did talk him into another letter to explain *this* letter. The man is crazy. He won't issue orders that stick. He will pound on the desk and shout." And then, more wearily, Hughes scribbled the pregnant word that overshadowed all their thoughts now: "Bombs."

Hostility at SHAEF toward Montgomery was boiling over. On

July 23, Tedder wrote that despite the brave words used in Montgomery's orders, nothing was going to be done; he urged Eisenhower to move his headquarters to France now, to make sure that his orders were obeyed. The air marshals were furious that Montgomery had still not captured airfields for them southeast of Caen. General Morgan, who had always demanded that the strategic breakout should be made at Caen, was vociferous. Harsh words were used in the conferences. Kay Summersby wrote in her diary: "Letter from Tedder, greatly concerned regarding lack of progress on land front. . . . Tedder believes Monty is making a grave error in continuing to make only limited attacks on British fronts while professing to be seeking decisive results on American fronts. Tedder has written several letters on same subject." The word *professing* was an indication of how low American esteem for Montgomery had fallen. But Eisenhower refused to be harried into premature criticism of the British commander. Years later, rereading Tedder's intemperate letters shrieking for Montgomery's dismissal, Eisenhower would comment: "From June 30 onward I'd say that my most valued operational adviser was Bradley. Tedder's impatience was understandable but his advice was often wide of the mark." Omar Bradley, who well knew the grand strategy underlying Montgomery's operations, approved them—but kept quiet.

In France it was pouring with the worst rain since D-day. The mud was thick and slimy, oozing round the tank treads, sucking in trucks up to their axles. Bradley had to send word to London that he had again put off the Cobra attack because of the bad flying weather.

At Southwick House, while Eisenhower had a word with Montgomery's chief of staff, General de Guingand, Butcher had an illuminating talk with de Guingand's American aide, William Culver. Butcher asked, "What really stopped Montgomery's attack?" Culver replied that Montgomery and his commanders were so conscious of the Empire's ebbing manpower that they hesitated to commit an attack where a division might be lost. To replace even one division was practically impossible. "The commanders feel the blood of the British Empire, and hence its future, is too precious to waste in battle," was Culver's view.

It was true. Preserving British lives ranked high in Montgomery's mind. On July 22, in his "Notes for Minister of Defence," he addressed himself to the complaint that the army's equipment in the field had proven deficient. "There is often a tendency to de-cry equipment and weapons, instead of getting on with the job and making the best of the tools provided. I doubt if the British War Office has ever sent an army overseas so well equipped as the one now fighting in Normandy. When the tactics are good, and weapons and equipment are properly used, we have found no difficulty in defeating the Germans in battle—other things being equal." He expressed appreciation of the air support which he was getting and of the medical services. Then he gravely warned: "Casualties are slowly mounting. As the war proceeds, the manpower situation will necessitate that some units and formations have to be disbanded."

On July 24, Churchill got his wish—to visit Montgomery again. "My dear S of S.," Montgomery wrote to Sir James Grigg, the Secretary of State for War. "The P.M. spent a good deal of his time with me and I gave him every facility to do what he wanted. We talked about many things and he asked me for some facts which he could 'work into' his speech in the House on 2nd August. I told him that in his speech he must pay a great tribute to the War Office; such a tribute has never yet been paid and it is high time it should be paid—publicly. He said he would do so. Yours ever, Monty."

Grigg replied gratefully to Montgomery for this letter, and added: "Political affairs—international ones, I mean—are not going very well. I can't get out of my head the idea that the Americans and the Russians are going to frame us in the end and that unless we make up our minds for a generation of hard work and self-denial (and no Beveridge) we shall be left in the position of the Dutch after Utrecht in 1713."

Several days later, Grigg wrote to his father: "We are going to have a baddish time when the war is over. Both the Russians and the Yanks are jealous of us and will try to reduce us to a third rate power. They won't succeed of course, but it does mean that all these promises of a good time to be had by all won't materialize and that the people who believed them will be pretty sour for a bit. Incidentally these b——y Yanks are beginning to crab Montgomery because they say he is making them do all the fighting. It is an absolute outrage because I know for a fact that the plan is working out as he designed it from the beginning, that we were all along to be the hinge and the Americans the door. But our journalists fell into the trap and I am afraid some of the jealous Airmen help too. However at the moment he has Winston's confidence. I hope W. will speak out on Wednesday. I am on excellent terms with Monty and he is full of thanks to the War Office. By the way, Winston is getting very old and *very* tiresome. I don't think he will last much longer."

Grigg's pen was busy through the end of the month. To Montgomery he denigrated the press, particularly the American press. "The Americans at the best of times would do their damnedest to write down our effort and to write up their own, to laud others and diminish you. But an election year isn't the best of times anyhow. And further I am convinced that Coningham is continuing to badname you and the Army and that what he says in this kind is easily circulated in SHAEF via Tedder and again that Bedell—who seems to have become very conceited and very sour—listens too readily to the poison. If I am right then you will have no comfort until you have demanded and obtained the removal of Coningham from any connection with Overlord whatever. He is a bad and treacherous man and will never be other than a plague to you.

"If I may presume further, I should force Eisenhower to come out into the open the next time you see him and refuse to put up with dark and fearful hints. Indeed I should make the accusation that the rumours are started in his own headquarters."

Eisenhower went on a fishing trip with Bedell Smith and Jim Gault in the late afternoon of July 24. It was late when he returned to his caravan and went to bed. At one A.M. Butcher came crunching to the sleeper caravan along the cinder path, in his slippers and bathrobe, and said that Churchill was on the telephone. "God damn," said Eisenhower, but threw a robe over his pajamas and trod the cinder path to the office tent where the scrambler telephone was. Butcher heard Churchill's voice lisping indistinctly, and then Eisenhower replied: "What do your people think about the slowness of the situation over there?"

Evidently Eisenhower was testing Tedder's suggestion that Montgomery should be fired and wanted to gauge Churchill's response. The talk lasted over half an hour. The next morning, Eisenhower told Butcher that Montgomery had obviously sold Churchill a "bill of goods" during the Prime Minister's recent visit to him. "The P.M. is supremely happy with the situation," he said. That put a different complexion on things.

During the morning, Tedder telephoned Eisenhower and said he was going to come down in the afternoon to pursue his favorite subject, the sacking of Montgomery. Eisenhower told him that he had talked with Churchill and that the Prime Minister was satisfied with Montgomery. Tedder said, "Uh-huh," in a tone of voice that implied that he believed that Churchill had sold the Supreme Commander a bill of goods as well.

Before Eisenhower left to fly to Normandy—where he was going to spend the day with Bradley and watch Cobra—he told Butcher: "Get Bedell on the telephone and get him out of the meeting if he's in it, and tell him not even to hint at the subject we've been discussing"—meaning the sacking of Montgomery.

At Thorney Island airfield, near Portsmouth, a dispatch rider caught up with Eisenhower and handed him a letter from Montgomery. It was apologetic: the weather was "quite frightful," they had not seen blue sky for days on end, there was ten-tenths cloud, and air operations were virtually closed down. He described his intentions, though in vague and unmilitary language. "What might happen finally," he concluded, "cannot be foretold. My aim would be to 'crack about' and try to bring about a major enemy withdrawal from in front of Brad." That was where he wanted the "really big victory," while Dempsey's army would make a series of left-right-left blows to keep the enemy guessing.

The weather experts had said that July 24 would be fine for the air force. Accordingly Leigh-Mallory selected that day, and Bradley agreed that the Cobra attack would begin at one P.M., after saturation bombing of the defenses beginning at noon. During the preceding night Collins had stealthily retracted his troops from the road that marked the battle line, as a safety measure.

What followed was unforgivable. The weather on July 24 did not live up to the forecast. Leigh-Mallory, flying to Normandy around mid-morning, found the sky so overcast that he ordered the attack postponed. Scrubbing an attack by so many planes at the last moment—most of them in the air—was no easy job. "I was at my control center west of Caen," General Quesada recalled thirty-six years later. "One of the wing commanders in my Ninth Fighter Command, Colonel Macauley, heard about the shortfall of the bombs, and on his own initiative, he was able to use a frequency that the bombers would hear, and repeatedly told them to stop the bombing. He aborted the mission. He took a hell of a risk in doing it, because for all practical purposes he called it off without getting anybody's approval. About ninety percent of the bombers did abort. I think he saved hundreds, maybe thousands, of American lives."

Even so, what happened to the infantry waiting to go in was sufficiently horrible. General Courtney Hodges' diary describes the mood on the ground vividly. Hodges' party had set out from his command post at 10:50 A.M., with himself and General William Simpson riding in a Jeep, followed by two air force generals and the commander of the Mexican air force, who had been invited to this unique display of American muscle. Many war correspondents joined them. Lieutenant General Lesley McNair—who had come from America to take over Patton's "ghost army" in England for Fortitude, and was now in Normandy merely to observe—left their group and went on ahead, halting his car only a few hedgerows from the German lines. Around noon, the first foursomes of P-47 dive bombers appeared; a mighty thud and a pillar of black smoke half a mile away marked the end of an American ammunition truck they had mistakenly hit. Another P-47 group arrived and dive-bombed only five hundred yards away from them. Hodges took these mistakes of war philosophically. Then, while the generals adjourned to brew coffee in a cottage kitchen in a village called Vents, the heavy bomber squadrons arrived, firing rocket markers. The generals heard the shrieking crescendo as the first stick of bombs whistled straight at them; the bombs detonated a few hundred yards away, killing seventeen GIs in the 120th Infantry Regiment down the road. This was now no joke. General Brereton, also in Hodges' party, looked at his watch. "It's exactly 12:50," he shouted. "Make a note of that, colonel. We'll check on that bunch!" Farther forward, McNair had almost been killed—he was very deaf and had not heard the bombs screaming down. His aide had hurled him into a ditch only just in time.

The whole air attack was over almost as soon as it began. As the generals left, puzzled at the abrupt termination of the bombing, infantrymen were trudging back up the road saying the attack had been called off. General Leland S. Hobbs, commanding the 30th Division, was furious at the fiasco and told Hodges so. "The Air Corps came north-south, not east-west along the St. Lo-Periers highway as planned," he said. Back at VII Corps headquarters they learned that

Leigh-Mallory had canceled the attack shortly before noon and that Bradley had subsequently called off the infantry assault.

"A lot of the blame should go directly to Jimmy Doolittle," Quesada said years later, "because Doolittle insisted [on a perpendicular bombing run] and we asked that it be otherwise. The bombers started . . . aiming at the smoke, and the smoke was moving north, so they had the bomb line moving north"—that is, coming right over the American lines.

Half of the fighter-bombers had not received the improvised recall order and had completed their bombing runs. The first formation of five hundred heavy bombers had aborted. Most of the second formation had aborted too. In the third formation, more than three hundred released their bomb loads despite the poor visibility, causing many deaths and casualties among the American troops.

Bradley was furious. But he had the moral courage to make the decision to repeat the whole attack—regardless of the risk that the Germans would now be expecting precisely that. Leigh-Mallory agreed to remount the whole bombing operation, but he refused to order a parallel approach—there was just not enough time, he explained, to rebrief the thousands of airmen involved. The repeat Cobra attack would jump off at eleven A.M. the next day, July 25.

Eisenhower sent Bradley a letter which he described to Kay Summersby as a "strong message" of encouragement. He sent it through Montgomery, for whose eyes it was also intended. "A breakthrough at this juncture," he stated, "will minimize the total cost." As a hint for Montgomery's benefit, he urged Bradley "to pursue every advantage with an ardor verging on recklessness and with all your troops without fear of major counter offensive."

This time Leigh-Mallory's American deputy, Vandenberg, decided to fly over and observe from the air. He took off at 8:45 A.M. from Northholt airfield outside London, with his own deputy, Brigadier General Frederic S. Smith. They flew south toward the root of the Cherbourg peninsula, where Spaatz's bomber force was due to unroll a lethal carpet of bombs across the German lines for the American army assault to charge through. On the ground, General Collins had taken over a café at Goucherie as his command post. By nine-thirty, two thousand bombers were approaching, and the remaining windows of the café were beginning to rattle with their roar.

Courtney Hodges had taken a party of generals forward to the same cottage at Vents as before. At 9:36 the first P-47 fighter-bombers—nine groups of four each—screamed overhead to plaster the target highway and the ground south of it. The generals could hear the skies filling with the mighty drone of the first waves of B-24s. "We looked through the torn corner of the house to the north," wrote Hodges' aide in the diary they kept together. "As far as the eye could reach they came—flying in twelves. A mile past us, anti-aircraft fire came up to meet them, bad black spots marking their silvery white. One ship faltered, tried to regain the group, and then slowly floated down to the right; out of it blossomed three parachutes. A second one was hit more squarely— possibly in its bomb bay—for in several seconds it was one ball of red fire which fell straight down through the blue sky and this time there were no parachutes."

The first 500-pounders detonated only a few thousand yards from Collins. The ground around the café shook; seconds later, blast waves ruffled the starched lace curtains. High above them, in his airplane cockpit, Vandenberg looked down and decided that this time the bombers were dropping their loads in the rough area of the target. The red smoke marking the American front line showed quite plainly for the first twenty minutes or so of the bombing. But after that a pall of smoke and dust crept slowly north and obscured any marks identifying the front. The flak was heavy at first, but fell off until only one battery was left, placing silent puffs of black smoke into the air ahead of the thundering herds of bombers. Soon the smoke pall beneath Vandenberg became too dense for him to see even the flash of the bombs. He turned back toward London.

As 2,400 planes began dropping their four thousand tons of fragmentation bombs, high explosive, and napalm, fifty thousand troops gripped carbines and machine guns, listening for the signal to go in. When whistles sounded, however, they were not the whistles of company commanders signaling them to advance but the eerie, deafening shriek of bombs falling on their own lines. Again the 500-pounders cascaded into the leading battalions of the 120th Infantry Regiment. Hodges threw himself into a ditch beside the road for cover, and when he picked himself up several seconds later there was no sign of the generals who had been in his party. They had fled—anywhere to get away from the path the bombers seemed to be taking.

At 10:46 the last of the bomber groups came in. Its tons of bombs hurled hundreds of GIs into the air. At 11:30 the cataclysm was all over. The battle lines ahead were obscured by tornadoes of smoke and dust, and the air now throbbed to the concussions of exploding mortar bombs and artillery fire, and trembled with the distinctive rapid chatter of Schmeisser machine guns.

Hodges looked around for his colleagues. Nobody had seen McNair, which was alarming—he was one of the highest-ranking generals in the army. His aide had last seen him dive into a foxhole when the bombing started. The foxhole was found, and grim men with picks and shovels started to dig; but there was no sign of McNair. Meanwhile General Hobbs, whose 30th Division had this time taken ninety percent of the stray bombing, stumped up to Hodges, red-eyed with smoke, rage, and tears. "We're good soldiers, Courtney, I know," he blurted out, "but there's absolutely no excuse. No excuse at all. . . . The Air Corps was instructed not to drop unless they could see the highway."

Colonel Birks, his infantry regiment commander, telephoned Hobbs: the infantry attack had now begun, but his men were badly shaken by the bombing. He had been forward himself with a bazooka, but the Germans still had tanks there, dug in, hull down, and it seemed to him they were shooting more artillery now than had ever been shot before.

The American troops that plunged hesitantly into the still smoking Cobra area found the slaughtered remains of the Panzer Lehr Division. The bombs had tossed aside the heavy tanks, leveled slit trenches, demolished equipment. Demented German troops were staggering around the battlefield, jabbering incoherently. But to the right of the Panzer Lehr Division, the German 5th Parachute Division had escaped most of the bombing, and a handful of its formidable Panther tanks were hampering the American advance.

Late that afternoon rumors began reaching Hodges—that a lieutenant general had been killed, that the body of a "ground forces" general was lying up the road. Near a crossroads they found him. It was unmistakably McNair, the shoulder patch and general's stars showed it. He had been thrown there by the explosion of a bomb.

Hodges' diary entry for July 25 ended sadly. "This day," it said, "did not bring the breakthrough for which all had hoped. . . . There was no question but that the postponement of the attack from Monday to Tuesday, plus two successive days of bombing of our troops, took the ginger out of the front-line elements, and, as was to have been expected, all surprise element from the attack itself."

Early that evening Bradley telephoned Bedell Smith with the news of McNair's death. Soon after, he telephoned Eisenhower's headquarters, using a makeshift code, and Butcher hurried over to the Supreme Commander's trailer with the message: the 9th had gained 2,-300 yards from the starting point; the 4th, 1,200 yards; and the 30th, 1,300 yards. That was real headway. Cobra was stabbing deep into the German lines.

The bad news was that the bombing had killed 111 American troops and injured more than five hundred; a U.S. command group was wiped out, a fire direction center was obliterated, wire communications were shredded, and the troops terrified. Kay Summersby recorded: "The attack got off this morning. Not going too well, the air bombed our troops, E. says that we must press on with the attack and get going."

At 11:30 P.M. Churchill telephoned SHAEF's advance headquarters at Portsmouth, asking to speak to Eisenhower again—"if he isn't already asleep." The general was in his trailer but still awake. He went up the path to the telephone. "Monty sees eye to eye with me now, and I'm satisfied," he told Churchill. "But the battle is touch and go and there's hard fighting under way and more to come." Churchill invited Eisenhower up to London to lunch the next day at one-thirty.

The next morning Tedder arranged to see Eisenhower first. Tedder's rival Leigh-Mallory also telephoned Eisenhower's office chief and asked urgently for an appointment before the luncheon with Churchill—giving as his excuse that he was leaving for Normandy just after noon. Butcher noted: "Perhaps the air is ganging up on Ike before he sees the P.M." Trying to figure things out, he recalled that Eisenhower had written a generous letter to Sir Charles Portal a few days before, praising Leigh-Mallory; the air chief marshal, he said, had turned out all right and was a good cooperator, with a fighting heart. In general he wanted to withdraw any implication of doubt which he had expressed in preinvasion days to Portal about the controversial air chief marshal.

After these anxious visits, Eisenhower drove up from Portsmouth to Bushy Park, then into London for lunch at 10 Downing Street. He pleaded with Churchill to "persuade Monty to get on his bicycle and start moving." Churchill sent for Brooke and told him the Supreme Commander had complained about "your Monty's" stickiness and the reaction in the American newspapers—in particular about the grisly taunt that Montgomery was sparing British forces at the expense of the Americans, who were having all the casualties. Kay Summersby afterward told her diary: "[Eisenhower] discussed Monty's progress in France. The P.M. is most anxious to attack all along the front." Later she added, "E. has a conference with Tedder and Leigh-Mallory; the two air officers don't get along too well, but E. seems to always get them together." When Everett Hughes cornered him later, Eisenhower was brooding. "I am just a messenger boy between Tedder and Leigh-Mallory," he said.

Afterward Eisenhower wrote to Montgomery: "I reported to him [Churchill] your general plan for continuing attack in the Eastern Sector and he was delighted to know that you will have attacks on both flanks in that sector supporting the main effort down the middle. . . . He was very pleased. He repeated over and over again that he knew you understood the necessity for 'keeping the front aflame' while major attacks were in progress." He added reproachfully, "My news this evening on Bradley's attack is very sketchy and I have none at all on what is going on in the Second Army front."

McNair's death faced Eisenhower with unusual problems. It threatened to blow wide open the Fortitude deception scheme at a precarious moment. Ultra had shown that German intelligence had now identified in Normandy some units previously believed to be part of "Patton's army group" waiting in England to invade the Pas-de-Calais; as a result, two German divisions appeared to be moving down from that area to help the defenders in Normandy. For a while longer the secrecy was maintained. McNair's body was taken to be buried among the GIs, with no special ceremony. Marshall notified Eisenhower that not even the next of kin were being informed of McNair's death. McNair's pilot, however, had told many people in Washington the facts, and two days later it was announced that McNair had been "killed in Normandy by enemy action."

The death of McNair, one of the U.S. Army's most illustrious officers, led to an anguished Air Force inquest. With Bradley, Spaatz checked out the whole air support operation for Cobra. Doolittle presented the resulting bomb grid, showing where each of his 1,500 heavy bombers had unloaded. Spaatz glanced at it and could see that about sixty of the heavies had dropped short—but that was what he had warned Bradley, before the attack, to expect. Spaatz commented in his diary that these losses were less than might have been anticipated, given the conditions.

Others did not see it his way. Bedell Smith told Doolittle on July 27 that what was needed to correct "deficiencies" in bombing for ground support was "a commander who views that support sympathetically." The jibe seemed to be aimed at Spaatz. Vandenberg, who got to hear of it that day, noted: "Maybe Smith was egged on by [the] C-in-C [Leigh-Mallory] who resents [the] loss of control over the heavies."

One American could no longer stand the strain of working with the difficult Leigh-Mallory—Vandenberg's senior staff officer, Brigadier General Frederic Smith. He appeared to be suffering something like a nervous breakdown. Spaatz arranged to relieve him without prejudice and send him home. "He has been so upset over the C-in-C's personality and operational methods that this seemed to be the last straw," Vandenberg wrote in his diary on August 1.

Eisenhower stayed in London, braving the hail of flying bombs. During a letter to Mamie, he observed: "Up to this point I've been interrupted four times. First, an emergency conference with three generals on air problems. Second: a secretary with letters to sign to two commanders. Third: a telephone call from P.M. Just now: a date to decorate a general with Legion of Merit. This shows you what a slow business it is for me to write a longhand letter." There was cheering news about Cobra. Montgomery sent a triumphant message to Brooke: "The main blow of the whole Allied plan has now been struck on the western flank; that blow is the foundation of all our operations and it has been well and truly struck." On July 27 they all dined with Churchill—Brooke, Eisenhower, and Bedell Smith—and Brooke offered to go over to Normandy if necessary to assist Eisenhower in handling the testy British commander. He took pains to explain Montgomery's strategy of unbalancing the enemy in language that Eisenhower was able to understand, and wrote in his diary afterward, not without justification, "It is equally clear that Ike knows nothing about strategy. Bedell Smith, on the other hand, has brains, but no military education in its true sense. He is certainly one of the best American officers, but still falls far short when it comes to strategic outlook." Brooke put his finger on a basic element of Eisenhower's misconception. He evidently had some idea of attacking—or "engaging the enemy," as he called it—along the whole front. He wrote to warn Montgomery, "Unfortunately this same policy . . . is one that appeals to the P.M. Ike may, therefore, obtain some support in this direction." Over in France, this worried Montgomery—he remembered Bedell Smith once comparing Eisenhower to a football coach: "He's up and down the line all the time, encouraging everybody to get on with the game." That, reflected Montgomery, was a doctrine which could prove very expensive in human life.

Eisenhower returned to SHAEF after dinner vaguely pleased with the result of his top-level lobbying. Feeling that he had Churchill behind him, he sent a message to Montgomery, which he described to Kay Summersby as "very strong." The next day she wrote: "Message from Monty, he is fully prepared to go ahead."

The Germans knew what was at stake now at Saint-Lô. They knew that the Americans were within an ace of breaking right through and opening out into France and they fought fanatically to prevent it. The 2nd Armored Division alone estimated it had killed 1,500 German troops. Across the cratered countryside, now littered with the stinking, bloated carcasses of thousands of cattle slain in the bombing, the American troops advanced. The breakthrough was cleaner than they had hoped, and at noon on July 27 Bradley changed the orders: both Collins and Middleton were to push their corps through the gap toward Avranches, a little town on the coast, just above the Breton peninsula.

On July 28, as Bradley's tanks began rolling, Montgomery, anxious not to be upstaged or to appear laggard, sent this message to Eisenhower: "I have ordered Dempsey to throw all caution overboard, and to take any risks he likes, and to accept any casualties, and to step on the gas for Vire." It was an unfortunate choice of words, because Bedell Smith jumped on that word *caution,* taking it as an admission. Now at last, he later wrote, Eisenhower's insistence on all-out attack, east as well as west, was clearly being accepted "by all"—implying even by Montgomery.

After the breakout at Saint-Lô there was no stopping Bradley. Late on the afternoon of July 28 he called in his corps commanders and issued orders for the second phase, the exploitation. He was aware that the enemy was rushing forward reinforcements but he was confident he could smash them too. "As you can see," he wrote to Eisenhower, "we are feeling pretty cocky."

On July 30, for the first time in months, Eisenhower slept late. It was a sure sign that he regarded the Normandy crisis as past. He had decided to keep Patton's presence on French soil a secret a while longer. The man's name was like fresh dynamite, and he wanted the Nazis still to expect the dynamite to hit them in Calais.

CHAPTER EIGHTEEN

Something Spectacular

THE DYNAMITE was right there in the Cotentin peninsula. It was George S. Patton, Jr., at his reckless, thrustful best, believing in the protection of a divine hand, thinking himself immortal, piloting his own Cub three hundred feet above the lines, marching shoulder to shoulder with his infantry, halting to pry fearful GIs out of their "tomb-like slit trenches" and harry them into battle, profaning craven junior officers who had removed their insignia and covered their helmet markings so that they would not be called upon to lead their troops into battle, cussing out colonels for not pressing their men on, chivvying on generals to reconnoiter the battle areas in person. It was Patton, grabbing his binoculars and fixing them on the distant figures of enemy soldiers scurrying like ants across a hillside, and summoning fire against them.

Patton savored the moment when the world would learn that he was

231

here and hoped it would be soon. He was about to score a great victory. Of that he was certain. He was peaking, like a sprinter before the Olympics. "The lambent flame of my own self-confidence burns ever brighter," he wrote in his diary. And to his wife: *"L'audace, l'audace, toujours l'audace!* . . . When I eventually emerge it will be quite an explosion."

His frame of mind was clearly evident in two remarks he made at this time to the VII Corps commander. "You know, Collins," he said, "you and I are the only people around here who seem to be enjoying this goddamned war!" Then his face clouded momentarily. Obviously he was thinking of that slapping incident in Sicily and his other missteps. "But I'm in the doghouse, I'm in the doghouse! I got to do something spectacular!"

But the spectacle could not yet be a public one. Since McNair's death had decapitated the revised Fortitude deception plan, it was imperative that the Germans should not know that Patton was now in France. "Patton's army and the American army group will begin functioning the day after tomorrow, August 1," Eisenhower notified General Marshall by cable. "In the interest of cover and deception there will be *no* announcement of this for some time. In due course an appropriate statement will be issued."

By coincidence, on August 1 the command structure in Normandy was reorganized. Bradley stepped up to command an American 12th Army Group, composed essentially of Patton's Third Army and Hodges's First. Until the end of the month, however, for the sake of transition, Montgomery would continue to exert overall control. The American generals looked forward to the day when Omar Bradley alone would command them. Montgomery, for his part, used venomous language about them in a letter on August 2 to Sir James Grigg, who had evidently warned him to tread carefully in attacking his critics. "A good 'lash-out' all round is an excellent thing," wrote Montgomery, and he added mysteriously, "What we really need is an extensive use of weed-killer; we would then progress rapidly towards the end of the war."

For all his poisonous feelings, Montgomery was quietly satisfied that the campaign was now proceeding as he had always planned it. From the Ultra intercepts, he knew that Cobra had truly breached the German lines. His plan to hold the main enemy armor at the Caen sector, so that the defenses facing the Americans at Saint-Lô would be weakened, had been vindicated. Now would begin the mighty right hook into Brittany, and into France itself.

Shortly after temporarily laying aside his letter about "weed-killer," Montgomery picked up his pen and resumed it. "Here," he wrote, "the broad basic plan, on which we have been working for so many weeks, is now unfolding in the exact way in which it was intended. This is very gratifying. There were some difficult moments; that must always happen in battles, and it takes a little time to get the enemy where you want him so that you can hit him a colossal crack *somewhere else*. It was the same at El Alamein. And it is at that time that the commanders in the field want to be supported and encouraged, and the soldier's morale kept high. [But] in this case it was *at that time* that the press began a campaign which might have done great harm. This is one great battle, directed by one commander," he went on, "and designed to produce a great dividend. But one cannot tell them what you are trying to do, or how the battle is being forced to swing; the need for secrecy is too great. However, we are off now and I think the Boche will find it very difficult to stop us from bringing the full plan into effect, i.e., the swing of the right flank right up to Paris and pushing the enemy armies up against the Seine between Paris and the sea. And while this is going on we open up Brittany."

Now that the point of the American dagger had pierced the German lines, it was time to begin twisting the blade: Hodges was ordered to shift his thrust to the southeast, and to his right Patton began his advance. It was noon, August 1. Patton's Third Army now officially existed. His long, confidence-threatening wait since Sicily was over.

There had been times when he doubted if he would ever see war again. His best friend, Everett Hughes, wrote to Beatrice on August 2, "I have insisted for months that George keep his shirt on. For months and months I have stood up for him and his staff against *everybody*. I have succeeded in getting George into the fight at a time when we needed fighters. . . . I was fearful that he had been cowed by the fools who didn't realize that a fighter couldn't be a saint or a psychiatrist when the job was to kill Germans. Or cowed by those who didn't like pearl handled pistols, or fancy uniforms, or all the little idiosyncrasies that are George."

For the last four days of July, George had already been drilling through the crumbling German defenses, his two armored divisions plunging south, taking Coutances and then Avranches. The breach at Avranches was awfully narrow, but the armor pistoned through the bottleneck and burst out into Brittany, one division making for Rennes, the other for Brest.

By August 2, it was clear that Patton's armor was on a rampage. Before lunch, Eisenhower called out to Butcher: "If Ultra is right, we are to hell and gone in Brittany and slicing 'em up in Normandy!" There was an arrow on the map in the war room. It showed that Patton had already reached Rennes twelve hours earlier. Everett Hughes glowed with pride, again reflecting that it was he who had rescued Patton from the military trash can. The next day he wrote in his scrappy notebook: "Ike's two trips to France to burn up Brad . . . are paying good dividends in the way of an advance. Maybe he believed me when I said he had too many complacent generals." He added, "Geo is in Rennes: *'I have won the war.'* "

Patton raced on, heedless of his ever-lengthening flanks. Speaking a month later to newspaper correspondents, he would lightly dismiss the risk he had taken: "I have always been considered a damn fool and I still am. . . . I never worried about flanks. That was probably due to my long-felt masculine virility." Now, after weeks of stalemate, he was spearheading the drive into open France, sweeping around the Allied flank. Le Mans fell on August 8, and Patton—reluctantly, because he was greedy for ground—began to turn in to the north, closing the net on two German armies. Immense losses were being inflicted on them —the Fifth Panzer and the Seventh—but still no general retreat had begun. That, however, was just the way that Montgomery wanted it. The longer the Germans fought back, the more certainly they would fall into his net.

The success of the American operations, especially their bold thrust to the coast at Avranches, and the comparative slowness of the British operations left a sour taste in England. There was little in the news bulletins about Montgomery and the British and Canadian forces. For Britons, it was hard to take. One incident spoke for many. General J.C.H. Lee had established at Little Compton Manor in the Cotswolds, west of Oxford, a rest home for American officers—it had already handled 1,500 of them, six at a time, at American government expense.

Lady Alexandra Metcalfe, who owned and ran it, was half-American herself. But the news bulletins, day after day, spoke only of American army triumphs. On the last day of July, as the news of the American coup at Avranches was broadcast, she could stand it no longer. Without a word of apology to the American officers listening, she reached out and switched off the radio. Enough was enough.

Something of this anti-American resentment was overtaking Montgomery too. It did not escape him that now that the Americans had achieved their great breakthrough, the part that his strategy and determination had played in it was being overlooked. His irritability increased. He shouted at a British lieutenant general to clear out of his area, saying roughly, "I don't want to see your face." He also inflicted his feelings upon Captain William Culver, an American attached to his staff; Culver told Harry Butcher that his life in the British camp had become a misery for him. Montgomery never even invited him to dine at his mess.

Adolf Hitler, his body still torn and bruised from the assassin's bomb planted in his headquarters two weeks before, his brain still reeling from the shock and treachery of it all, knew what was at stake. Unlike his myopic generals, he knew how vital the possession of France was to his long-term strategy. He needed French airspace for the defense of Germany. He needed the submarine bases in Brittany for his new super type XXI and XXIII U-boats—submarines capable of traveling from Germany to Japan without surfacing. He needed the raw materials of France, he needed the French coastal waters to bring home the blockade runners, but above all he needed time—time to get the squadrons of astounding new Messerschmitt jet aircraft into service. Besides, if northern France were lost, he could no longer hurl his V-weapons against England. France was vital, worth taking the most momentous risks for. He had taken such risks in 1940, and they had paid off.

Unknown to Hitler, the similarity ended there. In May 1940, the Allies had not possessed the Ultra code-breaking organization that they now did at Bletchley Park, west of London.

On July 28, the Allies had learned from prisoners of war that Rommel had been seriously wounded by aircraft attack on his car; his place had been taken by another field marshal, Günther-Hans von Kluge. On August 2, Hitler ordered Kluge to counterattack savagely, to ram four

Panzer divisions across the breach that gaped from Mortain to the coast at Avranches, thus cutting off the long finger that Patton was thrusting with. With luck, Kluge might turn the whole American line. He might rout the entire Allied force—might Dunkirk them, as they had in 1940.

For the first days the German messages went by land line, and the Allies intercepted none of them. Then, on the evening of August 6, Ultra picked up radio signals that provided the first explicit indications that Hitler was planning a serious counterattack. That evening, word went out from England to the various Allied army headquarters that the Nazis were requesting night fighter protection for an attack by the 2nd SS Panzer Division through Mortain southwestward toward Saint-Hilaire. Since Mortain had just come into American hands, this meant that a counterattack was developing. Half an hour later a further Ultra signal went out, referring to an attack by no less than four Panzer divisions. Thus forewarned, the Americans were able to move their forces to thwart the German attack.

Patton, only just initiated in the wonders of Ultra, was skeptical. He wrote in his diary: "We got a rumor last night from a secret source that several panzer divisions will attack west from . . . Mortain . . . on Avranches. Personally, I think it is a German bluff to cover a withdrawal, but I stopped the 80th, French 2nd Armored, and 35th [divisions] in the vicinity of Saint Hilaire just in case something might happen." Forewarned by Ultra, the Allies had infantry and aircraft at just the right place, and the counterattack was demolished.

In July, General Marshall had informed Eisenhower that Henry Morgenthau, Jr., Secretary of the Treasury, and a party of experts were planning a trip to investigate currency problems in France. Eisenhower had sighed and replied that there was nothing to be learned in the little strip of land which his armies then controlled, "which is divided about equally between fighting fronts and a solid line of depots, with two main lateral roads completely filed with double columns of motor transport." Privately he added that these VIP trips were a pain in the neck. There just was not the space for visitors: Bradley's only guest accommodation consisted of one extra trailer and a couple of Jeeps, while Montgomery "usually simply refuses to see unwelcome visitors." He could hardly have made himself plainer. But Morgenthau had Roosevelt's ear and he was a powerful figure, so Eisenhower had no choice but to humor him.

Bedell Smith had secured for Morgenthau's son a comfortable army appointment near him, and the son was present when Morgenthau stepped off the C-54 at Prestwick on August 6. (There was to be "no mention whatsoever, at any time, about his son nor photographs including his son," Morgenthau's aide had stipulated.) Morgenthau's advisor, Dr. Harry Dexter White, was also in the party. They could not have picked a worse day for their visit—Hitler's counterattack against Patton and Bradley began during the night. They lunched with Eisenhower the next day at his Portsmouth command post. Kay Summersby eavesdropped and noted afterward: "Secretary Morgenthau and party for lunch. Quite concerned about post war policies in Germany and particularly anxious that we do not establish rates of exchange that might favour Germany." Morgenthau was proposing to inflict a punitive rate of exchange on Germany which would bankrupt it for all time, rendering it unable to rise again and make another war. This prompted the Supreme Commander to enlarge on his own views about the enemy, which he himself later quoted as follows: "The German people must not be allowed to escape a personal sense of guilt. . . . Germany's warmaking power should be eliminated. . . . Certain groups should be specifically punished. . . . The German General Staff should be utterly eliminated. All records destroyed and individuals scattered and rendered powerless to operate as body." Then he bade farewell to Morgenthau and thought no more of him. His hospitality was ill repaid. One month later, Morgenthau would put to Churchill and Roosevelt his notorious plan for the destruction of Germany's heavy industry and the chastisement of its citizens. The plan attracted worldwide opprobrium. In his own defense Morgenthau published a book, and in it he attributed the plan's origin to this lunchtime discussion with Eisenhower. Eisenhower did not forgive him for this breach of privacy and misrepresentation. In subsequent years Morgenthau often invited him to attend important functions, but Eisenhower always expressed his regrets.

On the afternoon of August 7—an hour after the departure of the Morgenthau party—Eisenhower flew over to France. A new headquarters had been found for him in Normandy, near Tournières. The site was in an orchard strewn with inedible green apples, a comfortable little cluster of trailers and tents—"near the spot where you and I camped with General Bradley," he wrote to his son a few days later. Harry Butcher wrote: "I am living in a tent with a straw carpet for a floor and liking it. . . . We have the peppiest little black tomcat you can imagine. Air Chief Marshal Tedder gave him to Eisenhower, who named him Shaef. Then we have at the camp a fine, tan colored cocker spaniel who belongs to Larry Hanson, the General's pilot. His name is Monty, meaning General Montgomery. . . . Shaef has no truck with Monty. He chases Monty away. Just now Monty was sniffing under the chair where Shaef was taking a sun bath. Suddenly Shaef jumped up, and out, and struck poor Monty on the nose. He was hurt, more so in his pride than in his smeller. . . .

"We are also going to have a cow. Ike has ordered one and insists it must give at least three gallons of milk a day. . . . Now the question is who will do the milking. He has suggested that this should be a responsibility of his naval aide, but I told him the navy gets its milk in cans."

Eisenhower's first visitor was his old West Point classmate Leroy Watson. He had been commander of the 3rd Armored Division but had fumbled his part of the fight for Avranches, and Eisenhower had busted him to colonel.

"We're going to send you back home," Eisenhower now told him.

"The hell you are!" Wap Watson replied. "I came over here to fight. I can fight just as good as a colonel as I could as a general. Give me a colonel's command."

Eisenhower, impressed, assigned him to a vacancy in the 29th Division. He told Kay Summersby: "I'm sure he'll come up again." Pretty soon Watson had earned his star back.

After a while Eisenhower drove down to Bradley's command post, which was now south of Saint-Jean-de-Daye. He wanted to have a look at the Cobra bombing area, and he passed not far from where McNair had been torn apart by American bombs. Every village he saw was badly battered with no sign of civilian life at all. Coutances showed heavy bomb damage. Montgomery was at Bradley's command post that afternoon, too, and assured Eisenhower that the Canadian attack southward from Caen was going well. Now it was Eisenhower who could take the initiative. He wanted Bradley to order Patton to wheel to the northeast now, the better to hound the enemy into a great pocket. The object, he said, was to destroy enemy forces, not gain territory. Bradley pointed out to Montgomery that the enemy could be encircled by Patton and Hodges from the south, and by the British and Canadian armies from the north. Montgomery agreed. The jaws of this giant pincer should meet at a little town called Falaise, about twenty miles south of Caen.

They discussed, too, the Nazi counterattack toward Avranches. It had begun during the night. The 30th Infantry Division had caught the full blow. There was unhurried discussion of how much strength to divert to meet this enemy threat and how much to push on through the gap, because the more, the better the chance of completing the encirclement from the south. Bradley decided that three divisions would be enough to deal with the counterattack, and rushed everything else south. Eisenhower agreed. While Tedder looked on approvingly, he assured Bradley that even if the enemy should get through to the coast and cut off the American thrust temporarily, he could supply two thousand tons a day by air. Their attitude was one of pure sangfroid. After all, they knew all Kluge's plans from Ultra. By now the 2nd SS Panzer Division had overrun Mortain and was engulfing the 30th Infantry Division, but they could not dislodge seven hundred men defending one particular hill, Hill 317; and artillery observers stationed on that hilltop were able to direct accurate gunfire onto the tanks below.

The war news on August 7 was dramatic. One corps of Patton's army was barging into Brittany with orders to take Brest; the other was swinging east to start the encircling motion toward Falaise. Yet nobody knew that he was in command. Butcher pleaded with Eisenhower that the time had come to release Patton's name to the world, to prove that Eisenhower had been right all along about Patton. Eisenhower shook his head. "Why should I tell the enemy?" he said.

Hughes had flown to France that day too. From the air, he could see the congestion on the roads, the bomb craters, and the shimmering dust cloud a mile high marking the terrain over which the American troops were advancing. The rains had gone, the weather had turned hot and dry. As luck would have it, none other than J.C.H. Lee was at the wheel of the car that was to take him to Patton. Lee drove at a crazy speed, and Hughes could only hold on with one hand and clutch his helmet with the other. Lee dropped off Hughes at Patton's command post, then roared off down the road. Hughes stepped into Patton's sleeping truck, which had been converted from an obsolete truck body. It had its own washstand, wardrobe, desk, map board, and 110-volt circuit. Patton showed him on a map how he was harrying his armored divisions south.

"One should never penalize a commander for making mistakes due to audacity," was his dictum, "but only for failing to take risks."

Hughes liked being with Patton, but on this occasion he found him edgy, perhaps because of a letter from Mrs. Patton, received a few days before. She had learned that Jean Gordon was in England, several thousand miles closer to her "Uncle Georgie" than she was, and had written to fire a shot across his bows. Patton had evasively replied: "The first I knew about Jean's being here was in your letter. We are in the middle of a battle so [we] don't meet people. So don't worry."

Hughes was able to jot a good deal of vintage Patton into his diary. Once Patton squeaked to him: "Strategy? Strategy is finding a sonofabitch whom you rank and telling him to take a place. And relieving him if he doesn't!" In another mood Patton made a remark which showed he had not lost his humanity. He had just called for saturation bombing raids on Brest and Saint-Nazaire—where tough Nazi troops were still denying these Atlantic ports to Eisenhower's troop convoys and supplies; now he turned to Hughes and commented soberly, "I have sealed the fate of a lot of French civilians." On August 10, Hughes scribbled words that were characteristic of the whole George Patton saga—the general was after all at the height of his rampage across France behind the German lines—"Geo still romping around."

A bit farther down the page, Hughes made the delicious inscription: "Jean Gordon off to France. [That] will please 'Uncle' Geo."

At midday on August 9, Eisenhower flew back to England from France—thanks to the inefficiency of the chief signals officer, one William S. Rumbaugh, his advanced headquarters there had virtually no communications facilities. He went to Bushy Park and spent the afternoon. The battle was going well, but he was not in a good mood. General Betts was waiting for him with more murder and rape cases. Almost as bad, he was taking long-range flak from Mamie about his secretaries. Eisenhower fired back at her a letter caustic enough to have rusted stainless steel: "I'm a bit puzzled over your outburst about me sending messages via aides and secretaries," he scrawled. "Naturally I cannot go to telegraph offices myself whenever the spirit might move me. Sometimes, over miles of bad telephone cable I dictate a short message to you with instructions it is to be placed on teletype at once. Naturally also it is an aide or a secretary that has to do the mechanical

part of the transaction. To save me I can see nothing wrong in this—
if there is then I'll just have to send messages when I get back to Main
headquarters which is infrequently."

He also saw Hughes, himself returned from France. He had phoned
Hughes to beg him not to get into anybody's hair during his coming
visit to the United States, where he was to check on the American end
of the unsatisfactory supplies organization. Hughes had assured him
that he was working *for* him and would do nothing to promote dishar-
mony—such as referring to Eisenhower's constant feuding with Lee
and the other generals on the supply side. "I appreciate the problem,"
Hughes had said, "and promise I'll not muddy any waters." Now,
before bidding Hughes farewell, Eisenhower again begged him to keep
his lips sealed in Washington.

At four-thirty he went to see Churchill, who was, in Butcher's words,
"still a bit pouty over [Anvil], still favoring diversion into Brittany."
Churchill's behavior these days was most odd. Montgomery too had
noticed something wrong with him when he spent the day with Churchill two days before, and had sent an agitated letter to Sir James Grigg.
"The P.M. visited me yesterday," he wrote. "He struck me as looking
an old man and tired and seemed to find it difficult to concentrate on
a subject for more than a few moments. He seemed restless, and unable
to make his mind up about anything."

"The war," continued Montgomery in the same letter, "is in a very
interesting state here; there are distinct chances of a good cop." This
was English understatement. Patton's army was cutting ahead fast.
Cooperation between his tanks and the tactical air force was outstanding, and when Spaatz and Tedder visited him on August 9 he sang loud
praises of the airmen. Both Patton and Bradley stated that the speed
of advance was due to the air preparation and particularly to the
excellent contact between the fighter planes and the ground column,
thanks to static-free VHF radio, a splendid device introduced by enter-
prising young Quesada. Patton was optimistic, though he did have one
complaint: Bradley had now ordered him to swing in to the northeast,
closing the net. Patton still felt he should be casting his net wider. He
told Spaatz that he felt he was cutting in too close. He would have
preferred to continue on the line to Paris and Berlin.

As for the other arm of the pincer, things were proceeding less
swimmingly. On August 5, there had been bombing operations in front

of the Canadian forces, to help them on their way. Vandenberg and Spaatz had balked at the idea of using American heavy bombers, and perhaps the British were just as glad; the Eighth and Ninth Air Forces had caused so many casualties to friendly troops now that they were sometimes referred to as the Eighth and Ninth Luftwaffe. RAF and RCAF bombers executed the mission; ironically, they inflicted quite a few casualties upon the Canadian troops. However, Montgomery firmly believed that the heavy bombardment had been essential. "To have attempted such a breakthrough without such preparation," he told Tedder and Spaatz, "would have cost me ten thousand men."

On August 7 the Allied attempt to encircle and smash the entire German army in France began in earnest, as the Canadian army started to extend the northern pincer. It jumped off southward down the road from Caen to Falaise with massed tanks and artillery. The attack made slow progress; much enemy strength was still present there. Yet the attackers remained confident. At a press conference at Montgomery's headquarters, de Guingand and the Canadian army commander, Crerar, stated that the war would be over in three weeks. Butcher told Eisenhower of that wild boast, so detached from any reality; Eisenhower regretted it, but there was little he could do.

That first night the British bombers battered the flanks, and the next day the Eighth Air Force sent strategic bombers in to flatten the area ahead of the thrust. Unfortunately two American bomber groups carved another bloody swathe among the Canadians.

In the five minutes between the end of the bombing and the renewal of the thrust, the Germans recovered their senses. In the next three days the Canadian attack advanced only eight miles, falling some distance short of their stop line—Falaise. That left a gap, one that would prove serious when the other arm of the pincer, the U.S. forces, came up to Falaise from the south. This latter movement was making great strides. Patton's presence was still blanketed in total silence, and his frustrated officers were convinced that this was a dark SHAEF plot to rob him of his triumph. But Eisenhower's attitude continued to be "Why should I tell the enemy?"

By late on August 9, the Nazi counterattack by four Panzer divisions toward Avranches had been defeated. Eisenhower knew—through Ultra—that great numbers of the German counterattackers were still massed in the area. He must send Patton under and around them quickly if they were to be trapped. For this, he urgently needed troops. "We are hurrying forward into the battle every unit as rapidly as it can arrive at the beach," he told Marshall. "Patton, Bradley and Montgomery are all imbued with this necessity and alive to the opportunity. Patton has the marching wing which will turn in rather sharply to the north east from the general vicinity of Le Mans and just to the west thereof, marching toward Alençon and Falaise."

To Everett Hughes, Patton reiterated his complaint that too small a net was being cast for his liking. "We are attempting to encircle the Germans doughboy fashion," he said, "rather than cavalry fashion." He wanted to continue farther south before beginning his turning movement to encircle the enemy. The terrain farther south was better tank country.

By August 13, the loop around the German forces retreating from their bungled counterattack was neatly tied—nearly. Patton and Hodges were coming up fast from the south, while the Canadians were still hacking their way down from the north, toward Falaise and the assigned meeting place on the stipulated boundary between the British and American army group boundaries. Inside the pocket were the remains of the Fifth Panzer and the Seventh Army. But the gap was still open between Argentan and Falaise and enemy troops were beginning to escape.

Patton was frantic. He began commandeering J.C.H. Lee's supply trucks as soon as they reached his army, loading them with troops, and rushing them forward to complete the encirclement. He boasted to Lee that all Eisenhower had to do was change the boundary; then he could push on north and take Falaise himself. Under its own momentum, Patton's XV Corps did in fact cross the boundary. Bradley's chief of staff, Leven C. Allen, telephoned a warning to Patton to halt at the agreed line. The risk of accidental clash between the two pincer arms was too great. And quite apart from safety considerations, normal courtesy left Bradley no choice. He had to wait until Montgomery sent a formal invitation to the Americans to continue the advance.

Patton telephoned Bradley's headquarters back, protesting that it was perfectly feasible for him to continue his thrust. Major General Allen repeated that Bradley's order was to halt on the line from Sées to Argentan and consolidate there. Unfortunately Montgomery issued no invitation, wrongly believing that the Canadians could more easily seal the gap from the north. Patton instantly suspected that Montgomery was behind the restraining order from Bradley and he put it down to "jealousy of the Americans or to utter ignorance of the situation."

"The XV Corps . . . has taken Alençon," Patton wrote in his diary on August 13, "and the Sées-Argentan line, and is in battle to the north. This corps could easily advance to Falaise and completely close the gap, but we have been ordered to halt because the British sowed the area between with a large number of time bombs [from the air]. I am sure that this halt is a great mistake, as I am certain that the British will not close on Falaise."

"Let me go on to Falaise," Patton told Bradley, "and we'll drive the British back into the sea for another Dunkirk!" Since Montgomery had been among those Dunkirked by Hitler in 1940, he was particularly stung to hear of that remark.

The next afternoon the Canadians began another big attack toward Falaise with four infantry and two armored divisions, called operation Tractable; once again the black-painted planes of the RAF Bomber Command were so dazzled by the unaccustomed daylight that they dumped many bomb loads upon the Canadian troops, killing a hundred of them.

Montgomery exulted to Sir James Grigg on August 14. "These are great days," he wrote, "and this week may well see great events. We have the great bulk of the German forces partially surrounded; some will of course escape, but I do not see how they can stand and fight seriously again this side of the Seine."

Many of the Germans did indeed escape, pouring through the quivering gap between the Canadians and the American XV Corps. Those who were too slow were finally trapped as the gap closed, and they were mangled by the massed artillery and bomber forces of the Allies. The losses inflicted on the Germans were such that Hitler had no hope of holding France with what remained. His disheveled army began retreating in disarray toward the German frontier and Belgium.

Bradley's halting of Patton's spearheads aroused controversy. But Bedell Smith would write, a year later, most fairly: "When two arms of a 'pincer' movement drive toward each other, there obviously comes a time when one or the other must halt, or one or both change direction if actual collision is to be avoided. In this case, the U.S. drive from the south through Argentan and Alençon was making speedy progress and cutting off or destroying many Germans. At Montgomery's headquarters it was realized that the possibility of collision was becoming imminent, and speedy coordinating action had to be taken. The decision was taken to stop the U.S. forces on the main east-west road, which Montgomery wished to assign to the right of the British forces as an axis of advance *across* the American front. Already there was considerable U.S. strength north of the road and everything had to stop in place. Guns could not fire; even though German columns were marching eastward across the U.S. front, Bradley, correctly, was adamant in refusing to let his forces get hopelessly entangled with the British and possibly, in the confusion of battle, actually engaged with them. The Supreme Commander was at Bradley's headquarters, and by personal decision upheld the wisdom of refusing to complicate the situation further by appeals to the 21st Army Group. Local commanders, on the spot, arranged to the best of their ability to act cooperatively as is necessary in the rapid pursuit of a routed enemy."

A few weeks after Falaise, the London *Daily Telegraph* published an interview with General Dempsey, commander of the British Second Army, in which he rather less fairly sought to blame the Americans for his slow pursuit of the enemy toward the Seine. "After the Germans' Falaise pocket disaster," he was quoted as saying, "I was forced to hold back our British Forces while the Americans, who had swung round the right flank, withdrew from my boundaries. . . . Eventually the Americans withdrew two divisions which had crossed my front before I could advance further. That delayed my forces for forty-eight hours. We made a crossing of the River Seine on August 26–27."

Reacting to Dempsey's charge, Bradley complained to Eisenhower. He pointed out that it was with Montgomery's specific approval that the American troops concerned, XV Corps, had advanced north as far as Argentan. A few days later Montgomery had urged the Americans to advance even farther north, to Chambois and Trun. "Dempsey," said Bradley, "knew of this move and jokingly stated he was going to beat us to Argentan." Collins's VII Corps by then had already arrived at the British-American boundary and had wanted to continue north. Bradley had halted Collins, and had told Hodges—Collins's superior—who had called him by telephone that night: "You cannot drive north without first getting permission from General Montgomery." The next day Montgomery had said that he thought it a good idea, and Collins had also pushed north of the Flers-Argentan road. Several days after Dempsey's remarks appeared in the London newspaper, Montgomery sent Bradley his profound apologies.

Now Eisenhower faced a duty which it took him pleasure to perform. The world had speculated on who was commanding the Third Army, which had performed this spectacular dash across France. He called a press conference, and announced that General Patton was that man— not left behind in England, but commanding an army, right out there in front. For Patton himself it was a moment that made all the months of humiliation and frustration since Sicily worthwhile. His name was in the headlines of every newspaper in the western world. Bradley too was proud of him. He would describe this general in these words: "Courageous, colorful, a great showman, sometimes shows anger too readily but really is very kind hearted, possesses high degree of leadership, bold in operations, has fine sense of feel of the battle, gets maximum out of his staff and achieves outstanding results, mentally and physically alert. One of our great combat leaders." It was an assessment which only Patton himself could have writ larger.

"General Patton's Third Army became operational just after the break-out at St. Lo," Bradley would recall in his same assessment. "The situation demanded bold action which would take advantage of the state of the disorganization of the German army. This ability to sense the nature of the resistance and act accordingly . . . was very ably furnished by General Patton. A more timid leader might have given the enemy time to reorganize. Throughout the remainder of the campaign he exhibited this bold leadership and ability to sense the strength of the enemy opposing him."

In his headquarters, far away in East Prussia, Hitler began to brood. Perhaps he would have time to reorganize after all. He pored over the maps, and began to think about the coming autumn, when the skies would close in and prevent the Allied air forces from bringing their crushing superiority to bear on his armies. When that time came, he would launch the mightiest counteroffensive that Europe had ever seen.

CHAPTER NINETEEN

Banging Away

THERE WAS no doubt about it: victory was in the air—a heady, danger-ous aroma which obscured all true realities. Sir Alan Brooke, writing in his diary on the first day of August, had reflected that it was the month which usually began wars, and he had asked himself rhetori-cally: "Wonder whether this one may look like finishing it instead?" On the next day he had written more soberly to General Henry Maitland Wilson, "It becomes evident that the Boche is beat on all fronts. . . . I certainly don't see him lasting another winter." Ultra's intercepts were confirming that glad prospect—reports of enemy tanks and equip-ment being written off, of casualties, of gasoline shortages—in short, of the Germans' hopeless situation. Exhilarated by the enemy collapse in France, Eisenhower advised the Combined Chiefs of Staff that he might be faced with the occupation of Germany sooner than expected. In the absence of any basic decisions as to zones of occupation, he hinted, he would push the three army groups into Germany shoulder to shoulder, with the British on the left.

By the middle of August the two unruly American armies were out in open France—Patton on the right, Hodges on the left. As Rommel had found in 1940, it was perfect tank terrain. The ground was hard, the sun shone, and great pillars of dust shimmered into the skies as the tanks and motor transport pounded forward in exhilarating pursuit. They rolled east with astounding speed. Soon the famous twin spires of the ancient cathedral of Chartres were glimpsed rising above the rolling plains of wheat. Soon they could be in Paris itself. Freed from the remorseless killing ground of Caen, the British Empire's armies could now turn to the northeast, to stamp out the V-weapon launching sites which had been tormenting London and to gain ports closer to Germany, ports vitally needed for what must surely be the last great offensive of the war.

On August 16, the Falaise slaughter was coming to an end. Kay Summersby, at Eisenhower's camp at Granville, wrote: "Canadian troops around Falaise. American troops enter Chartres. . . . The French report definite evidence of looting by our troops. A Brigadier-General is supposed to have taken a case full of silver. E. has given instructions that no statement of Patton's is to be published." Now that Patton's army was fighting forward, the Pentagon at last procured congressional permission for the permanent promotion of General Patton, which had been denied him in the wake of the ludicrous Knutsford speech affair.

In the United States, the announcement that Bradley had taken command of the 12th Army Group was greeted with satisfaction, but the agitation in the American press and particularly the *New York Times* grew when it became known that despite this, and even though Eisenhower had now moved his headquarters as Supreme Commander to French soil, the British general Montgomery was still in a position to dictate orders to Bradley. On August 18, Roosevelt was told by Morgenthau, who had returned from Europe, "The relationship between the American and British troops appeared to be good although there was a certain amount of talk as to why the British didn't get going and why we didn't have command of our own troops." General Marshall wrote a powerful message to Eisenhower saying that both he and Stimson felt that the time had come for him to assume what they called "direct exercise of command of the American contingent." Marshall added, "The astonishing success of the campaign up to the present moment has evoked emphatic expressions of confidence in you and in

Bradley." The Washington *Times-Herald* had printed a particularly
nettlesome story to the effect that Eisenhower was only a figurehead,
that all the commanders in chief were British, and, as Kay Summersby
quoted it in her diary, that "American generals had been demoted and
sent home but that a British general never was."

Visitors from Washington seemed to be permanently breathing down
Eisenhower's neck at his Normandy command post. On August 21 a
large party of Pentagon officials arrived for lunch with him, including
Stimson's undersecretary Robert P. Patterson and Lieutenant General
Brehon Somervell, the powerful U.S. Army supply chief. Somervell
later wrote an account in his diary: "Eisenhower very sanguine. Talked
of situation at front; also of his problems. Spoke of his trouble with
Churchill over Anvil plan." Afterward the visitors flew to see Patton.
"Patton's Hq near Brou," noted Somervell. "He is in trucks, parked in
a forest. Full of life, banging away. . . . Says he can have Paris for the
asking. . . . Wants to go straight through to Germany without stopping.
Has been three days ahead of Germans all along and wants to push as
fast as he can, before they can organize in front of him. Has no worry
about supply. Certain that he will go fast unless higher command stops
him. No worry about flanks. Has Germans on the run. Showed figures
on his casualties and Germans'—12,000 to 120,000." The next day, as
he left, Somervell summarized his impressions: "The commanders are
first-rate—Eisenhower, Bradley, Hodges and Patton." Somervell predicted that by bold action they could penetrate Germany by October
1 and finish the war in Europe. "The job now," concluded Somervell,
"is swift pursuit. Patton has the right idea—straight ahead, and let the
air forces take care of the flanks."

Montgomery, however, had ideas of his own. He too had victory
fever. On August 21 he issued one of his rare personal messages to his
troops, offering high praise for the brave fighting qualities of the Americans. "We never want to fight alongside better soldiers," he declared,
adding with reference to the recent inter-Allied squabbling, "but surely
it matters little who did *this* or *that.*" The Lord Mighty in Battle had
given them victory, said Montgomery: "The end of the war is in sight;
let us finish off the business in record time." Such exuberant remarks
were bound to introduce a damaging sense of euphoria. And indeed,
through that autumn the generals mindlessly squandered the chance for
early victory which the generals themselves had won.

On August 22 Eisenhower announced that he would assume the supreme command over both army groups from September 1. He would soon have to make up his mind on a directive to the army groups, on how he wanted them to deliver the coup de grace to Germany. But he had never been a battlefield commander; he was essentially a staff officer, preoccupied with logistics problems. He was not always flexible enough to recognize new opportunity when he saw it. Thus when Montgomery raised the specific plan for a single northern thrust via the Pas-de-Calais and the Low Countries into Germany's vitals, Eisenhower at first rejected it—because engaging the enemy all along the front was becoming a dogma for him, and for reasons of national pride. He wanted to give American troops a slice of the victory pie.

The row over this future strategy had begun to brew the day before —when Montgomery's chief of staff arrived to inform Eisenhower that his general wanted some American divisions placed under his command, to enable him to continue the northern thrust. The next day Montgomery himself wrote Eisenhower, stating quite simply that the quickest way to win the war was to advance northward, clear the coast as far as Antwerp, establish a powerful air force in Belgium, then advance into the Ruhr. Reminding Eisenhower, immodestly, that the great victory so far had been won by "personal command," Montgomery continued: "This is a *whole time* job for one man." He left no doubt whom he meant by that. He invited Eisenhower to come and discuss future strategy with him.

General Patton heard of Montgomery's plan when he visited Bradley the next day, August 23, to plead for two extra divisions for his eastward push to the Siegfried Line, the fortifications on the German border. He found Bradley about to leave to go see Eisenhower and Montgomery. Bradley told him that if Montgomery had his way, the Third Army would have to drive on as best it could with such resources —ammunition and gasoline—as remained. "He was quite worried," noted Patton later, "as he feels that Ike won't go against Monty and that the American Armies will have to turn in whole or in part [to support Montgomery]. . . . Bradley was madder that I have ever seen him and wondered aloud, 'what the Supreme Commander amounted to.' " The more Patton looked at the map, the less he liked Montgomery's plans. "I cannot understand why Monty keeps on asking for all four Armies in the Calais area and then [for a move] through Belgium, where the tanks are practically useless now [because of the numerous waterways] and will be wholly useless this winter. Unfortunately," noted Patton in disgust, "he has some way of talking Ike into his own way of thinking."

For a while Patton toyed with the idea of quitting. He suggested to Bradley that he, Hodges, and Patton should all threaten to resign; then Eisenhower would have to give way. Bradley offered a lame excuse which did not persuade Patton. "I feel that in such a showdown," Patton wrote, "we would win, as Ike would not dare to relieve us."

On the 23rd, Eisenhower drove over to see Montgomery, having first asked Bedell Smith to come over from England and meet him there. Montgomery, however, insisted that Bedell Smith should not be present, but he was. Montgomery told Eisenhower candidly that it would be a mistake for him to assume command of the land battle—as Eisenhower was planning to do at the beginning of September. "The Supreme Commander," he said, "must sit on a very lofty perch in order to be able to take a detached view of the whole intricate problem—which involves land, sea, air, civil control, political problems." He insisted that the land battle should be placed either in his hands or in Bradley's.

Montgomery then heaped criticisms on Eisenhower's broad-front strategy; he demanded that Hodges' First Army should be given to him for the big northern offensive into Germany he was planning, and that all supplies for Patton should be cut off in his favor. "Monty is being difficult about future plans," Kay Summersby observed, "wants about ten American divisions to help him in the Pas de Calais area. E. is going to give him five and no more." The disadvantages of a concerted northern thrust were as obvious to the Americans as the advantages were plain to the British. The enemy might amass a striking force and lunge into Montgomery's exposed flank; that might with one stroke convert the war situation. Ever the conciliator, Eisenhower reflexively began factoring all these pressures—from Montgomery as well as from Bradley and the turbulent American generals—in order to arrive at the algebraic sum thereof. The result was the customary Eisenhower compromise. It was a directive so wooly that Bradley and Montgomery each thought it had unduly favored the other. It would give Montgomery the task of operating to the northeast and "pushing forward to get a secure base at Antwerp." Hodges would be directed to thrust forward on Montgomery's left, his principal mission being to support Montgomery's advance. But the directive would still permit Bradley's army group to continue eastward.

Bradley was dubious about this plan, since it gave Montgomery the lion's share of the supplies; Patton was furious, and Hodges was also angry. His diary records on August 25 that he flew over for a morning conference with Bradley and Patton. "We are to strike northeast," the diary reads, "with the British taking care of the Crossbow [V-weapon] sites. . . . This is not a route which General Hodges wished to take, but at the time at least apparently there was nothing else politically to do."

On August 26, Montgomery wrote Grigg a crestfallen letter: "There have been some difficult times in this campaign; but I have always known that you and Brookie will stand firm as a rock behind us, and that knowledge has pulled me through. At the moment I fear that political and national considerations are influencing Eisenhower to take a course of action which is militarily unsound. I have tried hard to save the ship from going on the rocks and the compromise solution we have got will, I think, meet the case—because of the magnitude of the victory we have won."

Two days later the British Chiefs of Staff met. Sir Alan Brooke recorded that they argued about Eisenhower's strategy to split his vast force into two army groups, one heading southeast toward Nancy, the other northeast along the coast. For a commander to split his forces, Brooke felt, was basically unsound strategy and always had been. He angrily commented, "This plan is likely to add another three to six months on to the war." He decided to go and see Montgomery next day, and flew to Normandy. Montgomery—no doubt wishing him to see with his own eyes the injury he had inflicted on the enemy—insisted that Brooke drive forward, not fly, to headquarters.

The drive lasted three hours along rain-drenched roads that stank of horse cadavers—Chambois was a charnel house of broken tanks, trucks, carts, and dead pack animals. The enemy dead had been carted off for burial. Brooke had a long talk with Montgomery about Eisenhower and his willingness to let Montgomery have Hodges' First U.S. Army on his right, although it would remain under Bradley's orders. Brooke did not accept the concession as accomplished fact. "It remains to be seen," he said, "what political pressure is put on Eisenhower to move [the] Americans on [a] separate axis from the British."

On August 26 Eisenhower left his command post to see for himself the devastation at Falaise. After Falaise he set out on a circular trip. At Montgomery's headquarters near Gacé, the British commander told him that the best place to go and see damage was at the village of Aubry just south of Chambois. Gault wrote, "We were certainly not disappointed in the results, because the scene was one of masses of destroyed tanks, guns, transports and equipment of all sorts lying around, including many dead Germans and horses. The smell was tremendous. . . . This place was the point at which the Boche had tried to break out but had been caught by fighter bombers and fire from the V Corps." It was not an appetizing aspect. Kay Summersby wrote unemotionally that Saturday, "German dead were everywhere to be seen, especially at Chambois and Aubry. Horses and equipment were all mixed up. The stench was awful, the press who accompanied E. took numerous pictures."

Paris was about to yield to the Allies. The citizens had risen on August 19 and had made a deal with the Germans, allowing them to leave the city peacefully. De Gaulle's lieutenants were anxious that the political fruits should fall to them.

The next day Major General Jacques Philippe LeClerc, commanding the 2nd French Armored Division, arrived at General Hodges' First U.S. Army headquarters near Falaise at ten-thirty A.M., somewhat early for the one o'clock lunch to which he had been invited. "His arguments," recalled Hodges' diary, "which he presented incessantly, were to the effect that, roads and traffic and our plans notwithstanding, his division should run for Paris at once. He said he needed no maintenance, no more equipment, and that he was up to strength—and then, a few minutes later, admitted that he needed all three." The dour American general let LeClerc understand that he was to stay put until Hodges gave orders otherwise.

Eisenhower's plan was to bypass Paris to avoid delay, casualties, and injury to the city. This did not suit de Gaulle, who had arrived in France on August 20. Two days later he wrote to Eisenhower urging him to occupy Paris as soon as possible with French and Allied forces on account of the looting and rioting, "even if it should produce some fighting and some damage within the city." Shortly, Resistance leaders from Paris arrived with the same request. "E. does not want to take Paris," recorded Kay Summersby, "as it will take troops and supplies which we could use to defeat the Germans." He called a reluctant conference with Bradley, J.C.H. Lee, and the French generals to discuss the supply problem. Bradley argued that they were obliged to send troops into Paris, and Eisenhower had to agree.

Bradley raced by plane to First Army headquarters and told Hodges to occupy the city. Hodges recorded Bradley's message: "Paris, since Sunday noon, he said, had been under control of the [Gaullist] Free French Forces of the Interior which, after seizing the principal buildings of the city, had made a temporary armistice with the Germans, which was to expire Wednesday noon. General Bradley said that higher headquarters had decided that Paris could be avoided no longer, that entry of our forces was necessary in order to prevent possible heavy bloodshed among the civilian population, and he inquired what General Hodges could dispatch at once." Hodges sent for Gee Gerow, assigned LeClerc's division and an American infantry division to Gerow's V Corps, and packed them off toward Paris. LeClerc's division was more of a hindrance than a help—Gerow telephoned Hodges next day that the French drivers had become inebriated and were stopping in every town and holding up traffic all along the highway.

In Paris there was wild shooting and chaos, as Hodges' diary recorded on August 25, "between French political parties, collaborationists and anti-collaborationists." The aide to the commander of the 76th Field Artillery Brigade was shot dead by a Frenchman. The next day, just after Hodges had left for XV Corps headquarters in his Piper Cub, Gerow arrived at the First Army headquarters, his face as black as thunder: "Who in the devil is the boss in Paris?" he asked. "The Frenchmen are shooting at each other, each party is at each other's throat. Is Koenig the boss, is de Gaulle the boss? Am I, as senior commander, in charge?" Bradley's chief of staff General William B. Kean told him: "You are in charge." Gerow warned him there would be political repercussions. Even now de Gaulle's manipulations were not over. During Gerow's absence, de Gaulle ordered a victory parade of the French 2nd Armored Division through Paris. Gerow instructed LeClerc to disregard these orders, and told him to clean up the city. De Gaulle insisted, so the Americans—whose troops had borne their share of casualties in France—arranged to include elements of their own in the parade. It took place down the Champs Elysées. On the reviewing stand were Bradley, Koenig, LeClerc, and de Gaulle—who pointedly stepped off the stand before the parade was over, a deliberate insult which was not lost on the American generals.

Eisenhower considered the capture of Paris a mixed blessing—particularly after he learned that the BBC had announced that de Gaulle, by his very presence, had "liberated" the city. On August 26, Kay Summersby noted: "General Sibert (G-2) has just arrived back from Paris, the city is almost in our hands except for a little sniping. E. and Bradley decide to drive into Paris Sunday morning. Monty is sent a message inviting him to come along, but he declines." At the edge of the city Eisenhower and Bradley were met by General Koenig and driven to see de Gaulle. The imposing French leader had already taken over the old War Department building as his headquarters and had arranged a guard of honor on the stairs up to his anteroom. The men were in the uniform of the President's Guard.

Meanwhile, the southern American armies were all but at a halt. Patton's Third Army had lost its XV Corps to Hodges's First Army, which would now operate in support of the British and Canadian armies along the northern thrust. Hodges would also get the lion's share of the supplies, so Patton's Third Army—now extended along 300 miles of front—was virtually static, held up not by the Germans but by the lack of gasoline. The gasoline was in Europe; it had been landed, but it was still stacked in dumps around the unloading ports far to the west.

A few days later, on August 29, Eisenhower flew back from France to SHAEF main headquarters in England. The weather was bad, and his plane had to fly at barely a thousand feet all the way. He spent the next day working on a report to the Combined Chiefs of Staff on Nazi losses and reviewing with General Betts the usual dossiers; Eisenhower had to put his name to two more death sentences. In Lieutenant Kay Summersby's diary entry for the day appeared the first mention of a general supply crisis looming over the Allied forces in France: "E. is sending a statement to General Somervell on supplies that he needs, also stresses the point that it is imperative that they are kept up."

The time had now come—as always planned—for Montgomery officially to step down from his overall ground forces command, and to limit himself to the command of the British 21st Army Group. Inevitably it would look like a demotion, particularly coming after so much newspaper criticism of his slow progress. This had to be avoided. Eisenhower decided to summon the entire press and deliver a fine tribute to him. On August 31 he drove into London and at the Ministry of Information stood with Tedder before a big conference of newspapermen and told them just why Montgomery was losing overall ground command. It was his most generous statement yet about Allied cooperation. "Now," he said challengingly, "the time has come when we have broken out of that initial beachhead, and General Bradley is taking over his part of the job, reporting directly to SHAEF headquarters, and anyone that interprets this as a demotion for General Montgomery simply won't look facts in the face. He is not only my very close and warm friend, but a man with whom I have worked for two years, and for whom I have a tremendous admiration, one of the great soldiers of this or any other war."

General Montgomery, he went on, was as responsible as anybody else for the conception of the breakthrough at Avranches, the Falaise-Argentan pocket, and the crossing of the Seine. Eisenhower would not tolerate the slightest criticism of Montgomery's "slow progress" at Caen after D-day. "Every foot of ground he [the enemy] lost at Caen was like losing ten miles anywhere else," he declaimed. "Every piece of dust there was more than a diamond to him."

Eisenhower had a feeling of a job well done, as he sat down to prolonged applause. He had once again rescued the image of the Grand Alliance. As Kay Summersby drove him back to Bushy Park in his four-star sedan, however, he reflected that he probably had hurt many feelings too. Patton, as it turned out, was mortified by the reference to Montgomery as "one of the great soldiers of this war." That title was *his.* He had gone home and buried himself in paperwork.

But Churchill was jubilant. He wrote to congratulate Eisenhower: "Nothing could have been more straightforward, courteous and fair to us."

The next day, the press had a news item. Churchill had given Montgomery his *fifth* star. He was to be a field marshal.

CHAPTER TWENTY

Dragooned

A PROBLEM that caused Eisenhower great emotional difficulties was the projected Allied landing in the south of France, code-named Anvil. Stalin had suggested it at Teheran and Roosevelt had supported him. The ostensible idea was that Anvil should coincide with Overlord, to divide the German defenses. Stalin's real motives are easy to divine—he wanted to divert the surplus energy of the Allies in the Mediterranean away from the Balkans, where he had his own ambitions. Roosevelt's purposes were less clear. He in turn was fiercely supported by the U.S. Joint Chiefs of Staff, particularly by Admiral King, who was determined not to allow American ships and troops to become involved in any British-inspired Balkan adventure.

Churchill used some of his toughest arguments against Anvil, and applied his finest rhetoric to the matter. He maintained that Anvil was unsound, and should only be used as a threat, rather than mounted as a real assault. In February 1944 the British predicted that, after Overlord was provided for, there would be enough landing craft in the Mediterranean for only one division; even if there were enough for two, the British felt, the Anvil area was so far away from Normandy that the strategic "pincer" argument did not apply. Besides, since it was clear from Magic and Ultra that Hitler had unexpectedly decided to make a stand south of Rome, the Allies had no choice but to wage an even fiercer war in Italy—which made it unwise, they insisted, to divert resources to a new invasion.

Marshall regarded it as ironic that the British had now become so fiercely pro-Overlord while the Americans were the Mediterraneanites, a reversal of their previous positions. It was Churchill, after all, who had said, "When I think of the beaches of Normandy choked with the flower of American and British youth, and when, in my mind's eye, I see the tides running red with their blood, I have my doubts . . . I have my doubts."

Churchill continued to badger the Americans about the need to invade the Balkans. Throughout the spring and summer of 1944 he sent telegram after telegram to Roosevelt calling for an early Combined Chiefs meeting in London on this issue. Marshall was loath to go, and Leahy guessed that nothing good for the United States could come of it; together they headed off the idea. "This controversy is of long standing," Leahy wrote in his diary. "It is caused by American all-out concentration on an early defeat of Nazi Germany, and a British intention to combine with a defeat of the Nazis the acquisition of postwar advantages in the Balkan States for Great Britain."

The problem was that the Churchill-inspired landing at Anzio had run into a stalemate as German resistance stiffened. Supplying the beachhead was still soaking up all the landing craft available. When the British demanded an immediate decision on releasing the Anvil landing craft to boost Overlord, Admiral King told Roosevelt—as the record of their meeting shows—that more than enough craft were now available for Overlord. "With the terrific number of craft involved in the assault," he added sarcastically, "one would almost be able to walk dry-shod from one side of the Channel to the other." The decision was postponed for a month.

The British continued to pickaxe away at Anvil. Montgomery shared Churchill's views. On February 19, he wrote warning Eisenhower that the troops in Italy were tired and unlikely to take Rome soon. "Under these circumstances I do not see how the withdrawal of divisions from Italy for Anvil is possible," he said. He suggested dividing the Anvil resources between Italy and Overlord. "It would be far better to have a really good Overlord with a good choice of craft, a good reserve of craft, a good margin all round, and so on," he wrote. The next day Montgomery lunched with Churchill at Chequers. What Churchill told him about the Italian battle shocked him. "It seems quite clear that we are now engaged in Italy in a major war," Montgomery now wrote to Eisenhower. "It is not just a battle for Rome. We are suffering heavy casualties; but so is the enemy, and all this will help Overlord far more than would a reduced Anvil." Eisenhower was impressed, and was on the point of abandoning Anvil, but he decided to "saw wood" for a while instead. On March 21, he told Marshall that he had been asked to meet the British Chiefs of Staff the next day, and he added that he now also felt that the idea of launching Anvil simultaneously with Overlord would have to be abandoned, given the chronic shortage in landing craft. The Combined Chiefs accepted this, and Anvil was delayed.

On March 28, a telegram reached the Pentagon from General Sir Henry Maitland Wilson—"Jumbo" Wilson, who was as indolent as he was portly—blandly announcing that he had postponed his attack on the Monte Cassino position outside Rome by another month: bad news for Anvil.

On April 8, the Combined Chiefs met again in Washington to debate Anvil once more. Now the British Chiefs of Staff were refusing to proceed with Anvil preparations. Marshall told Henry Stimson about it. "I have come to the conclusion," Stimson observed, casting modesty to the winds, "that if this war is to be won, it's got to be won by the full strength of the virile energetic initiative-loving inventive Americans, and that the British really are showing decadence—a magnificent people but they have lost their initiative."

Rome's capture on the eve of Overlord caused little rejoicing among Eisenhower's staff. Everett Hughes entered this jejeune view in his diary: *"Rome fell at 9:15* last night. Germans withdrew to a position north of Rome! Hitler [having] spoiled Anvil, turns Rome over to us to be fed, releases some German divisions. Damned good strategic planning on Nazi part."

A week later, Marshall and his staff arrived in Europe to discuss Anvil. Overlord had now begun. Would strategic diversion benefits still derive from Anvil? To General Mark Clark, Marshall said thoughtfully, "We ought to give it a lot of consideration, because Eisenhower is doing so well up there that the landing in southern France may not be worth that much to the overall picture." But Eisenhower was reluctant to give up Anvil; he wanted every ounce of help. He had been given a mission to perform in France, and he was not interested in British or American global strategy. "I want all the insurance I can get," he told Clark, "and I always planned on a thrust in southern France, a one-two." The whole subject was discussed by the Combined Chiefs meeting in England on June 13. Afterward Commodore H. A. Flanigan, USN, confidentially wrote to Admiral Kirk: "It looks as if we are going ahead with Anvil."

Throughout June, Eisenhower was detained in England by bad weather, but this had its blessings because in England he could keep an eye on Churchill and thwart the British attempts to strike Anvil off the map. These climaxed on June 21 in a message from Jumbo Wilson to Washington arguing for a completely different thrust. The Allied troops, instead of sailing off to southern France, he said, should continue up the Italian thigh to Venice and then head east around the Adriatic to the Balkans and possibly Hungary. Stimson, sourly recording his observation that Jumbo Wilson was never far from a bottle, opined in his diary on that day: "The British with their Empire interest are anxious to throw our next blow into the eastern Mediterranean just as they were a year ago. . . . I am very confident that it would be a bad mistake from our point and that our country, which has now gotten its interest up in finishing the Germans in France, would be strongly averse to being shifted off to an enterprise in a region in which they would not see any interest." He also believed that the farther the Allies ventured into the eastern Mediterranean, the greater would be the risk of rivalry with Russia.

Eisenhower shared Stimson's suspicions. He told Wilson's chief of staff that he wanted Anvil quickly and he was against any Churchillian plan to attack from Italy through Trieste into Hungary. He repeated this the next day when he went to Downing Street for a conference with Churchill. Kay Summersby heard that they "discussed future Mediterranean policy. E. is flatly against move through Trieste." Four days later the two leaders conferred again. "E[isenhower] has decided to release equipment needed in Med. provided Anvil is to be executed," recorded Kay Summersby that day. "The P.M. is still set on capturing Trieste."

Thus the deadlock became formal. The Joint Chiefs in Washington refused to accept the British Balkan project, and insisted that Anvil must be set up for August; the British Chiefs of Staff shouted for Jumbo Wilson's plan, and voiced skepticism that Anvil could be set up in time. Stimson wrote: "[It] shows that they have not yet learned the lessons of American quickness and speed in planning and setting up amphibious operations."

Marshall was indignant at these frustrating delays, and he sent the British Chiefs of Staff a telegram which Stimson described as a ripper. Churchill aimed a no less powerful message at the President: "Our first wish is to help General Eisenhower in the most speedy and effective manner. But we do not think this necessarily involves the complete ruin of all our great affairs in the Mediterranean, and we take it hard that this should be demanded of us." Roosevelt replied that same day, siding unequivocally with his Joint Chiefs' demand that Anvil go ahead in mid-August and rejecting Wilson's plan to advance into the Balkans. "I really believe we should consolidate our operations and not scatter them," Roosevelt instructed Churchill. That same evening, Churchill fired off to Roosevelt a memorandum of tremendous length. And the British Chiefs of Staff pointed out in a subsidiary telegram that night that, if Anvil were abandoned, General Sir Harold Alexander had the chance of destroying Field Marshal Albert Kesselring's entire army in Italy. They added harshly, "We recognize General Eisenhower's responsibility for the success of Overlord itself, but we cannot admit that he has any responsibility for European strategy as a whole. This responsibility must rest with the Combined Chiefs of Staff and cannot be delegated to any commander-in-chief." The next day, Churchill telephoned Eisenhower, asking him to send Bedell Smith—whose strategic abilities were quietly estimated higher than those of his Supreme Commander—to talk it over with him. The Churchill diary shows this day: "1:30 P.M. General Bedell Smith to lunch." But Bedell Smith held fast.

Roosevelt turned up the heat. He sent a telegram to Churchill pleading, "My dear friend, I beg you let us go ahead with our plan." Roosevelt left no organ stop unpulled—from a specious reminder that they had both given their word on Anvil to Stalin at Teheran, to the hint that he might lose the upcoming presidential election over it. "For purely political considerations over here," he confided, "I would never survive even a slight setback in Overlord if it were known that fairly large forces had been diverted to the Balkans."

Churchill refused to be taken in. He had set his heart on the Balkan thrust—some said he was determined to prove that he had been right with his disastrous Gallipoli campaign in World War I. "The splitting up of the campaign in the Mediterranean into two operations," he replied to Roosevelt, "neither of which can do anything decisive, is, in my humble and respectful opinion, the first major strategic and political error for which we two have to be responsible." Neither friendships nor favors influenced his pen now. He recalled that in Cairo, Eisenhower had argued how vital it was to nourish an established theater. Now Churchill accused that same Eisenhower of having changed his mind. He predicted that only de Gaulle would profit from Anvil. Doing some organ playing himself, he described General Alexander in Italy as complaining, on the verge of tears, "The ghost of Anvil hangs heavily over the battlefront." American units, he lamented, were being wrenched out of combat for the new operation. He predicted doom for it. And as for that oft-mentioned promise to Stalin, Churchill now felt less generous than he had at Teheran. "On a long term political view," he said portentously, "he [Stalin] might prefer that the British and Americans should do their share in France in the very hard fighting that is to come, and that east, middle and southern Europe should fall naturally into his control. However it is better to settle the matter for ourselves and between ourselves."

Not wishing to be inelegant, Churchill made the mistake of sounding one conciliatory note. If, nonetheless, the Combined Chiefs should direct that Anvil must proceed, he said grandly, then the British would comply, but under solemn protest. The glint of victory in their eye, the Combined Chiefs so directed. They sent their directive to Jumbo Wilson next day: Anvil was to be launched on August 15. Eisenhower was pleased by this apparent capitulation.

One Sunday morning a week later, however, the illusion evaporated. Eisenhower drove up to Chequers and had ninety minutes with Churchill, who was resting in his bedroom. The Prime Minister gave him hell, to use the general's own robust description, for insisting on Anvil. Indeed, he revived the whole controversy. "He had lots of questions," Eisenhower informed Montgomery later, "most of which I answered by saying we were going to the offensive all along the line and would gain room and would kill Germans." Churchill invited him to stay for lunch, but Eisenhower declined.

So the battle over strategy had gone on. While Montgomery fought the grim killing match of Caen, while Bradley slogged it out through Saint-Lô and Patton's tanks prepared for their glorious breakout into open France, Winston Churchill battled against Dragoon—as the Anvil landing was now renamed. He shunned no tactics to that end. After a three-hour meeting and dinner with Eisenhower on August 1, Churchill telegraphed to Roosevelt that the general had agreed that the troops destined for Dragoon, now scheduled for mid-August, should be shipped instead to ports in the Brittany peninsula. These, admittedly, were still in German hands, but surely they soon would be freed, and through them the Dragoon troops could pour, to reinforce the beachhead armies. "Why should we bash in the back door," inquired Churchill persuasively of Roosevelt, "when we have the latch key to the front door?" Far better for ten divisions to be welcomed by American forces at, say, Saint-Nazaire than to have three divisions force a landing on the Mediterranean coast. The British Chiefs of Staff shared his view.

Churchill pressed his views on every occasion. On August 5, he lunched at SHAEF's forward headquarters, and fed milk from a saucer on the dinner table to the kitten Shaef. The ubiquitous Kay Summersby wrote: "The P.M. was in very good form, he and E. get along very well." However, "During luncheon Anvil was discussed. The P.M. does not want to go ahead with it. Message from U.S. chiefs of staff, agrees with E. that Anvil must go on." Her brief note did not reflect the vehemence of the argument. After lunch, under the canopy of Eisenhower's office tent, Churchill again pleaded—using all his powers of oratory—that history would accuse him of having missed a great opportunity if he did not have Dragoon shifted even at this late date from the Toulon area to the ports of Brittany. Harry Butcher was an amused observer. "Ike said no," he recorded, "continued saying no all afternoon, and ended saying no." But the argument was long and tough, and the Supreme Commander was limp with exhaustion when Churchill departed. "Although I have said no in every language," he told his staff, "the Prime Minister will undoubtedly return to the subject in two or three days and simply regard the issue as unsettled." He knew Churchill too well.

The British continued to manifest great inventiveness in finding arguments against the plan. Eisenhower stuck to his guns, backed by both Tedder and Ramsay, the naval commander in chief. Afterward, Churchill cabled Roosevelt that he supported what he now, craftily, termed Eisenhower's suggestion for the shift of Dragoon to Brittany. Eisenhower instantly checkmated that by a message to Marshall: "I learn that the Prime Minister has sent a message to the President relating to Dragoon. I will *not* under any conditions agree at this moment to a cancellation of Dragoon. . . . It is possible that the Prime Minister may have misconstrued my stated opinion on these matters, but I have never wavered for a moment from the convictions above expressed."

The Joint Chiefs of Staff rejected the notion and said so forcefully: nobody could predict when the Brittany ports would be freed—a prophetic argument, as it turned out, since Saint-Nazaire was one of the ports that Hitler would retain tightly in his grip until the war's end. Roosevelt also flatly turned down this last-minute idea of Churchill's. "It is my considered opinion," he said emphatically, "that Dragoon should be launched at the earliest practicable date." Churchill, cornered, replied the next day dramatically: "I pray God that you may be right. We shall, of course, do everything in our power to help you achieve success."

But it was false acquiescence; even now he had not given up the fight. When he saw Eisenhower on August 9, Churchill threatened to go to His Majesty and "lay down the mantle of my high office" if he did not get his way. Later Eisenhower recounted to Sir Hastings Ismay what had happened. Churchill, he said, had practically wept, and "in fact actually had rolled tears down his cheeks in arguing that the Americans were adopting a 'bullying' attitude against the British in failing to accept their—meaning primarily his—recommendations as to grand strategy." (In his postwar published version of the account, Butcher glossed over the harshness of the episode, adding—on Eisenhower's insistence—the words: "Both love the Prime . . . and their comment about him is like that of two admiring sons discussing a cantankerous yet adorable father." The bare wartime diary text has a different flavor.) Churchill again pleaded with Eisenhower to support the deflection of reinforcements to General Alexander, so that from Italy he could stab through the Ljubljana gap into "Europe's armpit," as he now termed the Balkans.

Eisenhower firmly declined. To him, Italy was a blind alley, and he wanted no more valuable forces diverted there. The episode had become a nightmare for Eisenhower. He was a soldier, responsible for the success of Overlord, and military factors, in his view, argued for Dragoon. True, if he had been a politician, he would have agreed with Churchill. Eisenhower would relate years later, in a letter to Al Wedemeyer, that the forces should have been used for a thrust to the northeast into the Balkans to forestall Stalin's ambitions in that area. "I told him [Churchill] that as long as the argument centered about the immediate *military* problem I was not only certain of the correctness of my view but was not permitted to deviate from that course."

The depth of Churchill's feeling of betrayal shook Eisenhower. Was this the beginning of a serious rift between Britain and America? He wrote him on August 11: "To say that I was disturbed by our conference on Wednesday does not nearly express the depth of my distress over your interpretation of the recent decision affecting the Mediterranean theater. I do not, for one moment, believe that there is any desire on the part of any responsible person in the American war machine to disregard British views, or cold-bloodedly to leave Britain holding an empty bag in any of our joint undertakings. . . . I am sorry that you seem to feel we use our great actual or potential strength as a bludgeon in conference."

Dragoon went ahead on schedule. All elements of the VI Corps landed near Fréjus, in southern France, at 6:00 P.M. on August 15, for a loss of fewer than one hundred casualties. Forty percent of the prisoners turned out to be Russians who had volunteered to fight for Germany against Stalin, but found themselves fighting the Americans and British. There was no firing at all upon the ships.

When the time came for Dragoon to be launched, Churchill did not let the fact of his long and bitter opposition to it cost him a grand entertainment. He hurried to a front seat for the show. After a day or two luxuriating in Capri, he boarded a destroyer which sailed to Fréjus, and watched as the three divisions went in. "At eight A.M.," the visiting American general Brehon Somervell noted in his diary, "we went on board the *Kimberley,* British destroyer. Met the Prime Minister there, and got under way. It took five hours to reach the French coast. Spent the day on the bridge. The Prime Minister was lively and talkative. Spoke of the main events of the war and of his opinion on operations. . . . Denied that he wanted campaign in Balkans, except on guerrilla scale and in support of guerrillas."

CHAPTER TWENTY-ONE

Loaves and Fishes

ON SEPTEMBER 1, 1944, the day Eisenhower learned that Montgomery had been made a field marshal, General Francis de Guingand wrote to Montgomery. "General Ike," he said cheerily, "told me this morning that he was trying to get you on the phone in order to congratulate you, but he has not been successful so far."

Montgomery, referring to the persistent problems the commanders had been having with communications, wrote back tartly: "I do not suppose that Ike . . . will be able to telephone to me for months." It was amost the truth. Eisenhower's headquarters, now at Granville, was four hundred miles from the battlefront and—amazingly enough—not even in radiotelephone, let alone telephone, contact with Montgomery's or Bradley's headquarters. This day, according to Kay Summersby's unflagging diary, he began planning to move closer to the fighting—to a site north of Paris.

Montgomery's promotion to five-star rank left Eisenhower's generals aghast. There was no such rank in the U.S. Army. General Patton wrote to Beatrice: "The field marshal thing made us sick, that is Bradley and me." Bradley said to Bedell Smith with far more violence than Smith had ever known from him before, "Montgomery is a third rate general and he never did anything or won any battle that any other general could not have won as well or better." Smith, by no means an unprejudiced observer, would later write in a letter to a friend that Montgomery would not have been worth a damn without Patton, and that he deserved the greatest censure for his "intransigence and behind-the-scenes conniving to enhance his own prestige and to obtain a major measure of the command."

This cannot be the verdict of history. It was a tragedy for the Allied effort that the strategic direction that autumn lay in the hands of these men: Eisenhower, Smith, and Bradley. Because of their feelings about the ascetic, friendless Montgomery, his voice was ignored by the strategists at SHAEF. Thus, while a rapid, single-minded decision to adopt one or the other of the thrusts proposed by him might yet have rapidly ended the war, Hitler was now allowed to catch his breath and regroup his armies for a stand at the German frontier.

Hitler had made stark strategic decisions late in August 1944. He had cut his losses. He had accepted the probability that the Balkans were lost, and had begun pulling his armies out of the southeast. He had also written off France—temporarily. His armies fell back on the Siegfried Line, a wall of pillboxes, barbed wire, and minefields built five years before. Gradually, the Allied armies fell behind in the chase, as the German supply lines grew shorter and the Allied longer. Still denied access to the main Channel ports, the supply-starved Allied armies were throttled in mid-pursuit, and their exhilarating offensive withered away. There was now little chance of crashing through the West Wall before the Germans could prepare a defense. As the Allied armies ran out of gasoline and ammunition, and as the rains and cold weather extinguished the last vestiges of even Patton's optimism, Hitler gained time and respite.

On August 22, Montgomery asked for a whole American army to be shifted to his right flank, to reinforce his northern thrust into Germany. Montgomery, "with his usual caution," as Eisenhower wryly put it in a confidential note for his own files—in itself a sign of growing edginess —felt that it was vital not to halt his operations toward Brussels and the deepwater port of Antwerp; thus he wanted the insurance of having all the supplies and men he needed. So Eisenhower had allowed himself to be persuaded and directed Hodges' First Army to advance more closely along Montgomery's right boundary.

Soon Patton's gas ran out. The gasoline was going up to Hodges' First Army to help Montgomery's thrust. Patton was obliged to stand where he was, to the southeast of Paris, capable of only minor reconnaissance missions. "The British have put it over again," he wrote in his diary. All the familiar paranoia—real or simulated—welled forth from inside him. He wrote to Beatrice, "I have to battle for every yard but it is not the enemy who is trying to stop me, it is 'They'. . . . If I could only steal some gas, I could win this war." Thought became deed. In typical Patton fashion, he had long since won over the blacks in the supply corps, and one of their truck companies now stole some gas for him that had been meant for other units. Soon he was resorting to ever more questionable methods of getting his own way.

The British began advancing rapidly into Belgium, aided by Hodges. Brussels was occupied on September 4. But there would be no alleviation of the Allied supply crisis until Antwerp could be opened to Allied shipping. Ultra intercepts indicated that Hitler had ordered frantic measures to prevent Allied ships from getting through to the port. Montgomery had neglected to take steps to clear the enemy out of the estuary leading to Antwerp, and the enemy's Fifteenth Army had now established positions in strength along both banks, and had begun extensive mining operations. Months would pass before the first ship could even approach the port of Antwerp. For this failure, the blame must be apportioned equally between Montgomery, who failed to secure the water approaches, and Eisenhower, who had failed to give him clear and unambiguous orders to do so.

The other deepwater ports—except for Dieppe, which was captured by the Canadians but was destroyed—were firmly in German hands, and some of them remained so until the last day of the war. Fanatical German troops still held Brest, in Brittany, now six hundred miles to the west of the fighting. One of the toughest Nazi paratroop commanders, Hermann Ramcke, had been given command there—he had lost all his teeth in a parachute accident and now had a mouth full of steel. Ramcke had forty thousand men, but many were only Todt Organization engineers and laborers. They had already inflicted four thousand casualties on the American VIII Corps and withstood weeks of artillery bombardment and saturation air attacks.

The ports had become a conflict of wills, a battle of national prestige. For Hitler, Brest was a symbol of his determination to reconquer France and then use this base for his new U-boat types, while for the Americans it was vital to show that they were invincible. Bradley told Patton in confidence: "I would not say this to anyone but you, and have given different excuses to my staff and higher echelons, but we must take Brest in order to maintain the illusion that the U.S. Army cannot be beaten." Patton agreed: once American soldiers put their hands to a job, they must finish it.

With the Channel ports still German, the Allies were forced to haul supplies hundreds of miles from Cherbourg and the gale-whipped Normandy beaches to the battlefront. The Allied bombers had destroyed the French railroad network so thoroughly that it would take months to repair, and supplies had to go by road. From Cherbourg to the front line a one-way trucks-only road network was set up—the Red Ball express highway. It was operated twenty-four hours a day and patrolled by military police who eliminated French civilian traffic and held down speeding and reckless driving by the truckers. Pilferage and loss of trucks along the highway was colossal. Red Ball helped, but still the armies were starved of the supplies they needed.

On Saturday, September 2, Eisenhower flew in his B-25 from Granville to see Bradley at Versailles. Kay Summersby observed in her diary, "E. says that he is going to give Patton hell because he is stretching his line too far and therefore making supply difficulties." He did not realize as yet that this was Patton's definite intention: to carry on regardless of any directives from above. Later that day the two army commanders, Patton and Hodges, came to see Eisenhower at Bradley's headquarters. Eisenhower kept talking about the future "great battle of Germany." He pontificated to them about Clausewitz, the great Prussian military philosopher—who had commanded forces, as Patton remarked in rejoinder, that were neither mechanized nor one quarter so numerous as the 450,000 men under his command alone. Patton tried to persuade Eisenhower to let the First and Third armies push against the Siegfried Line now, since the Germans had nothing left to fight back with. But Eisenhower stubbornly refused to divert the necessary gasoline and ammunition. Patton thought, "If we wait, there *will* be a great battle of Germany." He wrote it in his diary, but he probably did not utter it.

Eisenhower annoyed him more by marveling at the work done by supply chief J.C.H. Lee—whom Patton considered to have failed utterly, and perhaps even cost them the victory before winter, because of his inability to keep Patton supplied with gasoline. Patton wrote: "Ike is all for caution since he has never been at the front and has no feel of actual fighting. Bradley, Hodges and I are all for a prompt advance." The diary of Courtney Hodges confirms that this normally calm, taciturn, and retiring general was also deeply aggravated. He had driven over from his headquarters at Senlis, near the Belgian border. "A long conference with General Eisenhower, General Bradley and General Patton was held," Hodges' diary, written in third person, recorded, "and the results from General Hodges' standpoint were, to say the least, 'not altogether satisfactory.' . . . The whole plan is not altogether to the General's satisfaction since he believes he can whip the gasoline problem and that while the Germans are on the run there should be no halt for even a minute." The diarist added perceptively, "There have been so many changes in the First Army direction that indeed there seems at times as if those 'on top' did not have an altogether clear and consistent conception of direction from which they wish to cross the German frontier."

On the way back to Granville from this unhappy meeting, Eisenhower's B-25 broke a muffler and he switched to a small L-5. A gale started, and his pilot had to make an emergency landing on a beach near Saint-Jean-de-Thomas. Helping the pilot pull the plane up the beach, Eisenhower wrenched his leg badly. He had already damaged his other knee in August and spent time in bed. Now he was confined to bed once again.

Omar Bradley was nauseated by the decision to put the main push behind Montgomery. Thus began the great conspiracy between Patton and the army group commander to whom he had always referred disparagingly behind his back as "the tentmaker." Bradley immediately telephoned Patton, then went to assure him in person that he would give the Third Army half of any supplies available to his army group. Moreover, he said, he would assign four more divisions to Patton, and if Patton could now get across the next barrier, the Moselle River, then he would look the other way. In fact, he would not forbid Patton to punch right through the Siegfried Line and go on to the Rhine. Patton began to regard Bradley in a new light.

Montgomery was not satisfied that he had completely won, and continued to worry Eisenhower—in the sense that dogs worry bones—about the proper line of thrust. He sent him a telegram on September 4: "I consider we have now reached a stage where one really powerful and full-blooded thrust towards Berlin is likely to get there and thus end the German war." There were not enough supplies for two thrusts —both Montgomery's push to the Ruhr *and* Patton's thrust via Metz and the Saar. The field marshal demanded an immediate decision in favor of the Ruhr campaign. He added, "If you are coming this way perhaps you would look in to discuss it. If so delighted to see you lunch tomorrow. Do not feel I can leave this battle just at present."

The next day Eisenhower replied negatively. He had the day before begun discussions on taking Jake Devers' 6th Army Group—along with General Alexander Patch's U.S. Seventh Army, which also had landed in southern France—under his command. He had a broad vision of all three army groups moving together up to the frontier, shoulder to shoulder, and steamrolling slowly across Germany. Perhaps it was a delayed reaction to his talk with Bradley and the forceful General Patton, but he now reverted to his old position: he wanted to exploit what he called the German military collapse by breaching the West Wall—the Siegfried Line—on a wide front and crossing the Rhine. That is, he wanted to capture both the Saar *and* the Ruhr. He had come to the conclusion that it was time to get Patton going forward again, "so that we may be fully prepared," he wrote on September 5, "to carry out the original conception for the final stages of this campaign."

Patton, of course, was exuberant at Eisenhower's change of heart. "I hope to go through the Siegfried Line like shit through a goose," was how he poetically described his intentions to Third Army correspondents on September 7. To which he perversely added a now routine lie: "The perfectly phenomenal advance of the 21st Army Group under Field Marshal Montgomery has just completely buggered the whole show." Just whose "show" had been rendered nugatory—Hitler's or Patton's—was not obvious from the remarks. But that hardly mattered any more. Patton did not intend to stop again before he reached the Rhine.

In Washington, where nobody heeded the growing supply crisis, everything seemed much rosier. Carried away by the American radio and newspapers, the furloughed Everett Hughes speculated that Germany would be beaten by November 2. Beatrice Patton called on Hughes several days running, pleading with him to read out everything he had written in his diary about her George; Everett complied, but only partly. ("I tell her I'm busy," he confessed in that same diary.) Hughes left for London on September 3, bringing jackets, socks, gloves, mittens, coats, and other, less prosaic, gifts for Patton, Hodges, and Collins as well as a letter for Bradley that Bradley's wife had gotten to Hughes by what she termed a "nigger messenger." Hughes found himself flying back to Europe with a U.S.O. detail which included Bing Crosby and Fred Astaire. Once in London, he picked up J.P. and then made tracks for Cherbourg.

At Granville he found Eisenhower still limping badly. In the office trailer were Jake Devers and several officers from North Africa whom he had gotten to know well and who were being taken over by Eisenhower. It was like old times. They all lunched together—Hughes, J.P., Eisenhower, Kay Summersby, Colonel Tex Lee, and the newcomers. Hughes tackled Eisenhower about the growing public relations problem —the need to play up the American side of the battle in France.

"I can't do that," Eisenhower said, his eyes glazing.

"You had better," Hughes retorted simply. "You're not going to live in Europe all of your life."

He showed them the new 38 handgun he had bought for Georgie Patton, specially fitted with an ivory handle; he said waggishly that he had treated a WAC in Washington by letting her handle "George's ivory pistol," and they all guffawed. Hughes also told Eisenhower he had called Mamie by phone late on August 23, and she had sounded chipper. Hughes noted: "[Eisenhower] winked at Kay when I discussed Mamie." After lunch, Hughes told them all the latest wisecrack going the rounds of Washington—about how God had begun acting as if he were J.C.H. Lee—and the Supreme Commander laughed until his leg hurt. Then it occurred to Eisenhower that at five o'clock the aforementioned J.C.H. Lee was due to see him, about his Communications Zone —the American supply organization in the conquered areas—and the growing supply crisis, and it didn't seem so funny after all.

With Eisenhower's approval, Hughes moved his office as Chief of

Staff, European Theater, to Paris. He traveled from Valognes to Paris along the Red Ball highway—a fine conception, in his view, although far too many French were already being allowed along it for his liking. Thus Everett Hughes moved from rags to riches, from the muddy moonscape of "liberated" Valognes to a suite in the hotel George V with running hot water and liveried flunkies. "Luxury as conquerors thanks to George," he jotted—momentarily overlooking the semantic ruling by both Eisenhower and Churchill that the Allies had not come to France as "invaders." In Paris, communications were still atrocious, but that had not deterred headquarters staffs from joining the stampede to get into the city before all the best suites were taken. The 655 hotels occupied by the Germans had already been swamped by the Allies, Hughes noted, and more were being requisitioned daily. He moved his offices into the palatial Hotel Majestic. Some fool put up two signs, reading *HQ Com Z* and *HQ ETO,* in that order. Hughes had the order changed around before J.C.H. Lee could see the signs with Com Z first and take a liking to it that way.

The beauty of Paris, the girls, the late summer sun—all these seduced the Americans into a deeper euphoria. Hughes noted on September 5: "Liquor principal problem." To some generals that may have been true, but to the combat commanders other problems were more pressing: the gasoline and ammunition shortages were growing acute. J.C.H. Lee called conferences and answered criticisms that Com Z was not getting the supplies forward to the combat troops fast enough. Hughes told Eisenhower and Lee to advertise more; Com Z should tell the public about the Red Ball express, for example. Eisenhower replaced his public relations officer Tom Davis with Jock Lawrence. The upshot was better publicity—including a great piece about Lee in *Time* magazine —but not better supplies for Patton and Hodges. Hughes grumbled in his diary: "The old story—the combat troops can't or don't plan far enough ahead to enable Com Z to get the stuff in time. The supply man," he concluded, "must be a good strategist."

Paris made a delightful backdrop, however, for these arguments between the generals, and the spirits flowed. On September 6, Hughes sat up until one-thirty A.M., getting tight on Scotch and the best cognac —never a wise mixture at the best of times. Apparently unaffected, he and J.P. dined the next day with Henry Sayler, Eisenhower's chief ordnance officer, at his plush hotel. The conversation—to judge by

Hughes's diary—revolved around nonmilitary affairs. Sayler told him that Ordnance had three truckloads of cognac. Hughes was impressed but urged caution. "We want our wars wet but not wanton," he wrote that night privately, and liked the sound of that aphorism.

The public relations effort blinded the Supreme Command to the harsh realities of the supply crisis. On August 30, Eisenhower sent a congratulatory message to the Navy Department on the unloading figures so far: in the British area, 806,559 troops and 201,200 vehicles; in the U.S. area, 1,197,897 troops and 219,947 vehicles. And a total of 3,153,476 tons of stores. *Time* magazine talked of this logistics miracle as being in the American tradition—"begotten of a people accustomed to great spaces, to transcontinental railways, to nationwide trucking chains, to endless roads and millions of automobiles, to mail order houses, department stores and supermarkets; of a nation of builders and movers." On September 11, Lee showed Hughes a memo he had written to Eisenhower recommending that his sloppy Com Z troops wear regular field uniforms—high boots and helmets.

"I suggest you get the people to wear what they have—properly," Hughes replied. Afterward he told Anna Rosenberg, a civilian representative of Roosevelt who, for her visit to the war zone, was dressed as a WAC, about Lee's fussy pretentiousness, and she gasped to Hughes, "Lee can't be human." Hughes wrote her comment down in his notebook too.

In France, not much was happening of military significance. As could have been predicted, had SHAEF's intelligence officers heeded the Ultra intercepts, German resistance was meanwhile steadily increasing around the Albert Canal in Belgium, along the Luxembourg frontier, and along the river Moselle.

Eisenhower's SHAEF headquarters at Granville were so poorly equipped for communications that his new directive, with his change of heart, reached Montgomery in four parts, spread over the next four days. Thus it dawned only slowly on the field marshal that Eisenhower had switched back to the broad-front approach. He answered the parts he had received by September 6 as follows: "You can rely on 21 Army Group to go all out 100 per cent to further your intention to destroy enemy forces." But when he studied the rest of Eisenhower's directive FWD 13765, he noted that he could "not see it stated that the northern route of advance to the Ruhr is to have priority over the eastern advance to the Saar." He dictated a telegram to Eisenhower asking him to send a responsible staff officer to see him so that he could explain things in person. Eisenhower decided to go himself, although his leg was in a cast and he was barely able to move. He suggested that they meet at Amiens. Montgomery replied that he had an urgent operational meeting with his army commander, Dempsey, and "would be extremely grateful if the Supreme Commander could land at Brussels instead of Amiens."

Montgomery could see that time was running out, and he was becoming obstreperous. The more he received of Eisenhower's four-part message, the more he was shocked. On September 7, he began to holler for supplies. His message read: "Require an air lift of 1,000 tons a day at Douai or Brussels and in last two days have had only 750 tons total. My transport is based on operating 150 miles from my ports and at present I am over 300 miles from Bayeux." He was importing only 6,000 tons a day, half his daily needs. "It is clear therefore that based as I am at present on Bayeux I cannot capture the Ruhr." Even when he got one of the Channel ports near Calais, he would need 2,500 more three-ton trucks to enable him to push on to the Ruhr and Berlin. He referred specifically to Eisenhower's belief that while the ports of Le Havre and Antwerp would be sufficient for a powerful thrust into Germany, "no reallocation of our present resources would be adequate to sustain a thrust to Berlin." Montgomery disagreed. "I submit," he wrote, "that a reallocation of our present resources of every description would be adequate to get one thrust to Berlin." Then he asked again: "Would it be possible for you to come and see me?"

On Sunday, September 10, Eisenhower, Tedder, and Humfrey Gale, SHAEF's logistics officer, left for Brussels. As usual, Kay Summersby was partisan in her account. "Monty," she wrote, "is being most difficult, wants all the supplies." Eisenhower avoided going downtown into the Belgian capital. He hated cities and ceremony. In fact, his leg hurt so badly that the conference took place in his aircraft.

The first thing that Montgomery said was that V-2 rockets had started to rain down on London from the area which was his thrust's next objective. Eisenhower tried to assure him that he was giving priority to the northern thrust. Montgomery bluntly corrected him. "That is *not* being done," he said. Eisenhower then retracted, and said that he had not meant *absolute* priority, and that there was no way that he could scale down the other thrust into the Saar.

Montgomery wearily repeated his old argument: there were two possible plans, his own and Bradley's. Eisenhower had to decide which one to back. There just was not enough for both. Eisenhower clearly showed his vexation with Montgomery's analysis, and they parted with no clear decision, except that Montgomery's next major adventure— a plan for a mass airborne operation designed to capture three bridges including that over the Rhine at Arnhem—should go ahead.

When Eisenhower returned to his headquarters, his leg hurt him so much that he decided to spend several days in bed. Montgomery meanwhile thought over their talk and sent an obstinate, reproachful message to him: "Your decision that the Northern thrust towards the Ruhr is *not* to have priority over other operations will have certain repercussions which you should know. The large scale operations by Second Army and the Airborne Army northwards towards the Meuse and Rhine cannot now take place before 23 September at the earliest and possibly 26 September. This delay will give the enemy time to organize better defensive arrangements and we must expect heavier resistance and slower progress." He continued with an elementary lesson: "It is basically a matter of rail and road and air transport, and unless this is concentrated to give impetus to the selected thrust, then no one is going to get very far since we are all such a long way from our supply bases."

The result, as Montgomery later said, was electric. Bedell Smith went over to see Montgomery and inform him that Eisenhower had decided to act as he had recommended. The Saar thrust would be stopped. The truck transport of three U.S. divisions would be switched to supplying Montgomery's army group. It was the second time Eisenhower had changed his mind in a week.

This left General Patton out on a limb. He at once decided, conniving with Bradley, to get his own army so involved in its upcoming operations beyond the Moselle that not even Eisenhower would dare reduce its allocation of supplies, let alone halt the operations. The next day, September 11, Bradley came around to see Eisenhower and discuss the next month's operations. Bradley disclosed that Patton had just started a drive across the Moselle River, but promised that if Patton had not crossed it by September 14, the attempt would be abandoned. He wrote to Eisenhower the next day, confirming this. "I have told Patton to continue his attack," he said, "but that if by Thursday night he has not been able to force a crossing of the Moselle with the mass of his forces, that he will discontinue that attack." Bradley pleaded with Eisenhower not to cut Patton's supplies down below the 2,500 tons per day he was receiving. Part of the problem was that in the province of Lorraine, where Patton was now operating, the population was largely pro-German. Patton found it creepy. The French Resistance here was nonexistent—not that Patton had thought much of it elsewhere; he had told a press correspondent, who inquired how much the Free French partisans had assisted his advance so far, "better than expected and less than advertised."

Everett Hughes badly wanted to be with Patton again, but he had some difficulty in penetrating the bureaucratic fog—part alcohol, part incompetence—and finding out where Patton was. Nobody he asked in Paris could even tell him where Bradley's headquarters was. It was September 11 before he located Georgie—his headquarters was beyond Châlons—and telephoned him. Georgie said: "Come on over, and bring J.P." Hughes took her and the gifts he had bought in Washington for Patton—liquor, cigars, and a heavy fur-lined coat, as well as the 38 pistol he had allowed that WAC to feel. Patton took Hughes forward with him, his Jeep seldom making less than sixty miles an hour, with Hughes and the bulldog Willie eating dust next to him. Hughes observed: "Geo seems dissatisfied no matter how hard his commanders seem to be pushing. Maybe it works. . . . Geo says Eisenhower through —not a commander. Follows Monty's ideas—wanted to send U.S. troops to Lowlands." There were echoes of this in Kay Summersby's diary too. "E. is sending Bedell to see Monty," she wrote, "to find out just what we have to do. Monty's suggestion is simple, give him everything, which is crazy."

Eisenhower himself avoided Paris. He had been there only twice since Overlord, each time for just an hour. "I prefer camps to cities," he wrote to Mamie. Back in his headquarters, he stayed in bed, his doctors having ordered him to rest his knee. "It's just sore," he complained to Mamie, "and because of my age it is slow healing." The soreness made him crotchety. He kept rereading a letter from his brother Earl, who reported that newspapers at home were giving the impression that the armies were meeting virtually no opposition. Eisenhower replied in annoyed tones: "I do not know what the papers are saying that gives you the impression that battles are easy. I would guarantee that if any one of the writers of the stories to which you refer could have gone with me two or three weeks ago down through the Falaise gap, they would have changed their tune."

Hitler called it the West Wall. The Allies called it the Siegfried Line. It was the intensely fortified band running north and south along the German frontier. It would have to be breached or bypassed. Three Allied forces now approached. To the north, coming from Antwerp, was Montgomery. Two hundred miles below him, near Metz, was the stalled Patton. In between them was Courtney Hodges and his First Army. Joe Collins, one of Hodges' commanders, had not met real enemy resistance since Falaise, three hundred miles to the rear. Now his VII Corps was nearing the West Wall, heading for Cologne. Anxious not to lose momentum, Collins persuaded Hodges to let the VII Corps at least probe the outfield of the West Wall. Immediately ahead of his troops was the first big German city, Aachen, embedded in the wall itself. Ten miles to its southeast was the dense Hürtgen Forest. The corridor between the city and forest had been sown with concrete dragon's teeth and bunkers to halt any tank advance.

On September 12, Collins's corps crossed the border into Germany and began its probe. ("First Army gets through Siegfried Line to Germany," wrote Hughes, who was just visiting Patton. He added: "Geo jealous.") The bloody fighting that now began had nothing in common with the glorious tank thrusts of that summer. In the muddy, rain-soaked forest the Germans, well protected in pillboxes, took a large toll of Collins's tanks and infantry. Easy access to powerful heavy bomber support had spoiled the Americans during the long summer, and without it now they were no match for even these depleted remnants of the German army. Hodges allowed General Gerow's V Corps to probe the West Wall too, but Gerow was also thwarted. Throughout the rest of September and October the Germans and Americans in this sector would slug away at each other in the dripping thickets and depressing downpours.

On September 15, Montgomery wrote to his friend Grigg: "There is no morale problem here at present; when soldiers win great victories they do not bother over-much about the future. What really thrilled them all was the knowledge that by their exertions in the really terrific advance up to Antwerp they were over-running the launching sites for the flying bombs and thus liberating London." He added, "From 17th September onwards, things should be very exciting. And when we have the Ruhr I do not fancy the end will be far off."

Eisenhower appeared to share that view. On the same day he wrote a long letter to Montgomery, considering their next move after the capture of the Ruhr, the Saar, and the Frankfurt area. "Clearly," he wrote, "Berlin is the main prize, and the prize in defense of which the enemy is likely to concentrate the bulk of his forces. There is no doubt whatsoever, in my mind, that we should concentrate all our energies and resources on a rapid thrust to Berlin." Later in the letter, Eisenhower said: "Simply stated, it is my desire to move on Berlin by the most direct and expeditious route, with combined U.S.-British forces supported by other available forces moving through key centers and occupying strategic areas on the flanks, all in one coordinated, concerted operation." It was a good description of Eisenhower's beloved broad-front approach. In any case, all this heady talk of Berlin proved premature. Eisenhower had not even been able to get Montgomery to subscribe to the broad-front strategy for the present actions outside Germany.

Patton lamented in his diary, "Monty is still trying to make all the Armies attack in the Low Countries and against the Ruhr." Bradley sided with Patton. He was still smarting from Dempsey's public attack on the American army for "getting in his way" at Falaise. On September 15, Patton expressed himself more violently: "Monty does what he pleases and Ike says 'yes, sir.' . . . Brad thinks I can and should push on. Brad told Ike that if Monty takes control of the XII and VII Corps of the First Army as he wants to, he, Bradley, will ask to be relieved."

Fighting talk. Bradley muttered to Patton that it was time for a showdown, and Patton took him at his word and eagerly offered to resign with him. But Bradley hastily backed off. Bradley even let Eisenhower persuade him that Montgomery's strategy was logical—before any sustained drive into Germany could be supported, they would have to clear Antwerp and the Channel ports. A day later, Bradley telephoned Patton with word that Montgomery wanted all the Americans to stop so that he, Montgomery, could "make a dagger-thrust with the 21st Army Group at the heart of Germany." Bradley scoffed. "I think," he said, "it will be more like a butterknife thrust."

Patton told his diary: "To Hell with Monty, I must get so involved in my own operations that they can't stop me." He would start his own offensive, permission or not. Out loud he told Bradley, "Don't call me until after dark on the nineteenth."

Hughes, who with J.P. was still visiting Patton, had witnessed most of this. On September 16 he flew back to Granville and found Eisenhower still lame. He was now having to submit to ninety minutes of heat and massage treatment each day. Hughes, as Eisenhower's eyes and ears, made a report. He tattled on Lee's sloppy soldiers and Lee's failures to supply. "At present there is no buildup," he told Eisenhower. "The armies are just living hand to mouth." Then the two generals lunched with two admirals, Bertram Ramsay and Betty Stark, whom Hughes termed the "dumbest admiral I know except Kirk"; Eisenhower had to explain to him three times that each major German port was to be controlled by one Allied nation, and not by a joint mission.

The next day, September 17, Montgomery sprang three British and American airborne divisions on the enemy. He had them drop into a narrow corridor leading from his own front lines deep into German territory. Up this corridor Montgomery hoped to send an armored force and keep it going right across the lower Rhine, where the river was bridged at the Dutch city of Arnhem.

The operation had its curious features. For once, Montgomery's plan would be daring—involving 1,200 transport planes carrying some 16,-000 troops and their equipment, and two thousand gliders. It seemed uncharacteristic that so sudden, narrow, and enormous a venture should have been suggested by the Allied commander most noted for caution and lengthy preparation, and that it was supported by an American Supreme Commander most dedicated to a broad advance along the whole German frontier. But Montgomery had been clamoring for it for weeks, and Eisenhower may well have decided to let him have his way—if the gamble came off, they could all bask in the glory, and if it failed, it would silence Montgomery for some time. Curious too was that, in their hubris, SHAEF and Montgomery had ignored repeated Ultra references to the presence of two of the finest SS panzer divisions, the 9th and 10th, in the Arnhem area. In fact, an Ultra intercept on September 14 revealed that the German army group head-quarters, with Field Marshal Walter Model himself presiding, was actually in the outskirts of Arnhem.

On the first day of the airborne operations the weather was good and the planes flew 4,430 sorties. But the fighting at Arnhem was fierce. The British 1st Airborne Division was encircled. On September 19 the weather worsened, just when the division most needed a drop of reinforcements and supplies.

Eisenhower was in the dark. Communications from Montgomery were sometimes taking longer than letters from Mamie—on the crucial day of September 19 there was one from her complaining that he was not writing frequently enough. He wearily explained why. "You have seen in the papers two days ago we launched a big airborne attack," he said with perceptible sharpness. "Every time I have to order another big battle I wonder how the people at home can be so complacent about finishing off the job we have here. There is still a lot of suffering to go through. God, I hate the Germans!"

The messages from Montgomery were complaints that the crisis in supplies was jeopardizing his prospects, mingled with protestations that the battle was going to work out all right. "The British Airborne Division at Arnhem has been having a bad time," he acknowledged, "but their situation should be eased now that we can advance north-wards from Nijmegen to their support. There is a good sporting chance that we should capture the bridge at Arnhem, which is at present held by the Germans and is intact."

The gamble had been taken, but it failed. On September 25, Mont-gomery called off the operation. He had achieved two thirds of what he had hoped—he had pushed a thin corridor sixty miles long through the enemy position into the Netherlands, and he had secured bridges across the Meuse and Waal rivers. But he could not take the bridge across the Rhine at Arnhem, and that was the one that mattered. He had lost twelve thousand men and 228 transport planes. Two days later the hypertactful Eisenhower wrote to him without mentioning his disappointment. In fact, his tone was almost jocular. "My knee is improving rapidly," he said, "and I hope to be able to run up to see you very quickly."

Spaatz was angry about the Arnhem fiasco, and wrote to a friend on October 1: "We are all disappointed in the results of the airborne operation. . . . I would state that any deficiency in the operation was probably more the fault of the famous British General Montgomery than any other cause." After second thoughts, Spaatz cut this unqualified criticism out of the final letter that he sent. Everett Hughes was also upset about the failure, and wrote sardonically in his diary: "The air drop in Holland was a fiasco. British are glad it was their 1st [Airborne] Division that was captured, otherwise there would have been a stink about the U.S. having to help the British." Underlying both entries was a degree of concealed pleasure that the arrogant British commander had had his comeuppance.

Alarmed by the poor communications, Eisenhower moved on September 20 from Granville to Versailles, about twenty minutes outside Paris. Writing to Betty Stark to thank him for sending elastic socks for his knee, he explained, "I am going to be here only very briefly, as I am too far from the battle line." There were two messages from Montgomery that day, summarized pithily by Kay Summersby in her notebook: "(1) wants all the supplies, (2) also wants to keep the airborne divisions."

The next afternoon, Eisenhower visited Com Z in Paris. He was not getting good news on Lee. His ports were not unloading supplies at the rate expected—only 17,000 instead of 30,000 tons a day. The Red Ball system was breaking down—the cargoes were vanishing along the route, milked by the truckers, and trucks were breaking down under the strain and being abandoned. One day Hughes had waited in Paris to present a Distinguished Service Medal to a Red Ball truck driver, but the convoy had not arrived. Lee, who had given up his attempt to get his Com Z troops to wear helmets and high boots, again advised Eisenhower that he could guarantee sufficient tonnage for Hodges' First Army—which Eisenhower had given a degree of priority—only if the other two American armies stood still.

The strategic debate between Montgomery and Eisenhower, about the correct line of thrust for the Allied armies to take to kill the German colossus most swiftly, grew ever more convoluted. It continued throughout September—at great range, for the two men no longer met in person. It was one of the most crucial arguments of the war. Adopting the right solution might save the lives of tens of thousands of soldiers. Hitting the wrong one would prolong the war by many months. Montgomery harped on the narrow northern thrust. Eisenhower, for political as much as for strategic reasons, still inclined toward the broad-front approach, although he would not say so openly. The lesser British and American army commanders watched this duel with fascination and fury. Eisenhower could see that the American generals believed he was selling them out. Patton guessed that Eisenhower had no choice and that, since Montgomery would not take orders, the American generals would have to take orders instead.

In the debate, which was conducted by messages and letters, Montgomery used blunt language while Eisenhower was blander and more diplomatic.

On September 18, Montgomery wrote: "I consider that as *time* is so very important, we have got to decide what is necessary to go to Berlin and finish the war; the remainder must play a secondary role. It is my opinion that three Armies are enough, if you select the northern route, and I consider that, from a maintenance point of view, it could be done. I have not," he admitted, "studied the southern route."

Eisenhower replied on September 20, trying to appease: "Generally speaking I find myself so completely in agreement with your letter of 18 September that I cannot believe there is any great difference in our concepts." He assured Montgomery that he had never considered pushing into Germany with all the Allied Armies moving abreast; his chosen route of offensive was from the Ruhr to Berlin. Montgomery would lead the drive to Berlin, he said, supported by Hodges' First Army, while Patton and the other forces acted offensively to stretch the German defenders.

Even this did not placate Montgomery. He wanted *all* the other forces halted where they were, while his own offensive went ahead. He replied on September 21 in special code: "I can not agree that our concepts are the same and I am sure you would wish me to be quite frank and open in the matter. I have always said stop the right and go on with the left, but the right [meaning Patton] has been allowed to go on so far that it has outstripped its maintenance and we have lost flexibility." He begged Eisenhower to give Bradley a direct order to halt, adding, "If this order is not obeyed we shall get into greater difficulties." He signed himself, "Your very great friend, Monty."

Eisenhower seethed, but in silence. In fact, the well-built forts around Metz were still barring Patton's advance. And after days of rain, the

ground was getting slippery. So the prospect of an early Moselle crossing by Patton south of Metz was receding.

On September 21, Patton flew up to Paris to lunch with Eisenhower
and, incidentally, to try to thwart the plan to transfer his XV Corps to
the 6th Army Group; the 6th had landed in southern France—Dragoon
—and had worked its way up the Rhone to southern Germany, just
below Patton. It was felt that Patton's southernmost corps, XV Corps,
could be supplied more adequately by Devers, through Marseilles.
Patton wrote sourly to Hughes: "At the moment I am being attacked
on both flanks, but not by the Germans." (Upon learning a few days
later that Devers would definitely get the XV Corps, Patton wrote,
"May God rot his guts.")

Eisenhower, during lunch, must have discussed the Montgomery
problem in a way that pleased Patton, because on his return to his
headquarters at Nancy, Patton recorded: "Things look better today. Ike
still insists, for the present at least, the main effort must be thrown to
the British and the north flank of the First Army. However, he was
more peevish with Montgomery than I have ever seen him. In fact, he
called him a 'clever son of a bitch,' which was very encouraging."

Throughout October, however, Patton would have to sit.

At the same time, Montgomery began a prolonged and consuming
fight to regain overall ground command. The opening shot was a note
to Bedell Smith on September 21 which ended with the words, "I
recommend that the Supreme Commander hands the job over to me
and gives me powers of operational control over First U.S. Army." A
few days later, he would send Smith a wordy memorandum entitled
"Notes on Command in Western Europe." Eisenhower rejected the
recommendation on the thirteenth, and Montgomery wrote to him,
contritely, on the sixteenth: "You will hear no more on the subject of
command from me. I have given you my views and you have given me
your answer. That ends the matter and I and all of us up here will weigh
in one hundred percent to do what you want." This note he signed,
"Your very devoted and loyal subordinate, Monty."

Eisenhower was unimpressed. He told Hughes—and also Virgil Peterson, the Inspector General, who had arrived in Paris to call on Lee
—that he wanted more divisions in line but he could not get the trucks.
Referring to Montgomery's failure to clear the approaches to Europe's

biggest port, he also said: "I want Antwerp, but I have to depend on Monty."

"Why don't you promise Monty a promotion?" Hughes asked him facetiously.

"To what?" sniffed Eisenhower. "When the King was in North Africa, he said he was delighted to discover that Monty wasn't after *his* job."

On the afternoon of September 22, Eisenhower called a commanders in chief conference at Versailles—with Leigh-Mallory, Bradley, Tedder, and Ramsay—to examine the plans for an all-out attack on the Ruhr. Montgomery stayed away, pleading that the Arnhem battle was at a serious stage, but knowing too that he was not popular at SHAEF headquarters. "For operational reasons consider I cannot leave this front to attend your conference Versailles tomorrow," he had written, and sent de Guingand instead.

Bradley had just written a long letter to Eisenhower, showing that he too believed the number-one target in Germany should be the Ruhr industrial zone, and that the route north of the Ruhr was the best. It must have had an effect on the Supreme Commander. After the meeting, de Guingand sent his chief a message that Eisenhower was giving Montgomery his full support—that the northern thrust was to be the main effort. Montgomery recalled that, one month earlier, Eisenhower had refused precisely that strategy. They had lost one month. What the British commander did not know was that, even now, Eisenhower did not have his heart in the northern thrust and was allowing the American generals to subvert it.

Eisenhower, strained by the day's arguing, sent Kay Summersby into Paris to stop by Hughes's office and then went over there himself. Virgil Peterson and Hughes asked them over to the King George V hotel for a drink, but Eisenhower went one better and invited them all for dinner instead. They dined in Eisenhower's billet, which had previously been German Field Marshal von Rundstedt's. Hughes felt that Eisenhower often acted oddly in Kay's presence, and tonight was one of those occasions. Hughes was accustomed to the twosome, but he wrote in his diary, "I don't know what Pete [Peterson] thought." At one stage Eisenhower blurted out, "Have you seen Hodges?" Hughes inquired, "Why?" but got no answer. Then Eisenhower jumped on Brigadier General Paul R. Hawley, the chief surgeon, about the casualty airlift.

Hughes noted in his diary, "Getting nervous?"

The Red Ball truck convoy that Hughes had waited for finally arrived, and while photographers from *Stars & Stripes* took pictures, he awarded a medal to Corporal Bradley, a black driver, before his assembled comrades. Hughes made a little speech, then pinned on the medal. Everyone beamed, and the noncomissioned officer in charge, a Corporal Armstrong, explained to Hughes afterward, "It was the first time the men have been lined up—that is, except when somebody was looking for a man who had committed rape."

The supplies shortage was beginning to bite. At a Patton press conference, one questioner touched the raw nerve. "Is it true that Third Army has outrun its supplies?" he asked. And: "Are you getting your share?"

"Yes," snapped Patton with heavy irony. "But unfortunately we cannot make five barley loaves and three small fishes expand as they used to."

Somebody else asked: "Will the Nazis go underground when the Allies get to Germany?" Patton said: "Six feet."

But the old fire was not in him. The rains around Metz, coupled with J.C.H. Lee's failure to provide the supplies, had put it out.

On September 25, Bradley wrote to Eisenhower confirming that he had ordered Patton to assume the defensive. "At the same time, however," he added, "I have authorized George to make some minor adjustments in his present lines." Coincidentally, on the same day Sir James Grigg wrote to warn Montgomery: "I should like to know how much you are being injured by what I assume to be a fact, viz., that although Ike has assured you that your thrust gets priority his staff, ably assisted by [Humfrey] Gale [of the SHAEF staff, a Briton], are in practice disregarding his pledge."

Eisenhower nevertheless ordered Bradley to see Montgomery immediately to make plans for the First Army to join Montgomery's effort against the Ruhr. He wrote privately to Montgomery himself: "Naturally you and I realize that our present bid for a big prize must be considered as rather bold when compared to our general maintenance situation. However, it is amply worth the risk and the days of even reasonably good weather are rapidly flitting by us."

Eisenhower found himself thinking a lot about Mamie now. "Of course we've changed," he wrote stiffly to her on September 25. "How could two people go through what we have, each in his own way, and without seeing each other except once in more than two years, and still believe they could be exactly as they were. . . . But it seems to me the thing to do is to retain our sense of humor, and try to make an interesting game of getting acquainted again. After all, there is no 'problem' separating us—it is merely distance, and that can some day be eliminated. I'll be scared of you—but 'I'll like you'." "I'll like you" was what Kathryn Gerow, Gee's deceased wife, had always said.

The weeks of idle waiting, of mud, trench foot, rain, and inactivity, got on nerves. So did the dreadful communications. Eisenhower was still plagued by delays in receiving and sending messages. "Unless something is done immediately," he said on September 28, "I'll send General Rumbaugh home and get someone else." William S. Rumbaugh was the theater chief signal officer. Above all, the competition for the scarce gasoline and ammunition tore at previously solid friendships between the army commanders. The generals paid courtesy visits to each other, compared notes and plans, sharpened knives, and slapped each other on the back—feeling for the right place to plunge the blade when the time came.

Nine generals visited Patton on September 27 ("a big day for visiting fireman," he wryly told his diary). He did not mind General Spaatz, the air force commander, because he had him sewn up and in his pocket. But J.C.H. Lee was there—whose supply failure had enforced this accursed pause. Patton could not understand why Eisenhower would not get rid of Lee. "As usual," he wrote to himself, "Lee is a glib liar. Hughes was very much depressed at having to sit at the same table with him." Hughes, too, tried to fathom why Eisenhower put up with Lee. "Alexander the Great loved *flatterers,*" he wrote. Then, probably chuckling, he added, "He died at thirty-three and his empire was divided."

CHAPTER TWENTY-TWO

Crimes and Punishment

THE TWO bomber commanders, Toohey Spaatz and Butcher Harris, were anxious to get back to their attacks on Germany, and they had not been idle with their planning.

Harris had written to Eisenhower on July 18—the day of Goodwood —courteously but emphatically proposing that the big bombers should now be returned to their main task, which he saw as "knocking the weapons out of the hands of the German armies at the point of origin in Germany." The bomb plot against Hitler, two days later, had revealed undercurrents of discontent within the Reich, increasing the pressure for an all-out attack on German civilian morale. While the land battles were raging, Eisenhower disapproved. "Ike says," Spaatz noted on July 21, "he wants more precision, as opposed to morale, bombing." Still the high-level planning went on. Kay Summersby observed in her diary in the middle of the next month: "The CCS are working on a plan to bomb Berlin day and night when bombers are available from the battle front." Now it was Spaatz who objected, expressing opposition to what he called any indiscriminate bombing of Berlin.

But a new mood was overtaking the Allied Supreme Command in those first days after Falaise—days which had seen carnage on a nightmarish scale. Just as war was brutalizing the battle-torn combat troops, leading them to acts of cruelty of which they would never have thought themselves capable, it was now affecting the commanders with a callous impatience, a perverse detachment, a yielding to the convenience by which the end justifies the means. Eisenhower wrote to Spaatz on August 28 suggesting that such a Berlin raid might be executed under special circumstances, if there was an opportunity for a "sudden and devastating blow" with what he called "real promise of ending the war quickly."

This shift was just one of the changes now occurring in the world of the high commanders. The days of the Allied Expeditionary Air Force headquarters, for example, and of Leigh-Mallory as Eisenhower's air chief, were drawing to an end. On September 6, Hap Arnold wrote asking Eisenhower what was going to be done with the British air chief marshal. It would, Arnold said, be a problem to find a suitable employment for the man. "Naturally this is a problem for the RAF," he continued with a trace of irony. "Since they have over twenty Air Chief Marshals and Marshals of the Royal Air Force on their roles, I cannot feel that a suitable assignment for one of them is any insuperable problem." Eisenhower refused to join in the baying and howling against the British air chief. "I agree," he wired back to Arnold, "that under present circumstances we could get along without Leigh-Mallory's headquarters, but the fact is that through every day of this campaign Leigh-Mallory has proved his intense desire to cooperate and a very admirable grasp of the whole situation. . . . You should not be under any misapprehension as to Leigh-Mallory's qualifications and attitude. Admitting that upon first glance he seems to be a bit difficult, he is one of the type that never ceases." Arnold replied, muted: "I will not knowingly do anyone an injustice." The matter was soon solved. Leigh-Mallory left England a few weeks later to serve under Lord Mountbatten in the Southeast Asia theater; his plane was lost on the way out to the Far East.

The Combined Chiefs of Staff returned control of the strategic bomber forces in Europe to the respective British and American air commanders on September 15. In anticipation of this, Arnold had a week earlier asked Spaatz to submit a plan for the use of both American and British air forces in an "all-out, widespread attack, of perhaps six or seven days' duration, against Germany." As for the actual targets, Arnold added that he did not himself believe in obliteration attacks against cities, nor did he think that Berlin alone should be the target. The next day Spaatz talked the Berlin project over with Eisenhower. Spaatz later noted that Eisenhower gave him "instructions . . . that we would no longer plan to hit definite military objectives but be ready to drop bombs indiscriminately on the town when order given by General Eisenhower."

These bombing debates led to some strange entries in the annals of the war leaders. According to the minutes of the U.S. Joint Chiefs' meeting in Washington on September 14, Arnold "said that he understood the British objected to the Combined Chiefs of Staff recording their decision that Germany should be bombed for morale purposes." In other words, it should be done but there should be no record kept of the decision. The paragraph was amended to read: "General Arnold said that he understood the British desired that the Combined Chiefs of Staff endorse morale bombing of Germany." But even thus sanitized, the paragraph frightened some. Admiral Leahy "thought that it would be a mistake for the Combined Chiefs of Staff to record such a decision."

It must be said that at this time the German missile attack on London was just resuming, and no longer with mere V-1s. The V-2 weapon had arrived. This had been feared for months. Evidence had trickled into London all summer that Hitler was preparing a weapon far more sinister than the V-1 flying bomb—some kind of rocket, weighing apparently about fifty tons and carrying a ten-ton warhead that would wreck everything over a five-mile radius. This was no myth (although the figures were exaggerated). Agents had flown into Poland and picked up a section of one of the missiles from a rocket testing range. More fragments of a rocket had been obtained from Sweden, where it had crashed after a test flight. The V-2 was an appalling prospect for the British. In July their Home Secretary, Herbert Morrison, had reported to the Cabinet that 15,500 houses in London had already been destroyed by the V-1 and 691,000 needed repairs. Fifty thousand men were engaged in repair work; 229,000 people had been evacuated and half a million more had fled. Now a ghastly new rocket menace was looming, with the prospect that London, one of the biggest industrial cities in the world, might come to a total halt overnight—and that there might be uncontrollable public panic. Hospitals were already being cleared to accommodate 36,000 people, because up to four thousand casualties were expected every day. The Home Secretary said with typical understatement: "I fear the public will become angry."

Pressure, therefore, was mounting on the generals to capture the whole launching area along the Channel coast—now. On August 4, Eisenhower had received a directive from Washington ordering him to alter his strategy to include such a ground operation. "In the development of your plans for campaign in France," the directive read, "please ensure that due weight is given to the elimination of this threat."

Then the V-2 arrived. At the beginning of the second week in September, mighty detonations were heard in London. They were officially dismissed as gas explosions, but witnesses said they heard a supersonic bang preceding the explosion, and others heard the rushing sound of something coming to earth *after* the blast (an odd physical effect of supersonic missiles). On September 11, Spaatz sent a telegram to Arnold: "Explosions seem to have been caused by long range rocket projectiles. They were reported in England early evening 8th September. Sound location indicates projectiles came from Rotterdam-Amsterdam area. Radio search equipment heard no control signals. One possible radar plot as yet unconfirmed. Examination of one incident showed crater 38ft diameter and 8ft 8ins deep. . . . Projectile penetrated concrete road. Three persons killed, eighteen injured. Seven houses destroyed and blast damage extended approximately one quarter mile. Only small pieces found. Comparison of bits collected with parts of Swedish rocket gives reasonable identification of new parts for long range rocket projectile. Civilian interviewed by air technical officers stated he was in factory three and a half miles from point of impact and approximately one and a half minutes elapsed before sound of explosion reached him and he and other persons heard whistling sound similar to siren but of higher pitch. . . ."

The fear that the V-1s had inspired in the American commanders in England—and the grim prospect of an even deadlier rocket—resulted naturally in the idea of using old planes as pilotless superbombs: the plane could be packed with high explosive, the crew could bale out over friendly territory, and then a control plane could steer it onto some target. There had been initial experiments. They were not promising, but attempts were made to use these explosive-laden planes against the mysterious giant V-weapon sites. The trouble was that a clapped-out four-engined bomber full of high explosive could be more lethal to the men who had to fly it into the air than to its target. On August 12, a U.S. Navy robot-plane task force set out to wipe out Mimoyecques— a gigantic Nazi underground gun battery from which Hitler hoped to pump a thousand rocket shells an hour at London. A robot B-24 Liberator, crammed with explosives, was piloted into the air by a two-man crew and steered toward the point from which two mother ships would take over its guidance. The trial run came to a drastic end. After a few robot-controlled test turns, the B-24 suddenly blew up in a fireball and disintegrated into a puff of white vapor. There were few fragments big enough to hit the ground. The two crewmen were killed. One of them was Lieutenant Joseph P. Kennedy Jr., USNR, son of a former American ambassador to the Court of St. James's and brother of a future American president.

After that the American plan to use such aircraft for the bombing of enemy cities went ahead, but more cautiously. Arnold reported to Eisenhower on October 14 that the first bombers would be ready by winter: the pilots would bail out and the tail sections would be blown off over the target. There were immediate British objections—though not on moralistic grounds so much as because the British knew that Goering had available considerably more battered old planes than the Allies. The basic concept, however, did raise some eyebrows. Had not the American air force always prided itself on scrupulously attacking only military targets? Arnold chewed this matter over, then wrote to Spaatz: "I can see very little difference between the British night area bombing and our taking a war weary airplane, launching it at say fifty or sixty miles away from Cologne and letting it fall somewhere in the city limits." He favored turning them loose to land "all over Germany."

If the war had ended rapidly that autumn, as seemed possible during the Falaise battle, there would have been little need for these eccentric projects. As it was, they dissipated energies that would have been better devoted to concluding the urgent business on hand. Eisenhower, for his part, was enmeshed in the higher politics of planning the division and rule of postwar Germany, and this resulted in decisions and debates no less egregious than had occupied the generals over the rights and wrongs of bombing civilian targets.

Since seeing Roosevelt in his White House sickbed in January, Eisenhower had not given much thought to the problem of postwar Germany. On July 10, he told Lord Halifax, the British ambassador in Washington, who was visiting him in England, that the war leaders should be "shot while trying to escape." This, he suggested, would avoid the embarrassment and tedium of a trial. When talk turned to the enemy general staff, Bedell Smith agreed with Eisenhower that imprisonment was not enough. Harry Butcher noted: "There was agreement that extermination could be left to nature if the Russians had a free hand." At this, Eisenhower inquired, Why just the Russians? Zones in postwar Germany, he proposed, could be temporarily assigned to the smaller nations with scores to settle.

Roosevelt also touched on these problems that summer. At a stag dinner in honor of the Polish exile premier, Stanislaus Mikolajczyk, at the White House one day after D-day, the Joint Chiefs had listened with round eyes as Roosevelt related remarks Stalin had made to him about plans to "liquidate 50,000 German officers." Henry Stimson was particularly disturbed to find Roosevelt hell-bent on occupying northern Germany; that, thought Stimson, would invite trouble with the British, who wanted control of the great north German ports. He reminded Roosevelt of the large number of German descendants among his voters. "I felt," Stimson recorded obliquely in his diary, "that repercussions would be sure to arise which would mar the page of our history if we, whether rightly or wrongly, seemed to be responsible for it." Two days later Stimson jotted down notes which showed what he meant by "repercussions." Occupying the more congenial southern sector of Germany, he wrote, "keeps us away from Russia during occupational period. Let her do the dirty work but don't father it." Stimson was apprehensive about getting involved in what he called a "major humanitarian issue." But Roosevelt was hostile to the idea of occupying southern Germany; he feared his occupation army's lines of communication getting entangled in a Communist-led revolution that well could break out in neighboring France. He turned his back on the problem and concentrated on his election campaign.

In mid-August the War Department sent Eisenhower a draft paper outlining rather mild occupation policies, and asked him for his comment. Colonel B. Bernstein of SHAEF filched a copy of this draft and —bypassing regular army channels—sent it to his friend Henry Morgenthau, the Secretary of the Treasury, in Washington. This put the fat in the fire. Morgenthau was outraged by the leniency of the War Department approach. On August 23 he lunched with Roosevelt and told him his own, more stringent views about the control of Germany. Roosevelt repeated them at that afternoon's Cabinet meeting. Roosevelt, noted James V. Forrestal, the Secretary of the Navy, in his own diary, "said that he [Morgenthau] had just heard about a paper prepared by the Army and that he was not at all satisfied with the severity of the measures proposed. [Morgenthau] said the Germans should have simply a subsistence level of food—as he put it, soup kitchens would be ample to sustain life—that otherwise they should be stripped clean and should not have a level of subsistence above the lowest level of the people that they had conquered."

Stimson, who endorsed the gentler War Department approach, was horrified. "Morgenthau's proposal," he pointed out to his diary, "would lead to starvation for thirty million Germans."

Roosevelt said to him, "I'm meeting Churchill in September at Quebec. I expect all these questions will be settled then." Later, Morgenthau told Stimson that since Churchill, Roosevelt, and Stalin had already decided Europe's postwar frontiers at Teheran, it would not make much difference where Eisenhower's armies stood on the day the war ended. Stimson dictated this note for his diary: "Morgenthau told me of how he had learned in London that the division of Germany had been agreed upon at Teheran between the three chiefs. Although the discovery of this thing has been a most tremendous surprise to all of us, I am not sure that the three chiefs regard it as a fait accompli."

When Stimson called on the President again two days later, he found there were ideas of frontier justice drifting around in Roosevelt's mind. Stimson reminded Roosevelt of Stalin's words about liquidating the 50,000 German officers, and asked for directives. How was Eisenhower to deal with those categories proclaimed to be "criminals"? Should Hitler and his gang of racists and anti-Semites be simply liquidated? "Our officers," said Stimson, "must have the protection of definite instructions if shooting is required. Shooting must be immediate, not postwar." He felt that a Cabinet-level policy group should advise the President, and that a really competent political officer should be assigned to Eisenhower to guide him.

"The President showed some interest in radical treatment of the Gestapo," recorded a Stimson aide afterward. Roosevelt said that he would set up a committee consisting of Secretary of State Cordell Hull, Stimson himself—and Morgenthau. Roosevelt was obviously intrigued by Morgenthau's plan. "Germany can live happily and peacefully on soup from soup kitchens," he said.

Stimson abhorred the Morgenthau plan, which he felt too punitive. "I've been trying to guard against that," he noted privately. He and Marshall felt that the punishment should be visited mainly upon the Gestapo and the SS. "By so doing," Stimson reflected some days later, "I thought we would begin at the right end, namely the Hitler machine, and punish the people who were directly responsible. . . . I found around me, particularly Morgenthau, a very bitter atmosphere of personal resentment against the entire German people without regard to individual guilt, and I am very much afraid that it will result in our taking mass vengeance . . . in the shape of clumsy economic action." There was a danger, he stressed, that such a vicious program would obscure the guilt of the Nazis. That was the way to start a new war, he mused, not that at his age he would live to see it.

The special committee—Stimson, Hull, and Morgenthau—met for the first time on September 5, and it was the most difficult and unpleasant meeting that the Secretary of War could remember. Morgenthau outlined his grisly plan for Germany. Stimson found himself in a minority of one. "It's very singular," Stimson commented afterward to Marshall. "I'm the man in charge of the department which does the killing in this war, and yet I am the only one who seems to have any mercy for the other side." Marshall laughed sympathetically. Morgenthau, Stimson found, had spent weeks greasing the way, but Hull's ideas were no less extreme. "He and Morgenthau," wrote Stimson in his diary, "wished to wreck completely the immense Ruhr-Saar area of Germany and turn it into second-rate agricultural land regardless of all that that area meant not only to Germany but to the welfare of the entire European continent." The next day Stimson admonished President Roosevelt. "You should not burn down your house just to get a meal of roast pig," he said. He pointed out the economic fallacies and produced lengthy memoranda opposing Morgenthau. Roosevelt set them aside. Then—as Stimson later put it—Roosevelt "pranced up to the meeting at Quebec" taking only Morgenthau with him, while leaving Hull and Stimson behind. Stimson was furious that Roosevelt was ignoring the committee he had himself set up.

Supreme Court justice Felix Frankfurter hoped that Roosevelt in his wisdom would cast aside Morgenthau's proposals. Stimson did not share his hopes. "Here the President appoints a committee with Hull as its chairman . . . ," said Stimson, "and, when he goes off to Quebec, he takes the man who really represents the minority and is so biased by his Semitic grievances that he is really a very dangerous adviser to the President at this time." Stimson decided to go ahead and issue a directive to Eisenhower anyway. "Our troops are now in Germany," he pointed out to Hull over the telephone, justifying the need for haste. But events in Quebec overtook the Washington dissenters. Stimson was out of touch because a hurricane had torn down the telephone lines to his weekend house. Finally his deputy John McCloy got him on the phone and told him that, during dinner with Roosevelt on the thirteenth, "the Semites"—as he called them—had won. A memorandum authorizing the Morgenthau plan had been drafted.

The document—approving the conversion of Germany to an agricultural economy—was then "okayed" by the initials FDR and WSC, and dated September 15. The military men at Quebec were not consulted. Hap Arnold was purring because of bouquets from the President and the Prime Minister. "Prime Minister very complimentary about our Normandy and Southern France operations," he wrote in his diary, "after his violent opposition several months ago." In fact, Arnold's visit to Quebec was marred only by a visit to a Canadian army show at which, he clucked to his diary, "my sensibilities were shocked to see Negro men dancing and almost caressing white girls and a white man doing the same to a Negro gal." There is no record as to whether the racial sensibilities of Arnold—so similar to those of the men whose punishment he was helping to plan—struck his companions at Quebec as ironic.

When McCloy learned of the Morgenthau plan, he at once informed the navy secretary of it. "In general," wrote Forrestal, "the program, according to Mr. McCloy, called for the conscious destruction of the economy in Germany and the encouragement of a state of impoverishment and disorder." The effect on the already crumbling discipline of the U.S. Army was not difficult to predict, in McCloy's view.

It was an extraordinary decision—extraordinary as much for the manner at which the two leaders reached it as for what it prescribed. Both men were in fact quite ill. Hap Arnold observed in his diary at Quebec on September 16: "Thought that the President looked badly. He did not have the pep, power of concentration, could not make his usual wisecracks, seemed to be thinking of something else. Closed his eyes to rest more than usual." Churchill was also ill again. But the possibility of increasing British postwar exports at Germany's expense had animated him. When Anthony Eden protested the plan, Churchill became belligerent and snapped: "This is a matter of the good fortune of my people against the good fortune of the German people, and I am for my people." Sharp words flew. Churchill warned Eden not to return to London and stoke up the War Cabinet against him before he got home.

On September 17, an interim directive was issued to Eisenhower by the U.S. Joint Chiefs of Staff defining the nature of the regime to be set up after the Nazi defeat. Basically, Eisenhower was to ensure that the Germans realized they would never again be allowed to threaten world peace. "Your occupation and administration," the document read, "will be just but firm and distant. You will strongly discourage fraternization between Allied troops and the German officials and population." This vaguely worded document was amplified over the weeks by a string of ever-harsher directives from Washington as the Morgenthau plan began to bite. The political directive issued on October 14 stressed the elimination of the German officer corps: "General Staff officers not taken into custody as prisoners are to be arrested and held, pending receipt of further instructions as to their disposal." That sounded very ominous. Attached to the directive was a draft instrument of unconditional surrender for the Nazi leaders to sign when the time came.

McCloy described for Eisenhower the controversy surrounding the Morgenthau plan, and Stimson's hostility to it, in a secret letter on October 17. "Inevitably the Press and others oversimplified the issue into 'hard' and 'soft' schools," he wrote, "and immediately there was speculation as to who would be the High Commissioner and whether he would be of one school or the other. Mr. Morgenthau had his candidates and others had theirs."

The leaking of the Morgenthau plan in a New York newspaper led to an outcry in Germany. Nazi propaganda capitalized on it. Eighty million Germans were led to believe that if they lost the war, their nation would be systematically ruined and they themselves would be starved to death. German resistance, already stiffening, became desperate. The death toll among Allied soldiers increased. General Patton would tell General LeRoy Lutes, visiting his Third Army a few weeks later, "Some fanatical young Germans attack and die to the last man, refusing to surrender."

On November 20, Eisenhower sent a frustrated message to the Combined Chiefs of Staff. "German morale on this front," he said, "shows no sign of cracking at present. I am of the opinion that [the] enemy's continued stolid resistance is a main factor postponing the final victory which, in present circumstances, can only be achieved by prolonged and bitter fighting." One explanation of this German resolve, he said, was Nazi propaganda which had convinced every German that unconditional surrender meant the complete devastation of Germany and its elimination as a nation. He asked not for a reversal of the policy of unconditional surrender, but for more Allied subversive propaganda and deception measures. If the Allies could set the simple German soldier at odds with his commanders, as well as with the Nazi Party and the SS, that would be half the battle.

The CCS did persuade Roosevelt to draft a declaration suitable for issue to the German people, assuring them that despite the "overall iron discipline of the Wehrmacht and the stranglehold of the Nazi party over the individuals of the German nation," those people had nothing to fear from the Allies. But Churchill vetoed the declaration. He opposed giving any assurances to the Germans without consulting Stalin; and Stalin would undoubtedly insist on having "several million Nazi youth, Gestapo men and so forth for prolonged work." Moreover, argued Churchill, any such declaration would be taken as a sign of Allied weakness. German propaganda minister Joseph Goebbels, wrote Churchill to Eisenhower, "would certainly be able to point to the alteration of our tone as an encouragement for further resistance, and the morale of the German fighting troops would be proportionately raised."

Voices of reason continued to speak out. "The American people," Forrestal said to a meeting in January 1945, "would not support mass murder of the Germans, their enslavement, or the industrial devastation of the country." Stimson agreed with him. Forrestal asked why American soldiers should continue to have to pay with their lives, if everybody agreed that this cruel Morgenthau program was never going to be effected. The answer was, because the Allied governments refused to define the phrase out of which the Nazi propaganda was making so much capital: "unconditional surrender."

So the fight went on.

CHAPTER TWENTY-THREE

Bottlenecks

THINGS HAD gone so well for the Allies. German resistance was ranging from occasional to nonexistent. Paris was a pleasure, a splendid diversion from the rigors of high-level bickering and contesting for power. There were only two problems of any consequence; so they thought. One was supplies, and once that was solved—surely it soon would be solved—there would be no stopping the Allied armies. This raised the other problem, one resulting from the inevitable battlefield success: how soon would this war end?

One day in October, Montgomery visited the Canadian troops and had them all guessing as to how long the war would last. Then he gave them his own view. It all depended, he said, on whether the Germans brought their forces into action and offered a pitched battle this side of the Rhine; or whether they stepped slowly back, avoiding a pitched battle until well behind the Rhine, in which case, he said, the war would drag on into the spring of 1945.

Nazi garrisons still held the ports of Dunkirk, Lorient, Saint-Nazaire, and Bordeaux, so Eisenhower's armies still depended on Cherbourg. The Nazis still blocked the approaches to Antwerp too. In the mistaken belief that the great port was about to be opened, J.C.H. Lee had switched the port service troops—the unloaders—prematurely away from Cherbourg. The railroads were still unusable, thanks to Leigh-Mallory's transportation bombing plan. Red Ball had taken a toll on trucking. By late October nine thousand useless trucks with collapsed engines and broken suspensions sprawled outside a balloon hangar in Normandy—a dumb monument to Red Ball. The European theater lacked even tire repair kits. Everett Hughes read Eisenhower's appeal for tire conservation and scrawled across it: "A trifle late. Should have started when we came ashore."

As Eisenhower's "eyes and ears," Hughes paid a surprise visit to Cherbourg with the Inspector General, Virgil Peterson, to see what was wrong with the flow. "Pete disgusted," wrote Hughes. "Says that commanding officer of any similar project in U.S. would be fired if work did not go ahead faster." Hughes blamed Lee, whose inspections were never surprise but staged affairs with those being inspected forewarned by the itineraries he had expensively printed and distributed.

Hughes, appalled, got Lee to return to Cherbourg with him. On the way, he lectured Lee about how to make inspections, until Lee complained: "You're just an old schoolteacher." Forewarned yet again, the entire Normandy Base Section turned out in spotless uniforms to meet him. "Everybody in Normandy knows you are here," Hughes pointed out to Lee in frustration. "So what's the use!" He made a harsh comment in his notebook: "Lee has a hard job—the one of pleasing everybody including himself."

Hughes picked up a cold, which developed into a fever, and he was hospitalized in Paris. Ever on the ball, he got the doctors to describe how *they* got ready when they heard that Lee was coming on an inspection. Hughes reached for his notebook as they told him: "Dress up—stop all operations—liquor down toilets." He wrote it all down.

In Paris and Versailles, life was good, even though the coal was running out. Eventually Eisenhower called his ground commanders together to discuss the next phase of the war. A four-star car was sent to pick up Montgomery at Villacoublay military airfield and a three-star Packard Clipper for Bradley. Sir Alan Brooke came over from London. The commanders crowded into the SHAEF War Room and began by conducting an inquest into their campaign so far. Eisenhower himself nobly took the blame for Montgomery's failure to seize the approaches to Antwerp before attempting Arnhem; he had approved Montgomery's plans, he said. "The atmosphere," said Brooke in his diary, "was good and friendly in spite of some candid criticisms of the administrative [supply] situation."

The commanders then discussed the coming battle against the enemy West Wall. Eisenhower's strategy, as recorded by Brooke, consisted of opening up the port of Antwerp, then making a broad-front approach to the Rhine, crossing that river to encircle the industrial Ruhr region, the mighty arsenal of Hitler's armies. That, Brooke's notes continued, would be "followed by an advance on Berlin either from Ruhr or from Frankfurt, depending on which proved most promising."

Despite Eisenhower's charity at the SHAEF meeting, Montgomery was not tamed. With mounting irritability he blamed Eisenhower for the military stalemate, decrying the fact that he would not appoint one commander to direct the thrust to the Ruhr. Eisenhower was trying to run everything himself from SHAEF, he said, "by means of long telegrams." Montgomery fought back with letters handwritten with his broad-nibbed Parker 51 pen on pale blue note paper. The tone was at all times respectful, tinged with impatience when the going got rough. When the undercurrent was most acid, Montgomery would sign the letters, "Your very devoted friend." In them, he tried to show Eisenhower that, given the present supply bottlenecks, there was no way they could capture the Ruhr *and* the Saar *and* the Frankfurt area, as he was planning, before proceeding to Berlin.

At the same time, Montgomery kept up a running backup correspondence with both Brooke and Grigg, his military and political superiors in London. "The American armies have outstripped their maintenance and as a result we have lost flexibility on the front as a whole," he wrote to Grigg. "We are now unlikely to get the Ruhr *or* the Saar *or* Frankfurt. In fact it is my opinion that we have 'mucked up' the whole show and we have only ourselves to blame. It is a great tragedy, I did what I could; I have always taken my stand by my cable to Eisenhower of 4 September, in which I said we must concentrate everything in one terrific blow. I said that if we attempted a compromise solution and split our maintenance resources so that neither thrust is fullblooded, we would prolong the war."

When all else failed, Montgomery wrote the desperate memorandum

"Notes on Command in Western Europe," in which he lamented the wanton dismantling by Eisenhower of the command structure that had triumphed during Overlord. "With it," he wrote, "we won probably one of the greatest victories the world has ever seen." They had then gotten rid of the ground force commander—Montgomery himself— and then Leigh-Mallory as air commander. Eisenhower, he insisted, must appoint one ground commander now. "In battle," he explained, "very direct and quick action is required." Either Eisenhower should do that job himself, or he should name Montgomery or Bradley. "I would like to say," Montgomery told Grigg, "that I would be proud to serve under my very great friend Omar Bradley." Those were remarkably unselfish words for a field marshal to write—that to break a command deadlock, he would be willing to serve under a three-star general with only a fraction of his battle experience.

To his long letter to Grigg he added a postscript. "If the business is properly handled now, we could get away with it, I believe, and could finish the business this year—or as near as matters. But unless it is so handled and a very firm grip is taken, I feel we shall have only ourselves to blame."

Then he scrawled: "PPS: I think I have let off a good bit of steam in this letter and you had better *burn* it."

Eisenhower was not impressed by Montgomery's pressure tactics. On October 7 there was a letter from Montgomery saying, "It is my opinion that the present system of command is most unsatisfactory." To Tedder, Montgomery said: "The enemy has reacted very violently to our threat to the Ruhr and has concentrated strong forces against Second Army." Over the next two days, Eisenhower first emphatically disagreed with Montgomery, again demanding a broad-front assault on the Rhine, and then emphatically agreed with him: "I must emphasize that of all our operations on our entire front from Switzerland to the channel, I consider Antwerp of first importance." It was enough to make the austere field marshal's mustache twitch.

Montgomery was coming under increasing naval criticism for having failed to clear Antwerp. Admiral Ramsay's was the loudest voice. Montgomery cabled Eisenhower on October 9: "Dear Ike . . . Request you will ask Ramsay from me by what authority he makes wild statements to you concerning my operations about which he can know *nothing.*"

On October 12, Kay Summersby wrote in her diary: "Message from Monty. He wants to command the 12th Army Group." Eisenhower replied to Montgomery the next day in negative terms. Three days later, Montgomery sent off what appeared to be a capitulation. He had realized that the West Pointer was intransigent in his views on strategy and there would be no benefit in further upsetting him with this debate. He wrote an "Eyes Only" message assuring him grandly, "You will hear *no* more on the subject of command from me. I have given you my views and you have given your answer. That ends the matter, and I and all of us here will weigh in 100 per cent to do what you want, and we will pull it through without a doubt. I have given Antwerp top priority in all operations in 21 Army Group, and all energies and efforts will be now devoted towards opening up that place. Your very devoted and loyal subordinate, Monty."

Eisenhower replied the next day thanking him graciously.

October 14 was his fifty-fourth birthday. Eisenhower visited General Hodges' headquarters at Liege, Belgium. Bradley was on hand, and Simpson, Collins, Gerow, and Charles Corlett. Last to arrive was Patton, at a quarter to noon. It was a special occasion: King George VI was paying a call on the top American generals. Eisenhower spoke fine words of welcome to the King—saying that a prominent American had once gotten into serious trouble by saying that blood was thicker than water. But he felt the same. "If ever there is another war, pray God we have England as an ally," said Eisenhower, "and long live King George VI!"

That evening, in the chateau where Hodges housed them, the generals dined informally and pleasantly together. After dinner Simpson, a tall, thin, balding officer whose Ninth Army had just been moved to the front, retired to his third-floor room, and Patton walked in from his room just across the hall. Patton and Big Simp were good friends. Over cognac, Patton said, "It's a funny thing, you and I here now. We were at West Point together—and here we are now, both commanding armies." Then he remarked, without bitterness, "You know, you and Hodges and I are older foxes than either Eisenhower or Bradley, but we're going to do an awful lot of fighting for them." Obviously Patton had been giving the situation some thought.

Three days later Eisenhower went to see Patton at Nancy. Patton begged him for three million gallons of gasoline and five days' ration of ammunition. He was itching to get moving. In a letter a few days later he hinted that if Bradley could guarantee him two thousand tons of ammunition a day, he could attack at any time. He told Bradley the same, but the army group commander just listened and said nothing. He knew the strategic and supply position. Patton did not care to. He wrote, "Bradley is too conservative—he wants to wait until we can all jump together, by which time half our men will have flu or trench foot."

After five days on the road, which included a visit to Montgomery at his new command post in Brussels, Eisenhower returned to SHAEF at Versailles, to answer an enormous stack of mail from well-wishers, distant relatives, and countless children. "Today," he wrote Mamie, "I have had a letter from a six year old boy who says I'm his favorite soldier. . . . He ended his letter by saying he was sending also a big hug and a kiss for me." He was still looking for somebody capable of answering mail in his direct, simple style. Interviewed on a radio program, Bing Crosby had mentioned that Eisenhower liked hominy grits. Now Eisenhower had to sign a dozen notes a day just thanking people for their gift of grits. He kicked the electric heater in his quarters—it tried hard but usually failed. There was going to be a lot of freezing this winter. The Americans could supply the French economy with only one third of the coal that the Germans had supplied to them; there just was not enough transport.

One letter brought a lump to his throat. It was from his son John, now coming over from Fort Benning with a regular infantry division. John offered him congratulations on the progress of his armies. "I think," Eisenhower wrote in reply, "a man could far more easily be a hero to a whole nation . . . than he could to his own son."

The American XIX Corps had begun a relentless attack on Aachen two weeks before. For Hitler, Aachen, the first city in Germany to be attacked by the Allied armies, was a matter of prestige, a second Stalingrad. Its defenders took to the cellars and sewers, and the Americans had to fight it out street by street. They found by trial and error that the only caliber that could make an impression on Aachen's ancient stone buildings was the 155-millimeter howitzer. But 155-millimeter ammunition was running out. The few buildings that still stood were cheese-holed with artillery. The attacking troops were soon exhausted and demoralized, yet Aachen held out.

Eisenhower, one month before the invasion. Said Montgomery: "He has elected to take direct command of very large-scale operations, and he does not know how to do it."

Eisenhower's Irish chauffeur, Kay Summersby, and his terrier, Telek.

The British commanders were slightly amazed at the openness with which Kay Summersby appeared as Eisenhower's hostess and companion. The two of them are shown below, just after the war, in a London theater, with (from left) Eisenhower's son, John; a Miss Tony Porter; and Omar Bradley. At right, Eisenhower reacts to good news from the front.

Below, French General Jacques Philippe LeClerc leading Gaullist troops into an already-liberated Paris. At right, a dictatorial Charles de Gaulle ticks off a list of his requirements to a long-suffering Eisenhower; de Gaulle was considered a deep thorn in the Alliance. At bottom, celebrating Paris's new freedom, are: Eisenhower, French general Pierre Koenig, Omar Bradley, and Arthur Tedder.

On facing page, top: Secretary of War Henry Stimson visiting Eisenhower in England. "The British," said Stimson, "are showing decadence. A magnificent people, but they have lost their initiative." Bottom, Eisenhower at the wedding of a member of his office staff in Paris, unaware that at this very moment the Germans were launching their surprise Ardennes counteroffensive. Above, jubilating in Rheims over the signing of the German surrender (from left), are: Russian general Ivan Susloparoff; Eisenhower's deputy Frederick Morgan; Walter Bedell Smith; Kay Summersby; Eisenhower; his aide Harry Butcher; and Arthur Tedder. Butcher (right) also kept a candid diary, which Eisenhower forced him to censor.

On the other end of the chain of command, the ordinary soldiers lived or died according to the wars between the generals.

All along the front, the momentum was being lost. It was the same at Metz in Lorraine, an ancient fortress city straddling a traditional strategic route into Germany, a city which had not been captured for centuries. Here fanatical battalions of Hitler Youth troops were holding massive stone-walled forts against all attack. On October 18, Everett Hughes—who was again lying in the hospital, this time with a bad leg —wrote: "Aachen hasn't fallen yet and Geo [Patton] has had to withdraw . . . at Metz. Wonder who told him not to get men killed needlessly." A nurse brought Hughes a bouquet of roses, and he opened them with pleasurable anticipation. Perhaps they were from from J.P.? The card read, "So sorry, dear Everett." But it was from the abominable J.C.H. Lee.

Spaatz flew down to Nancy to see Patton and found him desperate to start moving forward again. He believed he had sufficient supplies and the punch to get to the Rhine, but "they" would not let him. Spaatz stayed the night, and spent much of it talking with Patton about the best way to use his heavies on the battlefield. Patton said that if and when he was given strategic air support, he would hold his infantry well back, dispersed, with its heads down in foxholes; and he would send tanks to lead the initial assault.

The next day, Spaatz flew on to Luxembourg to visit Bradley. Bradley told him he planned to start his big offensive toward the Rhine on November 10. Spaatz wanted it sooner than that. Hitler's jet fighters were appearing in growing force, and they threatened to drive Spaatz's daylight bomber formations from the skies. "To maintain our present air supremacy over the Hun," warned Spaatz, "will cost the strategic air force about forty thousand crew members. . . . So it's essential for the armies to get to the Rhine as quickly as possible so that we can secure additional airfields for our fighters."

Bradley thought it over. "We could advance our attack to November 5," he said, "if our meteorologists have an indication of good flying weather." Spaatz responded that his Strategic Air Forces would be willing to lay down a heavy barrage just where Bradley wanted it, if weather conditions permitted.

Weather was one factor. The other was ammunition. Hungry for it, Bradley went to Paris to demand of Lee's office that ammunition be put ahead of everything else. There was no need, he said, to move winter clothing forward yet—"the men are tough," Bradley told Robert "Big

John" Littlejohn, the chief quartermaster. "We must go forward as long as we can. And that means ammunition and gasoline must be given top priority." The fate of one ship, lying off Le Havre loaded with a million blankets, was typical of the supply chaos. Five different berths had been assigned to it, but always, just as it was about to unload, it was made to pull out so that an ammunition ship could get in. The army was taking a big risk, postponing the blankets and heavy clothing. If the winter proved to be a harsh one, then what happened to Hitler outside Moscow might happen to the Allies too. A further burden on the supply system was that SHAEF also had to provide for the liberated populations. Food was running low throughout France, Belgium, and Holland. The first people penalized were the German prisoners. Hughes decided their rations would have to be cut below those of the Allied troops. Since this contravened a basic rule of war, he advised Lee not to put "his staff's views on PoW rations on paper."

If only there were more ports. On November 3 the Canadians cleaned out the last enemy nests along the Scheldt, but the estuary was full of unswept mines, so the supply boats still could not reach Antwerp. Montgomery warned Grigg confidentially: "The Americans regard the acquisition of Antwerp as the solution to all our difficulties. I am afraid they will be greatly disappointed." Hitler was determined to add to the disappointment. He had ordered a major V-weapon assault against the port. General Marshall, too, was concerned. He warned Eisenhower against putting all his eggs in the Antwerp basket. Unconscionable damage would be inflicted on Allied hopes if a V-weapon destroyed even one or two ammunition ships, particularly one loaded with the secret VT proximity fuses, whose use he had now authorized for the European theater. On Hitler's orders, 5,500 V-1s and nearly 1,500 V-2 rockets would eventually be launched against the port. Ten thousand people would be killed and seriously injured—a quarter of them Eisenhower's troops. It would be almost December before Antwerp was finally cleared of mines and opened to the supply ships. By that time, for the principal purpose, it would be too late.

News of the supply breakdown—and its effect on early victory—was causing a political scandal in the United States. People began looking for scapegoats. Whereupon Eisenhower's staff, ordinarily so critical of each other, put aside their grievances, to a degree, and closed ranks against outside interference, prepared to defend even J.C.H. Lee. Marshall had again briefly visited France, and on his return to Washington he had urged Brehon Somervell to send over one of his best ordnance officers, and not just to troubleshoot but to remain in Europe and keep things running smoothly. Somervell chose the small, birdlike, energetic boss of the Sixth Service Command in Chicago—Major General Henry S. Aurand. The SHAEF intriguers made short work of him.

His plane arrived in Paris at Orly airport on a raw day at the end of October. It struck him as odd that no car had been sent to meet him. He had to take a cab out to Versailles. At SHAEF, for some reason, he had difficulty getting past the sentry. Aurand didn't take it personally; he merely assumed that major generals were a dime a dozen there.

Eisenhower assigned him as deputy to Major General Henry Sayler, SHAEF's ordnance officer. Aurand outranked Sayler—he was next in rank to Lee himself—but he did not grouse about being made Sayler's assistant. Sayler, after all, was a West Point classmate, and he had known him for years. Sayler, however, made it clear that he was not very pleased to see him. "I had the feeling," Aurand recalled later, "that I had to watch my step." Even his old friend Everett Hughes— an ordnance officer like himself—was noticeably cool. Somewhat subdued by his reception, he went downtown to his hotel. He found he had been given a room that was small, barely furnished, and unheated.

Aurand spent several lonely weeks inspecting the front-line ammunition depots—Bradley's, Patton's, Hodges', and Simpson's—trying to trace the bottlenecks in the ammunition system. Eisenhower, he soon gathered, was feuding with Lee—in fact he had told everyone that Lee had not been his choice for the supply job. Finally Aurand informed Hughes that his ammunition report was ready. Hughes, curious, invited Aurand to dinner. There were three major generals there that evening —Sayler, Aurand, and Hughes. Aurand, perhaps warmed by the wine, tactlessly chatted about the faults of the whole European command setup. (Later Hughes noted that he had spent the evening "listening to words of wisdom from . . . Aurand," adding sarcastically: "[He] told of things so lofty that Sayler and I were not supposed to understand —nor did we.") Then Aurand made the mistake of announcing the names of several top SHAEF officers who would have to be sacked. They included theater signals officer Rumbaugh, chief quartermaster

Littlejohn, and Sayler himself, who was sitting just across the table. That must have caused a tremor; Sayler was one of the old SHAEF gang.

On November 14, Hughes and Aurand went off to inspect Cherbourg. They argued for the first few hours of the trip, then lapsed into silence. Delayed by heavy rain, they arrived after dark, too late to inspect anything. They were obliged to return to Paris early the next morning, another sour and silent drive of two hundred miles. That evening Hughes slapped him on the back and invited him to dinner, and, unconscious that Hughes was about to plunge the knife, Aurand accepted. J.P. joined them, and Aurand found that he and she had many mutual friends in the Far East, where her husband was a prisoner of the Japanese. Hughes sat by darkly.

On November 19, Bedell Smith sent for Aurand, received him coldly, and handed him a terse note that Hughes had written Smith that day. Aurand, it said, had expressed such vehement and indiscreet disapproval of the setup in Europe that he was unfit to be part of it.

"You will be sent back," said Smith, "in your permanent rank of colonel."

"But what about my ammunition report?" asked Aurand.

"It is evident that you are prejudiced," Smith replied. "A more competent officer will do the job."

Sayler, in due course, took pity on poor Aurand, once he was no longer dangerous. He found him an office and a charcoal stove. It fell to Lee, however, to apply the final humiliation. One day he invited Aurand to go to the Normandy Base Section with him. It was in Cherbourg, a war-blistered city still plagued by soldier violence and very far from the Hotel George V and the Champs Elysées. Aurand listened in stunned amazement as Lee said to the welcoming committee, "I want to introduce all of you to the new Commanding General of Normandy Base Section, General Henry Aurand."

November was a busy month for Hughes, especially as a diarist. On November 4, he called on Eisenhower—who was, he confessed to him beguilingly, one of the few men he cared to talk to. He had come for lunch but stayed until late afternoon. Hughes had several things on his mind: "Advised [Eisenhower] not to issue any orders about feeding PoW and issue of liquor," was the first note he made. Then: "[He] gave me the first instalment of the book he is going to publish after he resigns after the last gun is fired. Oh, yea! I guess he thinks that being Chief of Staff after being Commander-in-Chief would be a come-down."

Another diary entry concerned one of the most delicate nonmilitary matters imaginable: "Discuss Barbara." Gee Gerow, the commander of V Corps, and an old and favored friend of the Supreme Commander, had just flown back to France after testifying in Washington before the official Pearl Harbor inquiry. He had returned to find the family of his French-born wife, Marie-Louise, under investigation by the French Resistance leaders. They claimed that one of her relatives, a woman named Barbara, had collaborated with the Nazis. Hughes had written himself a memo on October 16: "Must not get involved with Gee's relations—think they are collaborationists." The next day, Hughes noted, J.P. got "mixed up in the attempted arrest by French of Barbara and her mother. . . . Gee must be told!" Eisenhower could or would do nothing to help.

On November 3, Hughes had dinner with the Gerows; it was a desolate occasion. Barbara spent the evening crying softly and he himself, despite his best efforts, fell asleep in a chair. A trial date was set. On November 9, Hughes entered this note: "The Gerows [are] still under fire—and irritated French judge by being late for trial." Eisenhower inquired cautiously once or twice of Hughes about the outcome. But his headquarters declined to intercede, saying that it was not a security matter and did not affect them. "Pless [an unidentified SHAEF officer] says B. is collaborator," observed Hughes, "and that until French court proves her innocent she is guilty." On November 21, he concluded: "Marie and Barbara apparently clear." But there was continued harassment. On January 5, Hughes lunched with Eisenhower and Kay Summersby and they discussed the Gerow case. Eisenhower, whose refusal to intervene stemmed from his innate discomfort with politics, said he was baffled by the whole thing. "He could figure out no sound answer," recorded Hughes.

It was only one of many such cases in France; the witch-hunt had turned into a winter of long knives. In Belgium, too, the Resistance, founded and nourished by the Allies, had turned into a Frankenstein creature which they had trouble in controlling. On November 17, Kay Summersby wrote: "The Belgium Forces of the Interior are kicking against an order requesting them to hand in all their arms." Montgom-

ery's headquarters finally had to threaten force, and a few days later de
Guingand wrote to the SHAEF mission in Belgium to thank them for
their help in ending the "unpleasant affair," adding that Montgomery
hoped that they would not make the facts public. But the affair did not
end, and the Belgians continued to be difficult. After one tough meeting
with Resistance and Communist leaders, de Guingand extended an
invitation to them to visit the front. "I think this is a good egg," de
Guingand wrote Montgomery, "and we would send them up . . . to all
the nasty places." He added, "I think we had better make them do so,
and possibly have an accident en route!"

On November 5, Marlene Dietrich and her troupe lunched with
Patton and Jean Gordon at Nancy, and gave his officers a show. "Very
low comedy," complained Patton to his diary. "Almost an insult to
human intelligence." Dietrich's streamlined figure left Patton unstirred.
He had become something of a connoisseur of the European female
form, favoring the statuesque Norman and Breton women to the shape-
less Arabs, the overstuffed Italians, and the boyish English. French
women, he noted admiringly, reminded him of British locomotives,
with two buffers in front and powerful driving wheels behind.

Later that day, Hughes came over to see him, and Patton installed
him in the Grand Hotel. Hughes noticed that Patton was tense. He
had finally persuaded Bradley, two weeks before, to give his Third
Army its head. It was set to jump off in three days' time, and he was
counting on covering the 132 miles to the Rhine in the next ten days.
The army had all the supplies he wanted, except for overshoes and
socks, which worried Patton: the old army fear of trench foot was high
in his mind. The next day the clouds opened and it began to pour.
Hughes wanted to reminisce about Tunisia and Sicily and the breakthrough at Avranches, but Patton was too keyed up to chat. His brain
was full of the pep talks he was going to deliver to the 6th and 4th
Armored Divisions that afternoon. "We are going to win!" he would
declare. He reflected that he was now commanding half a million men
in their early twenties, while he himself was fifty-nine. Alexander the
Great, he knew, had died at thirty-three believing there were no more
worlds to conquer; Napoleon and Hannibal were finished by forty, and
Wellington was forty-four at Waterloo.

The army would march before dawn. At three A.M. he woke with a start. It was raining hard. Feeling the usual pre-battle stomach nerves, he browsed through Rommel's famous war book, *Infantry Attacks,* for half an hour. From its pages, Rommel lectured Patton, informing him that once in September 1914 it had rained on him too, but the Germans had still advanced to a great battle victory. He fell asleep again at 3:45 A.M., but an hour and a half later he was wakened again by his artillery barrage. Soon his four infantry assault divisions would be going over the top. If they penetrated, then the two armored divisions would go through the gap. The objective was the Siegfried Line, sixty miles ahead. The main obstacle was the forts at Metz.

"The rain had stopped," Patton wrote in his diary later that day. "And the stars were out. The discharge of over 400 guns sounded like the slamming of doors in an empty house—very many doors all slamming at once." The noise woke Hughes over at the Grand Hotel. Eisenhower and Bradley both phoned encouragement. "I expect a lot of you," the Supreme Commander said. "Carry the ball all the way."

Hughes drove back to Paris, obliging Jean Gordon with a lift in his car. If the attack succeeded, Patton would not have much time for her. But the Germans were well dug in, the rains streamed down, and the Third Army slithered to a halt. On November 10, Hughes noted: "Third Army not thru yet. V-2s hitting London, V-1s hitting Antwerp."

November 12 was Patton's fifty-ninth birthday. The day before, as a sort of birthday present and to cheer up the doleful warrior, Hughes sent Jean Gordon back to him. But Patton had his own therapy. He celebrated the day, as he wrote to Beatrice, "by getting up where the dead were still warm." "I saw so many dead Germans that it actually made me sick . . . ," he wrote to his sister Nita, "I believe about 800. They were all neatly piled like cordwood along the side of the road waiting to be buried by our Graves Registration units."

The Germans and the rain dampened his spirits. That day he went to church, heard the worst sermon yet, and ordered his chief of chaplains to "have the offender removed." The chaplain went, but the rains stayed on. The Moselle ran its highest since 1919. It flooded its banks and washed away trucks, airplanes, and a hospital platoon. Patton captured only one bridge intact, at Pont-à-Mousson, but he was not discouraged. Trench foot was causing big trouble. When Eisenhower telephoned him that day, to ask what he would like, Patton thought not of himself but of his men: he asked for woolen socks and for dubbin to waterproof their shoes. Eisenhower immediately passed the request on to J.C.H. Lee, and Lee—the fear of God now instilled in him by all the attention from Washington—called back the next day: "Socks went up to Patton's troops last night."

Despite violent air attacks and twelve days of bloody fighting, the forts at Metz and the city itself stayed in German hands. Patton's attempted breakthrough had failed. Montgomery was sarcastic, but Patton still had defenders. A friend wrote Hughes, "Tell Georgie that all the market needs to send it into a peace panic is to learn that he is on the rampage again. The Dow-Jones average slipped three points when he started storming Metz. Patton for President clubs will be forming soon." The writer continued, "Really, the slapping incident has helped to glamourize him. However, I suggest that next time he should pick on a general. Why don't *you* be the victim?"

Hughes put the suggestion to Patton and said that if he liked it, he should come to see him. "I will go as far as to let you boot me if you think it would do any good," he said, "for I am still pro Patton."

Patton replied in the same vein. He denied any political aspirations. "As you know, at the close of the war, I intend to remove my insignia and wristwatch, but will continue to wear my short coat so that everyone can kiss my ass."

It would be mid-December before the last fort capitulated and before Patton could think of pressing on. Hitler, meanwhile, was preparing a challenge that would test Patton's skills to the utmost.

CHAPTER TWENTY-FOUR

Grit

EARLY IN November 1944 Montgomery wrote Eisenhower, obediently asking permission to go to London to see his dentist. In fact, he wanted to see Alan Brooke. He had drafted a new document, "Some Notes on the Present Situation," in which he had renewed his attack on Eisenhower—this time on the Supreme Commander's directive of October 28. They had to face, he said, the facts; the overall plan could not succeed. He repeated for Brooke all his arguments for "one tremendous left hook," but explained that he could not himself keep hammering away at Eisenhower because relations between himself and all the American generals were so cordial—"they have, in fact, never been so good"—that it would be folly to jeopardize this harmony now. "On no account," he wrote to Brooke, "must these good relations be endangered; this is the first and great principle on which I work."

He added, "I have therefore come to the conclusion that I must now refrain from any further criticism, and must get on with the business as laid down by General Eisenhower. He knows my views; he has made up his mind; he carries a great burden and a great responsibility, and we must all weigh in 100 per cent and help all we can." Having said that, Montgomery left no doubt as to his disenchantment with Eisenhower's strategy. "We must all now be quite clear that we have to face up to a winter campaign in western Europe, with all that that implies. I believe that if we had not made mistakes we might well have finished the business off this year. But now I do not think it is possible, unless some miracle happens."

In London, Montgomery did what he could. He slipped his memorandum to *The Times*. He lunched with Brooke—but Brooke shared his opinion of Eisenhower's strategy already. "I agree," Brooke resignedly told his diary afterward, "that the set-up is bad, but it is not one which can be easily altered, as the Americans naturally consider they should have a major say."

The breaking point was approaching for the Allied troops, both in the air and on the ground. During the summer, several hundred American pilots, their courage abraded by the horrific odds against their survival, had set down their aircraft in Switzerland or Sweden and been interned. Arnold was worried about this evidence of "intentional evasions of further combat service." Combat fatigue was also overtaking the American infantry. Eisenhower was angry, visiting one field hospital, to find most of the wounds were self-inflicted. Combat casualties were bad enough; so were the losses to trench foot; but there were also great numbers of these casualties of the mind. There were practical, human reasons for them. In World War I, a rifleman could count on being pulled out after two weeks of battle, for rest and recuperation; but in this war he got no respite. One reason for the American II Corps' success in Italy during May had been the replacement system devised by General Marshall. Instead of waiting for a division to get run down in battle before pulling it out of the line for rehabilitation, the Americans alone among the Allies rammed fresh troops into that division during the fight as fast as they were needed; as a result, morale had stayed high. By November 1944, the manpower situation no longer allowed that. The GI divisions stayed in the line, and as the old faces vanished, the ranks thinned and morale drained away.

Eisenhower tried to keep on top of the problem. He told his son in one letter how to train his brand-new infantry platoon. "Go around and see every man, see that he gets into warm, dry clothing . . . that he gets a good hot meal and that his weapons are in tiptop shape. Shoes, socks and feet are of tremendous importance, and you should try to wear exactly the same kind of materials as your men do when in field training or in combat. By pursuing these methods you will not only have a splendidly trained platoon, but one that will follow you anywhere."

These rules were ignored by many of American platoon commanders. Driving around France as the rain poured down, Eisenhower was annoyed by their callous thoughtlessness toward their men. He passed convoys of open trucks in back of which infantrymen huddled, frozen and dejected, because nobody had thought to order that the top cover be raised. He saw troops bivouacked in shivering tents only a short way from a warm, substantial shelter earmarked by the officers for themselves. His mail made him fear that the army was rotting in the rain. On November 6, Eisenhower wrote his commanders and gave excerpts from some of the letters. "Unit commanders," he quoted one man as saying, "disapprove leave for enlisted men, but give it to officers freely." "When enlisted men are out of the battle line," wrote another, "they are given no opportunity to see any of the country over which they have been fighting, but officers travel everywhere without restraint and in government transportation." "Officers can get whiskey rations at the front, but the men can't even get cigarettes," complained a third. "On board transports," wrote a fourth soldier, "thousands of men are jammed into a small space while officers and nurses have the advantage of large deck space." "Officers' food is much better than the men's."

There was no end to the list of beefs. Eisenhower ordered his commanders to ensure that all officers and enlisted men received equal treatment. Generals were to travel by ship sometimes and even by road, with the stars on their cars covered, to see what conditions were. And liquor stocks looted from the Germans were to be distributed equally to officers and men. Everett Hughes, who spent most of his pay on liquor, protested loudly, noting on his copy: "Tried to keep Ike from sending this. Failed."

That second week of November found Eisenhower on the road again. He spent twelve days visiting his troops. In his directive of October 28 he had rejected Montgomery's pleading for one rapier thrust against the Ruhr and ordered instead a general offensive along a two-hundred-mile front, with the main thrust north of the Ardennes region, by the First and Ninth armies through the Aachen gap toward Krefeld, Cologne, and Bonn. He had also directed that "when logistics permit," Patton should renew his attempt to capture the Saar. Logistics, as we have seen, did not permit, but Bradley had still impishly allowed Patton to launch his thrust at the beginning of November, thus robbing Eisenhower's major effort north of the Ardennes of all hope of success. But air support for the First and Ninth army offensive would be bigger than anything since D-day—the entire Eighth and Ninth air forces and the RAF heavies would saturate the ground defenses, and seventy-five battalions of artillery and rocket launchers would join the barrage too. But the weather had to be just right for this great air offensive.

Meanwhile Hodges' infantry was meeting resistance as it moved forward; every village and wood was defended by pillboxes, and soldiers could not get close enough to place demolition charges on them because the Germans were even calling down mortar and artillery fire on their own pillboxes. The infantry were faced by minefields, by eight-foot concertina rolls of barbed wire, and by murderous small arms fire. In a village called Schmidt the buildings were shelled until only the basements were left, and even those had to be cleared in hand-to-hand fighting with fixed bayonets. Sometimes the infantry clawed over only three hundred yards of ground in a whole day's bloody fighting.

On November 8, snow began to fall along the First Army front. The long-range weather forecasts for the area grew worse, and the date for the offensive receded.

Eisenhower's memory flicked back to the football matches he had gone to and how it always seemed to rain on Saturday during the season. He wondered if Mamie still went. How much wouldn't he give to go see the Army–Notre Dame game. That reminded him that his knee was still sore; because of it, he had been getting no exercise, and that was making him paunchy. This war seemed to last forever, he reflected. When he called back at his advanced camp at Rheims— established, tantalizingly, beside a golf course built by a big champagne merchant—on November 11, he found an embittered letter from Mamie, who had just learned that John was returning to Europe as a brand-new shavetail, a platoon commander in the 71st Infantry Division. Platoon commander was not a profession on which a life insurance broker would offer cheap premiums. Mamie was taking the news badly, and her letter talked of the beating she had taken through Eisenhower's "dirty tricks."

Ike decided not to take this lying down: "You've always put your own interpretation on every act, look or word of mine, and when you've made yourself unhappy, that has, in turn, made me the same. It's true we've now been apart for two and a half years, and at a time and under conditions that make separations painful and hard to bear. Because you don't have a specific war job that absorbs your time and thoughts, I understand also that this distress is harder for you to bear. But you should not forget that I do miss you and do love you, and that the load of responsibility I carry would be intolerable unless I could have the belief that there is someone who wants me to come home—for good. Don't forget that I take a beating, every day." He was sick of getting letters from other women begging him to send their men outside the battle zone; he could not yield to Mamie. "So far as John is concerned," he told her, "we can do nothing but pray. If I interfered even slightly or indirectly he would be so resentful for the remainder of his life. . . . Please try to see me in something besides a despicable light—and at least let me be *certain* of my welcome home when this mess is finished."

In mid-November, Brooke and Churchill came by train to Rheims. Brooke was still unimpressed by the Supreme Commander: "He went over the dispositions on the front and seemed fairly vague as to what was really going on." Nor was Brooke edified by the curious lunch table menage, with Kay Summersby presiding and Mr. Churchill on her right; it was not the kind of thing that could have happened in the British army.

On November 16 the weather cleared enough for the big Bradley push to the Rhine, the one they had been planning since October. The First and Ninth armies attacked at 12:45 P.M. in the vicinity of Aachen. First 1,100 American heavy bombers went in, and later in the afternoon 1,150 RAF Lancasters pummeled the defenses. For once, there were no shortfalls, no Allied troops killed by their own planes. But the enemy troops were dug in so close to the American lines that they were not badly affected either. "You can't tell anything about an attack like this for forty-eight hours," Hodges said that night. He found out sooner than that. The German resistance was intense. The next day, Tubby Barton of the 4th Division told him that one German platoon was killed to the last man—"they just refused to surrender or retreat." Progress was slow and painful, but Bradley professed to be pleased. "No one," he said on the phone to Hodges five days after the attack began, "but the most optimistic stargazers expected that we would crack the line in twenty-four hours and dash to the Rhine in the manner of the Saint-Lô break-through." Bradley, it seemed, had been gazing at the stars; they were nowhere near the Rhine, and a breakthrough it was not.

On the rain-sodden ground, the infantry battle was a protracted agony. After listing the meager infantry advances that had brought Hodges' forces to the edge of the Hürtgen Forest, just beyond Aachen, the First Army's unofficial diary noted apologetically: "This reads perhaps small in type, but into these yardage gains went thousands of shells, tons of bombs, and many lives."

The air force continued to steamroll ahead of the troops, but the returns were diminishing. On November 28 the 474th Bomb Group slapped sixty-seven out of its cargo of seventy napalm bombs right into one village called Kleinhau, burning it to the ground. But for two more days the Germans holding the blackened ruins fought back. To intensify the ordeal for Hodges, his headquarters at Spa was right beneath the V-1s being fired at Liege and Antwerp, and on some days more than a hundred droned low overhead. His diary on November 29 described one "clearing the house by only a few hundred feet and causing such vibration that a mirror was wrenched from a third story wall and hurled across the other side of the room; the second gliding in to a loud three-point landing about a mile away from the house lifting the floors a foot or so before setting them down to rest. The last explosion also took several windows out of the Britannique hotel, splattering glass far enough to cut the sergeant sitting at the information desk."

Once they were inside the dark and impenetrable Hürtgen Forest, the Americans commenced a soul-destroying fight through the neolithic jungle of leafless, fallen trees and stinking, shell-churned slime. It was the kind of slow, stamina-testing infantry battle that doesn't make history, but that remains indelibly impressed on the memories of all those troops who fought it. It would continue until the end of November.

Montgomery had neither seen Eisenhower nor spoken to him by telephone for a month. That struck him as odd. In fact, when he thought of it, he realized that he had been with him only four times since the end of the Normandy campaign. He had given Eisenhower his word not to bother him anymore. But he was troubled by the clear signs that Eisenhower was steering his war machine into static trench warfare more ghastly than even World War I had seen, and so on November 17 he wrote complaining to Sir Alan Brooke instead. Eisenhower, he wrote, "is at a Forward Headquarters at Rheims. The Directives he issues from there have no relation to the practical necessities of the battle. It is quite impossible for me to carry out my present orders. . . . Eisenhower should himself take a proper control of operations or he should appoint someone else to do this. If we go drifting along as at present we are merely playing into the enemy's hands and the war will go on indefinitely. . . . He has never commanded anything before in his whole career; now, for the first time, he has elected to take direct command of very large-scale operations and he does not know how to do it."

It was a real scream of protest from the field marshal. He continued: "The Germans are bound to bring divisions to the Western Front— from Norway, from the Russian front and from elsewhere. . . . Bradley tells me the American ammunition situation is going to be worse and his allotment is already being scaled down; the reason is that the Pacific theatre is now coming to the fore and ammunition has to be diverted there; the Americans have not enough ammunition to give adequate amounts to two theatres—both going at full blast. So the urgency to finish the German war quickly is very great."

And with that he was back on his theme—the colossal crack at the Germans at just the right place. But what could he, Montgomery, do? He saw tens of thousands of Allied soldiers dying needlessly—but he had assured Eisenhower in a letter that he would let the matter rest. "I would be grateful for your advice," he pleaded to Brooke now, "as to whether you think I ought to take the initiative again in the matter. . . . I think we are drifting into dangerous waters."

Brooke raised Montgomery's long and desperate letter at the next Chiefs of Staff meeting in London. "Eisenhower completely fails as Commander," he agreed, writing in his own diary. "Bedell Smith lives back in Paris quite out of touch; as a result the war is drifting in a rudderless condition. . . . Am preparing a case, as we shall have to take it up with the Americans before long." But in his view it would be quite improper for Montgomery, having given his word, to broach the matter with Eisenhower himself. Brooke sent Portal, the Chief of Air Staff, to France, bearing a highly confidential letter to Montgomery, penned in terms of the most delicate reproach, urging him "(a) not to approach Eisenhower for the present; (b) to remain silent now, unless Eisenhower opens the subject." They would have to let SHAEF condemn itself by proving defective—a desperate remedy that would cost many, many lives. "I feel pretty certain," said Brooke with perverse pleasure, "that the results of the current offensive will provide us with sufficient justification for requesting the American Chiefs of Staff to reconsider command organization and the present strategy on the western Front." He also felt constrained to remind Montgomery that any ground commander would almost certainly be an American—which meant that Bradley would get the job.

Several times, Montgomery tried to lure Eisenhower out his way. When the Supreme Commander wrote on November 22, asking Montgomery's permission to visit Dempsey and Crerar, Montgomery approved, and added: "Perhaps while you are up this way we could have a talk together; there is much I would like to discuss." A meeting was arranged for six days later. Meanwhile, Montgomery began searching for some etiquette that would enable him to reopen the whole issue, despite his self-imposed promise to refrain. Suppose he *asked* Eisenhower for permission to do so? Brooke urged him not to. "Personally," he wrote, "I think you are wrong in doing so." Suspicious of the field marshal, Brooke wrote asking him for immediate word as to exactly what he was up to, and he sent this letter by special messenger. Brooke feared that a real crisis was blowing up, one that might have unforeseen consequences for Montgomery. During the Chiefs of Staff meeting on November 24, Brooke asked the secretaries to step outside and told his colleagues about the crisis. "Eisenhower," as Brooke put it, "though supposed to be running the land battle, is on the golf links at Rheims —entirely detached and taking practically no part in the running of the war." Matters had recently gotten so bad, alleged Brooke, that Bedell Smith and a few others had formed a deputation to Eisenhower and insisted that he get down to it and *run* the war. Eisenhower had said he would. The Chiefs asked Brooke to put the problem to Churchill.

Meanwhile, Montgomery remorselessly plugged away. On November 26 he arrived in London for an hour just to see Brooke. Together they hacked out a proposal that might just be workable: Bradley should be ground commander, controlling two army groups—Montgomery north of the Ardennes, and Devers south. Montgomery would have Patton's army in his group. Montgomery was scheduled to see Eisenhower in two days' time and, noted Brooke, "If *he* opens the subject, Monty is to begin putting forward the above proposals."

Brooke used plain language when he put the case to Churchill: "This last offensive could only be classified as the first strategic reverse that we had suffered since landing in France." He described Eisenhower's strategy as sheer madness.

Eisenhower spent several days with Devers. Eisenhower had never thought much of Jacob L. Devers, commander of the 6th Army Group. He was a West Point classmate of Patton and, like him, a keen polo player, but there the similarity ended. Asked by the War Department to rate thirty-eight of his highest officers, he put Devers at twenty-four, lower than several corps commanders; and Devers was the only one of thirty-eight he had anything negative to say about. Devers, he said, was "often inaccurate in statements and evaluations," and added, "He has not, so far, produced among the seniors of the American organization here [a] feeling of trust and confidence." It was a mystery that Eisenhower retained him—except that he hated to bust lieutenant generals, an aversion from which J.C.H. Lee was also profiting.

The weather was miserable and all his travel was by car, which took time and temper. Kay Summersby—proudly sporting her new bars as a WAC second lieutenant—drove and Jimmy Gault sat in front to map-read, which left the back of the car for the general alone. The hours usually passed in silence. Some of these roads, he reflected, perhaps staring at the back of Kay Summersby's neck, were the ones that he and Mamie had traveled during a vacation fifteen years before. Back at his forward headquarters, he jotted down a letter to her. All military wisdom taught against allowing a war on two fronts to develop and he had enough on his hands already, with Montgomery; and so he wrote: "I'm truly sorry if I've let my letters lately reflect any impatience with your messages. I really do know how upset and ill you've been. Anyway I love you heaps—if you'll just remember that, we shouldn't have any trouble understanding what we mean when our letters sound strange."

Constipation rather than starvation was ailing the supply system now. Eighty American supply trains carrying vital ammunition like 105-millimeter howitzer shells and mortar bombs were stalled east of

Paris, lacking both troops to unload them and depots to unload them into. Forty-eight percent of all American supplies on the continent were still logjammed back in Normandy. It did not help that five different languages were now being spoken in the combat railroad areas—American, French, Dutch, Flemish, and German.

On November 22 the influential American columnist Walter Lippmann lunched with Hughes in Paris and asked him his view of when the war would be over. Hughes replied: "A lot depends on Stalin, a lot on the weather and a lot on the Germans—Hitler is reinforcing the west with thirty divisions; he has, and is using, large strategic reserves. Provided the Pacific demands don't interfere, the war will be won late in the spring."

Life in Paris for Eisenhower's generals was still a round of cocktail parties, Red Cross nurses, newspapermen, suspenseful trials of alleged collaborationists, and the Folies Bergères. As GIs flooded in, a frenetic black market was building up. By late November, 168 American soldiers were under arrest for currency offenses and operating a black market ring. Pilferage and currency counterfeiting were beginning on a large scale. Eisenhower had told Lee to pull his troops out of Paris and assured the army and corps commanders that he was going to "chase the SOS [Services of Supply] out of Paris and make it a well ordered rest center for combat troops." But the streets were still crowded with American soldiers, all of them with apparent reason to be there. At the races, the women were elegantly dressed, noted Hughes appreciatively, "also the young men," he added, feeling older as he wrote it. Everyone was smoking cigarettes, which on close inspection turned out to be the American brands that the enlisted men could not get at the PX any more. On the Paris black market they could be bought —for two hundred francs per pack.

Two hundred miles to the east of the City of Light, on Hodges' and Simpson's battlefields, the grueling fight was going on. About two thousand casualties were being outloaded to the United Kingdom each day. Hughes recorded that it was "raining, raining" and that the Seine was welling up to the tops of its banks. The Rhine was already in flood, making it an even more formidable barrier to invaders.

On November 28 the great meeting between Eisenhower and Montgomery at last took place. The setting was the field marshal's tactical headquarters at Zondhoven, Holland. It lasted for three hours, and the tone was fairly friendly. Montgomery firmly stated that the plan laid down in Eisenhower's last directive had failed. The Allies had in fact suffered a strategic reverse. Eisenhower agreed. He also agreed that they should now concentrate on one selected thrust. But he emphatically did not agree with Montgomery's unselfish proposal that Bradley should be appointed overall ground commander. Nor would he agree to the other proposals about dividing up the front between Montgomery and Bradley.

The following morning they talked again. "There is no doubt our discussion last night has left him worried and ill at ease," reported Montgomery by telegram to Brooke. "It is my impression this morning that he thinks Bradley has failed him as an architect of land operations." Montgomery believed that Eisenhower would now agree to revert to the successful Overlord command arrangement, whereby Montgomery called the tunes and Bradley and the other generals danced to it. Brooke read these reports from Montgomery with well-founded skepticism. "Ike," he observed in his own diary, "is incapable of running a land battle, and it is all dependent on how well Monty can handle him."

To nail things down, Montgomery wrote to Eisenhower the next day to put on record what they had talked about. "My dear Ike," he said. "We have definitely failed to implement the plan contained in the SHAEF directive of 28 October . . . and we have no hope of doing so. We have therefore failed; and we have suffered a strategic reverse. . . . This time *we must not fail*." He repeated that he and Bradley were a good team, and told Eisenhower he was keeping two days next week free for him for a meeting at Maastricht in Holland, at which time Bradley should also be present, and he concluded peremptorily: "Will you let me know which day you select. I suggest that we want no one else at the meeting except Chiefs of Staff, who must not speak. Yours ever, B. L. Montgomery."

Montgomery's curt letter made Eisenhower exceedingly angry. He replied tartly that he refused to look, as the field marshal did, upon the past performances of "this great fighting force" as a failure. Whereupon Montgomery withered slightly.

"I have never done anything of the sort," he wrote back in his own hand. He emphasized that he had taken as a basis for discussion the directive of October 28. "I said," he wrote, "we had failed to carry out the plan *contained therein.* When one reads that directive one has to admit that that is so."

Eisenhower meltingly replied, "You have my prompt and abject apologies for misreading your letter." In the meantime he had gone on to Bradley's headquarters in Luxembourg. To his staff he apparently misrepresented what the field marshal was asking for. Kay Summersby's diary said: "As soon as [Eisenhower] arrives he has a long talk with Bedell re Monty. . . . Monty is most anxious to have Bradley under his command, keeps on saying that there would be a lot of advantages etc., of course he is completely crazy even to think of such a thing."

Montgomery kept Grigg informed. "My dear P.J.," he wrote. "Some very delicate negotiations are going on here: designed to try and ensure that the war will not go on longer than is necessary."

An unfounded optimism must have betaken him, because he issued to his army commanders a request that there be no offensive operations on Christmas, so that it should be available to all officers and men as a day of rest. "They shall have opportunities to attend services as desired and to have their Christmas dinner undisturbed. . . . We will not ourselves take the initiative in offensive action on that day." When Christmas Day came, both Montgomery's and Bradley's officers would be fighting for their lives.

On December 4 Eisenhower wired Montgomery, agreeing to meet him with Bradley at Simpson's headquarters at Maastricht, "as near after eleven o'clock Thursday morning as we can get there." He insisted on taking Bedell Smith—"I will not by any means insult him," wrote Eisenhower, "by telling him that he should remain mute at any conference he and I both attend." When he saw Montgomery that Thursday, December 7, he was an angry man. Gone was the good-natured, avuncular diplomat, radiating bonhomie and Anglo-American accord; he was now the tough West Pointer who had reached his present position by being tough. In vain Montgomery urged that both his and Bradley's army groups should be sent thrusting into Germany north of the Ardennes; in vain he said, "I would willingly serve under Bradley."

It was soon clear that the Maastricht meeting would be a failure. Montgomery felt that the other American generals had "got at" Eisenhower. Eisenhower, he saw with chagrin, had reversed his opinion on all the major points on which they had agreed ten days earlier. Bradley's army group, Eisenhower announced, would be divided into two forces, deploying for attack in two different directions. Montgomery saw with concern that there would be a gap of one hundred miles in between, facing the Ardennes, held only by General Troy H. Middleton's VIII Corps.

They had an artificially cheery lunch and parted with gales of no less artificial laughter, after which Montgomery retired to his desk and penned to Brooke one of the most bilious letters of his career. It ran to over forty paragraphs.

It had particularly irked Montgomery that Eisenhower had brought Tedder with him to Maastricht, since during their three-hour drive back to Luxembourg to spend the night at Bradley's headquarters, Tedder and Bradley would obviously talk the Supreme Commander out of even the few concessions he *had* made. Later Tedder told Spaatz about the conference. "Apparently," noted Spaatz in his diary, "Montgomery pressed for command of all the forces—American and British —involved in the attack north and south of the Ruhr, and that all effort should be placed on that attack, even to the extent of stopping Patton." He dryly commented, "This appears to be a repetition of Caen and St. Lo, and the only hope of a breakthrough by the American forces is not under the control of Montgomery."

On December 7, Montgomery received by courier from Sir James Grigg a letter marked Top Secret, one of the most extraordinary yet to come from Grigg's War Office desk in London. "My dear Monty," he began. "It is a long time since I have written to you—the main reason being that I did not want to communicate to you any of my discouragement of spirit. If you ask what in God's name I have got to be discouraged about I answer: (a) a growing conviction that the Americans and the Russians *intend* that we shall emerge from this war a third rate power. Indeed they no longer take any pains to conceal their intentions, (b) a settled conviction that there is a lack of grip in certain quarters here which makes it quite impossible for us to take a strong line in this or any other direction." Grigg had been kept informed of Montgomery's strained correspondence with Eisenhower. "I am bound to say," he wrote, "that Ike's last letter looked to me much more of a skid than a wobble. I don't believe he means to deliver the goods. Anyhow I am beginning to reconcile myself to the German war lasting throughout 1945. How infuriating it all is—but much more for you than for me, and somehow you manage to be much the more placid of the two."

Upon Montgomery's return from Maastricht, he replied to Grigg. The conference, he said, "was a complete failure, and he went back on all the points he had agreed to when alone with me. Bradley and Tedder were there too; I played a lone hand against the whole three. That Tedder should take their side is too dreadful." He described Eisenhower's plan for winning the war as "quite dreadful" too. "It will not succeed, and the war will go on. If you want to end the war in any reasonable time, you will have to remove Ike's hand from the control of the land battle; and Bradley's hand also. How you will do this I do not know; but unless you do so, the war will go on. I hope the American public will realize that, owing to the handling of the campaign in western Europe from 1 Sept onwards, the German war will now go on during 1945. And they should realize very clearly that the handling of the campaign is entirely in American hands. We did quite reasonably well when it was in British hands. One must just keep plugging away at it; possibly some miracle will happen. But the experience of war is that you pay dearly for mistakes; no-one knows that better than we British."

Perhaps Grigg's reference to "a lack of grip in certain quarters" was aimed at Churchill. Anticipating precisely this deadlock, Churchill had sent a telegram to Roosevelt three days before asking for a meeting of the Combined Chiefs of Staff to discuss the stalemate in France. Marshall was not receptive to the idea. So Churchill and Brooke invited Eisenhower and Tedder.

Eisenhower proposed visiting London with Tedder on Tuesday morning, December 12. He arrived there a welcome visitor—because he had agreed to lend Churchill thousands of GIs in London to help the 120,000 men now working full time to repair the rocket bomb damage. But he left under something of a cloud, since he still refused to yield his position. They met at six P.M. that evening in Churchill's map room. The entire British Chiefs of Staff were assembled too, to awe Eisenhower. He was the only American present. He reiterated his whole vague plan for a double advance into Germany, but it was not convincing. Brooke told him that by violating the most sacred principle

of warfare, the concentration of forces, he had already brought them
their present failure. Eisenhower replied with platitudes. Overwhelmed
by a feeling of hopelessness, Brooke wrote afterward, "Quite impossible
to get the P.M. to understand the importance of the principles involved." They all dined, but nothing changed. "Amongst other things,"
noted Brooke in his diary, "[I] discovered that Ike now does not hope
to cross the Rhine before May!"

As a great power, Britain was finished. In terms of manpower, it was
already on its last legs. Brooke was desperate almost to the point of
tendering his resignation. But the next day Churchill showed that some
of Brooke's arguments had lingered in his befuddled brain, and he
called the War Cabinet together that evening. That May 1945 date
shocked the Cabinet too.

The meeting with Churchill had ended at 1:35 A.M. As he never went
to bed much later than ten, Eisenhower awoke sleepy the next morning.
He had been on the move for days, by car and plane, with the bad
weather uppermost in his mind, and had forgotten even Mamie until
suddenly he realized with a guilty start that he hadn't written to her
since he didn't know when and he'd better sit right down and do that
now. It was getting harder to think of anything to write; he lived,
walked, and breathed "top secret, British most secret." He let out a
chuckle when he thought of all the talking the two of them would have
to do when this was all over: "We'll have to take a three month vacation
on some lonely beach," he wrote, temptingly. "And Oh Lordy, Lordy,
let it be sunny!! I don't believe how I'd ever kick about the sun."

Lieutenant General Brehon Somervell, chief of the Army Services
Forces, was a formidable, tidy-minded Pentagon bureaucrat who knew
how to impress Capitol Hill by submitting elegantly bound reports with
all the orders and papers clipped in perfect place. But now this normally
suave general was getting angry. Reports of the supply crisis were in
the Washington newspapers, and the finger was being pointed at his
door. He had fired the first barrel of his counterattack by sending over
General Aurand, but that shot had ricocheted. Now he fired the second
barrel.

On December 4, Major General LeRoy Lutes, his cool and efficient
director of Plans and Operations, found himself heading for Paris with
instructions from Somervell to investigate what the hell was causing the

ammunition bottlenecks. Lutes knew most of the generals. He had been present at that famous May assembly in St. Paul's School when Montgomery briefed King George and the invasion commanders. At Paris's badly bombed Orly airfield, he was met by a big lieutenant general of impeccable appearance, who snapped a salute at him. That was J.C.H. Lee, commander of the Communications Zone—the man whom rumor blamed for this supply *misère*. Lutes was installed in the fabulous Hotel George V. It was large and modern, and his room had a fine view over terraced gardens and a fountain, but it was chilly—there was little coal. Lutes reported in his diary: "I had a brief talk with General Lee, who seemed quite subdued and puzzled. I am sure that he did not fully understand the purpose of my visit." Lee assured him that supplies were "in very healthy shape." He invited Lutes to cocktails in one of his hotel suites—"He seemed to have several," Lutes observed.

The next morning Bedell Smith asked to see Lutes urgently. Smith did not like inspectors. (Only two days later Eisenhower would tell Everett Hughes that Smith wanted him to be the Inspector General at SHAEF. "That figures," thought Hughes, and he wrote in his diary: "I suppose Bedell wants me to report to him instead of Ike. He has always wanted that.")

Bedell Smith scowled at Lutes and said without prompting, "No one can say that supply here has failed." He repeated that supply at the front was satisfactory, then went straight on to reveal Eisenhower's disquiet about J.C.H. Lee. "But," said Smith, "at this stage of the war he has no intention of changing him. The principal difficulties are in clashes of personalities."

"How long are you going to be in France?" he asked Lutes pointblank.

"I am on loan for about a month," Lutes replied.

"That won't be enough," Smith said.

Lutes could see what was at the back of Bedell Smith's mind, and as he reported, he gave Smith "a very broad hint that unless they were willing to have a new commander in the Communications Zone I doubted if I would be made available." Smith insisted that Eisenhower had not selected Lee, or recommended his promotion—Lee had been foisted on him by Washington. When Lutes revealed that he *was* going to investigate Lee's competence, Bedell Smith changed his tune—the armies were in a chaotic supply position, supplies were now moving forward, but a terrific rail jam was building up east of Paris.

That evening Lutes walked around Paris. "There is much excitement among the French on political matters," he found. "The Communists seem to be working openly and swiftly to gain control of all the villages and towns." The French blamed this on the Americans. He added the observation: "The Parisians impressed me as merely tolerating Americans. As far as they are concerned the war is over."

The next evening, December 7, he was invited to a dinner with J.C.H. Lee. "As usual he had formal toasts and so forth." He was surprised at Lee's brusqueness with General Ewart G. Plank, the very capable Advance Section commander, who was responsible for distribution of supplies at the front. Then he realized that since Plank was not part of the supply clique in Paris and was indeed critical of it, Lee was leery of him. No matter that Plank was excellent at his job. "Apparently," Lutes deduced, "General Lee will back up his Paris staff to the limit, regardless of what happens."

General Lutes was provided with an aged English Wolseley car and a driver, and set off into the snowbound landscape to tour the front-line depots. His trip, as it happened, proved to be a unique survey of the American field commands on the eve of one of the great cataclysms of the war.

Despite the fierce infantry battle going on along the West Wall, he found that the depot commanders spent most of their time eating and drinking. Their stock records were nonexistent. They had made few plans for breaking the rail jam east of Paris, where rail cars, each holding fifty tons of supplies, were backing up at the rate of four thousand per day.

There was a blizzard as he entered the Ardennes forest. "The scenes," he wrote, "were exactly like those in the nursery rhyme books and many Christmas cards we have all been familiar with—fir forests covered with snow and now and then an ancient chateau back in the hills."

Bradley was out when Lutes arrived at the 12th Army Group headquarters in Luxembourg. He waited for him in the map room. Bradley slipped in behind him after a while and grabbed him by the arms. They greeted each other like the old friends they were, and Lutes gave him the fine American bourbon he had brought for him. Then they talked of the ammunition crisis. "He is very bitter on the subject," wrote Lutes afterward, "and says that the British wouldn't begin to consider an attack on only fifty rounds of 105mm ammunition per day. He said that normally they have 150, and that he wants 150 to 200 rounds per gun for his offensive operations." Bradley blamed Lee for the howitzer and mortar ammunition shortage. He invited Lutes for dinner at the Alpha —a very modern and plush hotel reserved exclusively for the use of his staff. They dined in the swanky main dining room, watched a movie, and turned in for the night. Lutes took out his diary and wrote down his impressions—the fine formal dinner with placecards set for each officer, the air of splendor and comfort. But something else had struck Lutes. It was something told him in confidence. "General Bradley," he recorded, "feels that it is entirely possible for the Germans to fight bitter delaying actions until 1 January 1946."

There was a baffling paradox, Lutes found, in the way the generals talked. All of the army commanders he spoke to echoed Bradley's gloomy prognosis, yet all talked as well of the low morale of the German prisoners and the tremendous beating the enemy was taking. Lutes gave his own view. "I do not see," he wrote, "how the Germans can hold out beyond spring."

After Bradley he went on to see Patton, driving through bombed and savaged villages where there were "always a few inhabitants woefully clinging to the remnants." East of the Moselle there were recent signs of battle—dead animals, shell craters lathered with fresh mud, strewn equipment. Patton told him they were having the worst floods since 1861. His army was still fighting in Metz and one fort was holding out west of the city. Lutes could see big fires on the horizon. He lunched with Patton in his home, the most palatial in Nancy. "He is bitter also on ammunition," reported Lutes, "and dislikes General Lee as much as ever. However, he is cocky and confident. . . . Says Germans not strong enough to make a strong attack." "General Patton," he wrote to Somervell, "states that as far as he is concerned he is going to drive as far as he can drive with his supplies, and then dig in. . . . Patton states that he trusts no one behind the Advance Section [of General Plank] and that he doesn't mind saying so to anyone from General Lee on up or down. He is very outspoken."

The supply crisis was very real, whatever Bedell Smith's assurances. Lutes noted that the armies had only about six days of supplies each.

"General Patton prefers to keep long on gasoline," he reported, "and short on rations, so he has eight days of POL [petrol, oil, lubricants] against three days of rations." Patton had just run a combat train all the way to Normandy and back—a round trip of eight hundred miles —to get the 155-millimeter howitzer ammunition he needed.

After Patton, Lutes lunched with Hodges at the First Army. "General Hodges," he wrote, "inspires me as a man who has never studied the supply side of the picture and does not desire to. He is a good soldier but intolerant of any supply deficiency." Hodges' mind was probably elsewhere. He spent a good part of that same afternoon with a prosperous Belgian—one Monsieur Francotte. The U.S. Army Ordnance Department was using the famous Francotte gun factory at Liege for the repair of its equipment, and Francotte had offered to make shotguns for Bradley, who was a fine shot, and for Hodges and Quesada—adding, cunningly, "Perhaps you could arrange to let me have some energy." They lent him an army generator. Hodges finally picked the kind of shotgun he wanted. "It should be a beauty," he wrote in the diary. Quesada ordered two.

On December 14, Lutes called on Simpson in Holland. Big Simp was an old-timer, but it did not irk him to fight under either Eisenhower or Bradley. He had first met Eisenhower at the Army War College; both were in the same class, and both were majors. Simpson's Ninth Army had now been given the job of clearing out Brest. "Simpson," Lutes wrote to Somervell, "is a very tolerant understanding type. He has no serious complaints and trusts Communications Zone to support him. Of course his is one of the newer organizations. He has a very tough fight ahead of him in an area populated by twenty million people. Each town and village is so located that it can support and enfilade the neighboring town or village. Therefore towns become strong points that have to be battered down either by air or artillery, and the weather over here in the winter prevents air operations most of the time."

The next day, Lutes drove on through the corps zones, along roads stacked high with ammunition, into Aachen, the former city of 170,000 people that had fallen late in October and was now dead. He toured the huge ammunition depot outside Liege, with its four railheads. The depot's colonel had his offices in a feudal Belgian chateau, its walls rich with tapestries and paintings. The young countess was out hunting game. He noticed the unkempt American soldiers in the towns and heard of the "alarm of villagers . . . over some of our American conduct."

It was the end of Lutes's survey. He summed up his views in a one-and-a-half-hour talk with Eisenhower—the first meeting with him he had been able to get—at the end of the month. "It was not news to him," reported Lutes. Eisenhower said he had never felt easy about the Com Z but he had tolerated it, and he did not desire to get rid of a lieutenant general like Lee unless there was a specific failure.

The mailman was bringing Eisenhower a deluge of Christmas cards and countless more boxes of hominy grits. He contemplated the heap of grits and reflected: "I wish some of them were *whole* hominy, as I really would like that better." His fan mail was getting to be quite a chore, particularly with a long name like Eisenhower to sign on fifty replies at a time.

A more welcome letter came from his oldest brother Arthur, a banker in Kansas City, Missouri, about their hometown, Abilene. He had driven out and found all their old pals still there—he had taken Sam Heller and Emmett Graham and Ralph Hoffmann for eleven dollars playing poker at Al Chain's house. At eight the next morning Arthur had called on Eisenhower's mother with a potted plant from Lucier's Flower Shop and a two-pound box of candies. She ate a piece immediately, then put the box aside, and Eisenhower knew that in two minutes she would have forgotten ever receiving it—she was getting a bit absent-minded now. The breakfast was good—ten pieces of mush with gobs of chicken gravy, and Arthur got all the Belle Springs butter that he wanted. Arthur had taken a peek at the old lady's bank account and assured Eisenhower she had spent only $160 since August, which was about right. Life was kind of slow in Kansas. "I went into Joner's place, but he was out," wrote Arthur. "Saw Howard Keel for the first time in fifteen years."

Eisenhower wrote back and asked him to send him about five pounds of what they in the family used to call puddin'. People in normal army supply channels, he said, did not know about the Eisenhower family's meat puddin'. He asked for a small box of cornmeal and one of whole hominy too. Arthur sent him eighteen pounds of cornmeal—coarse-ground by the old, old method, between two stones in a water-powered mill, somewhere in south Missouri.

Five inches of snow blanketed the Ardennes. At dawn on December 16, as a light ground haze rose from the white covering, Hitler's tanks poured in a torrent across the very roads that LeRoy Lutes had traveled only hours previously. The Führer was sending two powerful armies against the sleeping Americans. Like a dozing vagrant, torpid from endless dissipation and suddenly set upon by hoodlums, the Americans lurched into wakefulness to find the Fifth Panzer and Sixth SS Panzer armies bearing down upon them.

Hitler had timed the strike brilliantly; he had kept the secret well. He had chosen the weakest American sector, one held only by two inexperienced divisions. He focused the full fury of his artillery and airpower on a six-mile strip on the left flank of the VIII Corps. The Allies reeled under the unsuspected savagery of this attack. Hitler's aim was obvious. He was trying to pierce the Allied lines, stampede the Americans, thrust across the Meuse River, reach Antwerp, and cut off the entire British and Canadian army. If this plan succeeded, he would win the war in the west, because there could be no second Dunkirk miracle for the British.

"We cannot come out through Dunkirk this time," Montgomery sardonically informed Brooke in a letter, "as the Germans still hold that place." Brooke sent the letter on to Churchill, but tactfully excised that sentence.

CHAPTER TWENTY-FIVE

Grip

WHEN NEWS of Hitler's mighty offensive reached the commanders of Eisenhower's armies, they were caught offguard. It was hardly on the agenda. Eisenhower and his entire staff were attending a wedding. Montgomery was on the golf course. Bradley and Hodges were being tape-measured by a little Belgian gun manufacturer. Afterward all would claim, more or less indignantly, that they had known all along that a German offensive was quite possible.

The fact that two gigantic panzer armies—close to 600,000 men— had been assembling and training for weeks under the very noses of two Great Powers with almost total air supremacy and with the most modern and sophisticated code-breaking computers and intelligence networks, and that this attack had caught them flatfooted, was a scandal of considerable magnitude. Great effort was later expended on fudging the files to make it look as though knowledgeable reports had indeed existed. But the contemporary records are so detailed that there can be little doubt. Nobody, from the highest four-star general to the lowliest dogface infantryman shivering in his tunnel entrance in the

Ardennes and watching the snow settle across the mountains, knew what was about to happen as the colossal artillery barrage suddenly began. For some days, they had noticed that the hail of V-1s had diminished. They had assumed that the stocks were running out, or that the sites had been bombed to pieces. The guns too had grown quieter. Now the fire was opened with infinitely augmented violence—bombs, flying bombs, rockets, artillery and mortar fire, and strange, five-foot dartlike projectiles that had been shot from the "High Pressure Pump" —the gun that Hitler's scientists had originally designed to bombard London from the underground battery at Mimoyecques.

For some hours, the news of the German offensive was not taken seriously anywhere at army or corps headquarters. The early reports were sparse and not alarming.

At First Army headquarters in Spa's famous Hotel Britannique, Courtney Hodges occupied the office in which, in 1918, von Hindenburg had informed the Kaiser that World War I was lost. Hodges, Quesada, and Bradley had met there after breakfast that morning for the first fitting of the new shotguns which Monsieur Francotte had brought over from Liege. Francotte arrived, and they all began talking shotguns. While they were being measured for the stock and drop, aides kept bringing notes. Each note showed the attack was bigger than the note before had indicated. There was talk of enemy penetrations, of villages falling into German hands, of units encircled. Courtney Hodges gave his instructions, very low key. Bradley left for his headquarters in Luxembourg.

Montgomery's was perhaps the reddest face. Only yesterday, December 15, he had written to Eisenhower, "If you have no objection I would like to hop over to England on Saturday 23 December and spend Christmas with my son. I have not seen him since D-day." Even more damning, this very day he had signed a 21st Army Group situation report which could hardly have been more dismissive of the Germans: "The enemy is at present fighting a defensive campaign on all fronts; his situation is such that he cannot stage major offensive operations. Furthermore at all costs he has to prevent the war from entering on a mobile phase; he has not the transport or the petrol that would be necessary for mobile operations." He concluded: "The enemy is in a bad way." Having written which, Montgomery had flown off in a light airplane to nearby Eindhoven for a round of golf. After a couple of holes with the golf pro, Dai Rees, he got news that something was up, and flew back to his headquarters.

The morning of December 16, Eisenhower had received Montgomery's letter asking for permission to go to England for Christmas. With it came a marker, a reminder to Eisenhower that fourteen months earlier he had bet five pounds that the war would be over by this Christmas. "For payment I think at Christmas," Montgomery had handwritten on the marker.

"I still have nine days," Eisenhower wrote in reply.

Later that morning, Eisenhower, Bedell Smith, and most of their staff went to the Louis XIV chapel at Versailles for the wedding of Eisenhower's valet, Mickey McKeogh, to the diminutive, bespectacled WAC sergeant from Queens, Pearlie Hargrave. It was the first wedding there since the eighteenth century. It was followed by a reception at Eisenhower's house in Saint-Germain, at which lots of champagne flowed. The U.S. Senate had just announced Eisenhower's nomination to General of the Army, the newly created five-star rank. Hughes buttonholed him and said, "I couldn't bear the idea of having gotten drunk when you received the fourth star and not having a drink with you now that you received your fifth." Eisenhower invited him back for dinner, and Hughes brought a bottle of Highland Piper Scotch—in Hughes's eyes there could be no deeper mark of esteem. Five stars! The Supreme Commander foresaw problems: how was he going to fit them on his jacket? He would have to find someone to embroider them on.

Ever since late August 1944, Hitler had been planning for this moment.

Throughout September he had been counseling with his military and industrial experts on ways of building up the necessary striking power even while the desperate defensive battles were being fought in the forefield of the West Wall. Plagued by the side effects of his assassination-attempt injuries, and afflicted at the end of September by a ten-day bout of jaundice that put him in bed, he had nevertheless had his orderlies bring into his sleeping bunker the maps of the Ardennes, scene of his strategic triumph in 1940, when he had flung his panzer armies headlong into France. The maps were spread out on the foot of his bed, and to his strategic advisor, the balding, shrewd-faced General Alfred Jodl, he had outlined his secret plan for destroying the Allied armies in the west.

Hitler had detected a sector of the American front line that was very thinly held. It contained only three American divisions—the 99th, the 106th, and the 28th. The 28th had taken heavy casualties in the forest fighting; the other two had never seen combat before. Against them, under maximum secrecy, Hitler had drawn up two brawny German forces, the Sixth SS Panzer Army and the Fifth Panzer Army. By starving the rest of the front, he had provided these two armies with enough gasoline and ammunition for a long, desperate battle. And by instructing that all messages concerning this dramatic counterattack were to go by land line, not by radio, Hitler had unwittingly—or perhaps one should say intuitively—jabbed the eyes out of the Allies' intelligence system.

Hitler's plan was to crash these two German armies through the front line, liquidate the three weak American divisions holding that sector, then lunge westward and northward across the river Meuse. He would continue across Belgium and recapture Antwerp. That would split the British and Canadians from the Americans, both geographically and politically. He would deprive the Americans of their forward ammunition dumps—in fact, would wipe the British army off the map. And that, in turn, would change everything. It would mean the military defeat of the Allies in the west.

Hitler's gamble depended on many factors. He needed tactical surprise. He needed a long period of bad weather to ground the Allied air forces. Above all, he needed the Red Army to remain inactive on the Eastern Front until he had destroyed the Allies in the west. And Adolf Hitler would almost get his way. He not only surprised the Allies, he stunned them. For over a week the weather was the devil's own brew of rain, snow, low cloud, and fog. And for nearly one long month Josef Stalin stood by, watching impassively as the bloodstained armies staggered, locked in armored combat, across the Belgian countryside.

After the war, American generals developed agonized consciences about the failure to detect the German buildup. When the American army's official historian, the highly respected Professor Forrest Pogue, wrote the Ardennes chapter of his book *The Supreme Command,* which implied that American intelligence had been caught napping, he showed it for comment to General Edwin Sibert, Bradley's former G-2. Sibert, concerned for his reputation, hastened to tell Pogue that intelligence had had a mystery source which on this occasion had failed them.

Sibert said heatedly that if Pogue's draft were published with the criticism of him still present, he would ask for a Court of Inquiry to clear his name. Pogue was baffled. He thought Sibert was referring to ineffective agents. But Sibert meant Ultra, a secret to which Pogue was not privy. The line that Sibert and others were privately taking was that "this time" the oracle had let them down.

It was true that Ultra was not the only source of information on German intentions. The First Army G-2, Colonel Mont Dickson, had been close to discovering Hitler's plans and had drawn Hodges' attention more than once to possible enemy offensives. "G-2 reports," said the First Army diary on December 9, "keep putting emphasis on the fact that Sixth Panzer Army is drawing up . . . with at least three of its six armored divisions facing the First Army front. Reports from prisoners indicate that morale is high and that the Boche will soon be ready to stage an all-out counter-offensive. There is also rumor that Pressluft will be employed by its artillery"—an oblique reference to the HPP. Hodges grudgingly acknowledged that there is "no question but that a professional is now guiding the German Army in its efforts but he [Hodges] does not appear unduly concerned over the existence of these Panzer Divisions on his front." The next day Dickson issued estimate number 37, warning that the Sixth Panzer Army was poised and might be up to something unpleasant. These warnings were ignored. There was little excuse. Perhaps the general atmosphere of Paris and Luxembourg and Versailles, with the fine hotels, the entertaining, and the captured liquor, had dispelled all idle cares.

As for Ultra, it could have been useful once again, for Hitler's order was not flawlessly obeyed. Yet Ultra's clues went unheeded or unrecognized. On November 16, a German message was intercepted mentioning the *jaegeraufmarsch,* or fighter-plane concentration, in the central Rhineland; the text was not remarkable in itself, but that word was— it was used only before major attacks or offensives. The Ultra decode went out to the top commanders, including Eisenhower, Bradley, and Montgomery. On December 2, Rundstedt's Army Group B was heard asking urgently for fighter cover for troop movements to the west— which another message, later that day, revealed to be two *hundred* trainloads of troops including the Führer Escort Brigade, Hitler's armored pretorian guard. Other intercepted messages revealed urgent measures to scrape together thousands of trucks for the Sixth SS Panzer

Army, as well as aerial reconnaissance over Eupen and Malmédy and the Meuse crossings from Liege to Givet. In one message Berlin showed extraordinary concern because a division was delayed by just twelve hours in its transfer to the west. And from Ultra it was clear that tactical links existed between the Fifth Panzer, Sixth SS Panzer, and Seventh armies.

A year after the war Eisenhower, by now George Marshall's successor, would claim in an internal War Department memorandum that he and Bradley had discussed the likelihood of an offensive weeks before. Wisely, he had "unalterably opposed" publication of this memorandum. "I had received warnings from my intelligence system that there were indications that such an attack might take place," he wrote. "General Bradley actually traced on the map, many days in advance of the attack, the line to which he estimated the Germans could penetrate if they succeeded in concentrating considerable forces under conditions of very bad weather. . . . I refused to pass to the defensive."

This was not true. Lutes, coming from outside the theater, would report confidentially on December 20 to Brehon Somervell: "One thing appears certain to me and that is the Armies on the front were caught completely by surprise. I was through the very territory that the Germans are now operating only 24 hours before the drive was made. One of the first villages caught by German paratroopers was one that I had passed through, a short time before. I was allowed to proceed alone in a staff car through this country between Luxembourg and Spa. Bradley's staff did not anticipate an offensive in this sector so far as I could ascertain."

The farther back the observer was from the fighting man, the more complacently the situation was at first viewed. The infantry saw only tanks and winter-clothed SS troops bearing down on them across the snow. But when they tried to report to battalion headquarters, they found that communications in many cases were already cut by shelling and air attack. In the army and army group headquarters, those reports that did get through were discounted. The incredulous generals were convinced that the Germans were merely trying to interrupt the American attack toward Cologne. Hodges, a taciturn, soft-spoken general, called them spoiling attacks, designed in particular to disrupt his operation against the Roer dams.

Frantic appeals reached the Hotel Britannique at Spa from the 106th Division. Hodges' office diary, which is unlikely to have emphasized his weaknesses, used tactful words: "The General was neither optimistic nor pessimistic during the day." The diarist added guardedly: "It was unfortunate that during this busy evening, the General . . . had to entertain Lieutenant General A.E. Grasett, G-5 of SHAEF." Grasett and two other guests from Bradley's army group arrived an hour late, which did not help.

The 12th Army Group was equally unworried. Bradley too believed it only a spoiling attack, and traveled peacefully from Luxembourg to Paris late on December 16, either to discuss the need for replacement troops—which was Eisenhower's later explanation for the trip—or just "to spend the night," as Kay Summersby put it in her diary. The diary entry reflects the confusion of that first day, and the lack of overview: "[Hodges] First Army is attacking, the German has advanced a little, now only twelve miles from Luxembourg."

All this time the intelligence picture was hardening. At 10:40 P.M. Ultra sent out a message warning that the enemy II Fighter Corps had been heard ordering measures to "support the attack of Fifth and Sixth Armies" the next morning. Even this awesome disclosure—that Hodges was facing two panzer armies—did not trigger any urgent decisions. Bradley felt no constraint to hurry back to Luxembourg. He stayed in Paris and gossiped with Everett Hughes, who wrote in his diary: "Brad says Germans have started a big counterattack toward Hodges. Very calm about it. Seemed routine from his lack of emphasis."

At dawn the next morning Ultra transmitted its intercept of the famous proclamation Rundstedt had radioed to his commanders a day earlier, before the offensive had begun. "The hour of destiny has struck," it said. "Mighty offensive armies face the Allies. Everything is at stake. More than mortal deeds are required as a holy duty to the Fatherland." That did not sound like a simple "spoiling attack." Yet not even this could set alarm bells ringing right up the chain of command to the summit at SHAEF.

That day, December 17, General Kenneth Strong, Eisenhower's G-2, signed a Weekly Intelligence Summary which was obviously later doctored; it was duplicated on papers of several different qualities. Even so, it spoke only of the launching of "a diversionary attack on a fair scale" and added that it was too early to say much about it. It admitted that the attack appeared to be using all of the Sixth SS Panzer Army, but insisted that it was designed only to "relieve pressure from the Cologne-Düsseldorf and Saar sectors." Eisenhower, said a memorandum that he later dictated, "sensing that this was something more than a mere local attack," urged Bradley, who was still in Paris, to move the 10th Armored Division up from the south and the 7th Armored down from the north. Bradley passed the word on to Patton, who was not keen to give up his 10th Armored Division, but agreed. Apart from this, Bradley had still taken no decisive counteraction when, that second day of the offensive, he set out to return to Luxembourg. According to the diary of the unhappy General Hodges—to whom an intercept had now been brought reporting that seventy German planes were standing by on a Cologne airfield to drop paratroopers throughout his area—he tried several times to reach Bradley but was unable to until Bradley finally got back to Luxembourg "late that day." At seven P.M. Bradley at last acceded to Hodges' frantic request for help from the SHAEF reserve, the 82nd and 101st Airborne Divisions. The 101st went to Bastogne.

At midnight on the first day, unable to reach Bradley, Hodges had called up Simpson, the Ninth Army commander, at Maastricht. "I don't want to talk over the phone," he said, "but can you be up at my headquarters by 5:30?"

"Yes," Simpson said, puzzled, "I'll come up."

He arrived punctually at Spa in a Jeep with an armored car escort. The guard at the Hotel Britannique had been doubled. Hodges was in low spirits. He told Simpson that his troops were falling back before the Germans. Hodges' diary related: "The situation developed badly during the day and may be considered tonight to be serious if not yet critical." Captured orders and prisoners had been giving fragmentary impressions of the scale of the enemy effort. Then they brought in a German staff officer who had a map of the whole plan of attack. The map outlined its objectives; it showed the bulge that they were planning to make and identified at least the major German units—the armies and the corps.

Simpson tried to reassure Hodges. "Well," he said, "from what I see here, I don't feel too much alarmed. We are going to have to do some hard fighting, but I think eventually we'll stop this thing."

"I've been trying to get in touch with Bradley or Eisenhower,"

Hodges said rather pathetically, "and I can't reach either one of them. What I wanted to ask them is to order you to turn over a division to me."

"Hell, you don't have to!" Simpson replied, "I've got the 30th Infantry Division in reserve here. If you need it, I'll turn it over to you right now."

By now the First Army headquarters was in great tumult. Enemy tanks were reported at Stavelot, just nine miles south, and approaching one of the Americans' biggest gasoline depots—two million gallons of gasoline and only one engineer company to protect it!

The view from Paris, however, was serene. Kay Summersby's diary was nonchalant. On December 17 she merely noted: "The German is dropping paratroops in the Liege area. The going is still heavy. Bradley is leaving for Luxembourg."

Montgomery was also unflustered. He spent some time with the 2nd Canadian Division, presenting medals. After that he spent all day with the Canadian commanders, conferring about Veritable, the planned British-Canadian offensive toward the Rhine. N. Elliott Rodger, the Canadian brigadier, noted contentedly: "Found a new place to shoot pheasants within half mile of my caravan! Didn't shoot any though." Not until the next day did the external nastiness intrude upon this idyll. "Things began to hum," he wrote. But he added, "Out for half hour's hunting before lunch. . . . At 12:45 [First Canadian] Army told us to get 51st Division in hand for an early move."

It was the third day of the German offensive. "The situation is rapidly deteriorating," said the Hodges diary. Early that morning, however, he learned that Bradley had agreed to let him have General Matthew Ridgway and the entire two airborne divisions. The First Army's diary stated: "It is not yet known whether Twelfth Army Group fully appreciates the seriousness of the situation though both General Hodges and General [William] Kean talked with General Bradley half a dozen times during the day."

On this day a note of alarm began to creep into Kay Summersby's diary: "The German counterattack is bad. We can't use our air on account of poor weather. E. calls Bradley on the telephone. . . . The 106th Division is very badly hit. . . . [General] Strong reports that we have only located half of the German armor."

For Hodges, the nightmare was expanding. Tanks and infantry of the 1st SS Panzer Division were drawing ever closer to Stavelot and the immense fuel dump; it contained enough gasoline to keep a panzer division rolling for thirty days. That news galvanized even Lee into action—the Germans might poach upon his precious supplies. Hughes wrote: "Cliff L. [J.C.H. Lee] hastens forward to insure that depots are properly protected."

At three P.M., Hodges was told that the SS division was nearing Stavelot and driving toward Spa itself. There were only one roadblock and a few half-tracks barring its way. At four, Hodges emptied the Britannique and sent his entire headquarters staff, except for one officer in each section, out to help defend the road leading into the town. Colonel Dickson urged the shaken Hodges to escape in the Piper Cub that was standing by. But at the last moment the enemy spearhead turned away from Stavelot and veered off to the southwest. Thus they missed the almost defenseless First Army headquarters, and the huge gas dump too. Hodges ordered the headquarters to evacuate to Chaud-fontaine, ten miles west, near Liege.

The Stimson diary for December 18: "By this morning they [the Germans] had made quite a good deal of progress. So I had a talk with Marshall over that. We agreed that the Germans could not get very far. . . . Our people do not seem to be rattled and the American forces are closing in around the German salient and I think will stop it."

Stimson talked again with Marshall the next day, and the chief of staff was perfectly steady and clear. The complacency drained from the Pentagon's faces over the next days. On December 20, Stimson sat in on Marshall's staff conference. Afterward the secretary reported to his diary: "The news from France was bad today still, although our troops seem to be slowing up the breakthrough somewhat. Still it is a very formidable threat. . . . It may lengthen the war." By the next morning at ten-thirty, when Stimson addressed the regular press conference, the atmosphere was grave. But Stimson expressed optimism that "we will have them." He reminisced about the similar German offensive in 1918, and how the whole thing had burst like a pricked bubble.

Hitler's master plan had taken account of everything but George Patton. On December 18, Bradley telephoned Patton and told him to bring his top staff officers to Luxembourg for an immediate conference. Patton, sensing trouble, disattached Jean Gordon and sent her back to Paris in his personal plane to stay with Hughes's friend J.P. Then he climbed into his staff car and raced from Nancy up to Luxembourg.

There, Bradley showed him the latest map. It was a shocker. The whole American line was sagging, like a dam about to burst. "I feel you won't like what we are going to do," said Bradley, "but I fear it is necessary."

Patton knew what was expected of him, even before Bradley spoke. He would have to halt his attack on the West Wall. If he were Eisenhower, he would keep his nerve and let the Germans thrust fifty miles or more into the Allied lines—and then counterattack on both flanks and bite the bulge right off. Without hesitation, however, he said that he would start his 4th Armored Division rolling toward Longwy, one hundred miles north, at midnight. And he would send the 80th Division toward Luxembourg tomorrow morning. "I can also alert the 26th to start moving in twenty-four hours if necessary," he said.

While Patton was driving home—he hated driving home in the dark, especially since the roads were patrolled by trigger-happy MPs—conditions deteriorated. When he arrived back at Nancy, his chief of staff told him that Bradley had been on the phone and had ordered him not to wait until midnight but to start half the 4th Armored moving toward Longwy immediately. He had also requested that Patton telephone him the moment he got in.

Patton reached Bradley by phone at eight P.M.

"The situation up there is much worse than when I talked to you," Bradley said grimly. Tomorrow wasn't good enough any more—the movements must begin at once. "You and a staff officer," Bradley told him, "are to meet me at Verdun for a conference with General Eisenhower tomorrow morning at eleven."

Patton called his staff together at seven the next morning, December 19, and told them the change of battle plan, giving them the axes of attack. Then he drove off with a staff officer to Verdun. Verdun—an ominously evocative name. In World War I it was the scene of a months-long slaughter that annihilated hundreds of thousands of both British, French, and German youth. An eighteen-year-old Austrian corporal named Adolf Hitler was wounded there. Enormous military cemeteries still covered the hillsides.

Eisenhower had driven over from Paris, bringing Tedder; he was wearing his new fifth star as General of the Army. Devers was there too. While Eisenhower crumpled a cigarette pack and nervously reached for another, the SHAEF G-2, General Strong, began to brief them on the battle picture. The newest intelligence estimate was that this was a major Nazi effort. It was an attempt to push two lightning armored thrusts right through to Antwerp, capturing the major supply dumps around Liege as they went. Rundstedt had already committed twenty divisions, including five panzer divisions, to the push. Other attacks elsewhere on the front were not impossible.

There was only one solution, if Montgomery was not to be asked to come to the rescue—and none of the Americans wanted that. Eisenhower asked Patton to take command of a strong counterattack from the south. One year later, dying after an auto accident, Patton would get a telegram from Eisenhower recalling this crucial episode. "Bradley," wrote Eisenhower, "has just [reminded] me that when we three met in Verdun to consider plans, you and your army were given vital missions. From that moment on our worries with respect to the battle began to disappear. Nothing could stop you, including storms, cold, snow-blocked roads and a savagely fighting enemy. We want you to know that in your present battle we are supremely confident that your spirit will again bring victory."

"When can you attack?" Eisenhower now asked.

It was Patton's supreme moment of glory and recognition. Destiny himself had turned to him to save the American army. Without hesitation he shot back: "When? On December 22! With three divisions—the 4th Armored, the 26th, and the 80th." His response created commotion. Some of the generals were pleased, others frankly disbelieving. At this moment, Patton's forces were all tightly wound up to throw their punch due east. How could even Patton unscramble them in time, wheel them north, and then rewind the attack's mainspring to punch at right angles to the original axis?

As they left, Eisenhower was muttering. "Every time I get a new star," he said, "I get attacked." He had been promoted before the Kasserine Pass too.

"And every time you get attacked," replied Patton with a twinkle, "I pull you out."

Eisenhower returned to Versailles at once and wired Montgomery about the basic decisions reached at Verdun—to put Devers's troops onto the defensive along the southern sector of the front, and to bring up Patton to counterattack on the 23rd or 24th. His staff also sent a telegram to Bradley to remind him not to let any Meuse bridges fall undamaged into enemy hands. Bradley was nettled, believing that SHAEF was getting overprotective. "What the devil do they think we're doing," his chief of staff asked, "starting back for the beaches?"

The hope of keeping out the British dwindled. That same night, Bedell Smith telephoned Eisenhower. Strong, he said, now believed that the Germans had put their main effort into a thrust toward Namur, just forty miles from Brussels, and that the enemy might reach that city in two days. The entire British position was threatened.

Hodges's army was in disarray. The German offensive had cut its communications, and paratroops were operating in the Malmédy and Spa areas. While Hodges was pulling his headquarters back from Spa to Liege, a ghastly thing had happened: a V-1 flying bomb had dropped right on one of the staff trucks, leaving not a trace of either the three-ton truck or the fourteen occupants. When Hodges's last trucks rumbled out of Spa, the frightened mayor hurried to the city jail and himself released twenty suspected collaborators; the American flags were torn down, and pictures of President Roosevelt were removed in panic in case the Germans arrived.

At Versailles, at one A.M. on December 20, Eisenhower told Bedell Smith to send a telegram to Montgomery asking for his views. Should they give up ground in front of Hodges and to his left, in order to shorten the line and collect a strong reserve?

Montgomery had already begun to act independently. At 2:30 A.M. one of his officers had, on his orders, arrived at the new First Army headquarters, on the second floor of the Palace Hotel in Chaudfontaine, and asked that Hodges be awakened. Brought to Hodges's bedside, he informed him that the field marshal had moved the XXX Corps to where it could back up any retreat to the Meuse that became necessary. The XXX Corps had also taken charge of the bridges in the vicinity of Namur and Liege and were prepared to blow them upon call.

Montgomery was probably gratified at last to hear from the Supreme Commander, three days after Hitler's offensive had begun. The day before, he had sent Brooke a telegram which opened, "The situation in American area is *not* good." To Montgomery it appeared that the American troops were in full-scale withdrawal. "There is," he warned Brooke, "a definite lack of grip and control and no one has a clear picture as to situation. . . . There is an atmosphere of great pessimism in First and Ninth Armies due, I think, to the fact that everyone knows something has gone wrong and no one knows what or why. Bradley is still at Luxembourg, but I understand he is moving, as his headquarters are in danger. I have no information as to where he is moving. I presume Ike is at Rheims but I have heard nothing from him or Bradley. . . . I have myself had no orders or requests of any sort. My own opinion is that . . . the American forces have been cut clean in half and the Germans can reach the Meuse at Namur without any opposition." Montgomery pointed out how futile the command setup now was with the front bisected. He had therefore, he informed Brooke, told Major General Sir John Whiteley, the senior British officer on Eisenhower's staff at Versailles, that Eisenhower ought to place Montgomery in command of all the troops on the northern half of the front.

Brooke was aghast, and urged Montgomery, in a telegram, to tread softly: "I think you should be careful about what you say to Eisenhower . . . as it may do much more harm than good, especially as he is now probably very worried over whole situation."

When Eisenhower conferred the next morning at SHAEF with Tedder, Bedell Smith, Strong, and Whiteley, the German attack had moved to the top of his agenda.

The Allied front was in reorganization. Patton would begin ramming his army north into the southern shoulder of the bulge. But the German thrust was causing grave problems—the telephone links between Bradley in the south and his two armies in the north were already threatened. (Hughes prophesied in his diary, on December 20: "Probably another reorganization tomorrow, if I know my army. There must be motion—if not commotion!" He seemed to be enjoying the turmoil.)

Eisenhower was now forced to do precisely what Montgomery had been demanding for three months—make a decision that every American and many British members of the SHAEF staff could only regard as galling. He would have to put Montgomery in charge of those two American armies north of the bulge—Hodges' and Simpson's. This would leave Bradley in much-reduced circumstances south of the bulge, with only Patton under his command. Kay Summersby wrote, "E. called Monty on the phone and informed him of the new set-up."

The call was made at ten-thirty that morning. Montgomery could barely hear him. Eisenhower was very excited, roaring his words into the telephone so fast that Montgomery could hardly understand. Once, however, he heard the Supreme Commander shouting: "It seems we now have two fronts." Montgomery eventually perceived that Eisenhower was asking him to command the northern front. That was all Montgomery wanted to know. Eisenhower blustered on for a few more minutes—Montgomery had to shout "I can't hear!" once or twice—and the call was cut off before he finished. Montgomery later crowed in his memoirs. "This could not have been pleasant for my critics at Supreme headquarters," he said, "or for the American generals who opposed my ideas."

He acted briskly and decisively: within two hours of the telephone call from Eisenhower, he had issued orders in person to all the army commanders. He briefed Dempsey and Crerar at his own eleven A.M. conference; then he left for Hodges's headquarters, having told Simpson to meet him there.

At 1:30 P.M. Montgomery strutted into the Palace Hotel at Chaudfontaine "like Christ come to cleanse the temple," said a British officer who witnessed the scene. The windows had been blown out—a V-1 had blasted into the ground nearby only a few hours earlier. Montgomery found that neither Simpson nor Hodges had seen Bradley since the battle began. "There were no reserves anywhere behind [the] front," he reported to Brooke that night. "Morale was very low. They seemed delighted to have someone to give them firm orders." He at once reorganized the front so that he could extract a reserve of three divisions. "I have every hope the situation can be put right," he assured Brooke, "now that we have a properly organized set-up for Command and proper supervision and control can be kept over the battle."

This was no time to quarrel over nationalities. Montgomery put British troops under Simpson and shifted his Ninth Army to take over some of Hodges's front. Then he stationed British troops behind both American armies in case of a collapse. In particular, Montgomery asked Hodges for the most aggressive fighting corps commander he had, to mount the counterattack. Hodges knew only one general who fitted that description—Joe Collins, whose VII Corps had captured Cherbourg. Two of Collins's divisions were transferred to the Ninth Army, along with the British 51st Division, the three of them to act first as a reserve and then as the core of Montgomery's counterattack.

In London that afternoon, Brooke called on the Prime Minister and showed him Montgomery's overnight report on the crisis. He persuaded Churchill to telephone Eisenhower. But Eisenhower had already done what Churchill was going to propose—he had put Montgomery in charge. At six P.M. the Cabinet met to hear the news. "Cabinet took it well on the whole," recorded Brooke in his diary. "I rather doubt whether they realised all the possible implications."

Patton had driven up that morning, the 20th, to be with Bradley at his headquarters at Luxembourg, to plan the rescue operation by the Third Army. He found that Bradley already had interfered somewhat with his own dispositions, halting one division at Luxembourg without consulting him and also engaging a combat command of an armored division east of Bastogne—but given the emergency, Patton did not grumble. Shortly after he arrived, at nine A.M., the telephone rang for Bradley. It was Eisenhower, breaking it to him that Montgomery was going to be put in operational control of Hodges and Simpson—because, he said, telephone connections between them and Bradley had been disrupted. Patton scoffed. "As a matter of fact," he observed in his diary, "telephonic communications were all right, and it is either a case of having lost confidence in Bradley, or having been forced to put Montgomery in through the machinations of the Prime Minister or with the hope that if he gives Monty operational control, he will get some of the British divisions in [to the fight]. Eisenhower is unwilling or unable to command Montgomery."

He kept cool. The bulge was getting bigger? Then let it get bigger still. He told Middleton, the VIII Corps commander, to give more ground, so that the enemy would become even more extended, and to blow the bridges in such a way as to channel the enemy advance; then he would hit them in the southern flank. This was Patton—hanging onto the telephone, ordering self-propelled guns and headquarters and artillery and replacements moved about the map, cannibalizing antitank units, creating rifle units, shifting ammunition and hospitals and bridging units to the right places for when the fighting began. Since he had no staff officers with him, he ran the whole floor show by phone through his army staff at Nancy.

He was happy to do it—because he was killing Germans, outsmarting Montgomery, helping Eisenhower, to whom his destiny seemed linked, and proving himself a second Alexander the Great.

It was a hectic time for Hodges, who was old for this sort of trouble. "The weather was foul all day," the First Army's diary read for the 20th. "[V-1] Buzz bombs in countless numbers passed over the C.P., . . . the planes and the continual traffic moving up and down the main road make it difficult for the General to obtain the quiet which is necessary in the making of these vast decisions."

By now, the American generals had acute personal worries. The Germans had dropped 150 enemy parachutists into Hodges's area. They were wearing GI uniform and dog tags. Three had actually gotten to the Stavelot dump. When they were captured, they knew they could expect short shrift. One German officer asked for a pistol to commit suicide, "and thus held fast," said the First Army diary, "to his strange out-worn conception of honor. We shall cordially accommodate him."

But that was not all. A German officer captured in Liege had revealed that a killer squad in American uniforms and Jeeps, equipped with American weapons and IDs, was operating behind the Allied lines; some of its members were ostensibly transporting German "prisoners" to the rear. It was said to be led by SS Major Otto Skorzeny, and had the mission of assassinating Eisenhower. "These men are completely ruthless and prepared to sacrifice their lives," said Hodges' diary. "All personnel speak fluent English." They were carrying explosives, and some of them had a new type of hand grenade fired from a pistol.

Later on December 20, Eisenhower was warned urgently of reports that paratroopers in American uniforms had been seen at Epernay heading for Paris in a civilian vehicle. Skorzeny's name was already known to SHAEF. Its Counter-Intelligence Summary on December 1 included this warning: "Captured saboteurs emphasize impressive scale of Skorzeny's plan for sabotage and subversion. He . . . has created certain new units, apparently for para-military use." Bedell Smith passed the information to Eisenhower at the morning staff conference at Versailles. Kay Summersby: "G-2 reported that an attempt is to be made on E.'s life. Sixty Germans are supposed to be on their way to Paris for this purpose, they will be in Allied uniforms and will stop at nothing. E. is urged by all his senior staff members to stay in his office and not go home at all." For Eisenhower this was the final indignity. While a British field marshal now strode onto the stage and took charge, issuing orders to Hodges and Simpson, he himself had to loiter in his headquarters like a fugitive.

After that, security in Paris got so tight that Hughes, twice that morning, could not get into his own hotel because sentries did not recognize him. The second time, in a rage, he sent for the duty officer. That evening he stomped off to the Folies Bergères, taking Jean Gordon and J.P. with him.

When General Littlejohn got back to his headquarters at the Hotel Astoria, he found sentries with fixed bayonets all over the building. Littlejohn, a grizzly bear of a general with jug ears, bellowed: "Let's do away with them. If any Germans come, just send them up to me. I'll take care of them."

The next day, Eisenhower was still a victim of the security alert. Kay Summersby noted: "He is confined to the office building, which makes him mad." He lit another cigarette and wrote to Mamie: "This is the year's shortest day—how I pray that it may, by some miracle, mark the beginning of improving weather!" And he added mysteriously, "There are so many things about this war that cannot be told now—possibly never—but they should make interesting talk between you and me when we're sitting in the sun, taking our elegant ease in our reclining days."

He read the first reports from Montgomery about his conference with Hodges and Simpson. "The front," Montgomery had candidly said, "was in need of reorganization, and I issued orders on this subject. Elements of the 7th Armored Division with some other troops are still holding out in the general area about St. Vith, and there is no doubt that the brave work of these troops is slowing up enemy movement into the penetration area and westwards."

This day, December 21, was much colder, and the ground had begun to freeze. Two hundred miles to the east, at dawn, Rundstedt threw twelve fresh divisions into the battle, of which seven were panzer divisions. Now voices of criticism began to seep into Eisenhower's office. In his first guilty panic, he had ordered a news blackout—there was to be a forty-eight-hour delay in the release of any news. The effect on the French and Belgians was disastrous, he now was told. They feared this was 1940 all over again—when Hitler invaded France and Belgium by this same route. To find out what was happening, they began switching to German radio stations. Europe was awash with rumors. "Stories which start as mere rumors," Eisenhower was told by his staff, "are unfortunately often proved to be true at a later stage. . . . It is no use hiding the fact that the Germans have broken through and that the momentum of their counter-offensive is far from spent."

Nothing redeemed that day. Strong brought him evidence that Hitler was withdrawing divisions from the Russian front and shifting them to the west. Eisenhower's gloom deepened. He dictated a telegram to Marshall: "I . . . consider it essential that we should obtain from the Russians at the earliest possible moment some indication of their strategical and tactical intentions." Why was Stalin delaying his offensive like this? And why was he keeping the Allies in the dark?

CHAPTER TWENTY-SIX

Mad as Hell

THE DAY after Montgomery got command of the American armies on the northern flank of the bulge, Sir Alan Brooke sent him a warning not to rub it in—to anyone at SHAEF or elsewhere. But Montgomery found the advice difficult to follow. He had not been impressed by the American commanders' response to this crisis. He told Sir James Grigg: "I won't write my views on what has gone on here. I do not know of any ink that would stand what I would want to say!" In characteristic manner he continued, "Personally, I am enjoying a very interesting battle; but one ought really to burst into tears at the tragedy of the whole thing. Possibly in years to come certain people will turn in their graves when they think back on the past. There are some good sharp rocks ahead even now. At the moment I do *not* see how this is going to turn into what Ike calls 'our greatest victory.'"

The retreat by his own headquarters from Spa, the loss of many fine men, the knowledge that his First Army was taking the brunt of the attack, the fact that Bradley had not bothered to visit him during the first days of the crisis, all these bore down on General Hodges. The throaty rattle of the V-1s hurtling down their sky alley toward Antwerp grated on his nerves. Already at fifty-eight an aging, melancholy man, he absorbed much of the tragedy himself. Montgomery was worried by the general's lowering morale. It could be infectious. To the field marshal it was evident that Hodges was, as he put it, "a bit shaken early on and needed moral support and was very tired." He called on Hodges at Chaudfontaine on December 21 and asked if things looked better. Hodges assured him that they did. Montgomery decided to see the two army commanders, Hodges and Simpson, every day, to cheer them up. He communicated his views on Hodges to Eisenhower, and the next day Eisenhower sent Hodges a message. "The slogan is 'chins up,'" it said. To Montgomery, however, Eisenhower wrote, "I know you realize that Hodges is the quiet reticent type and does not appear as aggressive as he really is." And he hinted at the possibility of making changes on the American side, if Montgomery felt them to be necessary.

That day, December 22, at lunchtime, Montgomery returned to Hodges with the glad news that he had managed to deploy 150 British tanks along the Meuse, like clothespins on a clothesline, to defend the vital Meuse bridges between Namur and Givet. This lifted a tremendous load from the general's mind, said Hodges's diarist, adding: "Monty was chipper and confident as usual." He kept his own disquiet —particularly about the low troop strengths of Gerow's divisions, north of the bulge—to himself.

Three hours later Hodges pulled his headquarters farther back, to Tongres, to obtain "the peace and quiet which are necessary for the momentous decisions which must be made." By that he meant that it was safer on the other side of the river Meuse.

Simpson, Montgomery's other American army commander, had none of these morale problems. He found Montgomery a bit pompous but told Eisenhower bluntly a few days later, "I and my Army are operating smoothly and cheerfully under command of the Field Marshal. The most cordial relations and a very high spirit of cooperation have been established between him and myself personally and between our respective staffs."

Early on December 22, Patton's forces began their counterattack after a feat of regrouping and of staff work that was spectacular, given the short time. "We shoot the works on a chestnut-pulling expedition in the morning," he had written meaningfully to Beatrice the previous night. Eisenhower and his senior advisor, General Harold R. Bull, feared that Patton was attacking too soon, before he was strong enough —but Patton felt that it was now or never. His attack began at 6:30 A.M. on a twenty-mile front, and thrust seven miles. It was less than he hoped, but now the snow was coming down.

Montgomery did not hold high hopes for his rival. "I am not optimistic," he told Eisenhower, "that [the] attack of Third Army will be strong enough to do what is needed, and I suggest Seventh German Army will possibly hold off Patton from interfering with progress westwards of Fifth Panzer Army." He reassured Eisenhower that Hodges's army was "now reorganized and in good trim and we will fight a good battle up here." On the First Army's erstwhile front, however, Troy Middleton's VIII Corps was being shredded. Its tattered remnants clung like rats to breakwaters in an unexpected flood tide.

The 101st Airborne had dug in at Bastogne, the most important crossroads in the entire area, together with portions of the 9th Armored and 10th Armored, a couple of companies of tank destroyers, and some black artillery troops. Middleton had given the temporary commander of the 101st, Brigadier General Anthony C. McAuliffe, the simple order: "Hold Bastogne." This McAuliffe did, in a heroic stand that would shine with diamond light through the darkest days to come. On December 22, Ultra intercepted word that at noon the Germans had called for the honorable surrender of the town. McAuliffe replied with one famous word: "Nuts." The German commander got the gist, and Ultra learned that too.

On Saturday, December 23, the bitter cold froze away much of the fog that had stopped air activity, and 241 C-47s parachuted artillery ammunition to McAuliffe's troops in Bastogne. At Eupen, the First Army carried out the first executions by firing squad of members of the "Stielau" parachute group. Hodges's diary records: "The prisoners' last request was to hear Christmas carols, sung by a group of German women prisoners."

Back in Paris, Eisenhower was still pinned in his office, for security reasons. The city was swarming with military police. The hotel where Hughes worked had sentries outside and inside the front door, in front of the elevator, and at all its levels; Hughes refused to show his papers to an MP who could not produce his warrant card for him; he got in through the front door, only to be stopped on the third floor and forced to produce his ID card after all. His driver, Sergeant Brown, was stopped and challenged for his trip ticket. It was all a big nuisance until Hughes and his staff found a side door they could enter through and get to their offices without meeting any sentries.

Hodges had ordered Joe Collins to assemble two infantry divisions and one armored division along a fifty-mile front by midnight, December 23, for an eventual counterattack. Collins set up his corps headquarters at Marche, a small crossroads town. It was ominously quiet when he arrived. The division commander on the scene, Brigadier General Alexander R. Bolling, was confident that he could hold the line from Marche to Hotton, seven miles to the northeast. If he could, it would help block the Fifth Panzer Army. The Germans had to be stopped before they could capture a bridge across the river Meuse.

On December 23 Eisenhower dictated a long memorandum. It was clearly intended to cover him, if there were an inquiry. He explained why the Ardennes region had been so thinly defended, why Bradley's earlier offensive in the north had been suspended—because of the failure to capture key dams on the Roer which the Germans might demolish to wash away their attackers—and why Bradley had continued Patton's offensive to the disadvantage of the rest of the front. As for the intelligence fiasco, he admitted that his staff had noticed that German panzer formations in other areas were being withdrawn and replaced by low-grade infantry. "All Intelligence agencies assiduously tried to find out the locations and intentions of these Panzer formations," he claimed, "but without definite success." This was not true, and Eisenhower must have known it. He continued: "While it was felt that an attack through the Ardennes was a *possibility* . . . it was not deemed highly probable that the enemy would, in winter, try to use that region in which to stage a major attack."

On Sunday, Christmas Eve, Eisenhower was briefly allowed home to get a change of clothing. They had still not caught the killer squad, and his life was too valuable to put at risk. Before leaving for Saint-Germain, Eisenhower called Henry Aurand, down at Cherbourg, and asked him, as a personal favor, to look into the case of a valued platoon sergeant from General Stafford LeRoy Irwin's 5th Division who had gotten in trouble while in Cherbourg and was under sentence of death for murder and rape. The theater had reduced the sentence to ten years, but Irwin, a classmate of both Eisenhower and Aurand, wanted the sentence suspended altogether. "The papers are on their way by messenger," said Eisenhower.

"I am anxious to get him back," Irwin himself then told Aurand on the phone. "If you send him back, have him drive a new Jeep for me and report to me in person."

Aurand, the exiled and eager supply officer, obliged. He had a new Jeep made available. "I felt the warm glow of Christmas," said Aurand, "when I returned to my office after starting this sergeant on his way back to the Fifth Division." The glow was dispelled an hour later. A message came that a ship had been torpedoed off Cherbourg, a ship that his Normandy Base Section had not even known was due in. For hours they searched in the darkness for survivors. Seven hundred men from the 66th Division were drowned.

Curfew in Paris was nine P.M. On Christmas Eve, General Hughes and J.P. strolled to Notre Dame, ancient and spectacular, brooding on the darkened island in the Seine. The show that the Catholics put on, Hughes felt, was the best of any religion.

The Germans had reacted violently to Patton's thrust, forcing the 4th Armored to recoil several miles. Patton's soldiers were tired after attacking day and night, and the weather was no good. The bulge was growing. On its northern flank, the situation was fluid. Collins drove forward to see Bolling at Marche. The infantry commander was still confident, although the fighting was coming closer now, and some 116th Panzer Division tanks had penetrated almost to the Marche-Hotton road. As his Jeep whipped along, Collins was bitterly cold, but he was cheered to see that the sky was clearing. Any hour now the Allied fighter-bombers would appear in force. And surely the German tanks must run out of gasoline soon.

On his customary morale-boosting visit to Hodges that afternoon, Montgomery showed his concern about a threat emerging on Collins's flank. There followed a misunderstanding that could well have proved fateful. According to General William B. Kean, the First Army chief of staff, Hodges directed Collins to prepare to hold the line from Hotton to Andenne—a thirty-mile axis running northwest to the Meuse, near Namur—should his corps be forced back; but he would leave that decision to Collins. Hodges sent Colonel R. F. Akers by Jeep to brief Collins on Hodges' wishes. As, however, it would take Akers several hours to reach Collins, Kean telephoned the VII Corps chief of staff, a General Palmer, at about 3:30 P.M. to dictate the gist. To avoid a security breach, he spoke cryptically: he told Palmer to look on a map for two towns beginning with the letters *A* and *H*. An hour later, Kean phoned again in case Palmer had misunderstood him. "Now get this," said Kean. "I am only going to say it once. Roll with the punch." Palmer looked at the map again and spotted two towns with the designated initials, Andenne and Huy. But this line was over *thirty miles* to the rear of the other villages. This order, as construed, seemed to presage a major withdrawal by the Allies. Palmer rushed the message over to Collins with a footnote, "I think you had better come home." When Aker arrived in his Jeep, frozen to the marrow, he anxiously corrected the error, and affirmed that even that lesser withdrawal was only a recommendation, not an order, to Collins. To cover himself, Collins asked Akers to write down Hodges's recommendation. He then filed this document and ignored it.

What Collins did was to telephone General Ernest Harmon and direct his 2nd Armored Division not to withdraw but to attack. The First Army diary stated: "It appears that tomorrow may be a crucial day in the VII Corps sector, with Terrible Ernie Harmon's tank forces getting the chance of a life time to do the work which he loves." Harmon attacked on Christmas morning, and in a two-day running tank battle he destroyed the greater part of the 2nd Panzer Division. He had help. Pete Quesada's fighter-bombers were out in force. And the massed American artillery—now firing the deadly VT proximity-fused shells—drew the teeth of Hasso von Manteuffel's Fifth Panzer Army before it could reach the Meuse.

On Christmas Day, Bradley went to see Montgomery at Zondhoven. The field marshal had peeled off the layers of garments he usually wore and put on a smart uniform in Bradley's honor. Thus attired, he could not resist the temptation to gloat over Bradley's discomfiture. Montgomery found Bradley looking thin, worn, and ill at ease. "I was absolutely frank with him," he reported to Brooke that evening. "I said the Germans had given us a real 'bloody nose'; it was useless to pretend that we were going to turn this quickly into a great victory; it was a proper defeat, and we had much better admit it." Montgomery continued that what had happened was entirely their own fault—Bradley had allowed Patton to go too far, with the result that neither his nor the northern thrust had been strong enough. "The enemy saw his chance and took it. Now we were in a proper muddle." He looked disdainfully, but compassionately, upon Bradley, reflecting that until a year ago he had never commanded anything bigger than a corps in Tunisia. "Poor chap," he wrote. "He is such a decent fellow and the whole thing is a bitter pill for him. But he is man enough to admit it and he did."

Bradley stayed only half an hour, for what must have been an uncomfortable interview. He told Montgomery that the 101st Airborne had not yet been relieved at Bastogne by Patton, but it was claiming to have destroyed 150 tanks. He hoped to reach Bastogne from the south, but doubted that he could push farther without more troops.

Montgomery began whistling a tune familiar to Bradley: he said that if the Allies were to regain the initiative, given the present manpower shortage, they would have to hold shorter fronts in the south; the units pulled out in the south could be packed into a powerful punch in the north.

After supper Bradley visited Patton, and told him confidentially that Montgomery said that Hodges's First Army could not launch its offensive for three months and that the only attack that could be made was by Patton, who was, however, too weak; hence, they should fall back to the Saar-Vosges line, and perhaps even to the Moselle. Patton was disgusted at the prospect.

Still Montgomery postponed the counterattack by Collins's VII Corps. He was planning only a limited counterattack, near the "thumbnail" of the German salient, intending to extrude the enemy from the pocket, hammering them all the time, as at Falaise. Attempting a big bite across the base of the salient would be a risky operation. This was very much what Hodges felt too, but Collins, though Irish fighting spirit that he was, wanted to go for the big bite. On December 27, Hodges's diary noted: "General Hodges . . . went over at midnight the three possible attack plans submitted by General Collins; two of which have Bastogne as the objective, one of which has St. Vith. . . . General Collins frankly admits in the papers submitted with them that they will require some strength because of the exposed flanks. General Hodges has had enough of exposed flanks for the last two weeks, and it is thought that the most conservative of the three plans will be the one finally adopted."

From his southern side of the bulge, Patton was not happy with Montgomery's deliberate preparations for Collins's attack. "If Ike put Bradley back in command of the First and Ninth Armies," he believed, "we can bag the whole German army. I wish Ike were more of a gambler, but he is certainly a lion compared to Montgomery, and Bradley is better than Ike as far as nerve is concerned. Of course, he did make a bad mistake [during the period before the German onslaught] in being passive on the front of the VIII Corps. Monty is a tired little fart. War requires the taking of risks and he won't take them."

On Christmas Day, Eisenhower's mess provided a turkey. He wore the fancy slippers Mamie had sent him. She had sent him a needle threader too, perhaps worried by his talk of getting "someone" to embroider the fifth star on his uniform for him. Eisenhower confessed in his next letter: "I haven't tried the needle threader yet." She had also sent him some king-size cigarettes, and he kidded her: "When I smoke one of those cigarettes I'll have to have time to devote to the job. They're huge. . . . You'll understand, from the papers, that we're preoccupied right now."

Eisenhower and his staff conferred on the attack. Kay Summersby noticed, "E. is a bit low in his mind." The Germans had evidently been stopped, but Montgomery, as cautious as ever, sent a message to the effect that he did not have the strength to mount his counterattack yet. The next day, however, after they had held out against three enemy divisions for ten days, the bravery of the defenders of Bastogne was rewarded as Patton's spearheads crashed through and relieved them. "The German has shot his wad. Prisoners have had no food for from three to five days," he noted. "We should attack." This was easier written than done, given the present weather, grouping, and the manpower, fuel, supplies, and ammunition shortages. But Patton was cocky. He said, "The damn Jerries have stuck their heads in the meat grinder and I've got the handle."

Later that day, December 26, Hughes, Lee, and Lutes went off to Lille via Soissons. "Oyster soup with Ike, and then a game of darts," wrote Hughes in his diary. "He is in confinement. . . . Said he couldn't do otherwise than to give [the] two American armies to Monty."

His chief preoccupation was, Why had the Russians not yet attacked? Marshall sent a message this day, saying that Stalin was willing to see any senior officer that Eisenhower would send to Moscow. Eisenhower was worried enough about the prospects to send his own deputy, Tedder. He left immediately for London, but for days he was grounded by weather in Naples and Cairo, and it would be mid-January before he was ushered into the Soviet dictator's presence. The Russians' silence about their strategic plans gravely embarrassed the Allies. A newsman who spoke of that embarrassment, Merrill Mueller of NBC, was sent straight home and banished from the European theater. At the end of January, Churchill would send Eisenhower a message urging that the story should never be told, that there should never be any announcement about the relations with the Russians before the trip to Moscow —it would deeply shock American and British opinion.

In Washington, after lunch on December 27, Stimson walked back to the War Department and slipped into Marshall's office for a long private talk about an unthinkable possibility: what if the Germans pulled this gamble off? Marshall had been thinking the same thought. Rain and sleet lashed the office windows as they talked. Basic to both men's worries was the fear that they had created an army too small for the job—and that in consequence the infantry was becoming battle-fatigued. The German armies facing the Allies still equaled them in divisions. Should the United States begin raising new divisions now, for autumn 1945? "He said," Stimson dictated afterward, "that . . . if Germany beat us in this counter-attack and particularly if the Russians failed to come in on *their* side, we should have to recast the whole war; we should have to take a defensive position on the German boundary —which he believed we could do with perfect safety—and then have the people of the United States decide whether they wanted to go on with the war enough to raise the new armies which would be necessary to do it. . . . He discussed the importance of Antwerp as our main port in keeping this system of pressure up. Much depended on the failure of the Germans to obliterate that port."

Roosevelt had remained considerate throughout these two weeks. He had not embarrassed his Chiefs by asking about the progress of the battle. But in France, Hughes read the American newspapers and observed on December 30: "Papers wondering how we let Germans get set. I wonder too."

Later Eisenhower left for Brussels for a conference with Montgomery. It was a long and trying journey, because of the fog and delays. At Brussels, Eisenhower found that Montgomery had unexpectedly gone on to Hasselt. It was not the first time this sort of thing had happened. Swallowing his frustration, he followed him by special train. Kay Summersby learned the next day: "E. and Monty had a long talk. Monty wouldn't let his chief of staff be present. Monty still tried to convince E. that there should be one commander of the entire battle front, left no doubt as to who should be that commander. From all accounts he was not very cooperative."

At Hasselt on December 28, Montgomery told him that he hoped the Germans would launch a new attack. He would then drive them in on the rebound—a classic textbook maneuver. If, however, they did not attack, he would have Collins counterattack on January 1. Then they talked about the future—after the bulge had been deflated. Montgomery again said that the Ruhr was the main next objective, they must concentrate on it—all forces being under one commander. Brooke heard of the meeting, and did not like Montgomery's account of it at all—"It looks to me as if Monty has been rubbing into Ike the results of not having listened to advice!"

By the time Brooke wrote this, Montgomery had already struck. The next day, true to pattern, he followed the conference with a harshly worded letter to the Supreme Commander, demanding the appointment of a ground commander, "only because I am so anxious not to have another failure." He asked him not to mention one part of the letter to Bradley—because Bradley would oppose being under his control, and he warned Eisenhower that he would have to be very firm with Bradley on this matter. "Any loosely worded statement," said Montgomery, "will be quite useless." Montgomery himself proposed the precise wording: "From now onwards full operational direction, control, and co-ordination of [the operations of the two army groups] is vested in the C-in-C, 21 Army Group, subject to such instructions as may be issued by the Supreme Commander from time to time." He signed it, "Yours always, and your very devoted friend, Monty," and added a postscript: "Do not bother to answer this." Of this letter Kay Summersby tartly wrote afterward: "Monty left no doubt as to who should be the ground commander, namely Monty."

When Eisenhower returned from seeing Montgomery on December 29, his spirits were low. He called his staff together for a conference. "They are all mad at Monty," said Kay Summersby, "especially Whiteley. E.'s one aim is to keep the staff together. Tonight E. is leaving his house in St. Germain and is moving into a new one, which is three minutes from the office." Years later one of Eisenhower's staff described the ire which Montgomery's resumption of his demands on Eisenhower —at this crucial pass in Allied fortunes—raised at SHAEF against him. In an oral interview for the Eisenhower Library, Arthur S. Nevins, SHAEF's wartime chief of plans, said: "General Eisenhower was on the point of sending a message to the CCS asking for his [Montgomery's] relief. Montgomery's chief of staff de Guingand got news of this disagreement . . . and made a flying trip to headquarters and contacted Bedell Smith and together they worked out a solution. De Guingand persuaded Eisenhower and Tedder to hold up a message they were drafting to Washington; he told them he could straighten out Montgomery—that Montgomery didn't really understand how serious the situation was. De Guingand then went back and openly told Montgomery that he would certainly be relieved if the message went to the CCS, because no one would be willing to defend him—not even Churchill— if General Eisenhower couldn't get along with him. Montgomery sent a message to Eisenhower saying that he hadn't understood the situation and that he would cooperate "to the maximum." Montgomery signed the letter, "Your very devoted subordinate," and that, said Nevins, saved him.

From the wartime records, from Eisenhower's secret Montgomery file, and from private diaries it is possible to piece together the precise sequence of this crisis. On Eisenhower's return to his headquarters from Hasselt he found two things—de Guingand was there, and coincidentally there was a telegram from Marshall. It had arrived at 6:45 P.M., and it referred to outspoken newspaper articles in the London newspapers of the Beaverbrook group criticizing Eisenhower and Bradley and making Montgomery the hero of the Ardennes battle. "My feeling is this," said Marshall, his tones ringing authoritatively across the Atlantic. "Under no circumstances make any concessions of any kind whatsoever. You not only have our complete confidence, but there would be a terrific resentment in this country following such action." He said in closing: "You are doing a grand job and go on and give them hell." Eisenhower must have reflected that this was the same kind of false flattery that Eisenhower himself had used to buck up poor old Hodges. But it was powerful backing all the same.

When Eisenhower finally wrote to Montgomery, on December 31, it was a stiffly worded, handwritten letter ostensibly covering his outline plan for operations after the elimination of the bulge. It provided for great strength north of the Ruhr when the Rhine was crossed. "In these principal features it exactly repeats my intentions as I gave them to you verbally on the train, on the 28th," he admonished Montgomery. About one thing he was quite emphatic: he would never put Bradley under Montgomery's command. "You disturb me," he said, with renewed predictions of "failure" unless "your exact opinions in the matter . . . are met in detail." "I assure you," he wrote, "that in this matter I can go no further." He urged Montgomery not to let the schism grow to the point where an appeal to the Combined Chiefs would become necessary, because it would surely damage the Allied cause. He could speak no plainer than that: he was threatening to ask the Combined Chiefs in Washington which of the two of them was the more valuable to the Allied endeavor, Montgomery or Eisenhower. Having now received Marshall's letter, Eisenhower was in no doubt as to their likely answer.

It looked like game, set, and match for Eisenhower. Kay Summersby noted that day: "Bedell and E. agree that Monty has changed considerably since the day in Italy over a year ago when he said that he wanted to join the 'team'."

De Guingand had had a three-hour talk with Eisenhower the day before the reply to Montgomery. Now he rushed to the field marshal to warn him how "het up" the Supreme Commander was, and to tell him of Marshall's telegram. Montgomery decided to pipe down, as he put it, and at four P.M. on December 31, Montgomery sent Eisenhower, for his eyes only, a message numbered M.406: "Dear Ike, Have seen Freddie [de Guingand] and understand you are greatly worried by many considerations in these very difficult days. I have given you my frank views because I have felt [that] you like this. I am sure there are many factors which have a bearing quite beyond anything I realize. Whatever your decision may be, you can rely on me one hundred per cent to make it work and I know Brad will do the same. Very distressed that my letter may have upset you, and I would ask you to tear it up. Your very devoted subordinate, Monty."

There was a further *bonne bouche* for Eisenhower. In a second message, timed at 9:35 P.M. the same day, Montgomery told Eisenhower that, after consultation with Hodges, he was launching Collins's VII Corps counterattack at the first light in three days' time.

Security was still tight. Hughes arrived one morning at the gate of an ordnance depot, riding in his chauffeur-driven Cadillac with its two stars showing. A sentry stepped in front, with rifle at port arms, and demanded his ID. As he studied Hughes's papers, longer than usual, several civilians passed. Hughes irritably asked: "Who are those civilians who passed through the gate?"

"I don't know, sir," the sentry replied, "they ain't got no passes."

On the last day of the year, Stimson visited the President—Roosevelt was still in bed—and, with the aid of a contour map, briefed him on Patton's counterattack. They discussed the unpleasant British newspaper campaign for a British deputy commander. British divisions were now, Stimson pointed out, very much in the minority.

Roosevelt agreed. "Churchill always is a disperser," he commented; that is, he had dispersed his forces all over the globe rather than concentrate them on Germany.

Stimson played the same ball. "It's not unnatural that Churchill is a disperser," he said, "because he has to disperse his troops to protect the British Empire. On the other hand, we have to win this war. Nobody else can. And we have got to concentrate to do it on the place where we are doing it now."

Stimson told Roosevelt of the massacre of 150 U.S. troops at Malmédy by the 1st SS Panzer Division, as described by survivors.

"Well," replied the President cynically, "it will only serve to make our troops feel toward the Germans as they have already learned to feel about the Japs."

The strain on Eisenhower had not lessened as the threat of assassination began to fade and he was able to move with greater freedom. "This is a very trying period for E.," wrote Kay Summersby. "Everyone is feeling a trifle nervous not knowing exactly where the next attack is coming from. It is up to E. all the time to cheer people up. Not an easy job, he can never relax for a moment."

For a time it appeared that Eisenhower would have to pull his forces out of Strasbourg, the Alsatian capital seventy miles south of Saarbrücken, fifty miles southeast of Nancy. He told his staff, "We have not got the troops to defend it. If the French want to put some troops in the city that will be O.K." From the military point of view, Strasbourg was not worth defending. He ignored the political capital that Hitler would make out of such a victory—the Germans had long considered it a German city. De Gaulle was appalled, and his General Alphonse Juin told Eisenhower that the Germans would surround and take the city as soon as the Sixth Army Group withdrew, and that there were 3,000 Allied collaborators in the city who would be put to the sword. "He wants us to hold the line at all costs," wrote Kay Summersby on January 2. The French then sent LeClerc's division to defend Strasbourg. De Gaulle came on January 3, and "got heated to say the least of it," as Kay Summersby wrote. He stiffly told Eisenhower that if he pulled the two American divisions out of the Strasbourg area, "the French would go their own way." Eisenhower yielded, reluctantly, although he normally never allowed political considerations to override military necessity. Worried, he explained to his staff, "The French would have turned against us, if we had taken them [the two divisions] out."

To top it all, Churchill announced that he was coming with Brooke, and would stay the night of the third. That day, waiting for their arrival, Eisenhower wrote to Mamie. He had a guilty conscience—he had not written to her since Christmas. Every time he walked into his office he glimpsed the photograph in the corner, of Mamie and John. Now, because he knew that the two or three teletypes he had sent would not appease her, he saw the need to confess to having been very remiss.

"From your papers you will understand," he pleaded, "that we have been under some stress, and you'll understand that it has been hard to sit down and to compose thought applicable to a letter to one's best only girl." He hoped this soft soap would avert one of those griping letters from Mamie that he hated.

He had had a lot on his mind. Like Leigh-Mallory, Admiral Ramsay, the SHAEF naval commander, who was one of his closest friends, had been killed in an air crash. The day before, his plane had gone into a stall on takeoff from Villacoublay.

At about this time, Eisenhower had offered pardons to the American soldiers in military prisons if they would take up arms and fight. He was not encouraged to hear that only a few, those with long sentences, had accepted the offer.

On December 31, Montgomery had written to his friend Grigg: "My Dear P.J., . . . All is well and the Germans will not now get what they wanted. But they have given the Americans a colossal 'bloody nose', and mucked up all our plans; however, as we have not got a plan, I suppose they will say it does not matter!! Come over and see me some time."

Thus ended 1944, the year which the British had so urgently desired would bring an end to the fighting. Britain had banked everything on it: if the war were to go on until 1945, it would become an international bankrupt, stripped of manpower, bereft of material resources, and still fighting an implacable enemy, while allied to powers with little interest in the survival of the British Empire. This was what had underlain all Montgomery's exhortations to Eisenhower—the urgency of completing the campaign rapidly and cheaply, with a killer blow at Germany. Britain had no time for the slow, broad-front approach.

New Year's Day dawned with the drone of hundreds of aircraft engines, as Goering suddenly sent his entire fighter force on a surprise raid against the forward Allied airfields in France, Holland, and Belgium. Once again Ultra had given good warning, and once again the Allies were caught with their pants down—in fact, Montgomery's G-2 sent a pair of suspenders to the RAF tactical air commander's G-2. The First Army diary said: "Observers who were present at the Brussels field testified that more than 100 planes, closely parked in formation, were shot up and wrecked completely and by tonight the total was over 180." Among those destroyed was Montgomery's personal Dakota. Eisenhower at once gave him his own new Dakota, which he had just received. This act of spontaneous kindness was not lost on Montgomery. "If ever there is anything I can ever do for you," he wrote to Eisenhower in thanks, "to ease the tremendous burden that you bear, you know you have only to command me."

To Brooke he wrote: "I am now going to withdraw from the contest. It is clear to me that we have got all we can and that we shall get no more. I have told Ike that I have given him my views and he has given his decision and that I will now weigh in one hundred per cent to make his plan work. He is delighted and has sent me a very nice telegram in which he thanks me for my understanding attitude. So everything is very friendly."

These professions of amity were well enough, but echoes of the historic fracas still boomed distantly around the battlefield, like the last thunderclaps of a dying storm. Very promptly Eisenhower's generals heard of the letters that had passed between him and Montgomery. Patton would write, "I will not serve under Montgomery and neither, I think, will Bradley."

Patton himself believed that the enemy was finished in the bulge. His Third Army was still facing tough opposition as it pushed northward from Bastogne to Houffalize, but he knew how to encourage his troops. At a press conference on New Year's Day, he was asked about the enemy: "What about the concentration of armor?"

"They got damn little armor left—" he answered, "unless they have reproductive tanks."

As at Falaise, the neck of the pocket was still open. Patton had been battering his way up through Bastogne, trying to narrow the gap. Collins was aching to come charging down from the north, to close the gap altogether, but Montgomery wanted to be absolutely ready before letting Hodges unleash him. At last came the word: the VII Corps would begin its attack southward toward Houffalize, the proposed meeting point, on the morning of January 3. Hearing this, Patton scoffed in a letter. "Dear Courtney comes in at long last . . . ," he said, "and that will relieve the pressure."

Collins's VII Corps made a good start at 8:30 A.M. Once again the weather favored Hitler. The roads were icy and, despite the fact that gravel had been laid, tanks kept slipping off into the sides, knocking down the telephone poles, wrecking communications, and slowing traffic. But movement was adequate, and when Montgomery called on Hodges at two P.M., he kept remarking, "Good show, good show!" Houffalize was coming within reach. Facing Collins were three divisions of the II SS Panzer Corps. The ice grew more treacherous. Collins watched a tank force of the 2nd Armored Division deliver a frontal attack through a village, because the icy slopes on either side prevented any flanking maneuver. Dogged German infantry armed with Panzerfaust bazookas were dug into the basements of the houses. It took a barrage of eight-inch howitzer shells with delayed fuses, crashing through the rooftops to the basements of these houses, to clear the way for his advance. That afternoon he saw a caterpillar-tracked tank destroyer slither out of control sideways off the road and somesault downhill, crushing its driver to death. It was going to be a grueling, killing match all the way.

To the south at Bastogne, the tip of the other talon of the pincer, the fighting was getting fiercer as the enemy—and particularly the proud SS divisions—fought back against Patton. He wrote apprehensively on January 4, recalling the scandals he had brought down on himself in Sicily, "The 11th Armored is very green and took unnecessary losses to no effect. There were also some unfortunate incidents in the shooting of prisoners (I hope we can conceal this)." Not far away, a Waffen SS unit had killed many Americans in a shoot-out near Malmédy early in Rundstedt's offensive, and had laid the American dead side by side —like the cordwood heaps Patton himself had commented on earlier—just before being thrown back in a counterattack. American combat propaganda made an atrocity out of this—the famous "Malmédy incident"—the episode that Stimson, in good faith, had related to Roosevelt.

The closing stages of the Battle of the Bulge were preceded by the customary clash of views in the American command. Hodges favored the slow-but-sure approach. Spaatz, the strategic bomber commander, wanted a repetition of Cobra. On January 1 he arrived at Liege— despite the efforts of Patton's antiaircraft gunners to shoot him down —and asked General Hodges what air support he wanted for his coming attack. Hodges turned down the offer of carpet bombing in front of Collins's VII Corps attack, and asked Spaatz just to carry on as he had been doing. Spaatz told Hodges what he had told Bradley and Patton: "A spell of bad weather now will allow the Germans to build up again. So the best time to attack is immediately." After he left, he dictated a private note that General Hodges and his staff had not made a good impression on him; they seemed to lack aggressiveness. Patton turned a wary eye on the worsening weather and warned that if the Germans chose to put up a tough fight at Bastogne, they could blunt the pincer; far better, he argued, to attack closer to the base of the bulge. Then the Germans would take fright and try to pull out, which would make for an easier victory at less cost.

Appalled by the delays and the casualties his armies were taking, Eisenhower cast longing eyes to the east and wondered when the Russians were going to attack. There was no word from Moscow. Tedder was still en route, held up in Naples by weather. Eisenhower was nervous, and said: "His trip is of the utmost importance." To make matters worse, the American press had just broken the news that Montgomery was in command of American troops, so Eisenhower was now forced to release the story. "It has been a long and very tiring day for E.," noted Kay Summersby sympathetically on January 5. "He is beginning to feel the strain a little. Who wouldn't?"

That day Everett Hughes came for lunch with Eisenhower and Kay Summersby at Eisenhower's new house at Trianon, near the office. Eisenhower pleased Hughes by once again cussing the name of General Lee, when they turned to the appalling manpower shortage. "Lee has to have everything diagrammed," said the Supreme Commander. "And then he can't read the diagram!"

The overall situation was getting serious. One day Spaatz came and told Eisenhower of indications that the Luftwaffe had developed a kind of "ray" which could stop aircraft engines; more fundamental was the shortage of personnel replacements—"We are right down to rock bottom," wrote Kay Summersby on January 6. The next day General Ray Barker, of SHAEF, came back from Washington and reported to Eisenhower. Barker said he had told the War Department, "Unless we are supported more strongly, we may lose the war."

Patton, too, was dour. The heavy losses he was taking as he drove his troops north from Bastogne made him pensive. "We can still lose this war," he told his diary. "However, the Germans are colder and hungrier than we are, but they fight better. I can never get over the stupidity of our green troops." And in a letter to Beatrice: "Sometimes even I get skeptical about the end of this show."

Patton was planning to attack toward Houffalize with eight divisions on January 9. It would not be easy. The weather was still bleak and snowy. Driving back from Bastogne, his face bitten by the cold, he passed the last battalion of the 90th Division moving forward by open truck. The men had been riding in the blizzards for several hours, but they cheered and yelled as he drove past. It inspired him. "We simply have to keep attacking or he [the enemy] will," he wrote Beatrice. "I wish that great soldier Sir B. would do a little more."

On January 6, Field Marshal Sir Bernard Montgomery put away his wallet, grinning. The war had still not ended, so he had won another wager, this time from Grigg. "Cheque for two pounds received," he wrote back. "Thank you. The bet was a sitter for me!!" Then he told of how he was winning the Battle of the Bulge. "The real trouble with the Yanks," he wrote, "is that they are completely ignorant as to the rules of the game we are playing with the Germans. You play so much better when you know the rules."

Eisenhower now accepted the ineluctable fact that Montgomery's army group, with only 21 divisions, was too small for the job ahead. He allowed the U.S. Ninth Army—given to Montgomery, with the First, temporarily for the Ardennes offensive—to be placed more permanently under Montgomery's command. His new plan of campaign adopted all Montgomery's demands except for operational control.

The American generals were crestfallen and hypersensitive over their collapsed strategy. The British were jubilant. On January 7, Montgomery held a press conference. It created more ill feeling than any of his other remarks had ever managed to produce. He told the newspapermen he was perturbed about the sniping at Eisenhower going on in the British newspapers. He admitted that Rundstedt "obtained tactical surprise." He continued, "As soon as I saw what was happening I took certain steps myself to ensure that *if* the Germans got to the Meuse they would certainly not get over that river. . . . Then the situation began to deteriorate. But the whole Allied team rallied to meet the danger; national considerations were thrown overboard; General Eisenhower placed me in command of the whole Northern front. . . . You have thus the picture of British troops fighting on both sides of American forces who have suffered a hard blow. This is a fine allied picture." He continued in that manner, which many perceived as egregiously condescending, for half an hour before his peroration. "I would say that anyone who tries to break up the team spirit of the Allies is definitely helping the enemy. Let me tell you," he said, "that the captain of our team is Eisenhower." He took it upon himself to rebuke the press for their uncomplimentary articles about Eisenhower. "I would ask all of you to lend a hand to stop that sort of thing. Let us rally round the captain of the team and so help to win the match."

In effect, Montgomery had been belatedly responding to the flattering but unwelcome British publicity accorded to him just before Christmas, after the First and Ninth armies were placed under his control for the Ardennes offensive. The papers had championed him at Eisenhower's expense, which enraged the Americans, including Marshall, making them angry in turn with Montgomery. A few weeks later he would write: "No single incident that I have encountered throughout my experience as an allied commander has been so difficult to combat as this particular outburst in the newspapers. Both the Prime Minister and I tried with every device at hand to counteract this feeling but it was just one of those things that seem to cause a lasting resentment, due largely, I think, to the fact that the American troops here have their principle sources of information through the London newspapers and through the BBC." But that clamor was as nothing compared with the row that followed this press conference.

Chester Wilmot, Britain's leading war correspondent, wrote a dispatch about it that was intercepted by the Germans. They rewrote it, concocting some very anti-American comments and putting them in Montgomery's mouth, and rebroadcast it on their Arnhem radio station—a transmitter which pretended to be a British station. Bradley's headquarters monitored the Arnhem broadcast and mistook it for the BBC. That fanned the furor. But the Nazis were not alone to blame, and Montgomery later admitted in his memoirs that his remarks had been ill timed. And in any case his choice of words had been unfortunate. The Americans did not understand the English nuances when he described their frantic and harrowing defense against Hitler's determined onslaught as one of the most "interesting and tricky" operations he had ever handled.

For a time the uproar over the speech threatened to drown out the gunfire at Bastogne. Even Simpson, who had come to like the field marshal, found the speech offensive. Bradley was furious and confided to Simpson that he was just waiting for a chance to tell Montgomery off. Collins too, whose troops were still battling southward, was indignant. "The only time that Monty really got under my skin," he said years later, "was Monty's downgrading of the American troops at the time of the Battle of the Bulge. Now this is what just irritated the hell out of me and Brad. . . . He held that press conference and suggested that now that the British were masters, everything was going to be all right." In his memoirs, Collins pointed out that however reassuring it was to know that Brian Horrocks's corps was backing him up, in fact only one British division actually participated in the fighting. "That press conference so irritated Bradley and Patton, and many of us who fought on the northern front of the Bulge that it left a sour note to what actually was a great cooperative allied army and air effort."

As usual, Eisenhower's troubles in his two theaters of war, martial and matrimonial, coincided. On the day that Montgomery addressed the press, Eisenhower opened a new letter from Mamie—it turned out to be the gripe that he dreaded. He wrote to her at once. "It always distresses me," he said, "when I get a message from you indicating anxiety or impatience because I have failed to write. Please, please understand that I go through periods when I simply cannot sit down and write a note. To hold a pen is sometimes sheer mental, almost physical agony." He tried to paint a word picture of his situation for her—the exertions of the battle, the lack of exercise, the guards and snoopers everywhere. "There is even a guard in my upstairs hall." He did not want it himself, but his security people were insisting.

The next day, January 8, he got a phone call from Bradley protesting that the American sector was mad as hell about Montgomery's speech. De Guingand came to see Eisenhower and talked earnestly with him late into the night. The next day Hughes noted the anger in his diary: "Big play being given to fact that Monty commands First and Ninth Armies [and] Brad [only] the Third." Three days later Hughes wrote: "Monty/Brad controversy still being aired." On January 9 Eisenhower, after two telephone calls during the night from Churchill, decided to award Bradley the Bronze Star for his part in stopping the attack. The papers would give the award a lot of healing publicity.

In the meantime, the Americans in Paris seethed with anti-British feeling. Brigadier General O.N. Solbert, who lived just down the corridor from Hughes in the Hotel George V, muttered to him that the British would never destroy the Nazi army, since they wanted a strong postwar Germany—as a market for Britain's goods and as a buttress against the Soviet Union. He added, "The grant of two armies to Monty was a slap at Bradley."

After the morning staff conference on January 10, Eisenhower asked Bedell Smith and Whiteley to stay. The two pincer arms were drawing closer to Houffalize, and Jock Whiteley—the British brigadier on Eisenhower's staff—suggested that they should draw up plans now for Bradley to recover command of the First Army from Montgomery. Eisenhower agreed. "The Ninth Army commanded by Simpson will be left under Monty's command," noted Kay Summersby. "From the very first E. has always said that he would have to give Monty an American army, this was long before the German breakthrough. 21st Army Group has only got about 21 divisions. E. is afraid that Bradley will not like this arrangement, but after all it is not always possible in war to give way to personal feelings and ambitions."

There was still no news from Stalin. Strong, the G-2, said the next day at Eisenhower's conference: "So much depends on whether the Russians are going to attack. We sincerely hope that they will have started their offensive by the end of February. If not, the Germans will be able to release many divisions that were employed on the eastern front and send them against us in the West." At meetings with Bedell Smith and later with Eisenhower on January 8, General Spaatz stressed the need to be on the lookout for any signs that the Germans were regrouping to attack again. He saw a strong possibility that the Nazis would thrust straight across the Meuse to the Antwerp area. He strongly urged that oil targets should be made his first bombing priority when weather conditions allowed. Eisenhower finally agreed to this.

Hitler had meanwhile done what Patton himself would have done. He had sprung a diversionary attack on the Seventh Army, throwing a force of about a battalion across the Rhine in barges north of Strasbourg. Worried by this bridgehead, on January 10 Eisenhower asked

Bradley to stop Patton's Third Army effort in the Bastogne area. Patton grumbled, but obeyed. "This is the second time I have been stopped in a successful attack due to the Germans having more nerve than we have," he wrote.

A few days before Montgomery's speech, the British Chiefs of Staff had sent Marshall a powerful message alleging that Eisenhower was responsible for the Ardennes disaster—by his failure to keep Bradley from packing scarce resources into Patton's offensive into the Saar. This, argued the British, had unbalanced the whole line, and ran counter to Eisenhower's own agreement to break into Germany north of the Ardennes. The row cut across the nationality boundaries inside SHAEF, with all Eisenhower's British staff showing extreme partiality to him. Kay Summersby wrote on January 10, "It is very obvious that the British are doing their utmost to get the CCS to agree to one Commander, naturally Monty would be the person selected. I sincerely hope that General Marshall will agree to E.'s conception of future operations."

Marshall replied on the 12th. He pointed out the obvious—that since the Allied forces were composed mostly of American troops, therefore there should be an American commander. He did not perceive that he was thus implicitly suggesting that there was no American commander worthy of such a position on his own merits. But his verdict was authoritative. It was a knell for British hopes of controlling the war in northern Europe—and for empire.

Montgomery knew that he had lost the battle for the supreme ground command. But no one could deny that he lost like a gentleman. "I would like to say two things," he wrote to Bradley. *"First:* What a great honour it has been for me to command such fine troops. *Second:* How well they have all done."

January 12 was also the day that the great Russian offensive started. Within a few days the Red Army would have swept forward and captured Warsaw. The relief at SHAEF was palpable. In Washington, Stimson reached for the dictaphone: "This is a very good piece of news for we were all getting a little bit anxious about the slowness of Stalin in spite of the fact that we have been hoping and trying to be confident that [the Russians] would keep their word." The blight on the image of East-West cooperation could now be overlooked and forgotten.

Both Bradley and Montgomery desired to mount their next offensive north of the bulge. But when on January 15, at Eisenhower's request, Montgomery paid one of his very rare visits to him, they found his views unchanged. "We have got to defeat the German Army west of the Rhine," the Supreme Commander said.

Bedell Smith stayed behind after the conference to talk with Eisenhower about the American crime wave sweeping France—the stealing from the supply trains by GIs for goods to sell on the black market. To Eisenhower, this was hardly news. "I had over $100 of liquor stolen from Shellburst," he told Smith. Shellburst was his forward headquarters at Rheims.

Eisenhower was getting tired and grumpy. His health was not good. He was eight pounds overweight. To set an example he went down to donate blood, but the doctors had quite a job finding a vein to put the needle into. A doctor came to give him a checkup some days later and seemed pleased with his condition, although he delivered a stinging lecture to him on the number of cigarettes he was smoking. He was worried because Mamie had stopped writing—probably she had gone to Fort Benning and couldn't find the time to write while traveling. He did not complain, although he did inquire in one letter whether she had received the Christmas presents he had sent, the perfume for her and the leather billfold for John with the thousand-franc note tucked into it.

On January 16, Collins's troops thrusting down from the north met Patton's troops at Houffalize, and the pocket was sealed. There were not many Germans left in it by then, but it was obviously the end of the Nazi offensive. The enemy had lost about 85,000 men, estimated Strong; they had withdrawn with most of their formations intact, but they had suffered heavy losses in men and materiel. And they had begun to pull out of the bulge. Eisenhower put Bradley back in control of the First Army. "This," Patton felt, "will be very advantageous, as Bradley is much less timid than Montgomery." Patton saw German casualties lying tumbled in the snow, awaiting burial. They were colored a pale claret that had him wishing that it was color film in his camera as he photographed the corpses in their strange frozen attitudes.

Hughes was visiting Eisenhower's office one day at this time when Eisenhower told him, "Everett, George is really a very great soldier, and I must get Marshall to do something for him before the war is over." Hughes rushed lunch with the Supreme Commander and hur-

ried by plane to tell Patton these fine words at Nancy. Later he wrote
in his diary, "George looks fine. Sent JP a mousetrap, books. Gave me
back the pearlhandles. Until 1.30 we discussed Brad, Ike, Courtney, et
al and as usual agreed on their IQs. George also discussed his prowess
as cocksman. He is good—so he says." Hughes stayed with Patton a
few days. "Hellish country," he wrote, "lots of snow. Try to get George
to bed. But he says we are like two girls just home from boarding school.
We must talk."

The Americans got, as Montgomery said, a bloody nose—taking
nearly 70,000 casualties themselves. There had been serious losses in
equipment like infantry howitzers. What had gotten them into the
Ardennes disaster was poor generalship—which had left their front
overextended, with no tactical reserves—and above all the complacency
at SHAEF which had led them to disregard important intelligence. One
analyst in Washington pointed out that the SHAEF intelligence summaries for September onward had had a "tone of derision for all the
Germans had and could do." For all Marshall's loyal defense of Eisenhower, the Ardennes experience attracted powerful criticism. "To
date," wrote General L.S. Kuter, assistant chief of Air Staff, "Eisenhower's plans have appeared piecemeal affairs rather than concerted
actions, both from the point of view of employment of Ground Forces
and Air Forces."

What had rescued the Americans from the crisis was the cool example, on the days that counted, set by Montgomery for Hodges—and to
a lesser degree for Simpson. But the crucial work had been done, in the
final analysis, by the American fighting man, and these individual
soldiers had shown courage and perseverance, in the face of bitter cold
and personal deprivation, that more than outweighed the bumbling of
their commanders. Credit was due not only to the 101st Airborne,
spectacularly besieged at Bastogne, but to Major General W.M. Rob-
ertson's 2nd Infantry Division in the Monschau sector too: because if
the 2nd had not succeeded as it did on December 17 in slowing down
the Nazi avalanche before Krinkelt, at heavy cost in infantry casualties,
the Germans would have reached Eupen and perhaps even Liege that
day or the next, and Bastogne would have lost its significance. The
release of the VT proximity fuse for use in the battle had helped to tilt
the scales against the onrushing Germans.

The Ardennes battle had prolonged the war by many months, using up vital Allied supplies and reserves of manpower, and giving enemy morale a shot of adrenaline just when Hitler needed it. Kay Summersby on January 19 reported the bafflement at SHAEF headquarters: "German morale is very high right now. It has been ever since the breakthrough on December 16."

Marshall, worried by the mounting criticism of SHAEF, sent from Washington a high-powered general, Ben Lear, to find out what had gone wrong. Marshall told Eisenhower that Lear was stern and drastic but very soldierly. He suggested that Lear should be made "a deputy of yours" for command of the rear areas, with Lee subordinate to him. Lear arrived in Paris and telephoned Everett Hughes at Patton's headquarters to tell him that they were to work together. Hughes called on Eisenhower to protest that he did not want to work for Lear. He did his level best to make Eisenhower leave him where he was—as Eisenhower's eyes and ears. "I argue, he says no!" wrote Hughes afterward. "He wanted Lear as Deputy Theater Commander, as Commanding General CZ, as Inspector. He wants his best man to help Lear. That's that." Kay Summersby witnessed their argument. "Hughes," she wrote, "is a very difficult man to work with."

Hughes lunched with Lear on the 21st and was irritated by how little Lear knew. On January 23, Hughes noted significantly, "Lear's job just a mop up. To clean up after the mistakes are made. Who will get relieved? Brad, No. Hodges, No." Lee threw a dinner that night for Lear. "That settles everything," observed Hughes with dismay. Any friend of Lee's . . .

Writing to his friend Virgil Peterson on February 3, Hughes would complain: "Our classmate whose first name begins with B does not see eye to eye with me. . . . He has several youthful assistants who prowl around searching for errors without knowing the background and without knowing the organization. B. gets all excited when some man in the Communications Zone is cold. I suggested to him that he should go up to the front lines and find out how many men were dead that should not be. . . . My office continues to be a wailing wall, and I now have a new ashtray where we collect the tears."

Hughes's headaches were just beginning. Eisenhower believed that his were over. Montgomery asked for permission to go home for a few days' rest, and at the end of January he did so. He was on leash again.

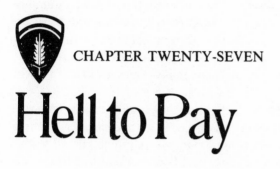

CHAPTER TWENTY-SEVEN

Hell to Pay

HITLER'S JET aircraft were patrolling the skies in increasing numbers.
They scared Spaatz and Doolittle. Even before the bulge was eliminated, they had told Eisenhower that it was vital to step up the attack
on the jet-plane factories. "It's going to take 10,000 tons of visual
bombing to set jet fighter production back by three months," they said,
"which is the absolute minimum if our own jet production is to catch
up." The sooner they could send the heavy bombers to deal with these
threats, the better. Eisenhower had said, "The present battle is still
critical, and it's going to need all the strategic effort we can give it for
the present." Spaatz, as always, campaigned ceaselessly for his air
forces, sending out books of damage photographs. He was hypersensitive about the way the armies were getting all the publicity. "Details
of the tremendous effect of air power," he wrote to Hap Arnold in
September, "have not been reported in the press." Bedell Smith did not
show the proper respect. The photos, he told Spaatz, "prove without
question that you have been a very busy woman."

In March there were reports that Messerschmitt jets were operating in formations of thirty-six at a time. One Messerschmitt pilot shot down forty-three American heavy bombers. Early in April a Messerschmitt factory test pilot, alarmed at the rate at which German pilots were being killed, flew a brand-new jet direct to Frankfurt, where he turned it over to the Americans. Soon he was describing to Arnold himself the chaos in Germany. "The war can't continue for more than two or three weeks," he said.

On May 10, just after the surrender, Spaatz and Vandenberg found themselves face to face with Hermann Goering, the Reich marshal who had commanded Hitler's air force from its inception. He was standing in a small office at the Ritterschule in Augsburg, wearing tan boots on his fat legs and a gray wool uniform with no medals but with epaulets displaying a large eagle, a small swastika, and crossed batons.

Spaatz asked, "Did the jet airplane really have a chance to win against us?"

Goering smiled, his blue eyes lighting his round, ruddy features. "Yes," he answered. "I am still convinced, if we had only four to five months more time. Our underground plants were practically all ready. The factory at Karla had a capacity of 1,000 to 1,200 jet airplanes a month. Now, with five to six thousand jets, the outcome would have been very different!"

Vandenberg chimed in to ask Goering if he could have trained sufficient jet pilots with the oil supply running out. Goering smiled again: "Yes, we would have had underground factories for oil. . . . The jet pilot output was always ahead of jet aircraft production."

That, in a nutshell, was what underlay the urgency to end the war. The longer it went on, the more difficult it would become to win. And Allied resources were not bottomless. At the end of January, Montgomery had written an agitated letter to Grigg about the lack of infantry reinforcements. He predicted a shortage of 1,850 officers by the end of March. He recommended "ruthless methods," including a comb-out of the RAF for officers. Grigg was able to offer Montgomery little comfort.

Eisenhower solved the U.S. Army manpower problem partially by transferring many of J.C.H. Lee's black service troops to combat roles. But the experiment did not seem promising. A black division fighting in Italy in February—the 92nd—had turned and run, clear proof in the army's view that black troops were unreliable unless led by white officers and NCOs. The blacks, it was said, simply would not either stand fire or stay out at night, whether under fire or not. Reflecting the prevalent army prejudices, General Marshall unkindly remarked to Stimson: "The only place they can be counted on is in Iceland in summertime—where there's daylight for twenty-four hours."

In February, Roosevelt, Churchill, and Stalin met at Yalta, in the Crimea, to divide up the world. Stalin had no trouble facing down the sick, aging western leaders. The decisions reached at Yalta left Eisenhower few strategic alternatives. It was decreed that east of the Elbe, the river that bisects Germany from north to south, the Russians would dominate. That would be the inviolate line.

The Chiefs of Staff conferences concurrent to Yalta rang with the absent Eisenhower's name, as the British attempted to nail him to a firm plan of operation. Marshall afterward told Stimson how he clashed with the British over their attempts to push Montgomery forward yet again to the exclusion of Eisenhower. "Marshall," noted Stimson on February 17, "who is always very tolerant in matters of dealing with the British, was finally quite aroused by this situation and evidently 'lit out' in the conference so vigorously that he carried everything before him. Montgomery has won the reputation of being a good deal of a self-seeker among our commanders at the front. He wants everything in the way of help and preparation of command and then is rather over-cautious in his advances.

"This time," he added, "I also found that Marshall thought that Eisenhower had been over-conciliatory in his dealings with the British in this matter. I have always been afraid of this."

Eisenhower had sent to the CCS his plan of operations for northwestern Europe. He intended to eliminate the enemy west of the Rhine, then seize bridgeheads over the Rhine in the north and the south. Then there would be a push north of the Ruhr, with a big force of about thirty-five divisions. It would capture the whole Ruhr industrial region.

The British feared that Eisenhower would delay his Rhine crossings until he had reached the river along its entire length, and protested. On February 10 the CCS reported their conclusions to Roosevelt and Churchill. "We have taken note of . . . the Supreme Commander's assurance that he will seize the Rhine crossings in the north just as soon as this is a feasible operation and without waiting to clear the Rhine throughout its length. Further, that he will advance across the Rhine in the north with maximum strength and complete determination, immediately the situation in the south allows him to collect the necessary forces and do this without incurring unreasonable risks."

This decision had been reaffirmed: to put the weight into the left shoulder of the offensive—Montgomery's armies. This came as a blow to Patton and Hodges, whose armies were on the right, planning an attack to penetrate the West Wall. But Patton had means of getting his own way. He knew how to attack without actually being allowed to. "Can I at least continue a reconnaissance?" he would call Bradley to ask. Bradley, knowing full well that Patton would develop a full-blooded attack, would okay it. It was almost a code language between them.

This sort of chicanery could not please Montgomery. He was counting on requisitioning some extra American divisions from the south, for his own Rhine thrust. If those divisions became enmeshed in battle, he would have trouble stealing them away. Worst of all, in Montgomery's eyes, would be if Patton and Hodges started their offensive before Montgomery could start his own. On January 24 the British had made what Patton interpreted as a devious attempt at emasculating the southern thrust by the American First and Third armies, so that Montgomery's prestige would not be dimmed.

What had happened was this. Hodges and Patton conferred at Patton's headquarters after lunch on January 24. Bradley joined them as they were agreeing on the new boundaries between the First and Third armies. "Just when everything had been satisfactorily arranged and Hodges said he could attack Sunday," Patton wrote later, "the telephone rang and General Whiteley [a British officer with SHAEF] called up Bradley and wanted to withdraw additional divisions . . . to help Devers." Devers's Sixth Army Group was having difficulty in cleaning up the Nazi pocket at Colmar.

Bradley was furious. "We would be giving up a sure thing for a side show," he barked. It was the first time that Patton had seen Bradley lose his temper. Gripping the telephone in his bony knuckles, Bradley snapped into it that if Whiteley wanted to destroy the whole operation, he could do so and be damned: "Go ahead and take all the corps and divisions!"

Patton stood right behind him and said loudly, knowing his voice was carrying down the telephone line, "Tell them to go to hell and all three of us will resign. I will lead the procession."

Bradley continued, his voice shaking. "There is more at stake than the mere moving of divisions and corps. . . . The reputation and the good will of the American soldiers and the American army and its commanders are at stake. If you feel that way about it, then as far as I am concerned, you can take any goddam division and or corps in the 12th Army Group, do with them as you see fit, and those of us that you leave back will sit on our ass until hell freezes.

"I trust you do not think I am angry," were Bradley's final words. "But I want to impress upon you that I am *goddam well incensed.*"

As he slammed the phone down, every officer listening rose to his feet and applauded.

A few days later, Bradley telephoned Patton and told him dourly to commit nothing until further instructions. Patton suspected Montgomery was behind the outrage. "Hell and Damn," he swore in his diary. "This is another case of giving up a going attack in order to start one that has no promise of success except to exalt Monty, who has never won a battle since he left Africa and only El Alamein there. (I won Mareth for him.)"

Despite such opposition, however, the big shift of emphasis to the north was beginning. Later Bradley told Patton that he would have to give up the 95th Division to Simpson's Ninth Army and probably five or six artillery battalions too. "This is not even Ike's plan," explained Bradley. "It has been forced on him by the Combined Chiefs."

Patton feared that the war might end with most of the American troops on the defensive, while Montgomery swept to fresh and noisy victories. Then he remembered that sweeping was not Montgomery's style. "Monty," he predicted, "is so slow and timid that he will find a German build-up in front of him and will stall."

For a while Patton had daydreams of grandeur. "I will be the first on the Rhine yet," he boasted to his diary. But the snows were thawing, the roads were disintegrating under his army's tread, and he knew his own dramatic battles were temporarily halted. He decided abruptly to go and see Hughes in Paris. It would be his first leave since October 1942. Hughes reserved a suite for him at the Hotel George V.

Ill feeling lingered on well after the Battle of the Bulge. Bradley came to see Eisenhower late on January 31, and when Eisenhower told him that they would now have to stop attacking in the Ardennes and mount an attack northward against the Roer dams, Bradley was bitterly disappointed, as Kay Summersby observed. "Veritable [the advance to the Rhine] . . . must go on," she wrote, "commanded of course by Monty. Bradley pointed out to E. that there are sixty-one American divisions . . . and that the American public is sore over Monty's continuous publicity in the press." After recalling the crisis which had resulted in the transfer of the Ninth Army to the British army group, she added: "Bradley tried his best to get the Ninth Army back. E. told Whiteley to call Monty (who is in London) and tell him that if any member of 21st Army Group should talk to the press, Bradley will be given command of Veritable. . . . It was quite a stormy conference at moments."

The next day this resentment was still smoldering. At the morning conference Bradley was still muttering about Montgomery. Eisenhower told the British brigadier on his staff, Whiteley, to phone Montgomery in London and tell him that Veritable must jump off on the eighth as planned. "Bradley is badly upset over E.'s decision to leave the Ninth Army under Monty," noted Kay Summersby afterward. "He sees the logic of E.'s decision, but the real trouble dates back to December and January when Monty got so much publicity in the press. Of all E.'s commanders, Monty is the one who has given him the greatest number of headaches. Monty has only come to Versailles twice for conferences, E. had always to send him a direct order otherwise he would send his chief of staff (General de Guingand)."

Montgomery had been planning Veritable since before the Rundstedt offensive. Immense quantities of ammunition had been dumped in forward areas, and accommodation been provided for troops. At the end of January, however, the thaw began. The roads turned into quagmires. The water level in the Meuse rose six feet in a day. But Veritable began on February 8 at five A.M. with a thousand-gun barrage that lasted ten hours. Ahead of the advancing troops, the ancient Rhineland towns like Cleves were thrashed by nine hundred bombers. Through the infantry battalions of the 2nd Canadian Division passed the assault divisions.

On February 13, Montgomery informed Grigg: "The battle up in the Reichswald forest area goes well. The problem is the mud and the floods, and not the enemy. The German soldiers are not fighting well; they surrender freely if given a suitable opportunity. Yesterday all that was left of a Para Bn (six officers and 200 men) surrendered en masse without firing a shot. They walked over to our lines south of Cleves."

The First U.S. Army made slower progress because on February 9, the day before the offensive began, the enemy had opened the floodgates on the Roer dams, releasing a torrent that the attacking troops could not cross for two weeks. Collins secured a weak foothold across the river, and despite heavy shelling his engineers constructed nine bridges. From this bridgehead near Düren, Collins sent his main armored force, the 3rd Armored Division, straight on to Cologne. He decided to advance on the great city, Germany's fourth biggest, from the northwest.

SHAEF was in the doldrums. With the American advance temporarily stymied by the Roer flooding, there wasn't much to do, and Eisenhower found himself inactive. He badly needed exercise, but he could not get out. Security would not let him walk too far—in fact, he had to stay inside a constricted area heavily guarded by sentries. There was nothing but a small circle to tramp around—like a prisoner in the exercise yard at Alcatraz. One bright feature was that the Soviet avalanche was now advancing across eastern Europe. "The Russians are still making good progress after their early spectacular successes," he wrote on February 11. "Lord knows they can't go too fast and too well for me. More power to them." Another happy thing was that his son was stationed nearby. He gave John a big weatherproof fur-lined coat for riding in Jeeps. Often he sat up late talking with him. "I've certainly enjoyed having him here," Eisenhower wrote to Mamie on February 11. Each time John came to spend the night with him, Eisenhower worried about his lad's forgetfulness. Perhaps he would grow out of it, he thought one day as he looked at the gloves and nice Burberry overcoat that John had left behind this time. He reflected, "I can't figure him out when he gets just sort of roaming about in his mind."

Patton was in Paris, on leave. Hughes noted: "Much Hoopla. Brought [Lieutenant Colonel Charles] Codman and Jean [Gordon] . . . to hotel for dinner. I guess Geo is thru with this war and has his eyes on China and a fourth star."

They still had lots to talk about. Hughes told him about the surliness of the French toward the Allies because de Gaulle had not been invited to Yalta. "De Gaulle wants to see FDR in Paris—" was the bon mot going round Paris, "FDR wants to see de Gaulle in hell." The two friends speculated about the end of the war, who would get the big commands in the Pacific. George would not get sleepy, and didn't go home until one A.M., so Hughes couldn't get any work done the next day. He lamented: "Geo is spoiled and demanding."

Patton enjoyed Paris. People recognized him everywhere, and that made him feel good. Bedell Smith had come down off his high horse and the two generals had gone hunting. The next evening, February 16, Hughes dined Patton at the Ritz with his aide Codman, Jean Gordon, and J.P. It was Paris cuisine at its best. Hughes told Patton of the "nigger soldiers" that Eisenhower had recruited, and wondered out loud how well they would fight. Patton was not choosy—he said he'd like to have some of them in his platoons.

They all drove over to the Folies Bergères after that, but the floor show got worse every time General Hughes saw it, which was not infrequently. "A man can get accustomed to naked women if he sees enough naked women," Hughes wrote. "But George had his mind on ——and a job in the Pacific, mostly on——, he can't talk about anything except that. He must be getting impotent." Patton himself noted in his diary that the show was so nude that nobody was interested. The manager had given them a box; they drank champagne backstage with him and his wife.

"My dear General," she gushed, "whenever you come to Paris, make the Follies your home. You can rest here always."

"I can think of no more restless place than the Follies," Patton replied, "full of about a hundred practically naked women."

The next day Patton went out to visit an old World War I flame, Eugénie de l'Horme. In World War I, she had been eighteen and beautiful. But she had changed a lot in twenty-six years; now she was a grandmother. After satisfying his curiosity, he went on a shoot with guns that Monsieur Francotte had made for him at Liege, with Bedell Smith, and returned with a bellyache which would not have hurt half as much if Bedell had not learned he was sick. He had spleen trouble. Hughes saw him off on February 18, after lecturing him: "Finish this job before you start worrying about the Pacific!"

Back at his headquarters, Patton had found little changed. The roads were still bottomless cocoa-colored mud, and nobody wanted to give him permission to go ahead and take cities he felt he could easily capture—like Bonn or Koblenz or Trier—because, as Bradley said, "higher authority" had decided to make the effort elsewhere. Bradley came to tell Patton personally about those higher orders. To Patton, Bradley looked very tired and no longer sure of himself. "I asked," wrote Patton, "if there was any objection to my making a run for Koblenz ahead of time or of taking Cologne if opportunity suddenly developed. He said there was no objection." By late February Patton was set to encircle Trier. But time was running out, and Patton had promised Bradley to stop at dark on February 27. He called him at dusk, but Bradley told him to keep on going until higher authority intervened. "I won't listen for the telephone," Bradley said. It was an odd way to run a war.

On March 1, Patton captured Trier. Bradley telephoned him from the Ninth Army headquarters, very pleased. Patton could hear Eisenhower's voice in the background, but Eisenhower made no effort to come to the phone. How Patton yearned for some word of praise from that ungrateful man. But Eisenhower was aloof, all powerful; he was Patton's "divine destiny."

The Ninth Army was the first to reach the Rhine at the beginning of March. "Shortly after we got over there," Simpson recalled, "I discovered a place right near the southern edge of the German industrial Ruhr, a very good place to cross the Rhine. Had I been under General Bradley, I would have just sent a division over there, just like that, but being under Montgomery [I could not]. Right from the start he made it very plain that if he had a plan to do anything, he didn't want anybody to do anything to interfere with that plan." There was no bridge, but there was a canal that flowed into the Rhine from Simpson's side; it would have been possible to load boats out of sight of the Germans. These assault boats could have gone down the canal and crossed the river. Montgomery turned the idea down. "Well, you get across," he pointed out, "but then what can you do?" Of course Montgomery had been planning his own crossing for a month. He did not choose to be upstaged.

At the end of February, Eisenhower wrote to Mamie. It got tougher every time. The moment he picked up a pen, his mind went blank. Mamie had been crabbing at him as usual for not writing, but now she had a new taunt—that he had exposed John to "moral dangers" during the summer. The alleged corrupter of youth apologized for his failure to write but added indignantly: "It's amazing to read what you have to say about the 'pitfalls' of last summer. He scarcely left my side, going I think to only one party—and that attended by a large number of people. So where he could have been in jeopardy, is beyond me." In fact he had found John overconservative and rather sedate.

The way that everybody slid the buck to him stuck in his craw. His brother Arthur forwarded an anguished letter from a Jewish friend trying to prevent his GI son from marrying a non-Jewish Belgian girl. How could he, Eisenhower, help? He replied negatively to Arthur: "I have thousands of worse things every day."

At about this time, even Everett Hughes was being critical of Eisenhower. Visiting Rheims, he and Tex Lee talked about the Supreme Commander and his failings. The man was too unwilling, they agreed, to say thank-you to his colleagues. Afterward, their talk turned to the enigmatic relationship between Eisenhower and Kay Summersby. Colonel Lee, who shared an office with the pretty second lieutenant, stated his view, after some discussion, that they were not sleeping together. That was not the view of old "Eyes and Ears." In any case, Hughes told Lee, "There is nothing we can do about it."

The strain was telling on Eisenhower. Hughes slept late the next day and called on him at eleven A.M. He had been invited to lunch. The Supreme Commander just continued reading, ignoring him, then leaned back and glared at him. "Shoot it," he barked. Hughes hesitated, then said, nonplussed, that he was there just to get a look at him. That got nowhere. The conversation turned to Madeleine Carroll and Marlene Dietrich, who were angling for invitations to SHAEF. Eisenhower flared up, and said: "I'll never ask Marlene Dietrich. She's just using the soldier for advertising." During their conversation—according to Hughes's notes—Eisenhower shouted and ranted and acted like a crazy man. Then he barked: "You're coming to lunch!"

"Yes, I have been invited," murmured Hughes.

Over lunch, the general's temper did not abate. He called out, "Where are the Spaatzes? Where's Toohey and Sally?" Twice he hinted at the cause of his ill temper: "Mamie gives me hell," he said.

Hughes jotted all these things down in his notebook. Then he summed it all up: "Ike: on defensive, guard up, worried, self-isolation. He has a chance to redeem if he gets across the Rhine."

The next day Hughes drove on to Dinant and saw Gerow in his billet at the Chateau Ardennes, a perfumery. Gee told him: "Ike is difficult in [the] office." He hinted that woman trouble was plaguing the Supreme Commander. "Mamie and Ike," Gerow told Hughes, "are not the same as you and Kate, or myself and Marie-Louise."

That same day, March 5, found Collins standing on a low ridge west of Cologne, thrilling to the spectacle. His binoculars swept the skyline and noted the smoking factory chimneys and the great twin-spired Gothic cathedral still towering above the haze, despite the thousands of bombs that had exploded all around. Two spans of the Hohenzollern Bridge had slumped into the Rhine. Two days later, the entire city up to the river was in American hands. Eisenhower visited Collins west of the city to congratulate him. Taking him aside, he told the general that, if the opportunity should arise, he was going to nominate Collins for command of an army. Collins said he was happy where he was: since D-day he had brought the VII Corps over six hundred miles from Utah beach and had taken over 140,000 prisoners, more than Patton's entire Third Army had captured so far. He wanted to have the privilege of leading his fine corps all the way to Berlin. All the same, he was grateful for the offer.

By March 7 Eisenhower's armies were on the Rhine, except for Patton's. That evening, Bradley phoned Eisenhower: in the First Army area, the 9th Armored Division had scored a spectacular coup—William Hoge's combat command had reached Remagen and found the railroad bridge still intact. German officers had fumbled their attempts to demolish the bridge, Hoge's troops had dashed across, and they were now punching out a bridgehead on the other side of the Rhine. In the first twenty-four hours, eight thousand troops of the 9th Armored and 78th Infantry divisions were passed into the bridgehead.

But already controversy was beginning. Remagen was nowhere near the spot chosen for Montgomery's main thrust. At SHAEF, General Harold Bull realized that this might distract from the big set-piece Rhine crossing being planned by Montgomery to the north, presently scheduled for March 23. To furious protests from Bradley and Hodges, SHAEF put the damper on major American exploitation of Remagen. The troops were to advance no more than the six miles to the Cologne-Frankfurt Autobahn, and there they were to halt until Montgomery was also ready to begin.

At a Cabinet meeting in Washington on March 16, Roosevelt said that he would like to be in command at the Remagen bridgehead. "The first order I would issue would be one directing General Montgomery to get a move on."

On that day Eisenhower went to visit Bradley. His plane landed at Luxembourg, and Patton hurried over to fetch the visitors to his headquarters. For dinner, Patton favored Eisenhower with the attentions of four pretty girls, from the crew of twenty Red Cross Clubmobile girls attached to Patton's headquarters. Strictly, their job was driving coffee trucks to the combat troops. To please Patton, the four girls had primped themselves up in Class A uniforms with white gloves, white scarves, dress shoes, and expensive perfume. Captain of the crew was Betty South, who made no secret of her admiration for Patton's "magnificent, tall figure." "There was arrogance unspeakable there," she described later, "authority unrelinquished even to his superior officer, the Supreme Allied Commander, whom he was toasting." But Patton knew how to ladle out the flattery. Eisenhower expressed surprise that some troops were disappointed not to see him.

"Hell, George," he told Patton, "I didn't think the American GI would give a damn even if the Lord Himself came to inspect them."

Patton smiled from the depths of those scornful eyes. "Well," he replied, "I hesitate to say which of you would rank, sir!"

The girls gasped at his egotism. "I was not altogether successful," admitted Betty South, "in keeping my poise as I watched the general's gentle, twinkling eyes full of infectious humor when something amused him change abruptly to flashing, angry blazes at something else which displeased him, and back again as quickly to frank, guileless, simple honesty. His agility in leaping back and forth between vulgar and shocking profanity and cultured, gentlemanly speech bewildered me. I was particularly hard-pressed to know what to do or say when he turned tearful eyes to me and spoke about God and prayer."

Jean Gordon was among the retinue. Subsequently Patton got another hostile letter from Beatrice. "Don't worry about Jean," he wrote back, "I wrote you months ago that she was in the Army. . . . I have seen her in the company of other Red Cross [girls], but I am not a fool so quit worrying."

Eisenhower enjoyed the evening with Patton's staff, and was extremely complimentary to Patton the next morning. "General Eisenhower," noted Patton, "stated that not only was I a good general but also a lucky general, and Napoleon preferred luck to greatness. I told him this was the first time he had ever complimented me in the 2½ years we had served together."

Eisenhower wrote to Mamie the next day: "He's always the same—and a good tonic." He added, "I've just gotten out of my plane after a hurried trip. It's almost time to close up shop for the day. . . . We've got another battle in progress—prospects look good, but I never count my Germans until they're in our cages or are buried! We keep pounding away."

Montgomery's planning for the big Rhine crossing was proceeding with as much attention to detail as for Overlord. An immense effort was going into the assault, to occur near Wesel. On March 16 he wrote to Grigg: "The following weekend the P.M. will be here; I didn't want him but he was determined to come; so I invited him in order to keep the peace!! Once we are launched across the Rhine anything may happen." Four days later he informed Grigg: "I am expecting the P.M. here on 23rd. He seems to be getting restless and querulous. Why he wants to go about in dangerous places I cannot imagine. He may quite likely get shot up. However, it is his own affair; I shall make it clear that he goes to these places against my definite advice; and then leave it to him. I shall be far too busy to attend to him."

In mid-March Hughes flew down to the Riviera, followed by Eisenhower. Bedell Smith had invited a dozen friends to join him there for a five-day holiday. The generals followed their Supreme Commander in ascending degrees of opulence. Big John Littlejohn, of whom Eisenhower was especially fond, traveled in a special train, with morning newspapers delivered at every stop; General J.C.H. Lee flew down, with his car following by train.

Soon afterward nine American army and air force generals were promoted to four-star rank. They included Bradley, Devers, Mark Clark, and Spaatz, but not Patton. Writing to Beatrice, Patton was philosophical—it would have been even worse if he and Hodges had been promoted on the same list: "I think I would refuse." Eisenhower was quite apologetic about it, but explained the need to retain the hierarchy of command.

Spaatz was engrossed in a promising poker game when the news was broadcast. Sally, Spaatz's lady, came in and said tantalizingly that she had just heard the broadcast but had caught only the names of Clark and Bradley. A quiet settled over the game. Sally returned shortly—the radio had quoted Bradley's aide as saying, "It's a well-deserved promotion." Everybody chuckled, and somebody said: "What aide would say anything less!"

She went off to telephone around, and presently returned. "General, sir," she said to Spaatz. "I just want to say that it is a well-deserved promotion!" For several seconds the poker game was threatened as everybody rose to congratulate the air force commander. Toohey's only comment was, "C'mon and deal!" It was the turn of Harry Butcher, who was now in SHAEF's public relations office. A month earlier Spaatz had taken Butcher for six hundred dollars, a serious embarrassment to his family. This night was more of the same. "I played poker with Toohey . . .," he wrote to his wife Ruth, "I shall have to delay the remainder of the reimbursement which I promised in my last letter."

A few days later Patton jumped the gun once again. He had boasted to Hughes that he had spoiled Montgomery's career by taking Messina. Now he decided to launch an amphibious crossing of the Rhine before Montgomery could start his epic undertaking near Wesel. He told Manton Eddy of the XII Corps to prepare to take his troops over the river near Oppenheim late on March 22, not far from where Napoleon had crossed in 1806—Patton, a student of history, liked that touch. The operation proved astoundingly easy. The 5th Division paddled across at ten P.M. and established a bridgehead against the 15th Panzer for only twenty-eight killed or injured. Bradley was still breakfasting the next morning when Patton's call came on the telephone.

"Brad," came the familiar squeaky voice, "don't tell anyone but I'm across."

"Across what?"

"Across the Rhine, Brad. For God's sake tell the world we're across. I want the world to know Third Army made it before Monty starts across."

On the far shore, Patton was torn by the sight of what the Allies had done. The wretched refugees were streaming past. "I saw one woman," he wrote Beatrice, "with a perambulator full of her worldly goods sitting by it on a hill crying. An old man with a wheel barrow and three little children wringing his hands. A woman with five children and a tin cup crying. In hundreds of villages there is not a living thing, not even a chicken. . . . Am I getting soft? I did most of it."

Eisenhower returned from the French Riviera. From Wesel, a little township on the Rhine, he watched as Bill Simpson's Ninth Army participated in Montgomery's majestic Rhine crossing. One million troops would cross at the point where the river flowed fast, five hundred yards wide. Two airborne divisions followed, and glider troops as well. A few days later Hughes noted: "George P. reaches Frankfurt. . . . Sending J.P. to Cannes. Vaughan and I going down Friday. I hope to get some sunshine."

One trouble, however, was that Patton now considered himself immortal. As his biographer Ladislas Farago graphically put it, Patton's values were getting mixed up—he spoke more and more of the beauties of war and the horrors of peace. It was as though the war were being fought for his own personal amusement and advance. A case in point was the extraordinary Hammelburg raid. Deeply concerned about his eldest daughter's husband, Lieutenant Colonel John Waters, a cavalry officer who had been taken prisoner after the Kasserine fiasco of February 1943, he decided to go and rescue him. He launched an armored task force of over three hundred troops, ten medium tanks, six light tanks, twenty-seven half-tracks, seven Jeeps, and three motorized assault guns on a daring raid to liberate the prison camp some sixty miles distant holding hundreds of American prisoners, including—he would later swear, by coincidence—Waters. Patton knew that Waters was probably at Hammelburg and he ordered this force from William Hoge's 4th Armored Division to set out before dawn on March 26. Both Eddy and Hoge objected, but he overrode them, and the force rolled off with twenty-year-old Captain Abraham J. Baum, a lanky, mustached former blouse-pattern cutter from Manhattan's garment district, in command. Major Alexander C. Stiller—one of Patton's buddies, who knew Waters by sight—rode with him merely, as he claimed, "for the thrills and laughs." The force actually liberated the Hammelburg camp, but at heavy cost, and on its way out it was ambushed and annihilated; Waters suffered an unpleasant groin injury when the sentries opened fire on him as he emerged from the camp to greet Stiller.

Bradley had authorized Hodges to put four more divisions into the Remagen bridgehead and to be ready to break out toward Limburg and then link up with Patton's bridgehead. Montgomery and Bradley would then throw a giant pincer around the Ruhr, Hitler's last industrial region now that the Russians had overrun Silesia. Hodges's troops jumped off against stiffening German resistance. The veteran 3rd Armored Division—commanded by General Maurice Rose, one of the army's most popular tank generals—formed the flying spearhead. At Paderborn, they ran into trainees from a tank school who had rapidly manned a defense line with Panzerfaust antitank weapons. The school's instructors had manned about sixty Tiger and Panzer tanks, and fought with unwelcome skill and fervor. Five nights later, on March 30, the battle was still raging. Collins spent that night in his Jeep. A few yards away from him, a young German soldier from a Panzerfaust team was dying of head injuries, his groans drowned out by the sound of an ammunition train flaming a few hundred yards farther away, sparkling and crackling like a giant firecracker.

Not far to the northwest General Rose's Jeep ran into four enemy tanks. He tried to career past, but the brutish tank swerved and crushed his Jeep against a tree. The tank commander ordered the Americans to discard their guns, and as Rose fumbled with his gun belt, the tankers decided to shoot him down instead. Collins was deeply grieved. He would never forget this tall, immaculately dressed officer. A few days earlier he had visited him at his headquarters on the outskirts of town. Collins asked Rose why he always had his command post in the last house in town, and Rose replied, "General, there's only one way I know to lead this division, and that's at the head of it!"

The noose tightened around Field Marshal Walter Model's army group in the Ruhr; on April 1, the encirclement was complete. With Collins's blessing, it became known as the "Rose pocket." There were more than 300,000 German troops in this bag. But the Americans never caught their commander because Model killed himself. Thus he followed Friedrich Dollmann, Günther von Kluge, and Erwin Rommel into the special Valhalla reserved for Hitler's finest battle commanders: all had committed suicide.

CHAPTER TWENTY-EIGHT

The Main Prize

OF ALL the controversies fostered by the war between the generals, the nastiest now came.

At the end of March 1945, General Eisenhower signed a new plan for the closing operations of the European war. It did not mention Berlin. That was remarkable, because in his letter to Montgomery six months before, September 15, Eisenhower had spoken unambiguously about the importance of Hitler's capital—"Clearly," he had then written, "Berlin is the main prize." At some stage Eisenhower had lost interest in achieving that prize. But nowhere had he said so explicitly to Montgomery—that is, until March 31. Bradley evidently knew the truth, and so did Hodges, because the First Army diarist noted as early as February 5 the odd fact that the Supreme Commander had laid a bet of ten dollars to thirty dollars that the Russians would be in Berlin by March 31. On that date, he would have to pay up, however, and until then, whether by design or accident, he had left Montgomery and Churchill in the unrectified belief that it was natural that the Allied drive would proceed to Berlin; this was the primrose path that he had mapped out for Montgomery, and now that he had revealed his real intentions it was too late to change his mind.

Of course, Eisenhower may have been too fatigued to follow normal procedures. The burden on him had not lessened in any way. But he made no effort to communicate his views to the British Chiefs of Staff, their commander in chief, or even their Prime Minister. When they had met at the crossing of the Rhine, their spirits had been high. They had met again on March 25, Eisenhower and Churchill and Bradley and Simpson, at the XVI Corps headquarters at Rheinberg. Kay Summersby wrote: "The P.M. had a long message from the Russians, accusing the Americans and British for not playing square with them over military operations. The P.M. said he was sending a long message to Stalin and is going to send E. a copy of his reply." That was how alliances should work—by consultation and the fullest information.

Quietly pleased at the success of his immense crossing of the Rhine, on March 27 Montgomery had proclaimed his own further plans. His directive stated that his armies would now make a bold drive to the Elbe, employing most of their armor. In a telegram to Sir Alan Brooke he explained further: "My goal is to drive hard for the line of the Elbe. . . . My tactical HQ moves will be Wesel-Münster-Herford-Hanover— thence via the autobahn to Berlin, I hope."

By that date, his bridgehead across the Rhine was thirty-five miles wide and twenty-five miles deep, and he had packed twenty divisions and 1,500 tanks into it. Hodges's and Patton's armies were sweeping around to meet Simpson's behind the Ruhr. Now they could make the long awaited thrust across the famous tank country of Lower Saxony, endless rolling plains, to the Elbe and Berlin.

On that morning Eisenhower had flown to Paris with Kay Summersby and held a press conference. "Takes several members of his personal staff with him," she noted. "Has a very good press conference. E. told the press that the war is going well and that we inflicted a heavy defeat on the Germans west of the Rhine. He also said that the German Army was defeated in the west. The Germans would probably make a stand in the mountains but nobody could tell for sure. E. spent the night at the Raphael Hotel in Paris." She did not say why he stayed at the Raphael instead of his house at Trianon.

They left at eight the next morning by car—Kay Summersby and Eisenhower. At SHAEF's forward headquarters at Rheims, two things happened: there was a letter from Montgomery, setting out his plans; and Omar Bradley came to lunch. As they ate, Bradley made clear to Eisenhower that he, for one, had other plans. First, he wanted his Ninth Army back—the one that had been turned over to Montgomery at the time of the Rundstedt offensive. Second, he did not want to advance to Berlin. Besides, with the Red Army standing on the Oder River only forty miles east of Berlin, while the Allies were still two hundred miles west, the Soviets would probably get there first. East Germany had already been granted to Soviet influence. Eisenhower asked Bradley what he thought about it, and Bradley, remembering Aachen, replied, "I think that to capture Berlin might cost us a hundred thousand casualties." He added: "A pretty stiff price for a prestige objective, especially when we've got to fall back and let the other fellow take over." (It was the same kind of butcher's bill calculation which, three months later, would persuade the Americans to drop atomic bombs on Japan rather than risk an invasion.) Eisenhower checked the directives that had been issued to him by the CCS. They said nothing about capturing Berlin. He decided to give Berlin a miss—he was getting sick and tired of this war anyway.

"E. did not have a minute to himself all day," wrote Kay Summersby. "Some member of his staff was in his office most of the afternoon. Bedell has not been feeling too good these last few days and has had to spend several days in bed. Long message from General Marshall re the sudden collapse of Germany. . . . G-3 [Bull] sends a message to Monty, re when Monty's force joins hands with Bradley's east of the Ruhr, it is proposed that the Ninth Army revert to Bradley's command." Then she added a note on the incident which was to cause the biggest row in Anglo-American relations in months. "E. has sent a message to Stalin, prepared by G-3, re co-ordinating our forces with the Russian Army. It has been a very long day for E."

The personal message that Eisenhower's G-3, Harold Bull, drafted for him to send to Stalin was numbered SCAF 252. It was obscurely phrased, but clearly assured the Russians that after encircling the Ruhr he proposed to concentrate his forces in Central Germany for an advance toward Leipzig and the upper Elbe, on which line he would await the arrival of the Russians. His purpose, he said, was to bisect Germany and then turn his main forces against the "National Redoubt"—a rumored Nazi fortress said to have been prepared for Hitler and Nazi fanatics in the Austrian Alps. In retrospect it was extraordinary that he made such ready concessions to Moscow, with no political authorization from either London or Washington. But Kansas plainsman Eisenhower feared no Russians—even later he would explain that he felt that in their generous instincts, in their healthy, direct outlook on the affairs of workaday life, the Russians bore a marked similarity to the average American.

Stalin was delighted. He telegraphed instant approval of Eisenhower's plan, assuring him that Berlin had lost its "former strategic importance" and that he would allocate only secondary forces to it in mid-May.

Churchill, however, was less than enchanted. Eisenhower's personal message to Stalin hit the War Cabinet officers with the impact of a V-2. It shocked the British Chiefs of Staff to see Eisenhower acting as though they and the CCS did not exist at all. As the noted historian Sir Arthur Bryant would later write, the British were thus forced to witness "at the dictate of one of their principal allies" the needless subjection of the whole of eastern Europe to the tyranny of the other. Because that is what halting on the Elbe would imply. "To start with," huffed Brooke on March 29 at the Chiefs of Staff meeting, "he has no business to address Stalin direct, his communications should be through the Combined Chiefs of Staff; secondly, he produced a telegram which was unintelligible; and finally, what was implied in it appeared to be entirely adrift and a change from all that had been previously agreed on." Churchill sent for his Chiefs at 5:15 P.M. to discuss this telegram and their reaction. Things looked ominous. The fat was in the flames.

One and a half hours later the scrambler telephone in Eisenhower's office rang—it was Churchill. Kay Summersby summarized the call as she listened: "He does not agree with E. [on] future operational plans . . . he wants to keep a large force under Monty."

The role assigned to Montgomery by Eisenhower's plan was a modest one: he would advance on Bradley's left, and turn north to cut off Denmark. Sent north into a Baltic backwater, Montgomery would go without much glory. Montgomery was cruelly disappointed. At eight P.M. on March 29 he telegraphed SHAEF, referring to Eisenhower's intention to change the command set up by depriving Montgomery of the Ninth Army. "If you feel this is necessary I pray you not to do so until we reach the Elbe, as such action would not help the great movement which is now beginning to develop."

Alerted by the unexpected violence of the British reaction, Eisenhower hurried to his office before eight the following morning—long before any of his staff were there—and drafted a message to Marshall. He said that Churchill had telephoned protesting particularly at the procedure he had used in communicating direct with Stalin. In tones of injured innocence, Eisenhower reminded Marshall: "I have been instructed to deal directly with the Russians concerning military coordination." He denied any change in basic strategy. "Merely following the principle that Field Marshal Brooke has always shouted to me," he added, "I am determined to concentrate on one major thrust, and all that my plan does is to place the Ninth U.S. Army back under Bradley for that phase of operations involving the advance of the center from Kassel to the Leipzig region. . . . May I point out that Berlin itself is no longer a particularly important objective." It was, he said, in ruins and the ministries were fleeing. So wrote Eisenhower to Marshall on March 30. And to Montgomery himself he wrote explaining his plan on March 31, and sharply concluding: "You will note that in none of this do I mention Berlin. That place has become, so far as I am concerned, nothing but a geographical location, and I have never been interested in these."

Not surprisingly, Kay Summersby closed her day's entry: "E. spent most of the day discussing problems with members of his staff." (Among his other problems was, as Bedell Smith now told him, that, as had happened once before, a trainload of German prisoners had suffocated to death.)

The U.S. Joint Chiefs of Staff replied slightingly to their British colleagues, referring to Montgomery's slow progress in Normandy and more recently north of Wesel—where the Roer dams' flooding had delayed the troops for thirteen days. Churchill was furious: British forces had suffered twenty thousand casualties since Veritable began on February 9, and to imply that the British were not taking their fair share of losses was a terrible slur on his commanders. On April 1 he summoned his chiefs to Chequers and drafted an icy protest to Roosevelt over Eisenhower's high-handed actions. "The British Chiefs of Staff," he explained, "were naturally concerned by a procedure which apparently left the fortunes of the British Army, which though only a third of yours still amounts to over a million men, to be settled without the slightest reference to any British authority." He added, "Nothing will exert a psychological effect of despair upon all German forces of resistance equal to that of the fall of Berlin. It will be the supreme signal of defeat to the German people." It was important, he stressed, not to let the Russians "liberate" both Vienna *and* Berlin.

That Montgomery was about to lose the Ninth Army to Bradley would leave him too weak in the north to achieve his objectives. The German resistance was becoming increasingly determined. Meanwhile Eisenhower was directing his armies not at Berlin but at Leipzig, one hundred miles to the south. Montgomery loosed off salvoes of telegrams at Brooke. Their tone was the same. "I consider we are about to make a terrible mistake," he said. "The great point now is speed of action, so that we can finish off German war in shortest time possible."

Churchill continued to mutter, but made up with Roosevelt. "My personal relations with General Eisenhower," he wrote, "are of the most friendly character. I regard the matter as closed." He ended with a Latin tag—*Amantium irae amoris integratio est* (Lovers' quarrels always go with true love). Brooke commented in his diary: "It is all a pity, and straightforward strategy is being affected by the nationalistic outlook of allies." But as Churchill said to him: "There is only one thing worse than fighting with allies—and that is fighting without them."

There are signs that Eisenhower may have begun to doubt his own plan. On April 7 he sent a message to the Combined Chiefs, inquiring whether perhaps he ought to advance on Berlin after all. "I am the first to admit," he wrote, "that a war is waged in pursuance of political aims and, if the Combined Chiefs of Staff should decide that the Allied effort to take Berlin outweighs purely military considerations in this theater, I would cheerfully readjust my plans and my thinking so as to carry out such an operation." The CCS did not reply.

Thus the Allied advance began to slow. At the end of March 1945, Bradley telephoned Patton to advance rapidly to the Werra and Weser rivers but then more slowly toward the Elbe. Patton was puzzled, and told him that any slowdown was dangerous: "We have the enemy on the run and should keep him that way." Patton cursed. Whenever Eisenhower and Bradley got together, he thought, they got timid: "I am sure that had a bold policy throughout been used in this war it would have long since been over." For the next days his Third Army effectively marked time, as it waited for the First and Ninth armies to catch up. Patton wrote to Beatrice, "Now I am waiting for Courtney and Charley so we will end the war in line. I could join the Russians in a week if I were turned loose. Damn equality."

Bradley's directive to Hodges ordered his army eastward along the Kassel-Leipzig axis until contact was established with the Russian forces. The great First Army advance began on April 5, paused while wrecked bridges across the Weser were replaced, then resumed a few days later with the veteran 3rd Armored Division again forming the spearhead. The Americans were now moving into the Harz mountains. They did not yet know it, but Hitler had evacuated his most important secret weapons factories into these mountains, where centuries of quarrying had formed tunnels that honeycombed the whole region. Near Nordhausen, thousands of slave laborers worked on bombproof production lines assembling V-1 and V-2 rockets and engines for jet aircraft. The advancing GIs stumbled upon rocket test rigs set up in the quarries, underground fuel stores, and preparations for the underground refining of gasoline, and they found concentration camps full of pitiful prisoners.

On April 5, lunching at Seventh Army headquarters in Darmstadt, Eisenhower confided to Hap Arnold that he was feeling the war. Arnold later noted: "It had taken a whole lot out of him but he forced himself to go on and would until [the] whole mess was cleaned up." After lunch Arnold drove down the Autobahn to Frankfurt to see Patton, who had his headquarters in an old barracks there. He was the same old Patton. "There's nothing in front of me," he told Arnold. "I could go right on through and join up with the Russians tomorrow, but headquarters is holding me back here until the army on our right catches up."

He knew he was way out in front. The day before, he told Arnold, a Nazi sniper had taken a potshot at one of his staff in this very building. "Yesterday," he bragged, "guerrillas in a town in my front refused to surrender. So I burnt it down."

Patton soon had more high-ranking visitors. On the evening of April 11, after inspecting a mine captured by the XII Corps in which much of the German gold reserve was stashed, and then a camp at Ohrdruf Nord where forced workers had been laboring under deteriorating conditions for the nearby munitions factory, Eisenhower and Bradley arrived at Patton's headquarters. Eisenhower dictated to Patton a proposed stop line, and explained the reasons. Patton felt it better not to set them down in his diary, but his chief of staff Gay noted them: "From a tactical point of view, it was highly inadvisable for the American Army to take Berlin, and he hoped political influence would not cause him to take the city. It had no tactical or strategical value, and would place upon American forces the burden of caring for thousands of Germans, displaced persons, Allied prisoners of war etc."

General Patton disagreed, saying: "Ike, I don't see how you figure that one. We had better take Berlin and quick, and on to the Oder."

On April 3 Simpson's Ninth Army was at last transferred from Montgomery's command back to Bradley's. The Russians had been halted on the river Oder for some weeks, east of Berlin. Simpson later said: "I could have beaten them into Berlin if I had been allowed to go."

At that time Berlin was about sixty miles from his leading unit. On the morning of April 15 Simpson got a message from General Bradley in Heidelberg asking him to fly straight down. As soon as Simpson got there, Bradley told him, "You have got to stop on the Elbe. You can't go into Berlin."

"Where did this order come from?" Simpson asked Bradley.

Bradley replied shortly: "From General Eisenhower."

On April 17, Patton called Everett Hughes in Paris and said he would be in that night. Hughes met his old friend as his plane landed. "He stopped to see Waters," wrote Hughes, "and then to dinner and night with me. For dinner had Geo . . . drank until weesome hours. Geo sore because Ike had cussed him out for taking a gold mine in Russian territory. Sore at Jean because she broadcast to U.S. that she is here! Bea heard it before Geo did and wrote him. Hell to pay!" Hughes got up late the next day. *Stars & Stripes* had announced George's promotion to four-star general, but Hughes had a hard time even getting him to read the news. "He is sore to be promoted as an afterthought," observed Hughes. "I don't blame him."

A few days after the Americans halted on the Elbe, the Red Army began its offensive from the river Oder toward Berlin. To the Russians would fall what Eisenhower had described, before his change of mind, as the main prize.

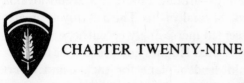

CHAPTER TWENTY-NINE

Parting of the Ways

HENRY L. Stimson was at Highhold, his country house, getting ready for bed, when the telephone call came. It was from an aide, Colonel William H. Kyle. A Top Secret cable had just arrived from General Eisenhower, Kyle told him. "The mission of this Allied force," it read, "was fulfilled at 0241, local time, May 7th, 1945."

"Does it include Norway?" Stimson asked.

"It includes everything."

That day Everett Hughes drove over to Rheims from Paris to keep a 12:30 lunch date with Eisenhower. In his eagerness he got there an hour early, but Kay Summersby took him right in. Eisenhower was jovial and heartily shook his hand.

"That's the only reason I came," Hughes exclaimed, "to shake hands!" He reminded Eisenhower of the day he had first told Hughes about Overlord. And now . . . And now, said Eisenhower, he had been up all night with Bedell Smith signing peace treaties! Hughes asked him what would happen to SHAEF, now that the war in Europe was won.

Eisenhower scratched his head and said he just didn't know.

Churchill kept phoning Eisenhower all afternoon. He wanted to announce the surrender that evening, but he couldn't get Harry Truman, who had become President upon Roosevelt's death less than a month earlier, on the transatlantic telephone. The next day, when the French newspapers proclaimed the victory, the headlines read to the Americans as if the French had won the war. Hughes and J.P. threw a little party for their friends and listened to Churchill's radio speech. Hughes remarked: "He sounded as though he were a little tight."

George Patton was still fighting—around Pilsen, in Czechoslovakia —when Germany surrendered. Several of his Third Army intimates were worried about him. He seemed increasingly eccentric, emotional, even unstable. Secretly they contacted Hughes and asked if he and J.P. would come over—they would send a plane for them—and divert George a bit. Hughes and J.P. arrived at Third Army headquarters in Regensburg, Germany, on May 11. Patton was living in a castle that was more like a museum, full of bric-a-brac.

Hughes soon gathered that Patton had had a scene with Jean Gordon —perhaps, he thought, about what would become of her now. But that evening, thanks in part to a huge bottle of champagne provided by a Red Cross girl named Marion Hall, they had made up. Later Patton mystified Hughes by telling him that Jean had handed him "a marked calendar." Patton went on unblushingly to inform Hughes that he had ordered nine condoms for his forthcoming trip to London—he had been encouraged to take some time off and relax. Before he left he achieved a victory over Soviet Communism: he met a Russian general in Linz, drank him under the table, and walked out under his own steam.

Flying into London on the 16th, he noticed that the city was much less battered than German cities he had seen. He checked in at Claridge's Hotel, then phoned Alfred Lunt and Lynn Fontanne to ask for two tickets to their current play, which he found "most amusing." News photographers came into the theater and took Patton's picture. "I think that they may have thought I was Montgomery," he playfully told his diary, "until I started to go out, when they found I was bigger." He was pleased to find that "the whole street for about three blocks was a solid mass of people waiting to see me."

The next day he gave an interview: "I simply stated that I was very glad to be in England because it always felt like home to me, which is a mild remark well-swallowed by the English." He had lunch at Claridge's with Lady Astor, "a very smart old lady."

Just after lunch, Harold Bull of Eisenhower's staff phoned Patton and told him to get back to his troops at once. It seemed that Tito was causing trouble, claiming northern Italy for Yugoslavia. Patton was to go down and rattle his sword a bit. On May 18 Hughes noted cheerfully: "Geo recalled from UK. He didn't need the nine."

Tito was quickly deterred, and later in May Patton was able to return to London to resume his endeavors. Back in Paris, he told Hughes that in London he had succeeded "four times in three days." He went on to remark that a busy man sacrifices a certain number of opportunities. He knew the exact number of opportunities that he had *not* sacrificed: "Seventy-one," he said.

· That evening Patton invited eight people to dinner at the Ritz—and had to fork over $180 out of his own pocket. He told Hughes he was scared to death of going back home to America. He left the next day. Jean Gordon was distraught. With J.P., Hughes took her back to his apartment so she could "have a good cry." When Patton returned to Paris on July 4, he told Hughes over sandwiches and Scotch in Hughes's room: "Beatrice gave me hell. I'm glad to be in Europe!" He added that he was damned well not going to the Pacific while Mac-Arthur was out there. Before they parted, he said: "Stick around, maybe you and I will run this theater."

There is no question that Patton had come to admire the Germans, the very people he had been fighting. Everything he saw of Russians, Poles, and Jews aroused loathing in him. Until the war ended, he had struggled to conceal these feelings, but afterward they were displayed in his opposition to the nonfraternization and denazification orders.

That May, in a letter to Beatrice, he called the Russians "a scurvy race and simply savages. We could beat hell out of them." He said that Hap Arnold shared his views about "the Mongols," as he called them. In July he wrote to Beatrice: "Berlin gave me the blues. We have destroyed what could have been a good race and we [are] about to replace them with Mongolian savages." In August he would note in his diary, about the Russians: "I have no particular desire to understand them except to ascertain how much lead or iron it takes to kill them." On August 31 he told Beatrice, "The stuff in the papers about fraternization is all wet. . . . All that sort of writing is done by Jews to get revenge. Actually the Germans are the only decent people left in Europe. . . . I prefer the Germans. So do our cousins"—meaning the British. By mid-September he was describing the Jews as "lower than animals"—he had by then toured many of their refugee camps and been sickened by the aspect. When a visit by ten Russians had been announced in September of 1944, he had gone to the front to avoid them, and left them staring at a map which told them nothing. Those whom he met did not impress him: Marshal Tolbukhin, conqueror of Hungary, he noted, sweated profusely; Zhukov had a primordial lower jaw like an ape. The aristocrat and wealthy Californian in Patton saw no reason to fear or appease the Russians.

Many of Eisenhower's generals worried about the future, but Patton was so alarmed about Russian strength that he wanted to carry the war into Russia now—he felt he could be in Moscow within months. David Astor told Basil Liddell Hart on May 22 that both Patton and Montgomery had said in private that if there was a danger of war with Russia, it would be better to tackle that danger now than to postpone it: at present, the British and Americans had the air superiority, and the American forces were on the scene and fully mobilized.

Eisenhower began planning his return. Mamie would be waiting for him in Washington. He ordered two tropical worsted summer suits to be delivered to him there. After a vast formation in Frankfurt on June 10, at which his assembled troops hailed their victorious chief and sent him on his way, he paid triumphal visits to London and Paris, then flew to the United States. In Washington he addressed a joint session of Congress, declaring that American security could be safeguarded only by amity between the Allies, backed up by armored might. In New York, six million people gave him the biggest reception in the city's history. At Kansas City there was a parade too, and his mother was on the reviewing stand. One of the reporters asked her: "Aren't you proud of your boy?" The old dear replied: "Which one?" Eisenhower made a speech, and as he spoke one old boyhood friend saw that he was holding onto his great big thumb with his other hand just as he always used to. The Eisenhower express roared on to Abilene. On the way, he got off the train at Topeka to greet a group of soldiers who had been awarded the Purple Heart. The train started without him and when he tried to jump it, he missed the steps and banged his weak knee. He returned to his hometown, Abilene, on June 21. One newspaper head-line read: ABILENE'S 6,000 SHOOT WORKS FOR MRS. EISENHOWER'S SON. Another said: IKE DEPLOYS MOTHER PAST SURGING CROWD. At the railroad station, a train bearing troops toward the Pacific slowly clacked by, and he shook as many hands as he could reach. One GI gave him a firm clasp and yelled, "I won't wash that hand until I get Tojo."

He held a press conference, vigorously denying that he had any aspirations to enter politics. That had always been his position. Once, in the summer of 1943, when a senator mentioned his name as a logical candidate for political office, he showed his irritation in a letter to his brother Edgar: "I can think of nothing that could more definitely damage a soldier's effectiveness than to have people at home begin to believe he was interested in political preference." He had had enough politics in dealing with the renegade French and Italians to last him the rest of his life. And he had laughed outright when he saw in the paper in October 1944 that Mamie had told a reporter that she could not say which political party Ike belonged to, and he wrote to her: *"Neither could I!!!"* He said that he did not know which was a dirtier business —war or politics.

After a holiday with Mamie at White Sulphur Springs, he returned to Europe. He got back to Frankfurt in July; he looked well, Hughes thought, but nervous. "Didn't discuss Mamie," Hughes remarked in his diary. Eisenhower did say that Harry Butcher, who had left his staff in August 1944, was getting a divorce. The Tedders came to say goodbye, and Tops promised Hughes a photograph. Hughes promised himself— now that the war was over, SHAEF had been disbanded, and the British and American commanders had been pried from each other's throats—to speak more kindly of people. "Kate bawls me out about criticizing," he wrote on July 24. "She is right."

This was a postwar posture that Montgomery, too, was learning to master. In late May he had made a public statement to the German people so tactless that even his old crony Sir James Grigg became exasperated. Grigg sent a Most Secret cipher telegram by one-time-pad to Montgomery, dated May 31: "Private. From Secretary of State for Field Marshal Montgomery. I beseech you in the Bowels of Christ to watch your step or at any rate your loudspeaker so long as SHAEF still exists. I have quite enough quarrels to cope with." On June 27, Grigg sent another Top Secret message to Montgomery: "Eyes Only . . . Do for goodness sake stop making speeches for a bit. We are getting fuliginous minutes from the Prime Minister nearly every day. The latest is contained in my immediately following. Anyhow there are plenty of people about who will rejoice to see mischief between you and the Prime Minister, and they aren't all Germans, Russians or Americans. There are, for example, an awful lot of near-Communists among the newspaper correspondents and there are certainly a lot of lice."

On the same date Grigg also sent to Montgomery, for his eyes only, this: "Prime Minister has seen an Associated Press report in the *Yorkshire Evening Post* of June 26th of a speech made by Field-Marshal Montgomery when decorating American officers and men in the last few days, in which he said that Britain was finished in 1941 and could not possibly have survived without American aid. The Prime Minister asks—(a) did the Field-Marshal actually say this? (b) if he did, he would like the War Office to tell him in no uncertain terms that he (the Prime Minister) entirely disagrees that this was the case. Further if the F.M. [field marshal] did say so, the Prime Minister would like his displeasure to be conveyed to him."

Montgomery denied the statement attributed to him, saying it was "utterly and completely untrue." He explained: "I went to Wiesbaden on 25th June to hold an investiture for American officers and men. At the end of the investiture General Bradley asked me to say a few words to the assembled recipients. In my talk I made two points. Firstly, I thanked American army for many kindnesses and great hospitality we had always received at their hands. Secondly, I said that the turning point of the war came when Axis powers committed the mistake in 1941 of attacking Russia and America. Up to that day . . . the British Empire had been just fighting alone against combined might of Axis Powers. The final defeat of Axis Powers was hastened when Russia and America had come in against them."

From all the evidence, especially the various unpublished diaries, it seems clear that whatever romance there had been between Eisenhower and Kay Summersby, it had flickered out, on his side, by the time he arrived in London early in 1944. From then on, for him, it was principally a matter of companionship, a remedy for loneliness. But she struggled to retain her bridgehead in his heart, and she clung to him all through their time in Europe. She was cruelly hurt by the inevitable and abrupt denouement. It took place in November 1945, when he told her at American army headquarters in Frankfurt that he had been ordered back to the United States. She took the news badly. She was "in a high state of nerves," according to Patton's diary. Merle Miller's *Plain Speaking, An Oral Biography of Harry S. Truman* quoted Harry Truman as saying that shortly after the war Eisenhower wrote to General Marshall that he wished to divorce Mamie and marry Kay Summersby. Truman was also quoted as saying that he personally ordered both the letter and General Marshall's uncompromising reply removed from Pentagon files and destroyed. But study of Eisenhower's papers reveals that this is improbable. For one thing, in October 1945 he had helped her to take out papers for U.S. citizenship; marriage, of course, would have conferred on her an automatic right to citizenship.

He wrote around to his influential friends, asking them to give his former private secretary a job, but warning that she could not type. She worked for a while at Fourth Air Force headquarters in California, yearning to see him. In May 1947 she wrote an article for the air base newspaper. It was a spoof interview with Eisenhower's dog Telek. The last paragraph quoted the dog's views on the great General Marshall, on "your airforce's bag man" Hap Arnold, and on "your razor sharp" General Spaatz. "They are all fine chaps," woofed Telek, "but in case you ever see anyone who can get word to Ike, tell him I miss him a lot, and I would give up my prospects of going to dog heaven just to have another long 'man to dog' talk with him." She sent Eisenhower the article. The message was plain, but he did not see her.

In 1948, she published a book, *Eisenhower Was My Boss.* It attracted more attention for what it did not say than for what it did. Eisenhower read only the first and last chapter, then put it aside. At the end of that year there was word that she planned to write her real story for *Look* magazine. Harry Butcher wrote to Eisenhower on December 13: "From Kay's visits with us in Santa Barbara it was obvious to me that she was [motivated] partly from need of money and, also, from pique." Two years later he heard that money was being raised by Democrats to tap her telephone in New York in the hope of discrediting Eisenhower's presidential campaign. The truth was that Kay had not heard from him for a long time, and Eisenhower wrote dismissively to Butcher: "I assure you that it is of no interest to me."

November 1945 was a sad month for Jean Gordon, too. She returned to the United States, never to see her beloved Patton again. On December 21, he died from injuries he had received in an auto accident. "I think it is better this way for Uncle Georgie," she told her friend Betty South. "There is no place for him anymore." There was no place for Jean Gordon either. In New York, two weeks after his death, she committed suicide.

After the war, the lid came down on the inside story of the fight between the generals. As early as the summer of 1944, the great partners in this coalition war had, severally and separately, begun hiding their cards from each other. A Top Secret British memorandum dated September 4 reveals that the War Office had created a new classification for documents, "Guard," to prevent the Americans from learning anything about "messages of far-reaching importance or controversial matters which must never become known to the United States." Such messages were to be sent in one-time cipher, which the Americans could not break. "No such message is in any circumstance to be handed to, or seen, by any American."

A sudden urge for confidentiality had also afflicted George Marshall. On August 18, he had written to General Handy urging fewer written records. There were some documents which should be preserved, but strictly under lock and key. "For example," he wrote, ". . . reference in historical writings to the bitter discussions which had arisen from time to time over various plans of campaign, allocations of material etc., etc., and particularly the views of the U.S. Chiefs of Staff and of their advisers regarding matters pertaining to the British or other Allied nations, would be highly inadvisable in the future. Otherwise we should sow definite seeds of bitterness that would be exaggerated and continued for years to come, to the great disadvantage of all possible British-American accord."

Marshall took as his precedent the proceedings of the American Constitutional Convention. Both Washington and Franklin had insisted on complete secrecy as to what actually took place in the discussions. And he pointed out that General Pershing still, in 1944, held World War I files which had never been released to historians. Writing on September 7, Marshall had made himself plainer. He would agree to the eventual release to the archives of the formal proposals made by the U.S. Joint Chiefs of Staff to their British colleagues. "They are not offensive documents," he explained, "though some of them may contain references to other nations that would not be helpful to the peace and serenity of the postwar period. But among these records are the minutes of the meetings and the statements of the Planners to the U.S. Chiefs of Staff, and it is to these in particular that I refer in my belief that publicity would be tragically unfortunate in its results."

Marshall had good cause for concern. The Joint Strategic Survey Committee, and its chief, Lieutenant General Stanley Embick, were almost pathologically anti-British. They sensed colonialist ambitions behind every British proposition, and they and their fellow planners in the S. & P. section of the Joint Chiefs urged policy decisions that seemed designed to force Britain to commit its dwindling resources to operations—like the frontal assault on the Continent, Overlord—certain to maximize its already substantial casualties. Many Britons regarded these decisions as an indirect way of slashing Britain's influence in postwar military affairs. Publication of these papers would certainly have caused outrage in London.

But embarrassing records did survive. When Eisenhower learned in 1945 that a diary had surfaced, which he had written at the War Department, he told Harry Butcher in writing: "Please destroy these personal notes of mine at once and keep no record of them whatsoever." He added, "The notes, made by me personally when in the Operations Division, have no place in the complete diary and they must not, repeat not, be seen by anyone." However, Butcher did not destroy them and they reveal Eisenhower's uncharitable remarks about both General MacArthur and Admiral King.

No sooner had the war ended than Butcher began publishing the thousands of pages of diary notes which he himself had dictated as Eisenhower's naval aide. The general suffered acute embarrassment and anger. True, the top secrets, the references to Ultra, and also personally offensive passages were deleted before publication, and many flattering sentences were incorporated which are not in the original diary text. Serial publication of the Butcher diary in the *Saturday Evening Post* in December 1945 caused Eisenhower endless soul-searching and he wrote scores of letters of apology. He did what he could to hold back Butcher. "You have already, of course," he wrote Butcher at Christmas 1945, "engaged to rewrite in the book the paragraph concerning Mr. Churchill to which I took such earnest exception. In going over the text I hope you will also give equal attention to anything involving any other foreign official, such as General de Gaulle, or Field Marshal Montgomery or others, where the promotion of bad feeling would be to defeat the very purposes that I strove so hard to advance during the war."

Eisenhower wrote a humble apology to Churchill for what Butcher had already made known. Churchill, holidaying in Miami, replied loftily on January 26, 1946: "I must say I think you have been ill-used by your confidential aide. . . . Great events and personalities"—meaning himself —"are made small when passed through the medium of this small mind." But he too added a note of apology about those times: "I really do feel very sorry to have kept you up so late on various occasions. It is a fault I have. . . ."

The already brittle Eisenhower-Montgomery relationship suffered too. The correspondence lingered on for years, becoming petty and cantankerous. Eisenhower pleaded with Montgomery on February 12, 1946: "In my personal files there are letters from you that show constantly how close we were. . . . It is true that those letters also reveal certain differences of conviction, but these . . . so far as I know have never been seen by anyone except myself and my own confidential secretaries."

After Alan Moorehead's biography of the field marshal appeared, it was Montgomery's turn to appease Eisenhower. In October 1946 Montgomery insisted that Moorehead had not had access to *his* confidential files, so how had he obtained the often acid correspondence between them which he quoted? "The more private letters," insisted Montgomery, "were not even seen by Freddie de Guingand." Eisenhower was baffled. He had kept his own red-hot Montgomery folder in a "Personal Secret File," locked away in his safe; many of the letters were not even mentioned in the official files of SHAEF, and many had been seen by nobody but Eisenhower himself.

Then Eisenhower published *Crusade in Europe.* It was chivalrously worded, but still caused a furor in England, and many newspapers sided with Montgomery. Montgomery's former chief of staff, de Guingand, whom he had unfeelingly bowler-hatted after the war, penned a favorable review for the *Sunday Graphic,* but the newspaper's military correspondent, Major Denis Hamilton, deleted his criticisms of the field marshal. "It was obvious," lamented de Guingand privately to Eisenhower, "that the gentleman had been to see Monty, for I saw all the old 'war cries'! I'm afraid Monty, in his endeavor to justify his *every* action, forgot that some of us could tell a very damaging story. It is a pity he is so sensitive." De Guingand then wrote warning his old chief that the little intrigues he had employed had done him no good, and he referred to "certain letters" which he had seen passed between Montgomery and Eisenhower, which might remove him from his present pedestal if published. Later, in Washington, de Guingand told Eisenhower in confidence of incidents that occurred in North Africa and in Normandy, and Eisenhower told de Guingand that if he had known of them they "could well have violently reduced my high opinion of Montgomery." Four days later he wrote a letter to Montgomery of unusual coldness; Montgomery's reply was brief to the point of rudeness.

Although their wrangling sputtered on for twenty years and more, it would be churlish to dwell on the differences between these two great commanders in chief. To maintain solidarity in a coalition war between two major powers was a frustrating, daunting, and unrewarding task; to do so during times of personal hardship, when many lifetime friends and trusted officers were falling, and in the awesome knowledge that the survival of more than just their army depended on their decisions, cannot have been easy. The victory which the Allies won, against fearsome odds, was due not just to the wonders of Ultra, the superiority of Anglo-American air power, and the rightness of their cause. It owed much to the fine generalship displayed by the senior commanders. Those who had failed were weeded out, sooner or later. Those who remained to the end, like Montgomery and Eisenhower, were unquestionably among the finest that their systems could produce. They were a match for each other.

After it was all over, on June 7, 1945, Montgomery wrote to Eisenhower these lines: "I owe much to your wise guidance and kindly forbearance. I know my own faults very well and I do not suppose I am an easy subordinate; I like to go my own way. But you have kept me on the rails in difficult and stormy times, and have taught me much." It is with those words that we choose to leave the battlefield on which the Allied generals fought their campaign.

Acknowledgments

THIS STUDY of the Anglo-American alliance was enriched by the fact that many of the warring commanders took pains to keep a record of what they were doing—whether with an eye to publication, like George Patton, or out of the classic diarist's itch to jot, like the man whom Eisenhower called his "eyes and ears," Everett Hughes. Some of the papers have been used by other historians—for example, those of Forrestal, Stimson, and Leahy; in each case, I worked from the often more complete originals. But many other, immensely revealing diaries have been neglected until now.

Why have these remarkable diaries remained unexploited? The answers are as varied as the diaries themselves. Some are subject to the most stringent rules of access. Years ago my very good friend the late Ladislas Farago heard that a certain man had some writings by Patton. The man turned out to be a clerk on Patton's wartime staff, and the papers turned out to be Patton's own diaries; after Patton's death the man had simply put them in a trunk. Farago used them in the writing of his biography of Patton, then showed them to the Patton family who,

416

embarrassed, had them locked away. Dr. Martin Blumensen very expertly edited them for his authorized version, *The Patton Papers,* but the originals, in all their vital candor, have not been available since. Farago, however, had managed to keep a copy of the 1945 Patton diary, which he used for his book *The Last Days of Patton,* and he generously allowed me to use it as well.

Others, like the diaries kept for the Supreme Commander by his naval aide, Harry C. Butcher, were subject to censorship—they were partially published, and it had not occurred to writers to go back to Butcher's original files. Yet many hundreds of pages, including the most rewarding materials, had been closed by the authorities. At this author's request they were released, including many pages withheld because of the personal and secret materials recorded in them by Butcher.

A third reason for the failure to use important diaries is their geographic inaccessibility. From the listing below of the archives and sources relied on, it can be seen how far-flung they are. Abilene, Kansas, site of the Eisenhower library, is not easy to get to; it requires a long flight and a long drive, to a town with sparse accommodation. Yet a Klondike of material exists there. Among the important diaries at Abilene are those kept by and for the First Army commander Courtney Hodges, and by Eisenhower's personal assistant Kay Summersby. Mrs. Summersby's two published books consist only of light and fairly inconsequential material, whereas her diary is a highly detailed and specific record of events, revealing her as a shrewd and perceptive woman.

The fourth reason is simply illegibility. Diaries that have lain for years under the noses of historians, as accessible as the Library of Congress on Capitol Hill, have been shunned evidently for no other reason than their intimidatingly awkward handwriting. Researchers evidently recoiled from the private diaries kept by Eisenhower's Boswell, Lieutenant General Everett S. Hughes, because they are written in a strange, spiky Gothic hand in a collection of unappealing, tattered little notebooks, their pages falling out. In any case, the diary has never been used, let alone published. Yet it contains some of the most dramatic—and often funniest—insights into persons and intrigues ever to emerge from Eisenhower's headquarters. It would—I must add—have been impossible for me to use this extraordinary source without the assistance of Molly McClellan, whose skill at transcribing the diaries' nine hundred pages for me qualifies her for the cryptographer's hall of fame.

A lot of the initial legwork for this book was done for me by Nicholas Reynolds in Washington, Charmaine Henthorn in Ottawa, and Wenona Bryan in London. When I set out on this investigation, many American colleagues generously helped me, with clues of their own. I received early and invaluable advice from Dr. Forrest C. Pogue, author of the magisterial work *The Supreme Command,* who guided me to the diary kept for Air Chief Marshal Tedder by Wing Commander Scarman, and from the official editors of *The Papers of Dwight D. Eisenhower,* Dr. Stephen Ambrose of New Orleans and Dr. Joseph P. Hobbs of Raleigh, North Carolina. It will be impossible to thank by name all the archivists who helped me, but I cannot forego mentioning Dr. William Cunliffe, of the Modern Military Records Branch of the National Archives in Washington, and Mr. David Haight, the archivist at the Dwight D. Eisenhower presidential library in Abilene, Kansas.

Time has robbed us of too many of the leading names mentioned in these pages of this book. But I had the opportunity of interviewing Sir Arthur T. Harris and his deputy at the RAF Bomber Command, Sir Robert Saundby. Among the other generals to whom I am indebted for their time are Mark W. Clark, James M. Gavin, Elwood R. Quesada, Henry S. Aurand, and Joseph L. Collins. I was privileged to correspond with Carl A. Spaatz before his death. Brigadier N. Elliot Rodger, of the Canadian army, kindly allowed me to use his unpublished diaries. I finally add a word of thanks to my editor and publisher, Thomas B. Congdon, Jr., for his care and skill in preparing the final manuscript.

Archival Sources

Abilene, Kan.: Dwight D. Eisenhower Library
H.S. Aurand papers
Raymond Barker papers
Harry C. Butcher diary and papers
   (The original diary was dictated by him up to August 15, 1944; the only
      other items he dictated were on January 27 and February 26, 1945.)
Harold R. Bull papers
Norman D. Cota papers
Dwight D. Eisenhower papers
John Eisenhower papers
   Letters to Mamie
Courtney Hodges papers
   Including: First Army war diary maintained by Major William Sylvan
      and Captain Francis G. Smith
C.D. Jackson papers
Mickey McKeogh papers
J.M. Robb papers
Kay Summersby-Morgan papers

Walter Bedell Smith wartime papers
    Box 7: Walter Bedell Smith, personal papers 1942–1944
    Box 8: W.B. Smith 201 File
    Box 19: Documents—Cables No. 1
    Box 19: Incomings No. 1 & 2
    Box 27: Outgoing March 1945
    Box 35: Buchenwald Inspection
    Box 19: Outgoing (Eyes Only) No. 3
    Box 19: Incoming (Eyes Only) No. 1
    Box 103: Stimson, Henry
    Box 103: Strong, Kenneth
    Box 104: Summersby, Kay
    Box 107: Tedder, Arthur
    Box 113: Ward, Orlando

Dwight D. Eisenhower, Pre-presidential Papers: correspondence with

Alanbrooke, Lord
Aldrich, William
Alexander, Sir Harold
Arnold, Henry H.
Baruch, Bernard
Bracken, Brendon
Bradley, Omar
Butcher, Harry C.
Churchill, Winston S.
Clark, Mark W.
Cunningham, Sir Andrew
Devers, Jacob L.
Gault, James
George VI, King
Gerow, Leonard T.
Gruenther, Alfred M.
Harger, Charles M.
Harriman, W. Averell
Harris, Sir Arthur T.
Hughes, Everett S.
Ismay, Sir Hastings
Joint Chiefs of Staff
Leahy, William D.
Lear, Ben
Lascelles, Sir Alan
Leigh-Mallory, Sir Trafford
Littlejohn, Robert M.

McNair, Lesley J.
McNarney, J.C.
Marshall, George C.
Montgomery, Sir Bernard
Morgan, Sir Frederick
Morgenthau, Henry, Jr.
Morrison, Herbert
Mountbatten, Lord Louis
Patterson, Robert P.
Patton, George S., Jr.
Pogue, Forrest C.
Portal, Sir Charles
Pyle, Ernie
Ridgway, Matthew B.
Roosevelt, Franklin D.
Sherwood, Robert E.
Sinclair, Archibald
Slessor, Sir John
Smith, Walter Bedell
Somervell, Brehon
Spaatz, Carl F.
Stark, H.R.
Stars & Stripes
Stimson, Henry L.
Strong, Kenneth W.D.
Summersby, Kay
Taylor, Maxwell D.

Tedder, Sir Arthur
Truman, Harry S.
Truscott, Lucian K.
Ward, Orlando

Wedemeyer, A.C.
Wilson, Sir Henry Maitland
Winant, John G.

Dwight D. Eisenhower, Pre-presidential Papers
  Box 122: Cables: CCS (October 1943–July 1945)
  Box 124: Cables: Marshall/Eisenhower, 1944–1945
  Box 125: Cables: Marshall/Eisenhower, 1945
  Box 125: Cables: SCAF (Supreme Commander, Allied Forces)
  Box 139: Conferences, Supreme Cdrs (Jan–June, 1944)
  Box 140: *Crusade in Europe,* documents
  Box 141: D-day
  Box 141: Diary Harry C. Butcher 1942
  Box 144: Diary Harry C. Butcher 1943–1944
  Box 145: Diary Harry C. Butcher 1944
  Box 146: Diary Harry C. Butcher 1944–1945, and diary of Kay Summersby, transcript
  Box 152: Messages to Officers & Men, AEF
  Box 152: Messages, etc. 1942–1947
  Box 152: Morgenthau Plan
  Box 154: Operation Neptune, June 1944
  Box 158: Speeches (1939–Nov. 1945)
  Box 160: Speeches and Messages, 1943–1945
  Box 165: Summaries: Personal Correspondence 1943–1945
  Box 165: Surrender, No. 1
  Box 178: Eisenhower, Arthur B.
  Box 178: Eisenhower, Edgard N.
  Box 179: Eisenhower, Ida S.
  Box 179: Eisenhower, John D.
  Box 180: Eisenhower, Mamie Doud
  Box 180: Eisenhower, Milton S.
  Box 181: Eisenhower, Roy
  Box 184: D-day Message
  Box 184: Checklist of W.B. Smith document collection

Cambridge, England: Churchill College
  Sir P.J. Grigg papers
  Admiral A.B. Cunningham papers

Charleston, S.C.: The Citadel
  General Mark W. Clark papers

Lexington, Va.: George C. Marshall Foundation
George C. Marshall, papers
> Correspondence with Ira C. Eaker, Charles de Gaulle, W. Donovan, Carl F. Spaatz, Bernard Montgomery, Dwight D. Eisenhower, William B. Leahy

London, England: David Irving Author's Archives*
Field Marshal Erwin Rommel, diaries and papers
Field Marshal Erwin Milch, diaries and papers
Brigadier N. Elliot Rodger, Chief of Staff, Canadian II Corps 1944, diary
Lieutenant General Everett S. Hughes, diary, transcript

London: Imperial War Museum
Bernard Montgomery, miscellaneous papers

London: Centre for Military Archives, King's College
Lord Alanbrooke, diary and papers
General Hastings L. Ismay, papers
B.H. Liddell Hart, papers

London: Public Records Office
WO 205, Records of 21 Army Group
> 5b, Correspondence and signals between Montgomery and de Guingand
> 5c, Chief of Staff D.O. correspondence April 1944–May 1945
> 5d, D.O. correspondence of C-in-C
> 5g, Directives to army commanders, March 1944–April 1945
> 5e, Signals, D-day to December 31, 1944
> 5f, De Guingand's file of personal signals
> 70, Overlord, outline mounting plans, April–May 1944
> 82, Cover plan, wireless, January–May 1944
> 83, Cover plan, wireless, May 1944–February 1945
> 114, V-weapons against Antwerp
> 117, Command and control, May 1944–February 1945
> 173, Fortitude
> 273, Second British Army, January–May 1945 conferences
> 307, Veritable meeting
> 497, Overlord, Command and Control

---

*These archives are available on microfilm from E.P. Microform Ltd., East Ardsley, Wakefield, Yorkshire, England.

498, Overlord, correspondence May 1944–1945
1020-2, Interrogation reports, German generals
WO 208,
3249, CSDIC
WO 291
172, SAC conferences January–June 1944
184, Fabius, March–May 1944
186, Tiger, April–May 1944
254, Overlord, demiofficial correspondence, Eisenhower-Montgomery
255-6, Overlord, conferences and planning papers
268, Overlord, presentation of plans to King, Prime Minister, and
    guests (May 1944)
274, German counteroffensive
439, Secret overseas radiotelephone system
588, SAC meetings April–May 1944, September 1944
594, SACF meeting arrangements, May 1944
645, Overlord movements, timetables, May 1944
780a, Intelligence on Seelion 1940, D-day 1944

New Haven, Conn.: Yale University, Sterling Memorial Library
Henry L. Stimson papers, I
    Box 143, correspondence
    Box 144, correspondence
    Box 145, correspondence
    Box 146, correspondence
Henry L. Stimson papers, II
    Box 172, official papers, including diary of Colonel W.H.S. Wright,
    May 26–July 8, 1944

New York, N.Y.: Author's Archives of Ladislas Farago
General George S. Patton, Jr., diary, 1945
General Hap Gay, diary

Ottawa, Canada: Public Archives, Ottawa
MG 30 E133 vols. 249–250, war diary, Andrew G. McNaughton, GOC-in-
    C, First Canadian Army
MG 30 E157 vol. 5, Henry D. Crerar, GOC-in-C, First Canadian Army; vol.
    6, files of personal letters; vol. 8; vol. 23: Special Interrogation Report,
    Field Marshal von Rundstedt; vol. 267, Mackenzie King correspondence;
    vol. 311, Earl Alexander correspondence

Princeton, N.J.: Princeton University Library
Hon. James V. Forrestal, diary

Stanford, Calif.: Hoover Library
General J.C.H. Lee papers

Washington, D.C.: Library of Congress, Manuscript Division
General Henry H. Arnold diary and papers
General Ira C. Eaker papers
General Everett S. Hughes papers
Admiral William D. Leahy diary and papers
General Carl F. Spaatz diary and papers
General Elwood R. Quesada papers
General Hoyt Vandenberg diary and papers

Washington, D.C.: National Archives
RG-59, Records of State Department
　　Box 13: H. Freeman Matthews, papers
RG-160, Records of Headquarters, Army Service Forces
　　Trips (10), General Somervell's trips 1943–1944
RG-200, Records of General Lutes
　　Records relating to various overseas missions, December 1944–April
　　　1946
　　Folder, ETO: Lutes's notes December 1944–January 1945
　　Folder: [Lutes's] Personal Diary, Mission to ETO, December 4, 1944–
　　　January 13, 1945
RG-218, Official files of Admiral William D. Leahy
RG-218, Records of U.S. Joint Chiefs of Staff
　　000.7 (22 Sep 43) Secs. 1 and 2, Publicity and Psychological Warfare
　　　for Overlord
　　092 USSR (22 Aug 43) Strategy and Policy: Can US and USSR cooper-
　　　ate?
　　092 USSR (27 Mar 45) US-USSR Relationship: USSR capabilities and
　　　intentions
　　123 Germany (20 Apr 45) Disposition of bullion and other property
　　　discovered by the 3rd Army
　　201 (19 Feb 46) G. Patton personnel file
　　201 (31 Jan 42) W.B. Smith personnel file
　　250.5 (14 Mar 44) Effect of trials of high French officials on French
　　　morale
　　312.3 (5 May 42) Procedure for handling copies of General Marshall's
　　　log and persons having access to it

320.2 (22 Apr 43) Axis estimate of enemy capabilities

323.361 Poland (25 July 43) Appointment of Gen. Sankowski [sic] as CiC of Polish Armed Forces

334 (23 Jan 42–17 Feb 45) CCS meeting

334 (1 Jan 43) French Military Mission

334 (9 Feb 42–2 Jul 45) Various JCS meetings

334 (15 Jan 44) Russian military mission

334 (11 Aug 44) Wave propaganda committee

334 (6 Sept 44) CCS meetings

334 (2 Feb 44) JCS meetings

337 (6 Jun 44) Discussion with British Chiefs of Staff re Overlord

337 (12 Sep 43 and 7 Dec 43) U.S.-British-Soviet conferences

337.19 Commander operational conferences

350.05 (12 Apr 44) Plans for Overlord and Rankin

353 (13 Jul 44) Behavior of Allied troops in Germany

353.02/15 Churchill visits

370.05 (8 Sep 44) German proposal to evacuate

373.11 (12 May 44)

373.11 (11 May 43) Belgium, bombardment of Antwerp by AAF

373.11 (12 May 44) Loss of life from bombing in France and Belgium

381 (13 Oct 44) Plans to break German lines in Italy and Western Germany

381 (12 Feb 44) Information on Crossbow

381 (11 Jan 44) Plans for Overlord and Anvil

381 (17 Oct 43) U.S.-British conference Sextant

381 (4 Oct 43) UN course of action in event of Russo-German stalemate

381 (20 Aug 44) Rankin

381 (24 Apr 43) Secs. 3–5, Overlord/Anvil files

381 (28 Feb 43) the Elkton plan

381 (13 Oct 44)

381 (11 Jan 44) Sec. 6

381 USSR (27 Feb 44) sec. 1–6, Red Army offensive action to facilitate Overlord

381 Poland (30 Jun 43) Military organization of Poland as factor in general Allied planning

381 (20 Aug 1943) Sec. 12 and Sec. 13

383.6 (21 Mar 45) Accidental deaths of number of German POWs

383.7 (11 Oct 44) Statements of persons in forced labor and concentration camps in Germany

383.7 (26 May 43) Exchange of goods with the enemy (cotton for rubber)

384.1 Germany (17 Apr 43) What does unconditional surrender mean as applied to Germany?

385 (25 Jun 43) Deception plans for Overlord

385 (3 Apr 44) Outline of political and psychological warfare for Overlord

385 (19 May 44) Plan Royal Flush

385 (10 July 1944) Germany Sec. 2

385 Germany (10 Jul 44) Synchronized psychological war plans for Germany

386 Paris (19 Aug 44) Paris, France: Proposal to spare Paris

387 Italy (6 Oct 43) Surrender terms for Italy

387 Romania (23 Oct 43) Sec. 1: Rumanian cooperation with Anglo-American forces

400.3295 Supplying material to Poland for uprising

RG-319, Records of the Army Staff

ABC 337 (14 Sep 44) Sec. 4: Octagon conference

ABC 381 (22 Jan 1943) Sec. 2

ABC 383.6 (16 Jun 43) Sec. 1b

ABC 384 Europe (5 Aug 43) Sec. 1b

ABC 384 Europe (5 Aug 43) Sec. 9b

ABC 387 Germany (18 Dec 43) Secs. 1–37

ABC 387.4 Italy (2 Sept 43) Sec. 8a

ABC 387 (11 Jan 1945) Sec. 1a

RG-331, Records of Allied Operational & Occupation Headquarters, WWII

File 201—Eisenhower, D.D., Vol. II

File 201—Smith, W.B.

SHAEF/SGS Files

000.93 Meetings

091.411 SOE

300.6/6 Supreme Commander memo 17 June

311.22/2

311.122 War Cabinet

322.011/2

337/11 Supreme Commander conferences

337/19 Supreme Allied Commander operational conferences

350.09/2 German appreciations

353.02/5 Morgenthau visit

353.02/15 Churchill visit

370.03 Progress of Overlord

381/Braddock

381/Overlord I

381/2 German counteroffensive
381 Market
RG-407, Records of Adjutant General's Office
Papers of 201 H & P (History and Precedents) Branch
RG-457: Records of the National Security Agency
Magic Diplomatic Summaries

Washington, D.C.: Navy Yard, Classified Operational Archives
Secretary of the Navy James V. Forrestal, records
Admiral A.G. Kirk, records
Fleet Admiral Ernest J. King, records
Fleet Admiral William D. Leahy, records

Index

Index

435

Germany:
Allied bombings of, 22, 67, 68, 74, 122-124, 289-293
demarcation of, 18, 32, 294, 295, 383, 399
Eisenhower's apology to high command in, 11
First Army in penetration of, 279
forced labor in, 403
French views on, 132-133, 134, 204-206, 207, 278
morale in, 22, 114, 115, 123, 289, 291, 299, 306-307, 340, 379-380
Morgenthau plan for, 237, 295, 296-300
Nazi propaganda in, 299, 300
possession of France as vital to, 235
responses to Overlord preparations by, 33-35, 77, 97-98, 100-101, 128-129
secret weapon potentials of, 7-8, 33, 67, 72, 97-98, 115, 123-125, 168-171, 291, 372
surrender of, 1, 405-410
Gerow, Barbara, 311
Gerow, Kathryn, 288
Gerow, Leonard T. ("Gee"), 143, 279, 391
in capture of Paris, 254
Cobra and, 216
at D-day rehearsals, 106-107
Overlord role of, 87, 154, 157, 158, 159
Gerow, Marie-Louise, 311, 391
Gestapo, 296, 299
French resistance and, 134, 136
Giraud, Henri, 203
Goebbels, Joseph, 299
Goering, Hermann, 293, 369, 382
Gold beach, casualties on, 160
Goodwood Operation, 193-198
failure of, 198, 212, 213
Gordon, Jean, 185, 191, 240, 312, 353, 392
death of, 412
in Paris, 313, 346, 353, 387, 388
Patton's departure for U.S. and, 407
Patton's quarrels with, 404, 406
Grasett, A. E., 342
Great Britain:
colonial interests of, 17, 23, 260, 369, 413
"Guard" classification in, 412
Overlord and Anvil resisted by, 15-18, 20, 21, 22, 27, 49-50, 257-266
scientific developments in, 9, 152
see also British forces
Greek islands, Overlord vs. operations in, 17, 20, 23, 24
Grigg, Sir James, 49, 103, 166
Montgomery chastised by, 409-410
Montgomery's correspondence with, 119-120, 174, 188-189, 198, 219, 220, 232,

241, 244, 252, 279-280, 287, 303, 304, 308, 326, 327-328, 355, 369, 373, 382, 386-387, 393
Guderian, Heinz, 56, 92
Guingand, Frederick de, 141, 164, 206, 218, 242
Montgomery-Eisenhower relationship and, 365, 366-367, 375, 386, 414-415
Montgomery's correspondence with, 165, 205, 267, 312
on "Panther and Tiger complex," 199, 200

Halifax, Lord, 203, 294
Hall, John L., 143, 154
Hall, Marion, 406
Hamilton, Denis, 414
Hammelburg raid, 395-396
Hanson, Larry, 238
Hargrave, Pearlie, 37, 338
Harmon, Ernest, 360
Harris, Sir Arthur ("Butcher"), 67-70, 121
Leigh-Mallory opposed by, 69-70, 78-79, 80
strategic bombing issue and, 67-70, 74, 78-79, 80, 118, 142, 194, 289
Hawley, Paul R., 286
Hayes Lodge, 36-37, 43, 74, 75
H-hour, 106-107, 113, 148
"High Pressure Pump," 337
Hitler, Adolf, 24, 29, 114, 115, 246
attempted assassination of, 210, 216, 235, 289, 338
Avranches counterattack ordered by, 235-236, 237, 238, 243
December offensive of (1944), see Bulge, Battle of the
France as vital to, 235
1944 strategy of, 33-35, 258, 259, 268, 314, 335, 338-339
Panther tanks and, 201
Stalin as viewed by, 17
weapons evacuated by, 403
Hitler (Montgomery's dog), 184
Hitler Youth troops, 307
Hobbs, Leland S., 222, 225
Hodges, Courtney Hicks, 1, 179, 183, 190, 233, 239, 243, 245-246, 384
Battle of the Bulge and, 336, 337, 340, 341-342, 343-345, 348, 350-351, 352, 353, 355-356, 357, 358, 359-360, 361-362, 367, 371-372, 379
Berlin drive and, 397
in capture of Paris, 254
Cobra and, 222, 223-226

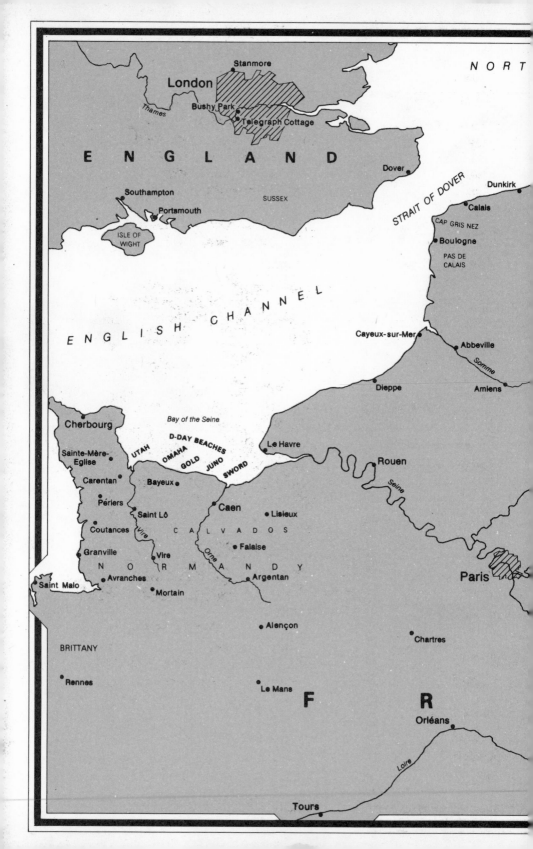